The Bloody Forest

THE BLOODY FOREST

Battle for the Huertgen: September 1944–January 1945

Gerald Astor

★
PRESIDIO

Published by Presidio Press, Inc.
505 B San Marin Drive, Suite 160
Novato, CA 94945-1340

Library of Congress Cataloging-in-Publication Data

Astor, Gerald, 1926–
The bloody forest: battle for the Huertgen, September 1944–January 1945 / Gerald Astor.
p. cm.
Included bibliographical references and index.
ISBN 0-89141-699-4
1. Huèrtgen, Battle of, 1944. 2. Schmidt, Battle of, 1944. 3. United States. Army—History—World War, 1939–1945. I. Title.

D756.5H8 A78 2000
940.54'213551—dc21

00-039145

Maps by Aegis Consulting Group
All photos courtesy the National Archives

Printed in the United States of America

CONTENTS

Acknowledgments	vii
Preface	ix
1: At the Westwall	1
2: The Attack Begins	10
3: Into the Woods	37
4: Stalled	53
5: Schmidt Number One	65
6: Schmidt Again	85
7: Turns for the Worst at Schmidt	105
8: Defeat Deepens	127
9: The Grand Disaster	148
10: The Start of the Great November Offensive	179
11: We Were There to Be Killed	203
12: Thanksgiving Celebrations	231
13: Costly Successes	256
14: Deeper into the Woods	273
15: Overlooking the Roer	300
16: Capture of the Dams	332
17: Postmortems	356
Roll Call	367
Bibliography	377
Index	381

ACKNOWLEDGMENTS

I am indebted to all of those veterans of the Huertgen Forest campaign who gave me their time and their recollections so freely. Their names are found in the section "Roll Call." I would also like to thank Colonels Tom Cross, USA Ret., and Richard Cross, USA Ret., for their efforts to afford me access to the personal papers and for their recollections of their father, Col. Thomas J. Cross, who commanded a regiment in the 8th Division. Benjamin Mabry was kind enough to give me access to tapes recorded by his late father, George L. Mabry, Jr., a 4th Division Battalion CO, as well as some personal papers. John Swearingen, who served under Mabry, also answered questions about himself and his commander.

Dorothy Chernitsky, as she has in the past, allowed me access to the sources for her book *Voices from the Foxholes.* John Marshall not only supplied me with his memoir and the details of his time in the forest, but also put me in touch with a number of his comrades from the 707th Tank Battalion. Al Burghardt, who fought with the 110th Infantry, responded to questions and sent me portions of his personal account of his military career.

Colonel Henry "Red" Phillips provided me with his memories and furnished names and addresses for others in the 9th Infantry Division. Chester Jordan, from the same organization, passed along his manuscript *Bull Sessions* and also freely answered questions. Ralph Hendrickson supplied a wealth of information on the 5th Armored Division. Donald Faulkner shared his memories and sent me clippings and reports that went beyond his experience with the 22d Infantry Regiment. Clifford Eames gave me relevant portions of his 800-page account of a 1st Division rifleman.

Norris Maxwell, one of the people who suggested I write about the Huertgen campaign, spoke frankly of his own difficulties as a member of the 121st Infantry Regiment and put me in touch with Stephen "Roddy" Wofford.

The 1st Infantry Division Association printed a notice in its *Bridgehead Sentinel* of my interest in hearing from men who engaged the enemy along the Siegfried Line. The 4th Infantry Division Association performed a similar service in its *Ivy Leaves*. Bill Parsons, editor of the 78th Division Association's *The Flash*, showered me with back issues, which enabled me to find memoirs of veterans from the campaign. Reverend Will Cook, from the 5th Armored Division Association, passed along copies of the *Victory Division News*. Bob Babcock gave me a copy of *History of the 22d Infantry Regiment in World War II* and newsletters issued by the 22d Infantry Regiment Society. Sidney A. Salomon supplied his monograph on the 2d Ranger Battalion, which covers the period of 14 November to 10 December 1944.

William Peña of the 28th Division not only gave me permission to quote from his book, *As Far as Schleiden*, but also answered my questions and furnished me with copies of letters from the German soldier Hubert Gees. In the same vein, Harry Kemp, from the 28th, also contributed valued information through his book, *The Regiment*. The 39th Infantry's Donald Lavender allowed me to quote from his monograph *Nudge Blue: A Rifleman's Chronicle of World War II Experience*.

Richard Blackburn loaned me the histories of the 13th, 28th, and 121st Regiments, among other items. Edward G. Miller was a gracious source through his book *A Dark and Bloody Ground*. George Wilson gave me a copy of his personal history, *If You Survive*. Albert Trosdorf of Merode, Germany, was kind enough to send me a copy of the memoirs of tanker Alvin Bulau. Dr. David Keough, with the U.S. Army Military History Library at Carlisle Barracks, Pennsylvania, pointed out relevant material in the archives.

Quotations from *If You Survive* by George Wilson (New York: Ballantine Books, 1987) are included by permission.

Preface

In the course of research and interviews while writing a series of books on World War II, I became increasingly aware of the campaign for the Huertgen Forest. While survivors of other battles sometimes criticized the strategy and the orders they were given, there was a depth of anger about the Huertgen that surpassed anything I had encountered elsewhere. The unhappiness with what occurred and the absence of much objective coverage in the memoirs of those in the top command slots convinced me to produce this history.

As I have reiterated in all of my books, which rely heavily on oral or eyewitness reports, there are always the dangers of flawed memory, limited vantage points, and the possibility of self-interest in such accounts. But the almost universal condemnation of their superiors' critical decisions by individuals who were under fire in that "green hell" offers a cautionary note on the accuracy and the truths of histories that draw from the official documents and the personal papers of the likes of Dwight Eisenhower, Omar Bradley, Courtney Hodges (who apparently left little in the way of records), J. Lawton Collins and others in similar positions.

On a personal note, the accounts of those who participated in the Huertgen combat triggered memories of my own service during World War II. I was an infantry replacement, and although I was fortunate to have spent my time in the European Theater guarding prisoners and hauling ammunition, I now realize how poorly I was trained, a condition that unfortunately pertained to many of those committed in the Huertgen and elsewhere.

I spent a great deal of my basic training period learning how to salute and perform close order drill. I had ample practice with an M1 rifle but never touched a BAR or the standard .30-caliber machine guns. When we practiced with a truck-mounted .50-caliber machine gun to shoot at a radio-controlled model airplane, we were not allowed to use tracers, making the aiming exercises useless. (A drone was too expensive to risk having someone shoot it down.)

I was schooled as an antitank crewman on a 57mm cannon, a weapon that was obsolete two years before I went on active duty in September 1944. At that, we had only a few days of practice with the piece. As infantry replacements, we were expected on occasion to be able to serve as riflemen. I never went through any training in house-to-house combat, which frequently characterized the efforts to capture villages in the Huertgen. I had no instruction for dealing with a pillbox. Nor did I, or anyone else I talked to, learn how to handle one's self when fighting in a wooded area, such as the Huertgen.

The cadre that instructed me had very little interest in how much I absorbed, because, under the replacement system, they would not go to war with me. Their lives would not be dependent upon my performance, because, while my contemporaries and I went overseas, they remained in a stateside camp. The historian Stephen Ambrose, among others, has criticized the entire replacement operation of the U.S. Army during World War II, in which individuals, often lacking even the rudiments of combat, were inserted into units rather than the possibly more effective procedure of bringing entire organizations with their own cadre of noncoms and officers in to substitute for those who required relief. That system would have ensured that the soldiers knew one another and those who led them would be aware of their capabilities. Ambrose suggested that, at the very least, complete squads or platoons should have been brought in, and substitution of whole companies and battalions would have been even better.

The experiences of those who were replacements in the Huertgen campaign demonstrate the awful failure of the system. But, as in the case of the command and control powers that held sway over the actual fighting, no one was ever held accountable for the disastrous consequences of tossing green, poorly schooled soldiers into the maw.

Each new war differs from that of the past, but to ignore what happened in the Huertgen enhances the possibilities for another bitter victory, if not a defeat.

1

At the Westwall

Optimism, an end to the war by Christmas, had infected the American forces by the first week of September 1944, as the Allied tide seemed poised to sweep the map clean of the Axis forces. In the Pacific, U.S. Army Gen. Douglas MacArthur and Adm. Chester Nimitz, MacArthur's seagoing counterpart, had all but destroyed the Japanese navy, recaptured almost all of the islands conquered by the enemy, and begun to assemble a massive invasion force designed to carry out MacArthur's boast of a return to the Philippine Islands. The homeland of the enemy was under siege from U.S. bombers.

In Eastern Europe, the relentless Red Armies pummeled the forces of the Third Reich after lifting the sieges of Moscow, Leningrad, and Stalingrad at horrific cost to themselves and the Wehrmacht. In the west, having evacuated Rome, the German legions continued to retreat northward. After a state of stagnation in the hedgerows of Normandy, following the invasion on 6 June, the British, Free French, and U.S. armies had broken out in a dazzling sprint that carried them to the very borders of Germany. The columns of tanks, accompanied by swift-moving infantrymen, who were supported by massive artillery and incessant raids from the air, shattered disciplined ranks of German soldiers, destroyed huge amounts of armor and ammunition, killed and wounded tens of thousands of troops, and raked in hundreds of thousands of prisoners. At the German border, the only question appeared to be whether the rampaging advance would need to halt for a few weeks to allow adequate resupply of ammunition and fuel before administering the coup de grâce.

First Army forces had begun to probe the enemy defenses at Aachen, and on 6 September, the First Army commander, Courtney

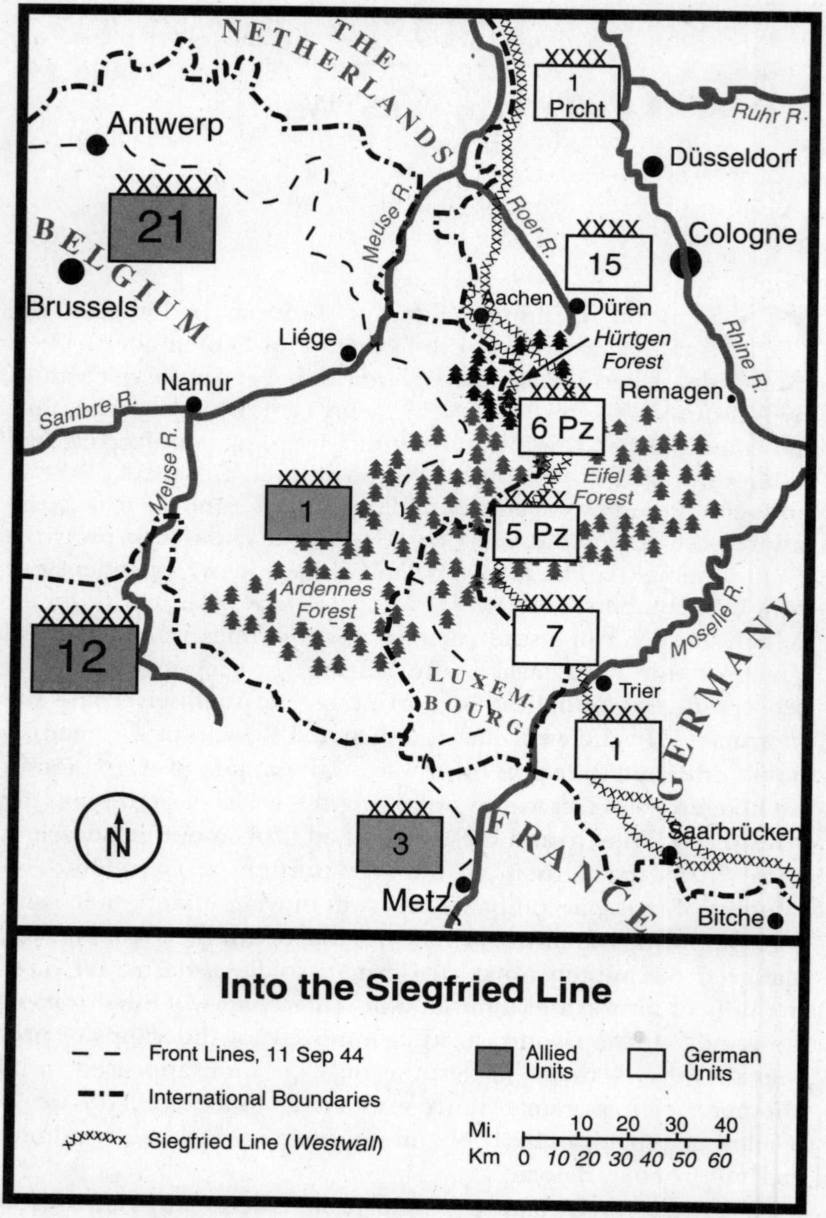
THE NETHERLANDS
XXXX
1
Prcht
Ruhr R.
Antwerp
Düsseldorf
XXXXX
21
BELGIUM
Meuse R.
Roer R.
XXXX
15
Cologne
Brussels
Aachen
Düren
Liége
Hürtgen
Forest
Rhine R.
Namur
Remagen
Sambre R.
XXXX
6 Pz
Meuse R.
Eifel
Forest
XXXX
1
XXXX
5 Pz
Ardennes
Forest
Moselle R.
XXXX
7
XXXXX
12
GERMANY
LUXEMBOURG
Trier
XXXX
1
XXXX
3
FRANCE
Saarbrücken
Metz
Bitche
N
Into the Siegfried Line
Front Lines, 11 Sep 44
International Boundaries
Siegfried Line (Westwall)
Allied Units
German Units
Mi. 10 20 30 40
Km 0 10 20 30 40 50 60

Hodges, having paused over a two-day span to sit for nearly four hours while the Marchioness of Queensberry painted his portrait for *Life* magazine, predicted the imminent demise of the enemy. According to Maj. William Sylvan, Hodges's aide-de-camp, "The general said tonight that given ten good days of weather he thought the war might well be over as far as organized resistance was concerned."

A sense of an approaching finale also infected some of the troops. Mike Cohen, a platoon leader in the 12th Engineer Combat Battalion, part of the 8th Infantry Division, recalled the coming of September. "We had led the advance to Rennes, then swung up toward Brest. It was truly brutal. The city was heavily defended by crack troops, granite walls, and lots of firepower. But when it was over, it was as if the war was over. The main force of the Allies had moved swiftly across France. The *Stars and Stripes* [military newspaper] reported that Patton had breached the Siegfried Wall in several places and the war was just about over.

"It was a time for rejoicing. It was autumn, the weather was balmy, the guns were still. The killing was finished. It was the time of the Jewish high holidays, Rosh Hashanah and Yom Kippur, and a prayer session was called on a sunny slope outside of Brest with a view of the blue harbor and a cluster of hospital tents. Despite the sincerity of my grandfather and the not-so-enthusiastic exhortations of my father [who left nineteenth-century Russia with its anti-Semitic raids by Cossacks and czarist pogroms], I was never very religious but this was very different. This was a nonsectarian emotion of brotherhood for everyone still alive and deep sadness for the guys who had been killed—our guys that is. I never could bring myself to regret the death of the enemies.

"We had a big party for the company, hired the jubilant French townspeople to prepare a great feast, and we ate and ate and ate and ate. Then, suddenly, the peace was over. We were back in our trucks and moving east. We wound up in Luxembourg and discovered the war was still going on."

The American commanders, the strategists and tacticians, had neglected a number of factors in their calculations of imminent victory. Only two days before Hodges's prediction, Sylvan had noted in his diary that, after a conference with Gen. Dwight D. Eisenhower, head of the Allied forces, and Gen. Omar Bradley, in charge of the 12th Army Group, which included Hodges's forces, "Both the Supreme Commander and General Bradley also are extremely worried over the gasoline situation, which is becoming more instead of being less critical." Sylvan reported that his boss was ordered "to curl up both the VII and XIX Corps," which, the aide remarked, handed the British ally and rival Gen. Bernard Montgomery, the "best use of east-west roads. The whole plan is not altogether to the general's satisfaction, since he believes he can whip the gasoline problem, and that while the Germans are on the run, there should be no halt even for a minute."

Omar Bradley, in his well-after-the-fact autobiography, implied that if Eisenhower had not allocated scarce gasoline for Montgomery's thrust to the north and given it to Gen. George Patton's Third Army, the American armor early in September might have pushed well into the Rhineland, the very heart of the Third Reich, instead of halting along the outskirts of enemy turf.

By dint of Patton's personality and the swift progress of his troops after the breakout at Saint-Lô, the Third Army's actions led to banner headlines and major news stories during the summer months. But the First Army, which furnished the beachhead through which Patton was able to enter Normandy, had achieved just as spectacular results. In the six weeks after the July offensive that smashed the German defenses, the troops under Hodges liberated Paris and pushed northeast to the border while contending with the largest segments of the enemy forces.

Between the First Army and the Rhine River lay the vaunted Siegfried Line (the German name for what Americans referred to as the Westwall), a stretch of fortifications that in some areas amounted to only a thin, single belt of fortified emplacements and in others, particularly in the sector fronted by the legions under Hodges, was a parallel series of bastions. A swift strong strike could penetrate and sweep to the Rhine. Although the textbooks and manuals stressed the importance of the terrain, the strategists were confident that technology and manpower could readily overcome whatever advantages the enemy could muster.

On 10 September, desperate to delay pursuit, the retreating Germans destroyed the bridges that spanned the Our and Sauer Rivers, which ambled between Luxembourg and the Third Reich. On that same day, on the heels of Hodges's assertion that all that lay between a final push and victory was "ten days of good weather," Sylvan said that a First Army staff conference described the supply picture as "extremely discouraging," and the situation mandated a delay in any concentrated attack on the Siegfried Line for a minimum of five days.

Nibbling at the border was the 5th Armored Division, a veteran force from the fighting in France. The combat log of the 71st Armored Field Artillery (AFA) of the division reported for 10 September: "The bridge across the Sauer River in Mersch was blown just as CCR [Combat Command Reserve, one of the three regiment-size units in an armored division] entered the town. [Battalion] registered by air OP [L-5 Piper Cubs flown by army pilots routinely as observation posts, spotting targets for artillery] and fired eight [battalion] concentrations. Expended 264 rounds. Many foot [infantry] and horses were killed and dispersed. Many horse-drawn vehicles were destroyed along with several automotive vehicles and guns. The Air Corps also had a field day attacking the retreating German columns as they raced east to the 'Fatherland.'"

A day later, the log of the 71st AFA reported a march of sixteen miles that bore it beyond the Brandenberg Castle in the Brandenberg Pass. "[Battalion] registered by air OP at 1630, B Battery, 71st. AFA was the first arty [artillery] unit to fire on German soil. Battalion fired interdiction and harassing missions throughout the night and expended 230 rounds."

On that same 11 September, around 4:30 P.M., the 85th Recon Squadron, dispatched six GIs and Lt. Lionel A. DeLille, a Free French officer serving as an interpreter, in a peep (the armored forces designation for jeep) and scout car to explore the territory between the positions of the 5th Armored Division and the enemy. The patrol cautiously moseyed forward to find out whether Wehrmacht soldiers occupied the pillboxes that threatened any advance.

Sergeant Warner W. Holzinger, leader of the group, recalled: "When we started out on our mission, we took my radio peep with us to keep in touch with the 2d Platoon and with headquarters. We worked our way down to Stolzembourg [a village on the Luxembourg side of the Our River]. From the citizens we learned there were no enemy soldiers in the vicinity. I have been thankful many times I could speak German.

"The enemy had blown to some degree the small bridge that spanned the Our River. Even at that, we were able to cross on it. We could have waded the river too." A dry summer had left the stream shallow.

"On the German side of the river there was a pillbox camouflaged as a barn. It's a good thing it wasn't manned. Lieutenant DeLille and I talked with a German farmer. He told us that the last time he had seen any German troops was the day before. He also told us that if we followed the road up the small mountain behind his farm, we would be able to see the first line of pillboxes. So, Lieutenant DeLille, Pfc. [William] McColligan, the German farmer, and I went into Germany about one and a half miles, where we could get a good view. We studied the pillbox area with our field glasses. None of them seemed manned. We returned to Stolzembourg, where we reported the information [by radio] to Lt. Loren L. Vipond [his platoon commander]."

Subsequently, G-2 at headquarters of the 5th Armored Division scrawled a transcription of a brief radio message received from Combat Command B, one of its three regiment-size armored units: "Dismounted patrols crossed into Germany at . . . 1815 hrs."

The frontier had been breached, but Holzinger's patrol returned to its base without occupying enemy turf. Subsequent probes confirmed the paucity of German troops, although one expedition from the 5th Armored observed soldiers leisurely marching in from the north, bearing machine guns and taking up residence in formerly deserted pillboxes.

The thinness of the foe's ranks whetted appetites for continuing the prewinter drive to the Rhine. The Allies were well aware of the most immediate obstacle to progress, the well-publicized Siegfried Line. The thickest fortification was along a radius anchored by the historic city of Aachen and enveloped a number of good-size towns—Stolberg, Düren, Eschweiler, Schmidt—and villages and hamlets, some no more than a crossroads, as well as some sizable rivers and tributaries with heavy forestry. The strongest section of the Westwall consisted of two chains of defenses, the Scharnhorst

Line, closest to the Allied troops, and the Schill Line, the deeper and more substantial array several miles back.

German engineers had artfully sited the more than 3,000 pillboxes, dugouts, and observation posts to exploit the full benefits of terrain—the lakes, streams, hills, gorges, forests, and other natural features. Within the confines of the biggest forts were living quarters for troops, arms and ammunition storage, concealed entrances, and, of course, firing embrasures. The concentration of such redoubts reflected the knowledge that Aachen and its surrounding territory acted as a gateway for the shortest route from the west to Berlin.

Some of the massive pillboxes, many of which were circular, would cause artillery and tank shells to glance off if they hit a rounded area. The structures were made of steel eight to ten inches thick, covered by a layer of concrete a foot deep. Concrete gun casements employed walls eight to ten feet thick. The German engineers artfully masked the apertures with mounds of dirt, which would cause 155mm rounds to ricochet. Machine gun bunkers covered open areas. Tank obstacles included ditches, eight feet wide and twenty feet deep, that were covered by pillbox weapons and rows of stalwart, six-foot-high, reinforced concrete barriers known as "dragon's teeth." Craters blasted in roads blocked vehicular passage. The defenses duly impressed intelligence specialists and strategists, but the first patrols revealed that the reeling Nazi armies had fallen back in such a disorganized rout that they had left much of the Siegfried Line unmanned or staffed with skeleton crews. When the fortifications were constructed in 1938, Adolf Hitler's propaganda machine trumpeted the Westwall as impregnable, a characterization swallowed by military leaders in England. That sense of inviolability helped convince the British to appease Hitler at the 1938 Munich Conference.

Unlike the French, who blindly trusted their equivalent Maginot Line to protect them against any invaders, the German generals understood that the Siegfried's major contribution to defense of the Fatherland lay in its power to delay an offensive until reserves could be rushed to the point of attack. And the demands on the Russian Front and in Italy and in France emptied the bunkers of even housekeeping crews, to say nothing of eliminating the mobile reserves expected to back up the defenses. To the top American commanders, the reports of those first patrols in September indicated that the Siegfried Line was a waste of concrete.

Even as Hodges plotted the offensive that would smash into the heart of Germany, on 8 September, only two days after his uncharacteristically confident boast, Sylvan informed his diary that Bradley was urging Hodges to dispatch some of his armor to the rescue of Third Army forces to the south: "The Boche had sent tanks into a Third Army Division CP and captured valuable documents." The 12th Army Group leader attributed the setback to the failure of Hodges's V Corps to drive ahead. Hodges alibied that the lack of gas stalled his troops. He insisted that the First Army should not be held responsible for Third Army problems.

The primary objective of the First Army was control of the Roer River, a stream that originates in the hills of the Ardennes, meanders through Monschau, a town near the Belgian border, broadens as it picks up a network of tributaries while passing through the city of Düren, and then curves northwest to flow into the Meuse River of the Netherlands. Beyond the Roer in Germany was a plain that extended to the last natural defense in the Deutschland—the Rhine. A few lone voices from intelligence suggested that the command consider the strategic importance of a group of dams, particularly the pair known as the Schwammenauel and the Urft. These dams controlled the flow of the Roer and several of its larger feeder streams. By opening the gates on the largest of these dams, the Germans could create massive flooding that would critically interfere with any offensive. But the plotters, from Eisenhower down through Bradley, Hodges, Joe Collins, and Leonard Gerow, basically ignored the threat posed by opening the floodgates and concentrated instead on the capture of real estate. There is, for example, no mention in Sylvan's meticulous notes of any intentions concerning the dams.

General J. Lawton Collins, V Corps commander under Hodges, when asked many years later whether the intelligence people considered the dams an important objective, responded, "They didn't, and they didn't recognize the threat they posed. We all knew there were some dams. We had not studied that particular part of the zone. They came as a surprise to most of the intelligence people in the army. There were two or three of them [actually, a system of seven such flood control structures]."

Poised to make the final blow at the Third Reich, what promised to be a swift triumph turned into a fiasco, as the American brass combined dubious strategic decisions with tactical blunders, which were compounded by a disregard for basic military axioms, an appalling ignorance of the situation, and the deadly germ of hubris. The competition to conquer the most land, score the highest body count, and collect the most medals is a not unexpected theme among military units at war. But, occasionally, that zeal overwhelms good judgment and results in deadly consequences. At the heart of the disaster that began to unfold in September 1944 was a great patch of densely packed, towering fir trees known as the Huertgen Forest, a man-made preserve. Actually, the seventy-square-mile area consisted of several forests—Huertgen, Wenau, Roetgen, Monschau, and smaller woods—but Americans lumped the entire sector under the name Huertgen.

Harry Kemp, who commanded a heavy weapons company for the 28th Division during its ordeal in the woods, said, "If one were to see it from the southeast outskirts of Aachen . . . it appears as a seemingly impenetrable mass—a vast undulating blackish-green ocean stretching as far as the eye can see." The official U.S. Army history covering this period, in which Americans confronted the Huertgen, states: "Upon entering the forest, you want to drop things behind to mark your path, as Hansel and Gretel did with their bread crumbs." Within this enormous stand of conifers, there was grim gloom. Sunlight rarely penetrated through the near cheek-to-jowl, interlocked branches. On the carpet of pine needles, American GIs bled in unprecedented numbers during a horrendous, five-month campaign that scourged seven infantry divisions, an armored division, and assorted other units. Referring to a World War I slaughter, Ernest Hemingway, who accompanied a regiment devastated in the Huertgen, christened the Huertgen "Paschendale with trees."

2

The Attack Begins

When General Hodges uttered his prediction of victory in less than a fortnight, the front of his First Army lay along a 35-mile-long axis from the Belgium-Netherlands border through Aachen, south through the Ardennes into Luxembourg. While the British war chief Sir Bernard Montgomery, to the north of the First Army, painstakingly marched toward the enemy border, the invasion of Hitler's Third Reich lay within Hodges's domain, because Patton's Third Army had stalled inside French territory, south of the Forest of Ardennes, some miles from the frontier.

As a cadet at West Point, Hodges had fallen victim to geometry during his first year. After he enlisted as a private, he earned a commission and received a Distinguished Service Cross for leading a reconnaissance into enemy lines while with the American Expeditionary Forces during the Meuse-Argonne battles of World War I. He progressed up the ranks until 1941, when Army Chief of Staff Gen. George C. Marshall named him chief of infantry at the War Department in Washington, D.C. Once the shooting began, Hodges was assigned as deputy chief of the First Army under Gen. Omar Bradley. When Bradley assumed command of the 12th Army Group, Hodges succeeded him as commander of the First Army. Bradley commented, "He was essentially a military technician whose faultless techniques and tactical knowledge made him one of the most skilled craftsmen of my entire command. He probably knew as much about infantry and training as any man in the army." Although Bradley offered such high praise, he also commented, "Courtney seemed indecisive and overly conservative." Bradley said that he hoped "my veteran First Army staff . . . would keep a fire under him."

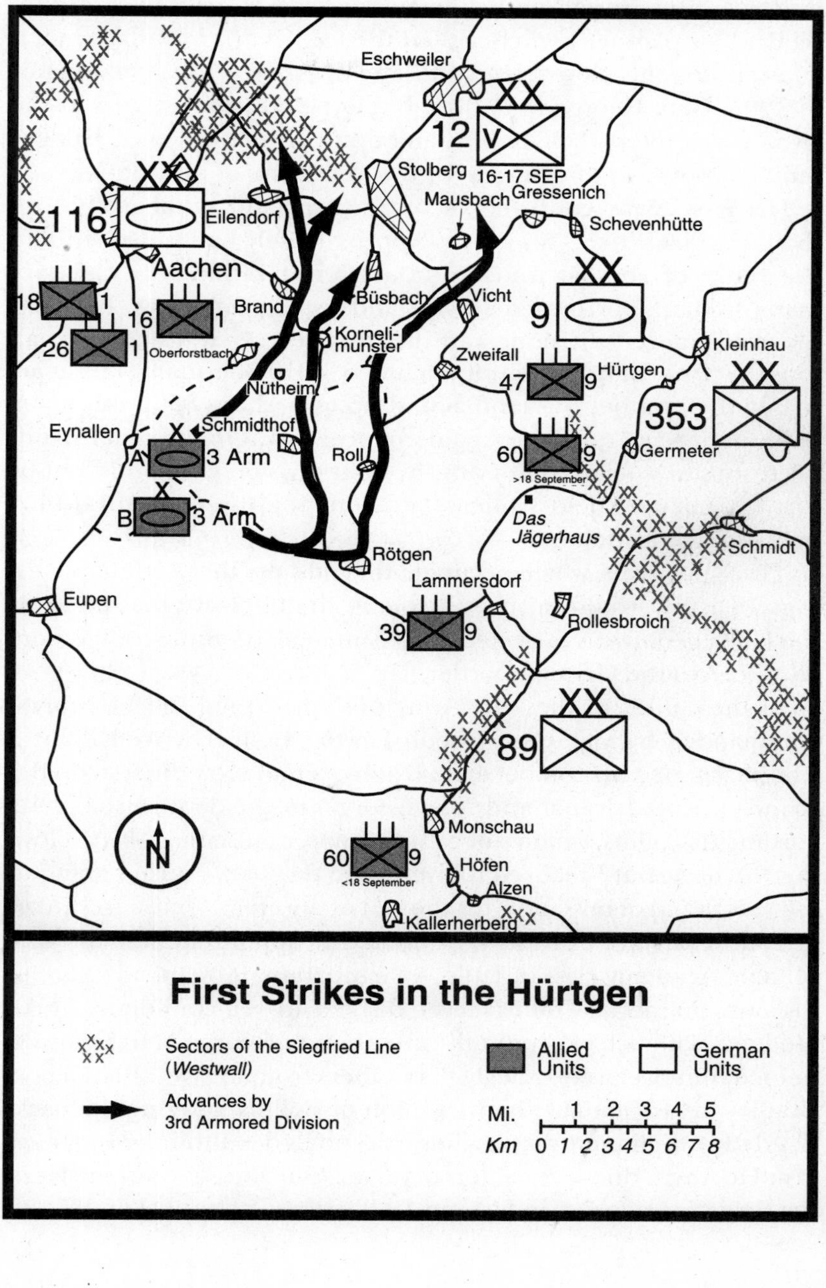

First Strikes in the Hürtgen

Now a fifty-six-year-old lieutenant general, Hodges was a stolid, meticulous planner and cherished the role of armor with as much conviction as his close friend and one of his West Point classmates in 1904, Gen. George S. Patton, Jr. He held a similar faith in the virtues of artillery. Unlike his flamboyant chum, however, Hodges built a reputation of concern for the well-being of his troops.

His First Army consisted of three corps and numbered more than 256,000 officers and men. Approximately half of these filled the ranks of combat units, although even within that category many soldiers performed service and supply functions. Between his two armored divisions and the attached separate tank battalions, his table of organization included 1,010 Shermans, but in actuality the number on hand added up to perhaps 850, with many badly in need of repairs or maintenance work. On the other hand, his troops were backed not only by their division's big guns, but by forty-six separate field artillery battalions and three chemical (4.2-inch) mortar battalions.

The XIX Corps, which occupied the most northern left flank facing Germany, would not play a role in the offensive that involved the Huertgen. It was expected to remain in place until Montgomery advanced to the German border.

At the center of the First Army positions stood the VII Corps, commanded by Maj. Gen. Joseph Lawton Collins, a West Pointer who sharpened his combat teeth leading an infantry division on the islands of Guadalcanal and New Georgia in the South Pacific. According to Collins, a native of New Orleans, Louisiana, "My first love was the navy. But I realized if I went into the navy, I wasn't going to see very much of my family for the rest of my life." While a freshman at Louisiana State University, he earned an appointment to the U.S. Military Academy class of 1917. An exuberant, forceful advocate of his own opinions, Collins never flagged in self-confidence. Like Hodges, Collins had caught the attention of George Marshall, who helped him rise more quickly than others from his West Point class. Bradley held a similarly high opinion of Collins, offering the backhanded compliment that Collins "was not a deep thinker or strategist. He was a 'doer,' an action man. . . . One of the most outstanding field commanders in Europe, Collins was without [a] doubt also the most aggressive. With a handpicked staff to help him, he seasoned an unerring tactical judgment with just enough bravado to make every advance a triumph. To these qualities, he added boundless self-confidence." Not everyone who encountered Collins would put such a positive spin on his character.

Collins was the sort of man Bradley expected to ignite the kindling under Hodges. He had a reputation for making frequent tours of the front and boasted, "Every day I was out in the field visiting as far [forward] as I could the critical point of action. Where the crux of the fighting was likely to be was the place I headed for." In the first days of September 1944, Collins directed the 4th Cavalry Group, the 1st and 9th Infantry Divisions, and the 3d Armored Division.

On the right-most southern flank, Maj. Gen. Leonard Gerow led the V Corps. Another West Pointer, Gerow had been a member of an advanced infantry officers' class at Fort Benning with Bradley, and they had graduated first and second, respectively. Gerow preceded Eisenhower as chief of the War Plans Division of the General Staff while Ike served as his deputy. He had almost no experience as a field commander (Eisenhower had none). When Gerow, a detail-obsessed draftsman with none of the bonhomie of his successor, was given responsibility for direction of the V Corps during its Normandy landings, some questioned the choice. However, Gerow's meticulous approach was augmented by an unexpected sense of the flow of battle. In the few months since 6 June 1944, he appeared to have the grasp of combat command well in hand. There was no doubt that he possessed a considerably less dynamic personality than his counterpart at the helm of the VII Corps or certainly the rambunctious Lt. Gen. George S. Patton, Jr., head of the Third Army who was then butting heads against a stubborn enemy defense on Gerow's right flank. Gerow's troops played a principal role in the D-Day landing on Omaha Beach, and within the ranks were the 102d Cavalry Group, the 4th and 28th Infantry Divisions, and the 5th Armored Division.

Directly committed to work with First Army operations was the IX Tactical Air Command, a component of the Ninth Air Force. Its fighter-bomber groups flew missions specifically requested by the ground forces and roamed the skies on "armed reconnaissance," swooping down on any enemy spotted from the air or in response to radioed requests. The Ninth Air Force furnished further aid with groups of medium bombers. The Royal Air Force also contributed its bombers to the effort.

During the staff conference on 8 September, where, according to Sylvan, the supply experts described dire shortages, Hodges's aide noted the arrival of the V Corps commander, Gerow, at 10 A.M.: "He was closeted with the general [Hodges] in an occasionally rather tempestuous discussion of V Corps Tactical Approach to the border. The general, knowing the importance that Gen. Bradley placed on the strength of the right flank [adjacent to the Third Army's positions], ordered the 112th Infantry to assemble in the area of the 5th Armored and generally layed [*sic*] out to Gen. Gerow the plan which he wished to see adopted for the attack. Gen. Collins came by car at 3 o'clock and for two hours they were closeted in the map trailer discussing the VII Corps's approach to the border."

On 11 September, Sylvan reported, "Shortly after 8:15, news from the V Corps that elements of the 5th Armored had crossed the frontier, approximately at the 42d horizontal. Gen. Hodges at once called Gen. Gerow who denied the fact, but later in the evening it was established beyond a doubt that patrols had crossed the border and stayed across the border. They had been joined in their respective sectors by patrols from both the 4th and 28th Divisions. No one claimed that the Siegfried Line or what there is of it had been pierced, but the fact remained that we were in Germany, the first to have that distinction." Within a few hours, the 16th Regimental Combat Team of the 1st Division [infantry working with armor from the 3d Armored Division] also trespassed on the Siegfried Line, capturing several pillboxes. But the advancing GIs reported that heavy obstacles lay ahead. Collins's organization had become the second corps to cross the border.

On 12 September, Hodges conferred with General Patton and the G-4 representatives, the staff responsible for supply. Sylvan noted, "It seems likely that we will have to halt for at least a short period." Sylvan also observed that in Eupen, a Belgian border town captured by the VII Corps, all of the civilians hung white flags from their windows and shops, "but were coldly indifferent to our troops in contrast to the reception given up to that point. Eupen was in disputed territory with a population that was strongly pro-German."

The hostility of the Germans was expected, but it also meant that the Allied armies could no longer, as they had in the past, count on much information from civilians. Based on what intelligence specialists could gather from such patrols as that led by Sergeant Holzinger, the experiences of the 16th Regiment troops, the questioning of a few prisoners and civilians, and intercepts of German communications, the First Army staff concluded that the Westwall emplacements were garrisoned mainly by service and second-line recruits of limited value for front-line combat but trained to man fixed defensive posts. Such troops were designated as SOS.

In his meeting with his superior, the ever-eager "Lightning Joe" Collins argued for his VII Corps to seize the initiative and plunge into Germany. To assuage Hodges's uncertainty, Collins proposed "a reconnaissance in force," which the army's basic manual on combat doctrine calls the "best means of clearing up an uncertain situation." In effect, the reconnaissance in force could probe defenses and mount attacks. The option of actually occupying territory would depend on the resistance offered.

Captain Armand R. Levasseur, the plans and operations officer of the 1st Division's 26th Regiment, wrote in a monograph well after the fact, "The men generally realized that the picnic, wine, and flowers campaign of France and Belgium was at an end. Now at least, the German was fighting on native soil, so resistance was expected to stiffen." However, Levasseur wrote, "the end now seemed within our grasp. Optimism was high, in fact too high in view of the tough battles that lay ahead. Sound tactical doctrine dictated that the enemy's defenses, reached at the close of a pursuit, which had turned into a rout, be penetrated as rapidly as possible. The enemy was to be given no breather to recover from the staggering blows struck in France and Belgium. For this reason no time was available for specialized training so valuable to the success of an attack on permanent type defenses. Also, at battalion level little was known as to the nature of construction, strength, or depth of the fortifications."

While the enemy was obviously gasping for breath, the First Army was also breathing hard, with many organizations like the 1st Division badly winded after more than ninety days of battle. Vehicles were worn out or seriously damaged, maintenance was far behind schedule, and the supply problems continued. Levasseur's comment about the lack of specialized training for dealing with the redoubts of the Siegfried Line is only partially correct, because the 1st Division, having fought in North Africa and Sicily and having confronted pillboxes and bunkers during the Normandy invasion, was an experienced outfit, although casualties had reduced the number of veteran soldiers. More to the point would be the absence of any significant instruction or experience in combat in a dense forest that housed massive permanent defensive positions.

These considerations aside, and persuaded by Collins, Hodges authorized both of his corps commanders to crack the Westwall. Collins, champed at his bit, giving the responsibility to a pair of combat commands from the 3d Armored and two battalions from infantry regiments of the 1st Division. The initial plan posed what might generously be labeled an "incongruity." While the top U.S. commanders plotted a drive toward Koblenz coordinated with the Third Army, and if V Corps hewed to a close association with Patton's bunch, it would be well split off from the bulk of the First Army.

Collins hoped to snatch the prize of Aachen, a town celebrated in German history, before the Nazi armies could regroup. Not only was the capture of Aachen valued because of the city's renown (it was the coronation city of the Holy Roman Empire and Charlemagne's capital), but it also would be the first major conquest on enemy soil. Furthermore, it held strategic worth because of its location in the Aachen Gap, an avenue through difficult topography to the north and in the southeast dense pine woods, the result of forestry preservation by the Nazi government. The Americans called this the Huertgen. The line that separated the VII and V Corps ran through the miles of these stalwart, packed stands of trees. On the southwestern outskirts of the sector was Monschau, which anchored another rough avenue toward the Roer River.

The German Seventh Army commander believed that his opposition would pinpoint Aachen as the major objective in an attack. Generalleutnant Friedrich August Schack, the officer responsible for the area that included Aachen, as well as the territory immediately south of the city, could muster only beat-up German divisions to counter any blows from the combined efforts of the American VII and V Corps. His 105th Panzer Brigade could field only ten tanks, and that tiny group had been shot up in its first encounter with U.S. armor on 11 September. The 9th Panzer Division, reorganizing after a drubbing in France, scrambled to defend Aachen but arrived piecemeal in small increments as the battle for Aachen seemed about to begin. Another division existed only on paper; all that was left of it was the headquarters staff. Retention of the entire Aachen sector devolved upon engineers, a few artillery batteries, a training regiment, a handful of local security people, and some remnants from armor and infantry outfits.

In charge of the actual defense of the city was Generalleutnant Gerhard Graf von Schwerin, who would fall victim to an incredible piece of mistiming. As he tried to move his hodgepodge of fighting men into place, von Schwerin discovered that the burghers of Aachen perceived the desperate state of their city and were panicky over a directive from Hitler that civilians evacuate the city. Although the Nazi dictator ordered the city emptied of noncombatants, he showed no inclination to abandon Aachen. He had personally ordered three full-strength divisions toward Aachen.

Von Schwerin, after vainly attempting to deploy his motley group of soldiers, decided the whole affair was fruitless. He foresaw a swift victory by the Americans menacing the city and no advantage in ejecting its inhabitants. Perhaps unaware that Hitler himself had demanded the people leave, the general tried to organize the local police to stop the evacuation but quickly learned that the local Nazi officials and the police had already fled. Army officers assumed the task of urging the populace to stay home.

Von Schwerin took it upon himself to write a letter in English to the American commander, whom he expected to enter the city. "I stopped the absurd evacuation of this town; therefore, I am responsible for the fate of its inhabitants and I ask you, in the case of an occupation by your troops, to take care of the unfortunate population in a humane way. I am the last German commanding officer in the sector of Aachen." Von Schwerin entrusted the missive to a telephone service manager, the only official he could locate who was still at his post. Unfortunately, at the very moment the Wehrmacht general chose to offer a surrender, the Americans turned away from Aachen. Von Schwerin's letter, preserved by the telephone bureaucrat, would haunt him.

Although not opposed by any significant enemy strength, Collins's reconnaissance in force, which he renamed an attack, stumbled. Roadblocks, the unfriendly ground, and small but sharp resistance from bands of stubborn defenders prevented the GI invaders from penetrating the Westwall. One battalion of infantry from the 16th Regiment, however, pushed well into the Aachen municipal forest, where they triggered a surprise counterattack from some eighty Germans. The 16th Infantry soldiers warily dug in to await further orders.

John Beach, a Californian who graduated from the U.S. Military Academy in June 1943, recalled, "I was a typical replacement officer when I joined the company on June 22, 1944. The company had been taken out of the line in our sector and enjoyed a brief lull in the action. The army, with considerable astuteness, had estimated the casualties on Omaha Beach would be 50 percent. It prepared for this by grouping replacements into packages of fourteen men each. Each such package had riflemen, machine gunners, and automatic riflemen. One platoon of these groups had been already assigned to the various units, even during the assault on the beach. They were fed into the gaps that existed. After the beachhead had been established, our package went through the regular chain of command before being assigned to Dagwood Red Charlie. Dagwood stood for the 16th Infantry, Red for the 1st Battalion, and Charlie for Company C.

"Our company was resting to the rear of the 1st Division near Caumont, dug in along the hedgerows that were so characteristic of this part of France. When I first saw Capt. Victor H. Briggs, he was occupying the only comfortable chair in the area, the front seat of his jeep, his long legs leisurely stretched over the dashboard onto the hood, as he enjoyed a cigarette. 'Good to see you, Beach,' he said, shaking my hand. 'We need replacements.' He pointed to a water can on the ground near the jeep. 'Have some coffee.' Captain Briggs's smiling face did not show the iron that was beneath. He had already been awarded two Silver Stars for his actions in North Africa and Sicily, a DSC for deliberately drawing fire on himself so his company might advance.

"I was given command of the first platoon, which held the right flank of the company. Technical Sergeant Floyd Newman from Seattle, my platoon sergeant, had been a private when the platoon entered Oran. My platoon guide, SSgt. Jim Dyer, from Indiana, was a veteran of Africa and Sicily. Charlie Company's rest was a short one. We moved up and occupied foxholes of a company we relieved. The sector was so quiet it was hard to realize the Germans were only about 300 feet away."

Beach gradually became friendly with another platoon lieutenant, James Horace Wood, a Georgian and former marine. Wood apparently thought the War Between the States was still an issue. "He would fight the Civil War at the slightest opportunity," recalled Beach. "He'd go back fighting Lee's battles when there was a lull."

Caumont may have been a peaceful scene, but Beach and his associates knew something big was in the air. Patton was reported to be in the vicinity, and there was talk of entry into Paris by the middle of July. The breakout occurred on 26 July, when 15,000 tons of bombs were dropped. Beach and his platoon fought their way toward the frontier, incurring casualties all along the way.

In September, he observed, "We moved through a town crossing the German border. A few kilometers beyond, Sgt. David Fehrenbach was the first man in the 1st Division to cross the German border, in the woods this side of Aachen. Immediately after that, we ran into a few enemy pillboxes and entrenchments, but they were not fully manned and the enemy surrendered after a brief struggle. We engaged a few firefights around Aachen, and I lost four men in the Aachen Forest. . . . There were now ten left from the forty which had started with me [at Caumont]. My platoon was down to twelve. When we pulled out of there, the next day I received sixteen men as replacements, which brought [the] platoon total to twenty-eight. We drove southward toward the city of Stolberg, southeast of

Aachen. The atmosphere was entirely different. Now we were in the enemy's home territory. No longer were there cheering crowds when we passed. For the most part, the houses had white flags hanging from them. The people were obviously not welcoming us but offered no resistance. The fight appeared to have gone out of them, with the exception of the children who hissed at us as we went past."

As the 1st Battalion of the 16th Infantry pushed deeper into the Aachen forest, they suffered further losses. The Germans captured Fehrenbach and his squad. In Company C a platoon leader went down, and Briggs assigned Wood as his replacement, naming Jake Lindsey to be his platoon sergeant. Continued casualties in and around Aachen due to intense fighting brought more replacements, and soon Beach, whose complement had dropped as low as fifteen, had forty-four men under his command. Activity gradually lessened in the 1st Battalion sector.

The 26th Infantry dispatched its 1st Battalion, aided by air strikes, to smash through the Scharnhorst Line with the aim of seizing hills overlooking Aachen. Tanks from the 3d Armored Division and armored infantry sought to break through on the right flank and take the high ground near Stolberg, about three miles or so east of Aachen. Colonel William Lovelady of Combat Command B (CCB) merged his 2d Battalion from the 33d Armored Infantry with most of the 2d Battalion from the 33d, plus a recon company, a tank unit, a platoon of armored engineers, a platoon of tank destroyers, a battery of M7 self-propelled howitzers, and a maintenance unit to form Task Force Lovelady. It jumped off around noon from Eupen in Belgium, traveling northeast toward Roetgen.

Moving slowly over muddy ground, Lovelady's lead element reached the unmanned customs station on the Belgian-German border shortly before 3 P.M. Lovelady radioed CCB headquarters that the task force had crossed the frontier. Brigadier General Truman E. Boudinot, CCB chief, told his radio operator, "Tell Lovelady he's famous! Congratulate him and tell him to keep on going!" Roetgen, a tiny enclave, passed into American hands with little resistance. It was the first German town to be occupied by the U.S. Army in World War II. From their vehicles, the history-making GIs saw frightened faces peeking out from their drawn curtains as the armor rolled through the main street. As in Eupen and thousands of other settlements, villages, towns, and cities, the ubiquitous white flags, often bedsheets, hung from the buildings.

On the far edge of town, the column approached a crater in the middle of the road. On the left, row upon row of dragon's teeth barred a detour in that direction. Steep hills blocked any opportunity to evade the gaping hole on the right side. When troops dismounted to examine the crater, a sniper's bullet cut down a company commander and signaled an outpouring of fire from other well-concealed German soldiers. GIs with machine guns in their trucks, jeeps, and tracked carriers could not roust the enemy, and the accompanying artillery could not drive off the foe. Despite orders to continue, Task Force Lovelady could not budge.

Elsewhere, the 3d Armored absorbed limited but stinging punishment. The task force of Combat Command A (CCA) encountered well-concealed antitank guns that knocked off three Shermans, temporarily halting further movement. A giant pit in a road walled by an adjacent cliff, solidly built roadblocks, mines, and the phalanxes of dragon's teeth shut down the other combat command.

To resume its attack, engineers with Task Force Lovelady filled the huge hole in the roadway with dirt but that quickly changed to impassable muck. The artillery then blasted an opening through the dragon's teeth on the left and the tanks rumbled toward the first objective, the village of Rott. En route the attackers approached eight pillboxes or bunkers. In every instance, the handful of Germans in residence immediately fled.

The GIs crashed through the relatively thin crust of the Scharnhorst Line and set their sights on Rott. But there they encountered a much more defiant defense. A Mark V tank, backed by antitank guns, opened fire. Task Force Lovelady quickly had four Shermans and a half-track knocked out. Only the superiority of numbers enabled the 3d Armored people to silence the Mark V, and once bereft of that weapon, the Germans retreated. A blown bridge across a stream near Rott stalled the advance for the night.

A few miles north of Task Force Lovelady, a smaller group, led by Lt. Col. Roswell H. King, moved toward Schmidthof, another village just beyond the Scharnhorst emplacements. There, however, pillboxes were clumped in greater density from behind a cordon of dragon's teeth. In addition, Schmidthof provided enemy observers excellent vantage points from which to call down artillery and mortars upon the Americans. Task Force King, with only sixty infantrymen, attempted an attack that was repulsed by the accurate and heavy German response.

A third punch, deploying tanks, tank destroyers, and an infantry battalion directed by Col. Leander Doan, hammered at positions to the northwest, closer to the Stolberg corridor.

Mortar shells denied engineers an opportunity to create openings in the dragon's teeth blocking Task Force Doan's tanks. Foot soldiers sifted through the concrete barriers only to meet withering machine gun fire from positions safely out of reach of the stranded armor.

The tankers discovered a rough roadway of stone and earth that allowed passage through the concrete antitank pylons. Led by a Scorpion (flail) tank, they proceeded slowly for fear of mines. The Scorpion floundered in the soft dirt, and only the intrepid action of its crew and a platoon leader who hitched up two mediums (Sherman tanks) to drag it out enabled Task Force Doan to maneuver past the dragon's teeth and start a rampage against the machine gun bunkers. But the infantrymen already pinned down could not disengage to protect the armor. The Germans, using the deadly *panzerfaust* (a one-shot rocket) disabled four of the tanks. To add to the attackers' problems, a German assault gun unit, committed to meet the threat of Task Force Lovelady, had detrained at Aachen and was diverted to contend with Task Force Doan. It arrived on the scene in time to destroy several more tanks. Within an hour, the task force had lost ten Shermans, half of its complement.

Combat Command A, the parent of Task Force Doan, summoned reinforcements, two more platoons of tanks plus a battalion of infantrymen from the 26th Regiment. German gunners quickly trained their sights on the additions, but, under cover of darkness, both tanks and foot soldiers advanced without serious losses. A torrent of shells from the armor killed, wounded, or drove off the opposition at the village of Nuetheim, just beyond the first band of the Westwall. There the task force paused for the remainder of the night.

The modest successes achieved by the 3d Armored's task forces were not replicated by infantry troops that attacked closer to Aachen. Two battalions of the 16th Infantry engaged in firefights around a series of roadblocks and coped with skillful delaying tactics by German units, which exacted a toll as they retreated.

Collins decided that, however tempting the jewel of Aachen, if he committed his forces to a drawn-out, house-to-house battle for the city, he might lose any opportunity to overrun the Westwall. Years later, he commented, "By this time we had a limitation on gasoline and a limitation on ammunition, and a serious question arose as to whether or not we would make our main effort to crack through the Siegfried defenses or to capture Aachen, which was just inside of my zone of action.

"I discussed it with [Maj. Gen.] Huebner [commander of the 1st Division], who urged that they go ahead to take the high ground overlooking the city." Huebner observed Aachen from one of those heights and remarked that it would be a "hard nut to crack." Collins ordered the 3d Armored, led by Maj. Gen. Maurice Rose, to press forward and breach both the Scharnhorst and Schill Lines, while the 1st and 9th Divisions' advances protected the flanks. Still confident he could defeat anything the enemy cared to risk, Collins, in recognition of the logistical difficulties facing the First Army, directed that the advance should go no farther than the west bank of the Roer River.

Bypassing Aachen, the VII Corps struck out in a northeast vector toward the town of Stolberg and a corridor through the Scharnhorst and Schill defenses. At the same time, the deployment of the Americans threw a cordon around Aachen itself. For the attack, the 1st Division received the assignment of isolating Aachen and protecting the left flank of the 3d Armored plunging directly toward Stolberg with the ultimate goal of taking Eschweiler. The new plan focused attention on the right flank of the main thrust toward the Roer, the Monschau corridor, a four-mile-wide, seven-mile-long plateau extending northeast. The ridge was in the midst of the dense wooded preserve known as the Huertgen Forest, and it was lightly sprinkled with small towns and villages—Huertgen, Schmidt, Vossenack, Hamich, Kesternich—names that would become terribly familiar to American soldiers.

Collins chose the 9th Infantry Division, another veteran of the North Africa campaign and commanded by Maj. Gen. Louis A. Craig, to secure the Monschau corridor and the right flank of the tanks and armored infantry aimed at the Stolberg corridor. The 9th's participation required a hasty move forward before it could enter the Huertgen Forest and the Monschau corridor. Once on the line, the 9th drew the difficult task of penetrating the Huertgen Forest, beyond which lay Düren, a city on the Roer.

Temporarily, the V Corps remained inactive except for a feint executed by the 5th Armored. The history of the division, *Paths of Armor,* notes, "V Corps ordered a show of strength to be made against the enemy's border defenses. At three in the afternoon all of the division's big guns, including the artillery pieces, tank and tank destroyer cannons poured out a thunderous barrage of steel that rocked the Siegfried fortifications. From Germany came no response." Instructions for a genuine offensive by the V Corps, coordinated with that of its neighbors to the north, arrived late. It was not until that evening that the 5th Armored commenced a bona fide attack, with the mission to capture the high ground south of Mettendorf, more than five miles inside Germany.

Task Force Lovelady resumed its drive on 14 September and rolled more than four miles through the countryside until it neared the Vechte River, southwest of Stolberg. Night had fallen, and, although the Germans had demolished the local bridge, armored infantry crossed the stream, heedless of sporadic mortar bursts and brief spurts of small-arms fire, taking advantage of the low water. They seized a clutch of the dreaded 88mm guns after the frightened gun crews hid instead of manning their weapons. Engineers next began to construct a bridge to accommodate the tanks.

Further progress meant breaching the more formidable Schill band of fortifications. Fortunately for the 3d Armored GIs, the sector they attacked held a Landesschutzen battalion, the third-rate, hastily cobbled together defensive forces. Under pressure, these Germans abandoned their posts during the night. When the American tanks rattled across the newly built bridge on the Vechte, they encountered no fire from the deserted pillboxes. Within an hour, the first American tanks clanked past the Schill Line's final bunkers. Task Force Lovelady had passed through both stretches of the Westwall.

The progress of Lovelady's unit aided the efforts of Task Force Mills—Maj. Herbert Mills had assumed command after Colonel King was wounded. At Schmidthof, the enemy, in danger of being outflanked, retreated, allowing Mills's armor to break through the Scharnhorst relatively unimpeded. But at the Vechte, Task Force Mills, instead of a reluctant Landesschutzen, met disciplined and determined Panzers whose four tanks and assault guns drove off the Americans.

Closer to Aachen, the 16th Infantry of the 1st Division broke through the Scharnhorst Line against token resistance, and when it took the high ground, the division surrounded the city on three sides. Karl Wolf, raised in Wethersfield, Connecticut, had entered the U.S. Military Academy as a classmate of John Beach in the summer of 1940. "I learned a lot at West Point about training and leadership that later came in handy during the war years," said Wolf. "Also [the Academy] taught me to strive to be a perfectionist and the necessity of always checking on things and planning ahead in every small detail." Following the attack on Pearl Harbor, classes at West Point accelerated, and Wolf graduated in three years. "With the war on, the big push among cadets was flying or joining the infantry. I failed the eye test for flying and then was determined to get into the infantry. Two of us were going to ask for the Marine Corps if we couldn't get the infantry, [but] we didn't have any problem getting into the infantry."

Wolf attended the Basic Infantry Officers School for three months, before his posting to the 76th Infantry Division. "I kept trying to get assigned for overseas combat duty, although after three months with the division, I was promoted to first lieutenant. In April of 1944, the division had to ship most of the officers overseas as replacements and I got my wish."

When Wolf reached England on 15 May, he was dispatched to the 3d Battalion of the 16th Infantry, 1st Division, preparing to assault

Omaha Beach three weeks later. Because he came to the organization so late in the war, there was no time to integrate Wolf into a rifle company, so he headed for the beach aboard a landing craft packed with battalion staff personnel.

The boat let them off among the X-shaped steel girders designed to obstruct landing craft. The first few men ahead of Wolf were cut down by German machine guns, which stippled the waist-deep water. Wolf glimpsed two soldiers killed by the guns and floating away. When Wolf finally climbed onto the beach, he noticed that the men around him wore division patches of the 29th Infantry Division. The navy had landed his boat a thousand yards from its designated location.

With the senior officer killed, Wolf assembled about a dozen men and led them toward their assigned destination. Along the way he saw all of the horrors of D Day: a soldier with an entire leg split to the bone, the upper half of another body, men drowning because fifty pounds of equipment covered their flotation devices, and a half-track and its crew disappear in a single mighty explosion. Wolf later temporarily led a rifle company but returned to battalion staff duty, then in August became the executive officer of K Company.

The outfit participated in the offensive of 12–13 September, which hacked its way into the Siegfried Line. "The Germans had been routed in Belgium and had not had time to set up the defenses in the Siegfried Line. Some of the pillboxes were not even manned. The regiment then attempted to go south of Aachen and ran into a fanatic German defense of its first major city under ground attack. The Germans used heavy artillery and mortar fire, and a new German division had been brought in to defend Aachen."

Wolf continued, "Our 1st Battalion had taken Münsterbusch and then had been ordered to advance on Stolberg. The battalion had lost 300 men in five days at that point. In Stolberg, which had been pretty well destroyed, the fighting was house to house. We came under fire directed from the German observation post on Crucifix Hill and the Verlautenheide Ridge. We held up our advance and dug in our positions."

The 1st Division had secured the flank, enabling Combat Command A to renew its advance northeast toward Eschweiler. Another battalion of those ersatz German soldiers quickly fled their bunkers, and the objective for the tankers, Hill 228 in the Schill Line, seemed ready to fall.

Suddenly, from well-concealed positions, a bevy of German anti-tank guns erupted with a volley of projectiles that shattered six tanks. CCA's commander, General Hickey, summoned reserves, including men from the 16th Infantry. After fierce exchanges, the Americans suppressed the resistance, and CCA tanks and armored infantry trundled beyond all but the final installations of the Schill Line.

By 15 September, the overall gains for the First Army offensive added up to a pair of narrow alleys through the Westwall. Although Hodges and Collins had agreed that the Stolberg-Eschweiler passage was their top priority and Aachen a matter for later attention, they kept their intentions somewhat disguised by an almost constant barrage of artillery fire into the city. General Shack, the German Seventh Army commander, nibbled at the bait, refusing to deploy the bulk of his 116th Panzer Division under von Schwerin to meet the threat in the Stolberg corridor.

At the start of the reconnaissance in force, four days earlier, Shack, persuaded that Aachen was in immediate jeopardy, ordered von Schwerin to take his understrength 116th Panzer Division and counterattack against the GIs of the 1st Infantry Division, now in the Aachen Municipal Forest, southwest of the city. In an embarrassing turnabout, von Schwerin, reluctantly accepting that Aachen would become a battleground, countermarched his troops to the city's outskirts.

Inside Aachen, von Schwerin coped with near hysteria among the citizens, a state of panic fueled by the absence of civil authorities, including the police. A committee of residents pleaded with von Schwerin to create some sort of bureaucracy to deal with administration of Aachen. Even as he considered the request, a direct edict from Adolf Hitler via military channels directed the town be evacuated, by force if necessary. The general started the process, while the Nazi functionaries and police, who previously had departed, returned. They discovered the letter of surrender von Schwerin had written and insisted he be tried as a traitor by a party "people's court."

Von Schwerin obstinately declined to appear. He put his trust in his soldiers and behind a wall of troops armed with machine guns hid in a farmhouse, believing he would be needed once the battle for Aachen began. When he and his superiors at last realized that the American focus lay elsewhere, he presented himself at German Seventh Army headquarters to account for his actions. Field Marshal Karl Rudolph Gerd von Rundstedt interceded to ensure that his fellow officer faced a tribunal of his peers, rather than one of Nazi party regulars. Von Schwerin received only mild punishment, assignment to an officer pool, and eventually worked his way back to a top command in Italy.

On 16 September, the First Army's VII Corps detected the unwelcome presence of the fresh, fully equipped, well-schooled Wehrmacht 12th Infantry Division. When the 3d Armored sought to renew its advance on 17 September, it collided with the newcomers and a stalemate ensued. A rain of American artillery pelted the 12th Division soldiers unmercifully, but the 3d Armored was too short of resources to continue.

South of the VII Corps, toward the Luxembourg border with Germany, the V Corps's 4th Division, a regular army unit that had arrived on D Day at Utah Beach, also cracked into the Westwall. Lieutenant George Wilson was a replacement with Company E's 2d Platoon, 22d Infantry Regiment. Wilson had not expected to find himself leading a platoon, because both the marines and navy had rejected him for poor eyesight. However, after the draft swept him from Michigan State, the college he attended on a football scholarship, the army was less fastidious. In fact, almost immediately after induction, he became a member of a special training group designated as probable fodder for Officers Candidate School (OCS).

Following completion of the OCS course, Wilson briefly served as a training officer and joined the 86th Division while it maneuvered through mud, rain, ice, and swamps in Louisiana before he and other officers shipped out as overseas replacements. On 12 July, Wilson, after several weeks behind the lines in France, rode in a truck to the headquarters of the 22d Infantry, the first 4th Division soldiers to wade onto Utah Beach.

Wilson's introduction to the regimental commander, Col. Charles T. "Buck" Lanham, was hardly reassuring. "He was a small, wiry man who looked as tough as he was gruff. He wasted no time in scaring the hell out of us. He stated flatly that the German resistance was very stubborn, and our losses were extremely high. He explained how tough it was to cross a field with the Germans dug in behind every hedgerow. 'As officers I expect you to lead your men. Men will follow a leader, and I expect my platoon leaders to be right up front. Losses could be very high. Use every skill you possess. If you survive your first battle, I'll promote you. Good luck.'"

Fortunately for Wilson and other newcomers, there was some time for instruction and practice in the techniques to overcome the hedgerow defenses. He received his baptism of fire, like John Beach, after the massive aerial bombardment on 25 July that wrought death and destruction on both Americans and Germans in the Normandy breakout. "Just west of Saint-Lô," wrote Wilson, "we came upon a dreadful sight. The destructive power of those thousands of five-hundred-pound bombs overwhelmed the senses. The dead from both sides lay twisted and torn, some half buried by overturned earth. Bloated cows with stiff legs thrust skyward in death lay everywhere, as did burned-out vehicles and blasted equipment. . . .

"When the order to move out had first come, my muscles had been taut with fear. After a while I realized that somehow my body was moving forward behind the tanks as my platoon took the lead. It seemed to me like the first few moments of a football game. As we advanced I began to feel my mind and body working together again—still very scared, but functioning."

Within twenty-four hours, he had shot his first man, a German sergeant abandoning his blazing tank, underwent the trauma of seeing his own men killed and wounded, and earned a Silver Star. Exactly one month after his first day of combat, Lieutenant Wilson rode slowly through the crowded streets of Paris to a wild celebration by the citizens, some of them brandishing weapons they had allegedly used against the Germans. The 22d Regiment then continued its pursuit of the enemy, gobbling up fifty to sixty miles per day against light resistance until they approached the border and its Siegfried Line of pillboxes and other fortifications.

"Colonel Lanham," said Wilson, "believed the best way to end the war quickly and save lives was to attack and attack. He also believed wholeheartedly that the boys of the 22d Infantry Regiment shared his spirit, that they could do the job if anyone could. The Siegfried Line was, to him, more an opportunity than an obstacle. He wanted his regiment to be the first Americans through the line, as they'd already been first across the border into Germany." (According to the official records, that honor belonged to the patrol from the 5th Armored Division.)

According to Wilson, the tactics prescribed for overcoming the bunkers, which provided mutual protection through overlapping fields of fire, required a coordinated choreography. "The vulnerable part of the pillbox was its rear. The crossfire support did not reach back there, and all they had was some barbed wire and whatever rifles and machine guns could be transferred to the rear trenches. The trick was to get behind a pillbox quickly. . . .

"The tanks and TDs [tank destroyers] also were to come up to within 200 to 500 yards of the pillboxes and plaster them with direct cannon fire against their firing apertures and steel doors. Artillery would fire hundreds of rounds onto the same targets. Many of the Germans thus would be pinned down and occupied with their own safety, and, it was hoped, would not be very effective against us.

"For close support, right up beside a pillbox, the infantry had two deadly weapons, flamethrowers and satchel charges. The flamethrower was operated by one man with a tank strapped to his back. The flame from the hose was huge, but the man had to get within ten to twenty yards of his target. If he could get close enough to an aperture, he could blind or suffocate those inside the pillbox. Some of the enemy might also be set on fire.

"The satchel charge had a long fuse attached to twelve pounds of TNT, six pounds on each side of a saddlelike bag. If it could be set off in one of the pillbox openings, it would kill or stun anyone inside. With both weapons, a man had to get in very close. Dangerous work, but it really paid off. Either close-in weapon could finish off a pillbox—providing the attacker could stay alive long enough to use them."

On 13 September, from positions around Saint-Vith, a Belgian town in the Ardennes, the regiment attacked and broke through, and it reached a position in the hills half a mile east of the Westwall near Sellerich. Lanham claimed that, given the go-ahead, the offensive could have been carried all the way to the Rhine. But the supply lines that stretched all the way back to Cherbourg could not feed the Allied war machine. Wilson learned later that the 4th Division possessed only enough gas to move each vehicle five miles, and only a day's supply of ammunition was on hand. There were rumors that everything was being given to Patton's Third Army, but, in fact, that organization also was starved for materials.

And despite Lanham's belief, there was plenty of fight left in the enemy. Wilson and his cohorts watched as a battalion from another division jumped off to capture Sellerich. "At first everything went exactly by the book, as tank-infantry teams performed beautifully, wiping out pockets of Germans in their path. We could see every move and heard the continual clatter of the tanks' machine guns and the crack of rifles. We could even hear the excited shouts of men in combat."

But suddenly the enemy wreaked a reversal. "German mortars and artillery, which had not been evident up to that point, suddenly came down hard on the infantry and tanks as they reached a small exposed area at a crossroad. There was no cover from the terrible barrage; the Germans knew the exact range and obviously had been waiting for the Americans to reach that point.

"The American tanks turned and raced back toward the woods to escape the slaughter, panicking the riflemen who chased after the tanks in confusion. The retreat was an uncontrolled stampede, and a great many casualties were left where they fell. Even at our safe distance we all felt sick. It could so easily have been us."

Although his company was forced to rely on a single map produced in 1914, on the following day the battalion attacked. At one point, Wilson and his colleagues ambushed a platoon of either poorly trained or careless soldiers. Huddled around a shelter to protect themselves from the rain, the troops had stacked their weapons some distance away. It was a slaughter.

"We had very little time to exult. In fact, even before I had time to report to Captain [Arthur] Newcomb or confer with Lieutenant Mason, the Germans hit us with a full platoon counterattack. They seemed to come from the woods, directly across the field from us.

"I instantly ordered my men back across the road and into the ditch, where they had some protection. The Jerries would fire at us as they ran toward us, and every few seconds they would hit the ground and fire some more. We tried to pick them off every time they got up to rush us, but the rain continued steadily and the visibility was poor.

"Some of them made it up behind the pines and fired rapidly enough to pin us down. I yelled at my men to throw grenades and return the fire. Then, Captain Newcomb ordered me to withdraw into the woods and rejoin the rest of Company E, so I moved along the line and got each squad to pull back two men at a time.

"Between the woods and the road was a strip of a hayfield about thirty yards wide. The hay was two feet high, and most of our men crawled back safely, though the last squad lost two men. Sergeant Williams, who had been shot through the neck around D Day and was returned to action only to get paralyzed at Le Mesnil Herman back in July, had a grenade land by him, and he became paralyzed again. So we had to drag him back into the woods.

"I yelled at one of the sergeants to hurry and get his men out of there. The sergeant thereupon stood right up in the open, for no reason at all that I could figure, and immediately was cut down by a German burp gun, a small machine pistol that fired so fast it sounded like a *b-r-r-r-r-ip*.

"To my mind the sergeant's girlfriend was responsible for the naked carelessness that caused his death. Just the day before he had shown me a Dear John letter he'd received from her. It was the most wickedly cruel letter I had ever read, and it morbidly depressed the sergeant. He was from the South, and this little wench told him, among similar tidbits, that she had been sleeping with a Negro, and that he was twice the man Sergeant Hester was.

"The rain still came down in torrents, and the Germans made no attempt to follow us into the woods. We had seen enough action for one day, so we dug in for the night among the tall pines. Each foxhole had to be big enough for two men, with one being on guard while the other slept, taking turns every two hours all night. The tree roots gave us plenty of trouble, but we managed with a few axes."

In the V Corps, Gerow also sent the 28th Division, led by Maj. Gen. Norman "Dutch" Cota, into the Westwall. Cota had been the deputy commander of the 29th Infantry Division when it hit the very bloody Omaha Beach on D Day and earned credit for having played a major role in spurring the men to vacate the killing zone at the shoreline. Like the 4th Division, the 28th also paraded through Paris upon its liberation. The division continued northeast to seize a Belgian rail and road hub named Bastogne before crossing into Luxembourg on the right flank of the 4th Division.

Ralph Johnson, a member of the Pennsylvania-based 28th Division, originally a National Guard outfit that was federalized as the war clouds darkened, had been asleep in a Virginia cornfield while snow covered his blanket when a nearby radio awakened him. "I cursed the operator of that little black box—tried to go back to sleep but the blast persisted, so I uncovered my head and tried to listen: Pearl Harbor—bombed."

Warrant Officer Johnson was assigned the job of assistant adjutant for the 110th Infantry Regiment and recalled the happy parade through Paris, which actually ended in a deadly firefight with rear guard elements evacuating the city. "As we hit the Siegfried Line early in September, the thought was that we would quickly reduce the bunkers and pillboxes, smash through the dragon's teeth and push to the Rhine River. During the early attacks on the pillboxes, it was necessary to send to the rear for a truckload of satchel charges of TNT, so named as the blocks of TNT were wired together with a handle similar to a small suitcase. As the load of charges was dumped in the Company F area, Capt. Robert H. Shultz had the nasty job of furnishing a detail to work the charges forward to the jump-off point for the attack. The mortar section was the only one immediately available, and Lt. William Whiddon and his men were tagged for the job. As they proceeded to move the charges, a tremendous explosion occurred and Lieutenant Whiddon and his entire detail of sixteen men were literally blown to bits. The cause of the explosion was never determined; however, it is thought that some Kraut slipped into the area and put a booby trap in the trailer containing the charges, and when the first one was moved, it detonated.

"Company F, 2d Battalion, commanded by Captain Shultz, was assigned the task of attacking and capturing a pillbox near Grosskampfenberg, Germany, by Maj. Harold R. Yeager, regimental operations officer. This was a stupid attack at the outset, as it did not have sufficient artillery support to succeed, and it cost Company F a total of 145 casualties, sixteen of the company remaining after the smoke had cleared away. That night, Captain Schultz and the remaining men of his company holed up in the pillbox, and during the night, the enemy counterattacked with flamethrowers and recaptured the pillbox. Captain Schultz and the others were taken prisoner."

Glen Vannatta had picked up his bachelor of science from Indiana University in April 1943 along with his second lieutenant's commission through the ROTC. After serving for a year with the 69th Infantry Division in Mississippi, he entered the stream of replacement officers pouring into England.

"I went to Normandy in early July and joined the 28th Division early in August, after they had five days of combat. I was assigned as CO of Company D, 110th Infantry Regiment, and started fighting in the hedgerows the next day. Initiation into combat was very confusing with hedgerow-to-hedgerow fighting, where enemy rifle and machine gun fire coupled with mortar and artillery made every move life threatening. My emotions were to be scared all the time but driven to do my duty regardless of risks.

"During the Siegfried battle, while I was in temporary command of B Company [rifle], we received a group of perhaps twenty replacements, who got caught in a German artillery shelling behind us and about half were casualties. The others were put into foxholes and their 'buddy' gave the 'orientation,' probably with considerable profanity. I believe but cannot assert that many of them seldom or never fired their weapons."

Communications Sergeant Ed Bergman, a member of the ill-fated F Company of the 110th Regiment, recalled, "We crossed the border into Germany at Supach, when my company was designated as the point company and reinforced with armor and given the task to probe eastward as a reconnaissance in force with the regiment deployed behind us. Company F met stiff resistance at the town of Heiderscheid and was troubled by roadblocks. We continued on until we made contact with the Germans' Siegfried Line at Grosskampfenberg.

"On September 13th the 2d Battalion launched its attack. After penetrating through the dragon's teeth, we came up against the line of pillboxes. My Company F fought for and captured six pillboxes in its assigned sector by September 13th. The next morning the Germans counterattacked. They killed off our outside security. We were unable to defend the pillboxes from the rear side [the Americans occupied those they captured]. They then blew in the rear doors with their version of the bazooka, backed up tracked vehicles with mounted flamethrowers, and cremated what few survivors were left. The company commander then surrendered what few survivors were left."

Obviously, the Germans could no longer be regarded as impotent and the 28th had a taste of the misfortune that lay ahead. Nevertheless, Sylvan's diary reported apparent progress: "4th Division advanced over German soil through heavily mined areas and successive roadblocks. Artillery fire was heavy here, as nowhere else. 28th Division found similar situations. Both the 4th and 28th Divisions six to seven miles inside enemy territory."

The foe along the Westwall now offered increasingly stiff opposition, even though the defenders mainly came from the Landesschutzen, or home guard. They were far from crack, experienced troops, but the pillboxes, bunkers, interlocking fire, dragon's teeth, barbed wire, and mines transformed them into a deadly enemy. The American strategists underestimated the strength of the Westwall. The First Army apparently believed in the World War I doctrine that an attacker with a three-to-one advantage in numbers could overwhelm fixed emplacements. Many German experts theorized it would require a six-to-one ratio. The U.S. tacticians had not reckoned with the enormous amount of concrete poured into the structures. Both the new 90mm antiaircraft gun, developed to match the excellent German 88, and the 75mm and 76mm guns mounted on tanks and tank destroyers chipped at but did not rupture the walls of the pillboxes. Many of the camouflaged emplacements were so artfully concealed that intelligence had not detected their presence. And as Levasseur remarked, the situation at the Siegfried Line demanded that GIs have the know-how to come close enough to their targets before they could destroy them.

Although the offensive had already slowed and the men up front knew they faced an uncertain future, a mood of optimism percolated through the command headquarters and overflowed to shape the public perception. Radio stations in the United States and music halls in England sounded a new tune, "We're Gonna Hang Our Washing on the Siegfried Line!"

But on 17 September, an action hundreds of miles away brought direct consequences on the First Army drive toward the Roer. Field Marshal Sir Bernard Montgomery, in a daring and, for him, an uncharacteristically radical plan, mounted Operation Market Garden. Thousands of paratroopers and glider-borne troops struck behind the enemy lines in the Netherlands, while British armor attempted to crash through the German defenses. Although the Allies had liberated the deep-water port of Antwerp in Belgium, it was useless, because the Germans still held the Schelde estuary, a fifty-mile passageway that lay between Antwerp and the North Sea. If Market Garden was a success, Antwerp, a lesser distance to the front than Cherbourg, could be used to funnel supplies and reinforcements. Furthermore, once the region was secured, it offered a pathway to outflank the Westwall and the Rhine and act as a shortcut to Berlin. Hastily plotted and activated, Market Garden took top priority when it came to fuel, ammunition, and air support, which would have a direct impact on the ability of the First Army to muster sufficient strength to continue its advance.

3

INTO THE WOODS

Strategic and tactical planning on the most elemental level stresses the absolute necessity to protect the flank of a unit as it attempts to advance. As veterans of World War I, Hodges and Collins could recall a devastating attack in 1918 on the American Expeditionary Forces' flank from an enemy that swept down from the Argonne Forest. On the right flank of the drive toward the Roer, via the Stolberg corridor, was what American soldiers called the Huertgen Forest. The dense trees extended over a seventy-square-mile triangle formed by Aachen, Düren, and Monschau. Through the forest, a pair of ridges, separated by the deep gorge of the Kall River, ran from the southwest to the northeast in the direction of the Roer. The high-ground timber had been cleared, making both ridges excellent observation and artillery sites.

To negate a possible flank attack from this area, Hodges and Collins tossed in another blue chip, the 9th Infantry Division, commanded by Maj. Gen. Louis A Craig. A regular army outfit bloodied in North Africa, and further experienced through hard fighting across France, the division was well below its normal strength. It had moved so swiftly across France that replacements could not catch up. The crossing of the Meuse River on 5 September had all but wiped out the entire 2d Battalion of the 60th Infantry, which could account for only twenty-five men from the three rifle companies, two machine gun platoons, and part of the communications unit deployed during the fighting. With a single experienced company commander and four noncoms still on their feet, the 2d Battalion lacked adequate leadership. Unable to draw from its depleted brother battalions for replacements, the 2d could only appoint people from the scant number left and any promising newcomers. Most of these were soldiers drafted from antiaircraft units and less schooled in infantry tactics. The other battalions of that regiment could barely muster about 40 percent of what was listed in the table of organization. Neither of the brother regiments, the 39th and 47th, could field anything close to full companies. The dearth of infantrymen persisted despite an increased flow of replacements.

Making things more dangerous, training the latest arrivals was nearly impossible, because the regiments were almost constantly engaged with the enemy. The supply and fuel shortages mentioned by Sylvan altered the combat effectiveness of the outfit. During an engagement just before the start of the First Army offensive, a lack of gasoline denied support for the 60th Infantry armor. There was not enough ammunition available for a major battle, and some GIs had to supplement their K and C rations with food captured from German soldiers.

In its weakened condition, the division nevertheless was responsible for a seventeen-mile-wide sector, far more than field manuals list as the maximum. Furthermore, the overall mission called for the 9th to carry out an incredible feat—clearing the entire seventy square miles of forest, from a starting point at Monschau along a northeast axis toward Düren. The strategists were emboldened by intelligence that reported much of the forest soldier-free, and where units of the Wehrmacht were detected, they seemed staffed with recruits still in training, men otherwise unfit to serve in normal combat duties, so-called "volunteers" from occupied lands on the eastern front and skeletal organizations short on artillery and ammunition.

On 14 September, the 47th Infantry Regiment entered the campaign on the right flank of the 3d Armored. The foot soldiers, following in the wake of Task Force Lovelady, struck along the edges of the Wenau and Roetgen Forests in an effort to widen the breach in the Schill Line. The most immediate objectives were the towns of Vechte, Zweifall, and Schevenhutte, and the ultimate goal was the city of Düren on the Roer.

In the division history, *Eight Stars to Victory*, the narrative describes conditions that increasingly bedeviled the combatants. "The weather was anything but favorable on September 14th. A steady drizzle which began during the preceding afternoon had grown more heavy by the hour. Gradually the continuous rainfall increased in intensity, becoming a 'drenching downpour' which kept its strength until about noon of the 14th. By then the ground was a cold mass of mud; the damp, wooded areas had assumed a more forbidding appearance and the going became tougher on the foot sloggers, who had to keep continually alert for signs of the enemy."

The regimental commander, Col. George Smythe, a former West Point quarterback, directed the column that crossed the frontier at Roetgen and continued perhaps a mile and a half, where the 3d Battalion peeled off, heading due east into the Roetgen Forest. The two other battalions trekked toward Zweifall at the confluence of the Vechte and smaller Hassel River. There was little opposition and, unhampered by enemy fire, engineers quickly erected a temporary bridge over the Vechte to replace one destroyed by the retreating Germans. While the 1st Battalion occupied Zweifall, the 2d leapfrogged ahead, engaging in brief skirmishes with defenders, apparently acting as rear guards for a general withdrawal.

In the forest, a platoon sergeant, Charles A. Karnak, of the 3d Battalion, moved along a narrow road and spotted a well-hidden pillbox. A pair of enemy soldiers, apparently unaware of the oncoming GIs, lounged at the entrance. Karnak yelled at them to surrender and they complied, along with another fifteen inside the emplacement. A brief firefight ensued farther into the woods, but the Germans yielded swiftly, and the battalion bagged another forty prisoners.

Pushing farther, the lead elements of the regiment finished their day, six miles northeast of Roetgen, and the outfit was all the way through the first barrier of the Westwall. Shortly before dawn of the second day, nearly a battalion of Germans launched a counterattack against an American roadblock. Denied in their request to withdraw, the greatly outnumbered GIs put up enough of a fight to detour the foe in another direction. As the Wehrmacht soldiers marched in closely packed ranks, they blundered into the main body of the 3d Battalion of the 47th. First to see them approaching was SSgt. James La Barr. He aimed his carbine at the officer in the lead and put a bullet between his eyes. Other GIs opened fire and

Pfc. Luther Roush, on a tank destroyer, turned a .50-caliber machine gun on the Germans. Within an hour, the Americans shattered the entire unit, inflicting heavy casualties. The 47th advanced another three miles, fighting off counterattacks and infiltrators. On its way toward Vechte, the regiment discovered a map on a prisoner. It showed the exact locations of every emplacement in the Zweifall area, which helped the attackers capture Vechte and its surrounding hamlets.

Lieutenant Chester H. Jordan, son of a disabled father and a mother who worked in a beauty parlor in Dallas, led a platoon for Company K of the 47th Infantry. Jordan had entered Texas A&M University in 1939. He volunteered for military training while in high school and spent two summers at Fort Bragg, North Carolina, in a citizens' military training camp, where he learned field artillery. But after being called up while at Texas A&M, Jordan entered OCS, where he obtained a commission in the infantry.

In July 1944, as a replacement officer, Jordan joined the 9th Division on the eve of Cobra, the Normandy breakout operation that would be proceeded by a massive air strike. "Waiting for the bombers gave me some time to talk to Sergeant Sheldon [3d platoon sergeant and a veteran of the North Africa and Sicily campaigns]. I told him what he already knew—I didn't know poodly-shit about combat, and though I would take the responsibility and issue the orders, I wanted him to tell me what to order. I also said that when I felt like I knew what I was doing, I would probably ask less questions, but he should feel free to tell me what he thought whether I asked or not."

Jordan had barely finished his brief dissertation on their relationship when the heavy bombers began to unload, with one of the first explosions hurling both of them into the air. In one of the worst cases of friendly fire, the overtures to Cobra dropped thousands of tons on American soldiers. Jordan's company commander said, "I think the bastards got me, look at my right leg." Jordan examined him and found that a piece of shrapnel had pierced his canteen, and what he thought was blood was water flowing down his leg.

The newcomer turned to Lieutenant Squires, the executive officer who had earned a Distinguished Service Cross, Silver Star with cluster, and several Purple Hearts, of whom he said, "The men not only respected and loved him, yes, loved him, they were in awe of him. One of his most recent exploits was jumping on the top of a tank from a hedgerow, catching armed grenades thrown to him and dropping them down the hatch. Lieutenant Squires was on his knees next to the captain with his head bowed as though in prayer. I couldn't see a wound or blood anywhere on him, but he wasn't moving. A medic came up and asked him if he needed help, putting his hand on Squires's shoulder at the same time. When the medic touched him, Squires fell over stone cold dead." The executive officer was one of 111, including Lt. Gen. Leslie McNair, killed by the errant bombs, with another 490 wounded.

As the organization approached the border of Germany, Jordan had became accustomed to the grim life of a combat soldier. He recalled crossing the frontier on 14 September. "[It] didn't amount to much more than a freight station with a sign saying 'ROTT' hanging on it. We entered the Huertgen Forest, where we were to stay for the next two months. Most of the Huertgen Forest is a tree farm. The firs are planted in rows about eight to twelve feet apart. The trees are planted so close together in the rows that some mature trees form an almost impenetrable wall. At regular intervals both parallel and across the rows are firebreaks—a 150- to 300-foot-wide strip that was cleared of vegetation. Every so often we came to a cut-over area that had been replanted in seedlings. It was a crackerjack place for defense, but it wasn't worth a damn for offense.

"For two days we saw nothing but trees. We saw no Germans, no buildings, nothing. On the second day, we were so close to Zweifall that their air raid sirens sounded as though they were in the next row of trees. Our radios picked up their air raid warning—*Achtung! Achtung! Nord-Oest Deutschland*—et cetera. We were skirting civilization narrowly. I was reading *The Bishop's Jaeggers* [a racy novel by Thorne Smith] and enjoying it so much that I was delighted we had nothing to do but walk. But I worried that my laughter might alert the Krauts.

"On the third day my platoon was leading when we hit a nicely developed hiking trail. It was about eight feet wide with a curb on both sides and covered with pulverized stone. Presently, the hill fell away from the trail on the west side, and we got the longest view we had in a week. At the bottom of the hill was a road lined on the other side with buildings. People were going about their normal business without bothering to look up. We made no attempt to hide. As we proceeded along the trail, I saw a couple of boys walking along the sidewalk below in animated conversation. One was carrying a skinned carcass that he swung to illustrate his points. I said, 'My God, Sheldon. They are eating cats!' He reassured me that it was a rabbit. One of the buildings below had an ESSO gas pump but no customers. In fact, there were no vehicles standing or moving in our view. Even more important, there were no Kraut soldiers visible.

"Shortly, we came to a point where our ridge was cut by an intersecting road. The path turned east, so we had to leave its comfort. There were park benches on the path and an apple orchard, so it looked like a good place to take a break. We stacked our guns by the bench and filled our helmets with apples. This combination of getting out of the woods for a change, a pretty day and a chance to see it, vicarious peeping, and good apples gave our stop the atmosphere of a family picnic.

"It was cut too damn short by a soldier exclaiming, 'God damn, look at that!' On the road below us walked a German officer completely engrossed in a map he held in both hands. None of us had ever heard of a Kraut officer going anywhere alone, so we expected the shit to fly at any minute. We grabbed guns and ran or fell down the steep slope. It was a German colonel, who was not only surprised but pissed off something terrible. We de-souvenired him and sent him back. I learned later he was from the German 47th Division (same number as our regiment) and was reconnoitering for positions to place his outfit. He got his dander up in the rear because they weren't showing proper respect. They forced him to walk in front of the escorting tank like the peons.

"We crossed the road and went up the hill to the next ridge; the hiking path reappeared. The buildings below were now on both sides of the road, and a swift mountain brook ran between us and the backs of the buildings. Sergeant Myers was the last of my platoon to cross the road, and as he did, he heard a motorcycle coming down the road from the east. Obviously, a courier chasing after the colonel. Myers knelt next to a tree and fired. He blew the rider into the ditch, and the bike continued to the Schevenhutte road. When the entire platoon was lined up along the path above the village, I called a halt and radioed for instructions. They said, 'Take the village.'

"We did a left face and raced down the hill to the village. Our speed was the product of the steep hill rather than combat zeal. As we ran through the backyards, I looked for the handiest back door. The one I opened led into a small commercial kitchen and then directly into the taproom of a small hotel. The only inhabitant was a dignified old man with a large mustache who was wearing a frock-tailed coat and a shirt with a winged collar. I motioned him behind the bar and had him draw beer for the three of us in the room. I was getting ready for the second round when I heard rifle fire outside. I went to check.

"As I emerged from the bar I could see the machine gun section standing by the church on the Gressenich road, and I walked over to inquire about the shooting. The section had been going down the road to set up the MG when a Volkswagen jeep with four Kraut soldiers came barreling by. The Germans waved and our men reciprocated, and both realized at the same time that they were fraternizing with the enemy. They had managed a few rifle shots, but the car had turned left at the church and headed for Düren. By the time our men had gotten back to the corner, the Germans had abandoned their jeep at the creek and disappeared into the woods. I walked down to the creek and found that the small bridge had been blown, which occasioned their abandoning their transportation. As I walked back to the village, a P51 pinned me against the church wall and dumped its .50-caliber clips on me as it fired at the rest of the company."

Jordan and his platoon briefly explored Schevenhutte, a Y-shaped town that sat in a valley surrounded by hills. The base of the Y pointed southeast to Kleinhau, a hamlet deep in the Huertgen zone. The right arm of the Y led northeast to Merberich, some four miles from Düren, while the left limb headed toward Gressenich. As an integral part of the defenses, Schevenhutte housed a massive concrete bunker with accommodations to suit a company of soldiers. Within that structure was a telephone, still connected to other German units, including some that were stationed in the Westwall.

Jordan remembers, "The German jeep evidently did not share their information with anyone, because for three days German soldiers on leave wandered into the village looking for a brew or what have you. Battalion sent a German-speaking sergeant to man the bunker phone. He would hear about the Krauts gathering at a particular spot, and as soon as they had assembled would saturate the area with artillery fire. The Germans would then call for ambulances, and they would shell the access roads. The Germans would get into arguments on who was responsible for the fuckup, and he [the German-speaking sergeant] would exacerbate the mess. He was able to maintain this for several days before they tumbled to the party line."

The platoon led by Jordan, occupying Schevenhutte along the fringe of the Huertgen, had advanced to only about seven miles from where the Roer bellied out to pass through the strategic city of Düren. Jordan's description of what his small group experienced, their relatively easy and uncontested hike for three days, is not only in marked contrast to what happened to other 9th Division GIs, but also suggests that the enemy was often as confused and uninformed as the Americans.

Elsewhere, the 9th Division's initial attacks produced less satisfactory results. Southwest of the 47th, GIs from the 60th Regiment captured Camp Elsenborn, an installation that prior to 1940 housed a Belgian garrison and that would become a focal point during the Battle of the Bulge three months later. From there the Americans sought to advance on a ridge between Hoefen and Alzen, a pair of hamlets astride the Westwall, southeast of Monschau. There, however, pillboxes spewed concentrations of small-arms and machine gun bullets, obliging General Craig to bring up reinforcements. For nearly five days the defenders stalled the attackers, and it was not until tanks arrived to provide support that the Germans were driven out of their positions and the ridge between Alzen and Hoefen secured.

Northeast of Monschau, the 39th Infantry butted against a strong point in the Scharnhorst Line. The start of what would develop into a bloody ordeal is suggested by the log of experiences reported by the 39th Regiment's 3d Battalion commander, Lt. Col. R. H. Stumpf, and Capt. A. V. Danna, commanding officer of Company I. Incidentally, a note by the interviewers who interrogated Stumpf and Danna two months after the September offensive stated, "Officers and ranking noncoms of this battalion who were there at the time of this action have almost all been killed or evacuated."

On 14 September, the statement of two officers declared, "The battalion moved with two companies on tanks and TDs and shuttled the third, while the heavy weapons and headquarters units were on trucks. Three trucks had been stuck the night before and the column was short on gasoline.

"As they advanced through the woods of the Kozener Wald, a few snipers and one machine gun were encountered, but these were dusted off when the tanks fired into the trees along the road. At [Road Junction 942234] the 1st and 2d Battalions had turned sharply northwest in the direction of Roetgen, but the 3d bn continued east 800 yards before hitting another road which led directly north and which would connect with the forward elements of the regiment as they moved east from Roetgen. This section of the road had not yet been cleared of the enemy.

"As the 3d Bn approached the highway . . . it encountered the first enemy roadblock, consisting of a locked iron gate across the railroad and a number of mines. A platoon of the 15th Engineers attached to the battalion came up and removed the mines, and the tanks crashed through the gate. Stumpf had put out a security squad on the flank of the column in the direction of Konzen, and it engaged the enemy at a distance of 500 yards in a firefight. The skirmish did not develop into anything serious, however. At 1000, having been held up by the roadblock about an hour, the column continued north.

"Before the tail of the column could pass the point of the first roadblock, the leading elements hit another obstacle. This consisted of trees felled across the road, but it was neither mined nor covered with fire. The tanks moved up and looped cables around the trees, since they furnished both the strength to move the logs and protection [against] any mines under the logs.

"Five hundred yards farther north a third roadblock was hit, of trees and mines. The large crater in the middle of the road at this tree block was made passable by a tank dozer. Stumpf radioed for engineers to make the road suitable for heavy traffic, while the engineers pulled the mines, and the tanks dragged off the logs."

Early in the afternoon, the column passed through three more sets of obstacles, and it reached the road junction at Fringhaus. Its companion battalions, coming from different directions, marched through Fringhaus about the same time of day. Stumpf now received another mission, to follow the 1st Battalion toward Lammersdorf and, from that town, to push farther east toward Rollesbroich, on the other side of the Scharnhorst Line.

On the heels of a company from the 1st Battalion, which veered north, the 3d Battalion's K Company, supported by tanks, advanced through the center of Lammersdorf. Stumpf remarked that the Americans did not realize the Germans retained control of a knoll north of the town, and his narrative reported that Company K "received no enemy opposition through the center of the town, but as it reached the end of the heavily built up part and turned the bend in the road, it came under enemy mortar and 75mm AT [antitank] fire. The tanks fired at the AT gun and probably knocked it out."

The battalion commander committed I Company to the battle. "K Company moved forward along the scattered houses, as the enemy continued to use mortars and AT fire on their position. It advanced about 200 yards, with one platoon on each side of the road, and almost reached the dragon's teeth. Since it was getting dark, however, it did not try to breach the obstacle but held this position for the night.

"Meanwhile, I Company attacked in two columns along parallel trails leading northeast from the main road. The plan was for I to conduct a flank movement from the north on the enemy position and thus secure the area from the rear. I Company came under fire from the pillboxes and emplacements to its front as soon as they left the highway in Lammersdorf. The enemy used small arms at this time. [I Company] was able to advance no more than 200 yards before it became too dark to see. It then held its position for the night.

"Throughout the development of the attack by the 3d Battalion, the entire right flank was open to attack by the enemy from the southeast. Therefore, L Company was brought up to act both as a reserve for the battalion and as protection of the right flank. L Company set up a thin line from the railroad tracks on the west to a small trail near the dragon's teeth on the east and began to receive some fire from the southeast.

"By night, the entire battalion was thus deployed and under the fire of the enemy. One section of heavy machine guns were, as usual, with each company and the mortars were set up in the rear. The section of tanks with K Company fired at enemy positions, while the other section remained in the town to guard road crossings with the TD platoon. The AT guns were set up to hold the defense on the open flank to the southeast. L Company began to get long-range artillery fire, but K Company and I Company as yet received nothing heavier than 50mm mortars."

On the dawn of the third day, the enemy developed a counterattack against I Company. The Americans drove off the Germans and fought forward along two trails while under fire from pillboxes. Tanks and tank destroyers forced the bunkers to button up until the infantry could envelop them. But even though they were neutralized, I Company managed to gain only 300 yards, and the enemy small-arms and mortar fire remained heavy. Similarly, K Company could measure its success only in a few hundred yards.

The following day, 16 September, saw another very strong counterattack by German soldiers on I Company. The Teutons captured several GIs and swarmed over the lead outpost. Mortars and riflemen repulsed further efforts. I Company, with tanks in immediate support, then reversed the situation, and the enemy broke. A large number of them were taken prisoner, but K Company again struggled to maintain its positions because of small-arms fire and finely pinpointed artillery and antitank shells. The resistance continued to stiffen. Soldiers from L Company, hidden by a smoke screen, cleared a minefield through a gap in the dragon's teeth. But when a tank unit started through the opening, a mine blew up the first one. During the night, German engineers had remined the passageway. Almost an entire day was lost as other mines detonated during efforts to clear away the disabled tank and open the narrow gap.

Having regrouped, K Company renewed its thrust into the Scharnhorst. At a road junction a pillbox pinned down the company. Those at headquarters insisted that the map of the sector showed the emplacement arrow marked a different field of fire. The embattled company commander radioed, "To hell with the arrow. It's shooting on me."

Help appeared in the form of I Company moving along a trail that led toward the pillbox. Approaching from a different direction than that of K Company, the startled GIs suddenly realized they were on top of the fortification. When they called on the inhabitants to surrender, the reply came in the form of a rifle grenade out the door. The position seemed impregnable, with the Germans able to shoot through the door and its machine guns housed so deep in concrete tunnels that grenades thrown through openings could not do damage.

A prisoner taken by K Company agreed to speak to his comrades. He pleaded with the troops inside, telling them to think of their wives rather than continuing the war. They refused to yield. From the rear, out of reach from shot or shell by the pillbox, a tank dozer started to push dirt over the top, filling up the entrance halfway. The Germans were told they had five minutes to surrender. When the allotted time passed with no response, the dozer sealed the pillbox, burying the defenders.

The creators of the Westwall had correctly noted that a plateau without the natural impediments of heavy forest growth behind the border at Lammersdorf would provide easier terrain for an attacking force. Accordingly, the military engineers packed the Westwall in the Lammersdorf vicinity with an abundance of concrete fortifications to compensate for what nature omitted. Between 1,200 and 1,500 soldiers, albeit drawn largely from a training regiment, manned the weapons in the redoubts. When the 39th Infantry emerged from Lammersdorf, a murderous assortment of small arms and mortars from well-protected positions met them. The deadly outburst pinned down the GIs. Subsequently, a series of flanking maneuvers, tanks, and mobile guns managed to carve a narrow pathway through the Scharnhorst. However, the enemy retained control of a stretch of this band of the Westwall between

Monschau and Lammersdorf, exposing the 9th Division to assaults on its flanks. Under these circumstances, the hoped-for avenue through the Monschau corridor to the Roer remained unavailable.

In the first days of the offensive, the mood at First Army headquarters was sunny. Sylvan spoke of the successes on 14 September. He wrote, "1st Division advanced within 3 kilometers of Aachen, surrounding the city on three sides. 3d Armored Division approximately 5 miles due east. 9th Division made good progress during the day, 47th Infantry smashing well over the German border. V Corps advance spotty, some pillboxes completely unmanned."

He also indicated the involvement of the two other U.S. divisions hammering at the Westwall: "4th Division made excellent progress. 2d Bn, the 22d Infantry reporting it passed all fortifications. The 28th Div. Infn. 6 miles inside the border, 112th approximately 3."

With movement slowed and the casualty count climbing, First Army headquarters pondered a disturbing report from the 1st Division's 16th Infantry. The message spoke of Germans approaching in a column of twos, "as far as the eye could see." All along the line GIs heard heavy vehicle traffic behind the front. Worse still, Task Force Lovelady from the 3d Armored, seeking to gain further real estate, cropped up against a contingent of tanks and self-propelled guns that in quick order eliminated seven medium tanks, a tank destroyer, and even an ambulance. Colonel Lovelady, with only a baker's dozen of Shermans still operable, less than 40 percent of the normal complement, received permission to button down for the night. Both CCA and CCB of the 3d Armored could progress no farther.

On 15 September, Sylvan sounded an ominous note. "Col. [Benjamin "Monk"] Dixon reported today, based on intelligence he had, the Germans now resolved to throw in everything on the present line in an attempt to hold the Americans before they could crack the defenses along it. The statement seemed borne out by the slowing down of all corps. In the V Corps . . . Gen. [Hodges] noted the three divisions spread out on an exceedingly wide front. Progress made by the XX Corps of 3d Army on its right flank is slow. It doesn't appear to cover the right successfully."

The anxiety expressed by Sylvan is all the more significant because on the same day the 47th Infantry captured 400 prisoners while penetrating the Westwall's first band. A day later the outfit achieved its immediate mission by breaking through part of the second barrier near Schevenhutte.

As could be expected, the demands of Montgomery's Operation Market Garden affected the First Army. Sylvan reported that Omar Bradley flew to headquarters for a long and, for the most part, secret conference with Hodges. "On the established facts of supply, both the [fuel], ammunition, and food continues to become more critical. We are now not even holding our own. It was acknowledged that we would probably have to slow up or altogether halt our drive into Germany in the very near future." In a desperate attempt to alleviate the deficits, Hodges arranged for emergency supply by air, requesting a minimum of 3,000 tons of ammunition.

Top commanders blamed the shortages of the vital fodder of war for the failure to break through to the Rhine and, to some degree, the lack of aggressiveness of the GIs against determined resistance. Because all of the evidence indicated that the Westwall was either sparsely defended or inhabited by second- and third-rate soldiers—physically limited men fit only for the SOS or fortress defense troops, members of the Landesschutzen or home guard, recruits still in training, and a few staff or cadre personnel—the top brass insisted that the weight of the U.S. forces should have been able to smash through the Westwall and surrounding forces to the objective of the Roer. Formidable fortifications at Omaha and Utah Beaches had not stopped the D-day landings. But there were significant differences when it came to the German border.

When the Allies invaded the Normandy beaches, massive, reinforced concrete pillboxes, similar to those in the Westwall, confronted them. But the naval vessels offshore, with their five- to sixteen-inch guns smashed the fortifications with projectiles that weighed as much as a ton. The First Army could not call on ships to hurl shells, nor could the Air Corps pinpoint well-camouflaged targets hidden in the woods.

The thickness of the Westwall pillboxes defied even the feared *Jabos,* the name Germans bestowed on P-47 fighter-bombers that ravaged their ranks and vehicles during the campaign across France.

George Wilson from the 22d Regiment of the 4th Division noted, "One day we heard the pillboxes to our front were going to be bombed by our P-47 fighter-bombers. To get a better view of the dive-bombing, less than half a mile from our area, some of us walked through the woods and mines to the old farmhouse we had found on our night patrol.

"We climbed up the back side and lay with just our heads above the roof line. Grandstand seats on the fifty-yard line. It was a tremendous show. We watched spellbound as the P-47s came over at ten thousand feet and then, one by one, tipped their wings and dived straight down at the pillboxes.

"The drone of the planes' engines became a thunderous roar as they sped earthward. My heart seemed to stop, and I held my breath waiting for them to pull up out of the dives.

"When it seemed suicidally late, they released their bombs and somehow managed to level off just a few hundred feet from the ground. The bombs hit smack on top of the seven-foot-thick concrete-and-steel pillboxes. From our angle we could see no damage at all. No roofs were caved in, no huge cracks appeared. Probably the Jerries had hellish headaches from concussion, but nothing was visible. All the great show did was raise dust."

Although GIs underwent extensive training in house-to-house combat, they received far less instruction in the techniques to approach and incapacitate a pillbox. The bazooka rocket was a useful tool, but one had to be close enough to put a round through an embrasure. Unlike the marines in the South Pacific, who enthusiastically adopted the flamethrower, incidentally developed by army ordnance specialists, the Americans in Europe were not abundantly endowed with the weapons that were so effective against Japanese bunkers. GIs in the 9th Division allegedly found flamethrowers ineffective against the massive fortifications of the Siegfried Line. The thickness of the walls insulated against the heat generated by flamethrowers.

Because the prescribed methods for assaulting pillboxes and concrete bunkers were not working, the 9th Division's 15th Engineer Battalion experimented with various approaches and finally concluded that the only effective technique involved an attack downward through the top. Using captured enemy "beehive" charges, the engineers blew away the five-foot layer of soil that covered the emplacement. Then the Americans tied together four beehives and detonated as many as a half dozen consecutive charges to create a hole in the concrete two and a half feet deep. Into that went 200 pounds of TNT. The concussion brought surrender.

The procedure, however, required GIs to get near enough to climb on top of the fortification. Any attempt to approach one of the bastions still had to cope with interlocking lanes of fire from other bunkers, tanks, and snipers. In addition, those directly involved in deploying troops and armor were discovering that movement, particularly in the wooded areas, was often much more difficult than anticipated. Blown bridges created bottlenecks and slowed advances. What appeared on a map to be a road frequently proved to be little more than a narrow, dirt track incapable of handling heavy traffic, even without the menace of enemy guns.

4

STALLED

Less than a week into the offensive in the forest, the Germans began to exact an increasing toll on the attackers. Although the platoon led by Chester Jordan entered Schevenhutte with little opposition, it soon faced a now vigorous enemy.

Jordan remembered, "I was not allowed to loll around the beer hall for even one more beer. We were sent up the ridge toward Gressenich. At first, we picked up the hiking trail, but by dark it had quit on us, and we were trying to guide on the road. The orderly tree planting had played out with the path, and we were now banging around in natural growth. Suddenly, it sounded as though we had walked into the middle of a German military convention. There was laughter, wood chopping, metal pounding, and, worst of all, a pack of barking dogs. I very quietly radioed the company, and they said, 'Hold what you've got.' That is not what I wanted to hear.

"I told the men to spread out, and if they wished to dig, to do so without [a] sound. I had the radioman switch off the radio, because I didn't want any electronic screams coming from our neck of the woods. We lay there listening to the German noises and dreading the moment when those damn dogs got a sniff of us. They should have been able to smell us in Düren.

"As we tried to melt into the earth there came another gut-wrencher. On the road below us, a Kraut unit sounded like they were doing a Jodie drill as they double-timed in the direction of Schevenhutte. My God, were those bastards singing as they ran into battle? Evidently no, because we heard no rifle fire. They must have been going to man the pillbox. We had a fearful, fretful night.

"When it got light the next day (it was not very bright in those woods at midday), I found the entire platoon was within a thirty-foot circle—one 60mm mortar shell would have wiped us all out. I called the company, and they said hold until further notice. They also said there was no chow of any kind.

"I had the men spread out so that it would take at least two shells to get us. Silent digging was mandated by their fellow man. Not only was the soil rocky, but it was full of roots that made it impossible digging. I didn't even try. Since the spot we were in was indefensible, it was imperative that we not be attacked."

For the isolated platoon, the day passed with the continued sounds of the Germans at work nearby. "The only thing I had to eat in my bag," said Jordan, "was a D ration bar and one of the compressed fruit bars from a 10-in-1 ration. I ate the fruit bar and it tasted like a banana. It took enough of the edge off my hunger that I didn't have to face the D ration until evening. By then I was starving again. I took a bite of the bar and put it right back in my musette bag. I was not hungry enough yet.

"I fantasized about food all night. I retasted every good steak I had ever eaten. Even peanut butter cropped up in my memory, but it must have been from home. I don't think I ever saw any peanut butter while I was in the army. Hunger even drove fear into a second-place position, but I never got hungry enough to take another bite of that D bar."

For a second day, Jordan and his people remained in their position, whispering to one another while starvation pains racked their stomachs. Just before nightfall, welcome word came from company headquarters, ordering the troops to fall back and dig in along a ridge overlooking the village. They settled down in a site well protected by tightly packed fir trees. Between them and Schevenhutte, now occupied by others from their battalion, lay a no-man's-land covered by enemy weapons.

"To get food and ammunition, we had to send carrying parties across this no-man's-land at night. From time to time the Krauts were waiting for them. After the first three days, the other platoons were getting mass attacks every night. Sometimes the Krauts went right through to the village but then [retreated] with tremendous losses. Every morning we would stack their dead on our trucks like cordwood to be hauled away. Our hill was not easy to attack, and if they got Schevenhutte, they would have us anyhow.

"My squad leaders had to rotate the distasteful and dangerous duty of providing the nightly carrying party. One night the Krauts met them in the valley with accurate machine gun fire. The squad leader and another man were wounded. They told me that as they loaded the squad leader into the meat wagon, he was shouting obscenities about my parentage, my intellect, my character, and consigned all to hell.

"After a week of constant attack, the Krauts evidently decided that they didn't have enough men to keep attacking, so they settled down in a siege. The platoon that had taken the brunt of these attacks on the south side wanted a quieter sector, so we starting playing musical hills. All the transfers took place at night, and although we were in the area for two months, I never returned to the village in daylight. The only time I spent there was what it took to walk through. I was never in the company CP and had no idea where it was located. My runner knew and that was enough. I cannot even remember who the company commander was."

As Jordan reported, the salient achieved by the 47th Infantry Regiment provoked furious responses from the other side, and it was obvious that the left flank, extending toward the Stolberg corridor, was vulnerable to an enemy thrust. The 1st Division and associates from the 3d Armored attempted to drive through the Schill belt of defenses and straighten the American line.

But first the armor and infantry outfits needed to plug a gap between them. Under the direction of CCR (Combat Command Reserve) of the 3d Armored, Maj. Francis Adams headed the 1st Battalion of the infantry, while Lt. Col. William Hogan commanded a tank battalion. They formed a task force with the mission of clearing elements from the Schill Line to enable the VII Corps to reach a desired posture adjacent to the embattled 9th Division troops.

The Adams-Hogan group hammered through the fortifications at Mossback, southeast of Stolberg, only to hear that a savage enemy counterattack had driven back comrades from the armored infantry, and many of them appeared trapped on a hill at the village of Weissenburg, a mile from the larger town of Diepenlinchen. CCR ordered a rifle company to rescue the beleaguered soldiers. Under Capt. Allan B. Ferry, C Company of the infantry, supported by a tank platoon, set out on the mission.

At Diepenlinchen, Ferry's command met a firestorm from German defenders. As darkness fell, Ferry pulled back his forces and, under the cover of night, conducted a reconnaissance that had the virtue of a stealthy approach. To avoid noise that might alert the foe, Ferry left his tanks behind, while just before dawn, he and the foot soldiers worked their way through rock piles along a slope.

The column neared Weissenburg, and a morning fog lifted to reveal a full company of Germans headed down a trail toward the Americans. Ferry immediately ordered a tactical withdrawal, hoping to negate the enemy's higher-ground advantage. His lead element prepared to cover the retro movement. Suddenly, from a factory mining complex they had skirted, heavy automatic weapon, artillery, and mortar fire slammed into the GIs. Ferry passed the word that the soldiers should continue their retreat, but he and some companions in the rear were trapped and forced to surrender. Most of the survivors holed up in Diepenlinchen and refused to run up a white flag, although under extreme pressure by Germans who controlled the streets.

Hogan and Adams immediately struck back. They plotted a two-pronged assault to retake Diepenlinchen. Supported by mortars and artillery, they engaged the Germans in house-to-house combat and routed them, taking forty-nine prisoners. In the thick of the battle, an 81mm mortar platoon expended all of its ammunition. Urgent pleas for resupply passed up the chain of command until finally a truckload of the precious ordnance arrived the following day, having been driven from Paris, 200 miles away.

The victory did not lessen the tenacity of the foe. A day later, as Company B from CCR hammered into the thick walls of a factory area north of Diepenlinchen, furious exchanges occurred amid piles of rock and rubble. Major Adams contacted the regimental commander with the message, "It is recommended that my [battalion] be returned to the unit so that I can get replacements and reequip. My unit has suffered heavy battle casualties, and yesterday and today I am beginning to get men suffering from combat fatigue. As of this A.M. my fighting strength was as follows: A [Company] 99; B-91, C-62, D-86." He was well below 50 percent of the standard table of organization.

Adams continued, "I am still attacking today against an objective that is very difficult to take. I shall undoubtedly suffer further heavy casualties today. At the present rate, I am rapidly losing my combat effectiveness. I would like to return to the outfit so that I can get my battalion back in shape."

His plea brought no immediate relief. Lieutenant Colonel Hogan, as the senior officer in the task force, ordered Company A paired with a company of his tanks to strike at Weissenburg. As soon as the attackers came out of the woods and into open ground near the village, a storm of enemy fire engulfed them. Hogan said later, "I have never seen such a concentration of German artillery before or since." The foot soldiers and the armor retreated back to the relative safety of the forest.

Undeterred, CCB's commander, Brig. Gen. Truman E. Boudinot, directed the task force to go at Weissenburg from another angle. Hogan demurred, noting he had considered that alternative and rejected it after his personal reconnaissance revealed the ground too soft for his tanks. Boudinot rejected his subordinate's misgivings and told him to proceed.

With only sixty-two men left from Company C, whose Captain Ferry had been among those captured in the first abortive attempt to occupy Weissenburg, the deployment followed the route questioned by Hogan. Heavy shelling greeted the GIs and the accompanying four tanks. The soldiers fell back, but the Shermans, just as Hogan feared, bogged down in the mud. The tankers abandoned their vehicles after rendering them useless.

Boudinot refused to quit. He arranged for a concentrated artillery preparation to precede another attack. While the infantrymen from the 1st Battalion assembled at the edge of the woods, the big guns from all VII Corps artillery within range opened up. Unfortunately, several salvos fell short, resulting in tree bursts that showered the Company A soldiers, who promptly scurried for cover.

The barrage halted while forward observers attempted to register the artillery for the appropriate distance. After a half-hour delay, the shelling began again, and, in a dismal repeat performance, the explosions walked back toward the GIs, who could only seek protection anew. As if oblivious to what befell their companions on foot, the tanks clattered off on schedule. A burst of cannon fire hit two of them, and a shoulder-fired *panzerfaust* knocked out a third. Without infantrymen to protect them against this kind of menace, the tanks retired.

A subsequent analysis of the problems besetting this last sortie revealed that the 105mm self-propelled howitzers committed to the preattack shelling had been stationed in muddy ground. Every time they fired, the recoil sank the rear mount deeper in the mire. The failure to adjust the guns because of these circumstances led to succeeding rounds dropping closer to the American lines.

Around midnight, Hogan dispatched his tanks to a site where they could blast away at the forest positions of the enemy. The darkness and the surprise nature of the action lessened the opportunity for German foot soldiers to use their antitank rockets. Because the outburst from the Shermans was so unexpected, the armor could withdraw before the enemy responded with counterfire.

At dawn on 20 September, a murky fog hovered over the ground. Captain Levasseur, the S-3 for the 1st Battalion of the regiment, proposed that, instead of the planned combined assault of tankers and foot soldiers supported by artillery, the troops exploit the poor visibility in an assault with fixed bayonets. He argued that the Germans, after a night of pounding from the tanks and some artillery fire, might not be fully alert.

Company A moved out quietly on its own and nabbed thirty-three prisoners, many of whom were asleep in their foxholes. The captives mentioned that the American armor in its midnight foray inflicted many casualties. Less encouraging, the interrogations revealed the presence of first-line troops, shifted from East Prussia by railroad and untouched by Allied planes, grounded because of poor flying weather. Furthermore, rather than playing a solely defensive role, the units, from the German 12th Infantry Division, entered the forest with the objective of driving the Americans back from any penetration of the Schill Line.

Soldiers from the 9th Division relieved the battered, thin ranks of the 1st Battalion of the 1st Division's infantry. Task Force Hogan shifted to an assembly area near Mossback, and the men received a hot meal and time to sleep. But a day later they prepared to attack Stolberg.

Sylvan's diary tersely noted, "Report of bitter house-to-house fighting in Stolberg. Numerous counterattacks, company or battalion size, which were met and repulsed without loss of ground."

That success notwithstanding, the American command continued to believe the offensive was jeopardized by the continued and strong presence of the Germans in the Huertgen, from where a flank attack could fall upon the VII Corps. Collins later explained, "We did our best to break through between the Huertgen Forest on my right and the city of Aachen, to break through the Siegfried defenses while there was a chance of doing it. We didn't succeed because we didn't have the artillery ammunition for one thing. The air was being pulled off to other missions. It was hard to get as much air support as we would have needed . . . and we were just stymied. There were second-rate troops in the German defenses, in the Siegfried defense, but don't let anybody tell you that the Siegfried defenses weren't formidable."

With the approval of Hodges, Collins committed the 9th Division's 39th and 60th Infantry Regiments to cleaning the Germans out of the Huertgen and thereby eliminating the threat to his right flank along the Stolberg corridor. The division's other regiment, the 47th, remained busy defending itself in Schevenhutte, the farthest penetration toward the Roer.

The 39th, in the vicinity of Lammersdorf, west of the Scharnhorst Line, pressed its attack without significant success. An attempt by the 2d Battalion to envelop the defenders drew such heavy small-arms and artillery fire that the troops withdrew.

The 1st Battalion of the 60th Infantry, operating to the northeast, inside the Scharnhorst in front of the Schill, tried to take control of road junctions north of Zweifall. The plan called for the troops to pass through the Huertgen toward Germeter, cutting off the supply routes to the Germans. In the roseate view of the intelligence specialists, resistance was expected to be "negligible." The timetable set the jump-off at noon, with arrival in the objective of Germeter by 6 P.M of the same day. It started out according to plan. The first steps through the woods went unchallenged, and the Americans delightedly passed a string of unoccupied pillboxes. Suddenly, the lead scout signaled a halt. A German machine gun opened up, and then a storm of fire ignited, much of it from cleverly camouflaged pillboxes that housed determined defenders. The Americans advanced perhaps 700 yards against fierce resistance. They would not reach Germeter at six o'clock; they would not get there for more than a month.

As the attackers blundered about in the damp, cold gloom of the woods, it did not seem to matter which direction the attacker chose in the depths of the forest. The defenders appeared able to deploy their resources wherever needed. Complained one discouraged soldier, "The enemy seemed to be everywhere, and in the darkness of the thick trees and the confusion, the firing seemed everywhere." A battalion commander asserted, "If anybody says he knew where he was in the forest, he's a liar."

Under the thick carpet of pine needles, the defenders concealed wood-cased *schu* mines that went undetected by metal-oriented mine detectors. The antipersonnel devices blew off feet and other parts of the lower body, leading to mordant nicknames coupled with sex organs.

Company A wandered onto the wrong trail, becoming hopelessly lost and eventually surfacing in a sector manned by the 39th Infantry. It took a day for A Company to trek to its prescribed position. A pillbox confronted Company B, armed only with grenades, rifles, and BARs (Browning automatic rifles), plus a few bazookas, rather than the appropriate satchel charges and heavier guns mounted on tanks or tank destroyers. The soldiers gamely peppered the bastion with all they had at their disposal, and the Germans obligingly surrendered. But shortly after the company commander installed his command post in the bunker and summoned his top people for a strategy session, an inexplicable explosion demolished the site, killing or wounding many. When dazed survivors staggered around outside, German soldiers from nearby positions picked them off.

The defenders mounted a strong counterattack that mingled opposing parties so closely that mortars could not be used. When the action broke off, both sides had been severely mauled. A series of these counterattacks devastated the 60th Regiment.

The towering, closely grown evergreens introduced a new source of danger—the tree burst. Although the United States was introducing its proximity fuzes, which, instead of relying on contact with a solid mass or a timing mechanism, detonated shells when they neared an object, the Germans still used the old style of explosion on contact. In the forests, the shells burst against the treetops. Men trained to drop prone on the ground then exposed their bodies to a deadly rain of shrapnel and wood splinters. Other than a well-covered foxhole, the best protection came from the lea of a tree trunk, and GIs adopted the posture of tree huggers.

Another grim lesson learned was the reduced effectiveness of supporting artillery. A battalion of field guns tried to aid the GIs but could only target 300 yards ahead of the friendlies; otherwise tree bursts would shower the American soldiers. Unfortunately, the German defenders occupied positions only fifty yards beyond the troops. The big guns could not hurt them.

The 60th Regiment continued to batter its head against the Huertgen wall for ten days. Not even with the commitment of a battalion borrowed from the 39th could the attack gain any major territory. Although the highway between Lammersdorf and the village of Huertgen had been cut, neither the 60th nor the attached battalion from the 39th possessed the strength to resume the offensive through the forest.

Southwest of the 9th Division, in the V Corps zone, the 22d Regimental Combat Team, from the 4th Division, had remained in a static position from 18 September to 3 October. The Germans counterattacked vigorously and frequently but without materially denting the American lines.

But the advance of the 4th Division, like that of other U.S. units had ended. George Wilson said, “We were, in fact, too thin and spread out for a solid breakthrough. Our wild, thrilling rampage through France, Belgium, and into the Siegfried had been too fast and far for our supply lines. We were lucky to have enough ammunition and food for the day.” With no orders to continue forward, the GIs busied themselves with refinements of their foxholes, piling logs atop them and scrounging branches to serve as mattresses on the increasingly muddy ground.

About one week after their drive bogged down near Sellerich, the 22d Regiment, with Wilson, pulled back, leaving to the enemy the bloody ground they had taken in the woods. The outfit moved northwest into the Schnee Eifel forest, a position that placed another thickly wooded area between the GIs and the Germans. While not in an attack mode, Wilson and his platoon engaged in the highly dangerous activity of patrols, both in daylight and at night. At the end of the month, Wilson's promotion to first lieutenant, promised by Colonel Lanham if Wilson survived his first day in combat, came through. Wilson carefully pinned the silver bar underneath his collar, where it would not be seen by a sharp-eyed German sniper.

On the right flank of the 4th Division line, the 28th Division from Luxembourg continued its efforts to breach the Westwall. Bill Peña, a 1942 graduate of Texas A&M with a degree in architecture and a lieutenant's commission through the reserve program at the university, served as a training officer for two years before the casualties in Normandy required his presence in Europe as a replacement.

Like John Beach with the 1st Division, Peña moved forward as part of a package of men to the 28th Division. Assigned to the 109th Regiment, Company I, he reached the outfit by jeep. He recalled, "On the way [to the battalion command post], the driver pointed out a small bridge over the Our River. This was the spot at which the boundaries of Belgium, Luxembourg, and Germany all joined. With a map I could tell where I was. The CP turned out to be a small concrete bunker on German soil east of the Our River and part of the Siegfried Line."

Although I Company currently occupied a defensive position, only a few days before, on 15 September, the outfit assaulted the perimeter of the Westwall at Sevenig. "[That] resulted in the capture of six pillboxes to our front—some of them had just begun to be manned by the Germans. Unfortunately, the attack had weakened the company, and it was now low on ammunition. It was not able to resist the strong German counterattack which came before the position could be fully organized and strengthened. One particular enemy tank was deadly and demoralizing. One-third of the company men had been captured, killed, or wounded. The company commander was taken prisoner."

For the following two weeks, with the front inactive except for exchanges of artillery, Peña became familiar with his platoon as it was filled with replacements and became indoctrinated in life at the front. The 13th Regiment of the 8th Division relieved the 109th at Sevenig, just over the frontier with Germany. Peña and his company boarded trucks for a circuitous trip that crossed into Luxembourg and then northward through Saint-Vith to an assembly area near Elsenborn, just behind the border of the Third Reich.

The shifting about of the various U.S. divisions signaled the end of the thrust that began in mid-September. Collins argued, "We ran out of gas—that is to say we weren't completely dry, but the effect was much the same; we ran out of ammunition and we ran out of weather. The loss of our close tactical air support because of weather was a real blow."

The reference to a dearth of ammunition was certainly true. From D Day on, artillery units struggled to match the requests for their firepower with their stocks of shells. Limitations on firing started early in the Normandy campaign and steadily hampered the batteries. The manufacturing plants at home could not fulfill the enormous amounts authorized for unrestricted action by the heavy guns. The pipeline through the beaches and English Channel ports also could not meet the specified allocations. The wretched weather of the Channel toward the end of September and into October further disrupted the shipments. In the howitzer class, a principal form of divisional artillery support, the inventory could never adequately feed the maws of the 105mm, 155mm, 240mm, and eight-inch weapons.

From 27 September to 5 October, the 12th Army Group cut the ration of shells to 3.8 rounds per gun, per day for the huge 240mm howitzers and 3.1 for the eight-inch guns. When the 12th Army Group issued a directive to increase the amounts to units, the commanders learned that there were no additional shells in the supply depots.

Furthermore, the organizations initially committed to the Huertgen campaign, the 1st and 9th Divisions, were short on manpower, the soldiers available near exhaustion, both physically and emotionally from their previous running battles from Saint-Lô to the border, and their equipment, trucks, and artillery were all in poor shape.

The experts in the War Department had estimated that three out of four infantrymen would be casualties in the European campaign. The planners based the need for replacements on that estimate. But the calculations fell far short of the actual demands for fresh troops. Of the roughly 15,000 soldiers in a division, riflemen would amount to almost 3,250. At the extreme, the 90th Division, which landed elements at Utah Beach just as D Day ended, lost more than 100 percent of its riflemen and 150 percent of its officers within the first two months of combat. Other organizations counted losses well in excess of the numbers foreseen by the War Department.

There was a desperate shortage of men bearing an M1, even though a startlingly high number of the wounded, out of action an average of 120 days after being hit but able to return to duty, insisted on returning to their outfits and harm's way. The administrators of military personnel pools frantically sought to add foot soldiers to the ranks in Europe. By July 1944 the replacement system, combing through service units, eliminating slots in antiaircraft and coast artillery as no longer essential, and ending specialized programs, began to add candidates for the job of rifleman. But even though some effort to add to the pool had begun before D Day, providing the proper training and equipment required time.

The losses to the four divisions primarily employed to break through the Westwall were heavy, but the defenders had also paid dearly. Ten years later, Collins gave an interviewer the theory behind the hasty offensive against the Westwall. "If we could break it, then we would be just that much to the good; if we didn't, then we could be none the worse." From the standpoint of someone directing operations a distance behind the fighting, that might have been appropriate, but to the hapless foot soldiers in the killing ground the situation could hardly be termed "none the worse."

5

Schmidt Number One

Both the First Army's venture, which hurled the VII and V Corps against the Westwall with much less success than anticipated, and Market Garden, Montgomery's mid-September failed plunge by air into the Netherlands in the hope of an end run around the Rhine barrier, represented almost off-the-cuff strategy. It was not until 22 September that Eisenhower convened the army group commanders for a master plan to conquer the Third Reich.

The British strategists under Montgomery urged a strike by his 21st Army Group along the northern tier over the lower Rhine in Holland, bypassing the German industrial war machine's heart, the Ruhr Valley. The strategy envisioned the American 12th Army Group as support for the thrust, protecting the right flank and halting at the German Rhine near Cologne. That plan sat poorly with Omar Bradley, ostensibly for strategic reasons, but undoubtedly the Americans strongly believed their ally was out to steal the glory.

The head of the 12th Army Group proposed a double envelopment, which, in conjunction with Montgomery's forces, would encircle the Ruhr while also blasting through south of where the Main River flows into the Rhine.

Eisenhower, as he did so often, stroked sensitive egos and arranged to parcel out his assets to enable the competing interests to follow their desires. Montgomery retained the right to continue his drive based in Holland. With reinforcements piling up in England, the Americans introduced a new command, the Ninth Army under Lt. Gen. William H. Simpson. Considerably smaller than the First or Third Armies, it contained only the VIII Corps, and Bradley inserted the forces in what was considered a quiet zone, the Ar-

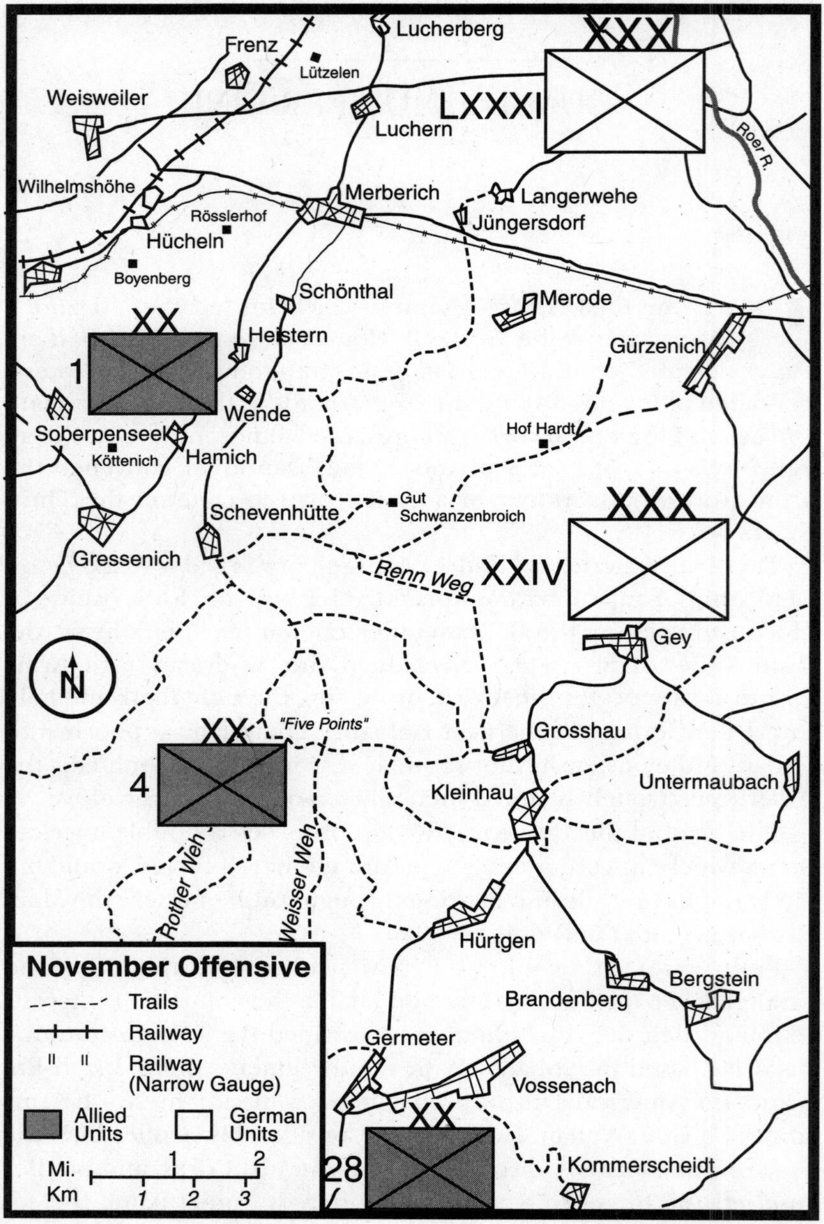
Lucherberg
XXX
LXXXI
Frenz
Lützelen
Weisweiler
Luchern
Roer R.
Wilhelmshöhe
Merberich
Langerwehe
Jüngersdorf
Rösslerhof
Hücheln
Boyenberg
Schönthal
Merode
XX
1
Heistern
Gürzenich
Wende
Soberpenseel
Köttenich
Hamich
Hof Hardt
Gut Schwanzenbroich
Schevenhütte
XXX
Gressenich
Renn Weg
XXIV
Gey
N
"Five Points"
XX
Grosshau
4
Kleinhau
Untermaubach
Rother Weh
Weisser Weh
Hürtgen
November Offensive
Trails
Railway
Railway (Narrow Gauge)
Allied Units
German Units
Mi. 1 2
Km 1 2 3
Bergstein
Brandenberg
Germeter
Vossenach
XX
28
Kommerscheidt

dennes south of Aachen and the Huertgen Forest. The placement reduced the frontage of the First Army by fifteen miles. The high command shifted Gerow's V Corps a few miles north, taking over the ground near Monschau previously reserved for Collins's VII Corps. With the front trimmed by fifteen miles, Collins could concentrate on the 9th Division in a renewed push for the Roer. Instead of banging away at the Stolberg corridor, the 1st Division focused its attention on the city of Aachen, which, with units from the XIX Corps, it would try to clear. The Stolberg corridor devolved exclusively to the 3d Armored.

The new deployment shrank the 9th Division sector from seventeen miles to nine. That, however, was a mixed blessing, because Gen. Louis Craig's troops now were committed to a campaign aimed at eliminating the enemy presence in the Huertgen and opening up a passage to the Roer via the woods.

Significantly, the strategy of those in charge remained concentrated on gaining ground and reaching the banks of the river. Major Jack Houston, the G-2 (intelligence officer) for the 9th Division, raised the subject of the dams. Their existence was well known; maps showed their location and aerial reconnaissance had produced photographs.

Sylvan duly confided to his diary on 29 September: "Supplies are slowly building up in desired quantities for the coming push." On 2 October, Major Houston notified his superiors that the largest of the structures, the Schwammenauel Dam and its powerhouse, were "targets of great importance." He pointed out, "Bank overflows and destructive flood waves can be produced by regulating the discharge from the various dams. By demolition of some of them, great destructive flood waves can be produced which would destroy everything in the populated industrial valley as far as the Meuse and into Holland."

Houston only mentioned the largest of the dams, but several others in the system also controlled water flow. The logical conclusion based on his report was that any troops who crossed the Roer downstream from the dams could be trapped, should the enemy release the confined waters. The intelligence specialists of the First Army, however, discounted the threat, saying that even "if all of the dams [were blown], they would cause at most local flooding for about five days, counted from the moment the dam was blown until all the water receded."

But an engineer with XIX Corps, who surveyed where that organization's men would reach the Roer, near Jülich, calculated, "If one or all dams were blown, a flood would occur in the channel of the Roer River that would reach approximately 1,500 feet in width and three feet or more deep across the entire corps front. . . . The flood would probably last from one to three weeks." Those soldiers caught by the surging water would be effectively isolated from the rest of the First Army and bridges would be wiped out. The XIX Corps officer vitiated the strength of his advisory to his superiors, observing that because the structures were all in the VII Corps sector, Collins's forces would be expected to seize the dams because the VII Corps would also be affected.

Certainly, the question of the dams seemed of little moment to either Eisenhower or Bradley. The latter, in his postwar autobiography, acknowledges the potential disaster of the Roer dams. "As long as he [Gerd von Rundstedt] held the huge Roer dams containing the headwaters of that river, he could unleash a flash flood that would sweep away our bridges and jeopardize our isolated bridgeheads on the plains of Cologne. Destruction of the 180-foot-high Schwammenauel Dam, engineers said, would swell the Roer at Düren by twenty-five feet and create a raging torrent one and a half miles wide. Clearly, we dared not venture beyond the Roer until first we had captured or destroyed those dams." But the statement is clearly a revisionist effort, because there was nothing in the plans of the September, October, and November offensives concerning the dams. All of the attacks followed a course that took them two or more miles northeast of the Schwammenauel and even farther away from the second most important, the Urft Dam.

There was no recorded discussion about the subject at Eisenhower's Supreme Headquarters, Allied Expeditionary Force (SHAEF) until late in October, when interrogators learned from a prisoner taken by the V Corps that, in Düren, persistent ringing of church bells would warn that the dams had been blown and residents should immediately evacuate to escape a flood depth of as much as twenty-five feet. In his autobiography, Eisenhower talks of the relevance of the dams in conjunction with the front line position of the Americans in December, but he, too, was writing well after the fact. Until December 1944, the ground forces in the personages of the supreme commander, the head of the 12th Army Group, and the commander of the First Army and his corps leaders at most regarded the dams as a subject of interest for the Air Corps, not themselves.

With its front line shortened to half that of September, the 9th Division prepared to advance toward Schmidt, a strategically located town, because its high ground overlooked the Roer and it served as a road hub. It was perhaps three miles beyond the Schill defenses, and the pathway to Schmidt ran through the Huertgen Forest.

The September offensive by the First Army, stopped with only meager gains, had cost both sides dearly. For the Germans, however, there was one major achievement; they had bought time to reorganize and to reinforce their defensive positions. That seems to have escaped the notice of the intelligence specialists. Major Houston, so prescient about the dams, estimated the German numbers at 5,000 (actually, the German strength was closer to 6,500, including some 1,500 in service or headquarters assignments), mainly drawn from home guard and replacement units. Houston described this as a poorly organized force marked by low morale but led by good officers.

Elsewhere, the increase in German resources was clear. Karl Wolf, with the 16th Infantry near Münsterbusch and west of Stolberg, recalled, "Just before midnight on October 3, the Germans launched the heaviest artillery barrage I was in during the war. Fortunately, we were in the pillbox [the battalion CP] and no direct hits occurred. I saw the report where regiment estimated between 3,000 and 4,000 artillery rounds were fired on our K Company position within a half hour. Following the shelling was an assault by German engineers and infantry carrying flamethrowers and demolition materials. They had four 88mm assault guns, two of which were carrying infantrymen in the assault force. Just a few nights earlier, we had layed [*sic*] antitank mines on the roads and crossroads in front of our position. One of the self-propelled guns was disabled by the mines. The other withdrew to where the other two had remained to deliver support fire. All three were eventually destroyed before the battle ended.

"The German infantry overran one pillbox that our men occupied. I remember getting messages from one of our platoons about being overrun and not being sure where our men were and where the Germans were. We requested support artillery fire from battalion to be brought down close to our positions, especially in the platoon area that had been overrun. Our regiment got the help of fourteen battalions of artillery to support us in repulsing the attack. We provided some help to our overrun platoon and drove the Germans out. I believe for a little while a couple of our men were actually held prisoners.

"Our losses were relatively light. Many German wounded and dead were found when morning came and we captured prisoners. That day we observed German vehicles picking up many more German wounded who had been caught in the open by our artillery."

Although the counterattack against Wolf and his colleagues had been defeated, it should have been obvious that the Germans had no inclination to yield an inch of their home turf. The general in charge of the Huertgen troops had also made excellent use of the pause in the fighting. His soldiers labored on field fortifications, built log bunkers, dug foxholes, connected trenches, strung barbed wire, set up roadblocks, and laid minefields to add to the heavier positions constructed as part of the Westwall.

What intelligence specialist Houston failed to appreciate was that even allegedly inferior soldiers, if solidly ensconced in massive pillboxes and bunkers behind mines and barbed wire, could wreak havoc on any offensive, particularly if it could not be well supported by armor, artillery, or air cover. Houston further misled his clients with an unjustified hope: "It is felt that should a major breakthrough occur, or should several penetrations occur, the enemy will begin a withdrawal to the Rhine River, abandoning his Siegfried Line." As the historian Charles MacDonald commented, "It was late in the Westwall fighting for this kind of thinking to persist."

General Craig, who set up his headquarters inside the forest, could call on only two-thirds of his organization for the proposed advance. The 47th Infantry remained clinging to Schevenhutte on the northeastern edge of the woods. Only the 39th and 60th infantries were available, and they could be committed because the 4th Cavalry Group replaced them as the guardians of the flanks for the Schevenhutte garrison.

Major William B. Sullivan, the 2d Battalion executive officer of the 60th Regiment, later pointed out serious weakness in his regiment. "It [the 2d Battalion] was now the strongest battalion, being about 75 percent full strength. It was almost completely new and devoid of combat experience except for what very little it had gained in its passive defense of Monschau." The personnel situation was a result of the battle after crossing the Meuse near Diant early in September. The combat there all but annihilated the 2d, which missed the 9th's subsequent struggles to penetrate the Westwall. Sullivan added, "The other two battalions were considerably reduced in size, being only about 50 percent of full strength."

Although much of the description of what happened during the first half of October is from the bloodless language of combat narratives and after-action reports, the stench of death and destruction permeates the words. The attack toward Schmidt, scheduled for 5 October, was to be preceded by a raid by eighty-four fighter-bombers from the IX Tactical Air Command. They were expected to dump their explosives on a trio of objectives. Their effort would be followed by a brief but intensive artillery barrage. As would happen so often during the entire Huertgen campaign, the weather obscured targets, and the airmen could not take off on schedule. A day later, at 10 A.M., the P-47 Thunderbolts roared in and dived on their targets, marked by red smoke, courtesy of American artillery.

It was almost noon when the two regiments moved out. They found the forest a mix of trees as tall as 100 feet, while in other areas, which had been cut down, replants had grown to ten feet. For the most part, however, the Americans struggled to see beyond a few yards, even at high noon. At night, a man could not see a trunk three feet away. Trails were nonexistent, except for a few narrow pathways artfully rendered useless by felled trees, and any tanks that accompanied the soldiers could move only along the firebreaks, likewise strewn with obstacles, which permitted no lateral action. Firebreaks were also well covered by enemy guns. Division artillery provided 155mm self-propelled guns but only where they could maneuver for a clear shot and then withdraw quickly. In any event, the steel and concrete pillboxes shrugged off these projectiles.

The lineup for 6 October placed the 2d Battalion in the lead, attacking southeast with the aim of taking control of the road network about two miles southeast of Germeter. The 1st Battalion was to follow, mopping up, while the 3d Battalion protected the right flank. Sullivan described the attack: "The 2d Battalion jumped off with Company G on the right, F on the left, and E disposed to the left rear to protect the left flank, there being some 2,000 yards distance between the left flank of the battalion and the nearest friendly unit.

"Despite the fact that the personnel of the battalion were surprised at the peculiarities of the forest, amazed at the actions of the enemy, and confused by combat in general, they managed to advance as a unit 500 yards against resistance on the first day. Artillery, which was very active on both sides, was very effective [against the Americans], because of the fact that it was nearly all tree bursts. It was very seldom that a shell burst on the ground." U.S. guns boomed an average of 5,000 rounds a day to support the GIs, but because of the proximity of the opposing troops, it was dangerous and difficult to lay shells directly on the defenders. The same held true when weather permitted the fighter-bombers to fly.

Sullivan reported, "Three tanks were available for use by the assault battalion but were not used because there was no way to get them up where they could be employed. There was a passable road which formed the left boundary, after the first day, but before it could be used, it had to be cleared of booby trap tank obstacles, which were defended by small arms from the other side of the road. The advance of the battalion had put in its possession a firebreak, which ran parallel to the front. The only possible effective use of the tanks was to get them up this avenue, from which they could poke into the trees far enough to get a shot at the enemy positions."

As Sullivan indicated, the foot soldiers met determined resistance and added little real estate—500 yards hardly satisfied the desires of Collins and Hodges. One company from the 2d Battalion of the 60th Infantry finished its first day with just two officers and sixty men still in condition to fight. After less than twelve hours, the company could muster only about one-third of its normal strength. The deadly tree bursts that Sullivan cited cost another battalion a hundred GIs.

On the night of 6 October, Sullivan and his fellow 2d Battalion heard the noises of axes chopping trees. "The morning of the 7th, when [the battalion] reinstituted the attack, they discovered the enemy had dug in deeply and covered their foxholes with logs. Artillery tree bursts failed to be effective against this type of emplacement, and artillery advantage now swung over to the enemy." Americans were learning painful lessons about forest combat.

Small improvements in positions resulted from maneuvers, but a day later, an attack failed to gain any ground. "To eject the enemy from its log-covered fighting positions, a large-caliber, direct-fire weapon was needed. The battalion commander [Maj. Lawrence L. Decker] realized this and took measures to get his three tanks into position where they could bring effective fire on the emplacements. He dispatched the three tanks, accompanied by a platoon of engineers and a platoon of infantrymen, with the mission of deploying in the front line firebreak and assisting the attack. This party had to capture two roadblocks, dismantle them, and generally fight every inch of the way. They arrived in the firebreak late morning of the 8th." Aided by this additional strength, the 2d Battalion overcame the most immediate obstacles to progress but continued to buck up against stiff and deadly resistance.

When American units as large as a company managed to slip through an opening and reach a clearing at the edge of the woods, they hesitated to proceed farther. Without the support of armor or artillery that could be directly brought to bear on defensive positions, any venture into open country would leave them exposed to withering storms of shot and shell. To enable these outfits to advance farther, engineers frantically hacked, hewed, and bulldozed routes to clear firebreaks and open trails in the woods. Until the engineers could complete their tasks, supply parties could only hand carry rations and ammunition, against the constant threats of mines, ambushes by infiltrating patrols, and the deadly tree bursts.

It took three days to manufacture routes for tanks and tank destroyers adequate for the requisite armor to join the forward companies from the 39th and 60th.

The defenders, of course, concentrated on openings provided by firebreaks, knowing they acted as channels for the tanks and outfits such as the 899th Tank Destroyer Battalion. In one instance, the latter fired and then charged across a 1,000-yard firebreak six times before the TDs could cross into a position to pour point-blank fire into the defenders.

En route to the ultimate objective of Schmidt, the 39th Infantry set its sights on a series of villages, including the last major one before Schmidt, Vossenack. Units of the 39th succeeded in crossing a stream known as the Weisser Wehe and neared the town of Germeter, while a battalion from the 60th achieved a position overlooking the settlement of Richelskaul. In the face of counterattacks, the American commanders held fast to their ground on the outskirts of these objectives. Engineers worked furiously to open trails that would allow armor and self-propelled guns to move up and protect the foot soldiers assigned to traverse cleared fields before assaulting the hamlets. Aware of the situation, the Germans sharply counterattacked along the flank through the woods and drove off the engineers before they could complete their task. Now the advantage of the forest passed to the entrenched Americans. Tree bursts scourged the German legions, killing and maiming many.

With tanks and tank destroyers in the field, the 1st Battalion of the 60th, led by Lt. Col. Lee W. Chatfield, stormed out of the woods into Richelskaul. The wedge formation of tanks, commanded by SSgt. Ralph B. Bertier, unleashed machine gun and 75mm cannon fire on defenders hunkered down in cellars of the handful of buildings and foxholes. A courageous German lieutenant surfaced long enough to hit a tank with a *panzerfaust,* but the rocket did minor damage. A gunner swiveled his 75 around and cut the officer in half. Terrified Germans either surrendered or fled. The battalion counted almost 100 prisoners, fifty corpses, and a dozen *panzerfausts* still operable among the booty.

For the 1st Battalion of the 39th, led by Lt. Col. Oscar H. Thompson, which menaced Germeter, the results were mixed. Two rifle platoons from the outfit occupied a couple of buildings in Wittscheidt, a tiny enclave along the road between Germeter and the village of Huertgen to the northeast. Suddenly, from other houses, small-arms fire hit the hapless infantrymen and then artillery smote the GIs. German foot soldiers attacked and overwhelmed the two isolated platoons. Thompson's people, bolstered by their tanks, retook Wittscheidt, but they found the body of only one American; the other forty-seven had vanished, presumably taken prisoner. Despite such losses, the American thrusts threatened to isolate Germeter, and, rather than allow the noose to tighten around its defenders, the Germans abandoned the village. It had taken five days to achieve the first major objective of the 9th Division offensive and cost more than 500 casualties.

On 10 October, from Richelskaul, the 39th Infantry, which had been slowed by rain, mines, roadblocks, and enemy fire, broke through for a surprising gain. Detouring around a manned pillbox, Company A plunged deeper into enemy country, capturing more than 100. Caution set in, and the outfit dug in, fearing they were too far out front and exposed. Unbeknownst to the GIs, they had actually outflanked a dozen pillboxes that were vulnerable to a rear attack. The opportunity passed, and other Americans advancing in the vicinity subsequently absorbed considerable punishment from those pillboxes.

The key to survival of the small salient hammered out by the two regiments was a road network that originated at a site known as Jaegerhaus (hunter's cabin), previously a hub for the enemy but was one of the few prizes taken during the September campaign. The junction was about a mile and a half southwest of Germeter, and the Germans regarded it as a primary objective to repossess.

To prevent loss of the Jaegerhaus position, the 1st Battalion, in an effort to secure the crossroads, attempted to advance 200 yards and eliminate a quartet of pillboxes zeroed in on road traffic. The operation began on 11 October with three tanks and a similar number of tank destroyers advancing into a clearing in front of the fortifications. The blueprint called for the tanks and infantry to lay down heavy fire, while the tank destroyers rumbled close enough to blast at the embrasures of the redoubts from point-blank range. What may have sounded feasible on paper proved frightful in practice. As soon as the 9th Division soldiers exposed themselves, intense automatic weapon fusillades pinned them down. It was not until dark that they could retreat to safety. The lead tank staggered with a disabling hit. Adding to the ignominy, the Germans dragged the abandoned Sherman off, and it was later seen firing at American lines.

The 3d Battalion of the 39th, under Colonel Stumpf, pushed off in the direction of Vossenack as part of a combined attack with the 1st Battalion, while the 2d Battalion remained in position to protect the northern flank of the regiment. Shortly before jump-off time, K Company reached an assembly position only to have a shell smash into the command staff area. This event necessitated reorganization before the offensive could begin.

Under heavy mortar fire, L Company, with K trailing, crossed the road north of Germeter and sifted through the woods to the east. The lead company advanced to the outskirts of Vossenack, and a patrol actually slipped into the town itself. The GIs saw large numbers of German soldiers in town and quickly retreated. Equally alarming, Stumpf received word of an impending counterattack, but the night passed without any sustained contact.

The following day, confusion, as so often happened in the murky depths of the Huertgen, fogged in the 3d Battalion. Stumpf first readied himself for a morning charge into Vossenack in partnership with the 1st Battalion, which would be aided by tanks. Told to stand fast, the perplexed commander then got word through a runner to retreat to the vicinity of Germeter.

The 39th's 2d Battalion followed the 3d with the mission to protect its left flank. Captain Albert Karre, the S-3 of the battalion, later reported, "All during the day the 2d Battalion contacted enemy who were probing with strong combat patrols. The battalion was subjected to intense mortar and artillery fire. The enemy attack was estimated at two platoons on a roadblock held by G Company and destroyed a light tank supporting G Company but was driven off. The enemy lost approximately twenty men killed and wounded but was driven off."

The following day there was a deluge of fire on the 2d Battalion, which protected so much frontage that its only reserve was a badly depleted ammunition and pioneer (A&P) platoon. Noted Karre, "The enemy attacked over a wide front of approximately 3,000 yards, employing an estimated reinforced German regiment. The attack was preceded by a tremendous artillery, mortar, and SP [self-propelled] barrage, which caused heavy casualties in all three companies and around the battalion CP and cutting all wire communications, leaving the battalion commander dependent entirely upon radio communication for contact with his companies.

"The enemy attacked with dogged determination in three waves of infantry, following closely on the heels of the barrage. The leading wave of enemy infantry was mowed down like ducks by E, F, and G Companies. However, the right flank attack of the enemy overpowered a road block. This attack [passed] completely around the left flank and reached a point twenty-five yards from the battalion CP before the A&P platoon could be employed. At this time, the A&P platoon, which was guarding the battalion CP, was immediately employed to stop the enemy attack in this sector. Drivers, radio operators, and one cook, who happened to be at the battalion CP, were also put into the fight to stop the tide of the German advance. In spite of this, one group of the enemy succeeded cutting the MSR [main supply route] and killed several medics who were evacuating wounded. The attack was stopped by the determined fight of the A&P platoon with heavy losses to the enemy.

"The second wave of enemy infantry attacked E, F, and G Companies with dogged determination, crawling and jumping over the bodies of their dead and wounded comrades. This attack was also stopped with severe losses to the enemy, E, F, and G suffering heavy casualties as well. During both of these engagements, our own artillery and mortars were constantly firing prepared defensive fires on dangerously close observed targets.

"In spite of these defensive fires, the fanatical enemy continued to advance and were only stopped when they reached our final protective line of light and heavy machine guns. Through this engagement, the clatter of artillery, mortar, and small-arms fire was incessant, to such a point that commands had to be given by hand and arm signal, one not being able to be heard by voice.

"The third wave of enemy attack was ferocious and intense, more so than the two previous ones, and came through mortar and artillery fire in their final bid to destroy our positions. They failed. However, due to the fact that we were maintaining a wide front and the casualties sustained caused gaps to exist on our lines, also because of the thickly wooded area and the limited fields of fire, the enemy was able at two points to penetrate our lines. However, they were not able to dislodge any of our men from their positions. Thus ended a second day's engagement with our fanatical enemy."

On 13 October, the infantrymen of the 9th Division renewed their assault, but an ambush devastated L Company only 100 yards from where K Company successfully moved along a narrow front. Already below normal strength, the battalion lost the bulk of two entire platoons. Stumpf directed K Company to swivel about and deal with the enemy in ambush. A furious series of firefights ensued, enveloping all four of the battalion's companies. Concentrations of mortar shells on the Germans drove off those who were not casualties. But the engagement ended any further progress by the 3d Battalion, which had been reduced to the equivalent of five rifle platoons instead of the requisite twenty.

Two days later, the 1st Battalion renewed the challenge to the defenders. Enemy action had shrunk the American armor to a single tank destroyer and two tanks, one of which refused to start. The stalled tank blocked the way out of the woods. The foot soldiers stubbornly set about their task without any armor. To their surprise, they achieved more than on the earlier try. A company commander and two of his riflemen actually climbed atop one of the pillboxes. Perched out of range of the weapons of the fortification, they futilely sought to convince those inside to surrender. Nothing availed; the inhabitants kept themselves buttoned up, undeterred by what the Americans could throw at them. Unable to overcome the bastion, the attackers, who had been under fire for all but a few days since their first day in France, abandoned their quest and retired to their original positions, having suffered severe losses without any territorial gains.

The defenders also absorbed appalling punishment. Hubert Gees, a seventeen-year-old runner for the 2d Company, Fusilier Battalion, in the Wehrmacht 275th Infantry Division, remembered being taught that "death on the battlefield is the most beautiful death. . . . To risk one's life for the Fatherland was the greatest honor of a young man. Right would be on our side, . . . 'Persevere, the new wonder weapons will soon be in mass production!'

"In the morning of 7 October, we moved along a curving road into the valley of the Weisser Wehe to counterattack the Americans of the 39th Infantry Regiment, who had broken through the day before. Our 2d Company attacked behind the bridge . . . in a southerly direction on the west side of the valley. We did not reach the point where we were to retake the bunkers, but remained flat on the ground under mortar and artillery fire, which was supporting the American infantry.

"The sad balance of the first day, thirty-five casualties, dead and wounded; more than one-third of our battle strength of 100 soldiers. Among the dead, my First Sergeant Zeppenfeld. In the days before I had shared quarters with him while we were in a rest area at the home of a farmer. He rests today in the Huertgen Soldiers Cemetery in Grave No. 584. After two or three days, Lieutenant Lengfeld took over our 2d Company.

"By the afternoon of 7 October, we had withdrawn to a tree line and dug in there. On the 8th of October we were attacked there by two armored vehicles, which came over a small summit and hit us from the rear. A courageous soldier knocked out both of them with a *panzerfaust.*

"On the 9th of October, our company once again withdrew some 600 meters in a southerly direction from the bridge. A continuous front was built up, in all haste. We had to dig in deeply, for the greatest number of casualties we suffered was from tree bursts. All available entrenching tools, the saw, axes, pickaxes, and shovels were in the front lines. We in the company troop had to dig deeply with our shallow spades into the slate stone with great effort.

"The main road toward Germeter was hell the entire day. Continuous infantry, artillery, and tank fire. The valley boomed in response. We received on a regular basis harassing artillery fire."

The Germans continued to adjust because of pressure from the Americans and the counterattacks by comrades. "Again we had to dig new foxholes in the slate stone with our primitive children's spades in the shortest time. There at midday, the first artillery salvo hit us. Shell noise and deafening explosions in the treetops over us came together. Instinctively, we had thrown ourselves into our shallow foxholes. The strong smell of gunpowder smoke stood over us. Our medical aid man was killed by a fist-sized piece of shrapnel in the back. One asked sarcastically whether this was 'the most beautiful death on the battlefield,' which we had been taught to sing in the patriotic songs. However, not everyone who was hit had the good fortune to die so quickly and painlessly.

"At twilight another artillery salvo hit us, during which a splinter went through a foot of our stretcher bearer. During the late evening a piece of shrapnel tore the lower thighbone of a comrade who was lying next to me in the foxhole. According to a medic from the aid station, he died the next morning of an embolism. An NCO did not return from the reconnaissance squad; shot in the stomach. Hardly a day without casualties.

"Over the front line area in the direction to Todtenbruch [Deadman's Moor], an American reconnaissance aircraft was constantly circling. We called them '*Krabe*' [crows]. Its crew drew artillery fire on everything they saw on the roads or tree lanes. Our horse-drawn supply wagon was completely destroyed.

"With leaflets and loudspeakers the Americans called upon us to surrender. Surrender? No, had we not sworn our fidelity to the Fatherland? However, the next morning the foxholes of some twenty replacements who had shortly before been attached to our company were found empty. These were soldiers of 'Volksliste 3,' more Polish than German." During a pause, Gees wrote home, "I have really been lucky that I have come through without a scratch. Pray only that this good fortune continues to stand at my side. . . . How wonderful it would be if one could return to his home in peace and quiet."

In the American lines, as the badly stricken 39th Infantry struggled to hold its positions, handfuls of replacements appeared. Frank Randall, a former Maryland National Guardsman, draft exempt because of two enlistments, had quit a "good job" after Pearl Harbor and volunteered for the army. Awarded a commission in 1943, he entered the replacement pipeline and surfaced at Company B, 1st Battalion of the 39th, "just fifteen minutes before an attack." Randall noted, "Fortunately, it was called off." Randall felt an esprit almost instantly. "I was well received by both the officers and men. Practically all of the NCOS, the CO, and Executive O were veterans of two campaigns in Africa, then Sicily and the Utah Beach landing, followed by Normandy. But I was accepted and had no problems with the men. I gave them my background to explain that I had no authority on combat and was warned by the NCOs about overexposing myself.

"I learned that this was a well-disciplined outfit, experienced and battle wise. The leadership was good at all levels, not only in the 39th, but throughout the 9th Infantry Division. The regiment had been led by a former classmate of General Patton's Colonel Paddy [Harry] Flint. He had been killed two months earlier while leading a company in Mortain. Colonel Flint had a motto for the regiment, 'Anything, Anywhere, Anytime. Bar Nothing.' He had it painted on the back of helmets and on vehicle bumpers. To the enlisted men, he was an idol."

Another replacement, Don Lavender, entered the army in 1943, as a draftee from Mason City, Illinois. Lavender, with one semester of junior college, entered an Air Corps flight training program after he completed infantry basic training. But in the spring of 1944, as anxiety about replacements grew, along with thousands of other cadets and men studying at colleges in the Army Specialized Training Program, Lavender abruptly received an assignment to the 78th Infantry Division.

Some four months later, he and some companions went to a replacement pool slated for overseas. He spent little more than a day in England before he stepped onto the floating dock off Omaha Beach. Lavender traveled east by train in the forty-and-eights—forty men, or eight horses.

"On an early October evening in 1944," said Lavender, "I arrived at Company I of the 39th Infantry with four other replacements. Darkness prevailed because it had been a dull day and the towering pines of the Huertgen Forest kept out any existing light. A jeep had already gone up to the line with hot chow, and we were to stay at the kitchen until the following morning.

"We bedded down quite early, for it had been a long tiring day on the trucks that brought us up to this area. Not long after, our artillery began firing from a short distance behind our area. We rested very uneasily, and one of the boys with us jumped completely out from his canvas cover when the firing began.

"Morning came almost too soon. We had a warm breakfast at the kitchen tent. Our first day in combat was just like every other day in the Huertgen—dark and rainy, damp and cold. A short time before noon, we started up the muddy road to the line in a jeep. The distance was only about three miles, but it seemed much further.

"When we reached the company area, we waited by the road, and our new company commander made it plain to us that this was the real thing—combat. He then directed us to our platoon leader, and we started the remaining distance on foot. As we walked, the platoon leader told us how lucky we were to join the company while they were in a holding position. He was interrupted by a burst of fire from the far hill, and he informed us that it was Jerry burp gun.

"The lieutenant was a slight man of dark complexion with a small mustache. He had a habit of pausing as he spoke to lick his mustache. A Georgian, he would hesitate at intervals and say, 'Ya hear? Ya hear now?' Men of the platoon questioned his nerve and some of them nicknamed him 'Foxhole Pete.' At a later day, he proved himself, however, and was wounded seriously in doing so."

At his platoon sector, Lavender met his squad leader and entered into the Huertgen life. "Most of the foxholes in this situation were prone shelters. They were long enough to lie down in and were covered with pine logs and dirt. Some of them had very small openings and could be entered only by lying down on the ground and crawling in head first. We spent the day getting oriented on the situation and asking questions. When we got the schedule for guard set-up, we stretched wires to the next foxhole so we could locate it in the dark. It rained that night as usual. There were two of us in our foxhole. When the man came to call us for guard, it was so dark he fell in on top of us. Our only guard pastime was to listen to the 'chop-chop' of our 60mm mortars as they dropped an irregular barrage on an unguarded draw to our front. It seemed like morning would never come.

"The dark of night in the forest was almost beyond description. A man couldn't even step out of his foxhole to relieve himself with any certainty that he would find his way back. Trees less than five feet away were not visible. It was not possible to throw a grenade at night without fear that it would bounce off a tree and come back into the foxhole. Resourceful GIs overcame this problem by placing stones on the edge of the hole in daylight so they could tell by feel the direction of a safe throwing lane in the dark.

"That evening, we were overjoyed to see the sun, but it only lasted for about an hour. We all shouted praise as a squadron of P-47s did a rumbling dive-bombing job somewhere to our front. Our liaison artillery Cubs were up too. The boys had many different names for them. They called them, 'Little Joe,' 'Sea Biscuit,' and several other names. The Germans never caused much trouble with their artillery when 'Little Joe' was up there.

"After about four days of the dampness in soaking foxholes, we were relieved for a one-night stand about 800 yards to the rear. It wasn't much better, except that we could put up a pup tent that kept us a bit dryer, and we were able to have small fires during the daylight hours. The little relief was hardly long enough, however, and the next day found us holding down our position on the line. It still continued to rain, and we were so well soaked that we couldn't find a dry match among us.

"Before combat, I had wondered if anyone would have to tell me to take cover when an artillery barrage first came in. I soon had the answer and found myself flat on my face with others when two 88 shells hit nearby. Everyone dug a little faster. We weren't quite as fortunate in these positions, as the approach route to our position was open to enemy observation, and we were forced to eat C and K rations. They could not bring up hot chow.

"During the dull damp hours of the day, we gathered in small groups, talking of anything that would get our thoughts away from our unpleasant situation. Frequently, we dwelt on rumors that we were to be relieved. The miserable weather and the apparent hopelessness of the situation led to a morbid feeling."

There is a curious absence of substantial entries in Sylvan's diary concerning the rebuff of the 9th Division during the first two weeks of October. While the troops of the 9th Division fought, bled, and died in the Huertgen, First Army Headquarters dealt with visits from VIPs and press interviews. On 14 October, when it should have been apparent that the offensive had broken down, Hodges acted as host for a visit from the king of England, Dwight Eisenhower, and Omar Bradley. Subsequently, other celebrities dropped by: Count and Countess DePinto and actor Tim McCoy. Sylvan remarked on hard fighting elsewhere, reporting a stiff counterattack launched against the 1st Division's 16th and 18th Infantries that brought heavy losses to the enemy around Aachen.

When the exhausted and chewed-up two regiments of the 9th Division sank back on their haunches on 16 October, the GIs had advanced less than two miles, for which they paid in the blood of 4,500 casualties. The dead, wounded, and missing included replacements who had fallen or disappeared even before anyone could call them by their names. After a week to ten days, the 9th Division soldiers welcomed their relief by the 28th Division.

6

Schmidt Again

By the middle of October, Omar Bradley no longer believed in a quick victory, and he spoke of a "time of utmost frustration in the Allied ground command." He noted, "Every day that passed gave the Germans more time and opportunity to build defenses." The only good news was that after a month-long siege, Aachen had fallen to the combined efforts of the 1st and 30th Divisions, with more than 9,000 prisoners taken in the city and its environs. However, both of the American outfits had suffered heavy casualties and would need a month to recuperate, refit, and replace.

On 18 October, with the offensive spearheaded by the two regiments of the 9th Division toward Schmidt all but shut down, Eisenhower held a strategy conference in Brussels. Having conceded the failure of the First Army's October push, Eisenhower, according to Bradley, informed the commanders of the American and British armies that he faced two options. He could order his fifty-four Allied divisions spread across a 500-mile-long front that started at the North Sea and ran to Switzerland, and to dig in and simply hold what they had. By spring many more American units would have disembarked in France to join the GIs at the front. Vast amounts of gasoline, food, ammunition, weapons, armor, and the other accoutrements of war should then be in hand. At the time of the Brussels meeting, British and Canadian troops were still struggling to oust the Germans from the Schelde estuary. Although the Canadian First Army, aided by a British division, ultimately overwhelmed the garrison that obstructed safe passage of the water route on 9 November, the mines sown in the estuary delayed for two more weeks the assurance that the route from Antwerp to the front was clear.

The alternative, said Eisenhower, was to fire up a November offensive relying on the manpower and materials on hand or available through the existing pipelines. Bradley asserted, "No one entertained seriously the proposal that we bed down for the winter." The fighting around Aachen, the abysmal results in the Huertgen, and the paucity of Siegfried Line penetrations testified to the determination and power still manifested by the Nazi government. There was a growing dread that, given any respite, the Panzers would multiply in unpleasant numbers, the battered troops would recover, the home guard units would become better trained, and the number of pillboxes and bunkers would be more numerous and defiant of Allied fire. The American Air Corps chief in Europe, Carl "Tooey" Spaatz, expressed anxiety over the ability of German industry to mass produce their new jet fighters, which posed a severe threat to his bombers. His fear implied that four years of British "area bombing" and two and a half of American strategic bombing had not sufficiently diminished the capacity of the Third Reich's aircraft plants.

Beyond the battlefield, a political factor influenced the decision. A stagnant, inactive front, said Bradley, would undoubtedly provoke Soviet ire, a reasonable assumption because the war on the eastern front showed no signs of abatement. In addition, the notion of a pause probably clashed with the traditional American preference for taking an action rather than sitting still.

Said the 12th Army Group commander, "Ike made his choice and predicated it in part on a measure of hope. We would hammer the enemy with all possible force in an effort to splinter his armies west of the Rhine. Perhaps then, when we reached that river, the morale of the Reich would crack and bring the war to an end. General Marshall [who, taking his cue from the optimism of Bradley, Hodges, and others in September, still retained a roseate attitude] had previously ventured this same, thin hope. Eisenhower and I both clung to it, though we sensed it was a fragile reed." (It should be remembered that when Bradley wrote this, the war was over and the virus of revisionism full blown.)

The First Army remained convinced that the residents of the Huertgen constituted a major threat to any offensive. To cope with the problem, the First Army staff shifted some of the responsibilities. What had been primarily a VII Corps sector now devolved upon the V Corps of Leonard Gerow. The new border between the two corps ran just south of the village of Kleinhau and north of Huertgen. That placed Schmidt entirely within the purview of Gerow.

There was no question that the battered 9th Division troops could play a role in this strategy. Replacement Pvt. W. George Knollenberg, who had completed basic training in August, entered an L Company, 3d Battalion, 60th Infantry, foxhole in the forest late in October, shortly after the debacle of the attack toward Schmidt. "We were a few miles southeast of Aachen, and I was one of forty replacements assigned to L Company, which with our addition brought the company strength to eighty men.

"After my first week, company strength was back down to about forty. We were subjected to heavy artillery and mortar fire several times each day. Most of the German 88mm shells resulted in tree bursts, which were deadly. We lost our company command and first sergeant from a direct mortar hit on the CP.

"My foxhole was positioned to the left of an M4 tank and about thirty yards to the right of a firebreak. The tank was dug in, and the crew served as forward observers for our artillery. The firebreak was covered by German machine guns. I was told there were dead Americans in the firebreak whose bodies could not be recovered. Our main mission was to provide protection for the tank and its crew.

"There was a single run of captured German concertina barbed wire strung in front of our position. The wire was in the cleared right-of-way of a road that paralleled our position. Being from a Wyoming ranch, where only fifteen months before I'd been building and repairing barbed wire fences, I guess it was fitting that I should be detailed to extend and improve our barbed wire defense. I did all the work myself, including toting the coils of concertina a couple of hundred yards from the rear. I had two riflemen covering me while I stretched the coils of wire and tied empty C ration cans with stones in them to the wire. I never understood how the two men could protect me, but since I never got sniped at, I guess they served the purpose.

"There was rain, sleet, or snow virtually every day. We did not have the new shoe packs, so trench foot took a heavy toll. I recall only one morning when the weather was suitable for the P-47s to operate.

"One morning I saw a lieutenant who wore a 28th Division patch checking our positions. The rumor was that the 28th was going to replace the 9th on line. A day or two later, we did in fact move back into Belgium, as fresh troops from the 28th took over our positions. We were told we were going to receive river crossing training." However, Knollenberg, because of a medical review of a previous mastoidectomy, was now classified for limited duty and left the 9th Division.

Don Lavender, the replacement who entered the Huertgen Forest and the 39th Infantry just after its ordeal, noted, "Rumors of being relieved were fulfilled in part when we were relieved a few days later [26 October] by the 28th Division. We were certainly happy to see them, and none of us felt remorse in leaving the Huertgen Forest. We walked about five miles in the mud that day before we reached our trucks, but the fact that we were being relieved made it much easier. The battalion settled into an area not far from Malmédy, a few miles from the Belgium-Germany border.

The 28th Division, the former Pennsylvania National Guard organization that took over from the 39th and 60th Regiments, received reinforcements for its assignment, including the 707th Tank Battalion, a pair of tank destroyer battalions, plus some engineers and extra artillery battalions.

The deployment of the three regiments from the 28th, which replaced the two from the 9th, formed a fan shape. The 109th Infantry presented a northeast thrust along the Germeter-to-Huertgen axis. The 110th aimed more easterly, in a drive through the middle to control a road between Schmidt and Strauch for supply purposes. The main gambit of the 28th sent the 112th Regiment after the prime goal—Schmidt. The V Corps offensive supposedly would assist a VII Corps division to capture Huertgen and a line of outposts northeast while on the way to the Roer.

The timetable scheduled the 28th to commence its attack as early as 31 October, while in the VII Corps, the 1st Division and the 4th Division, a regular army outfit that had secured Utah Beach on D Day, would power their way through the forest on northeast axes, left of the Keystone Division's attack with the 4th Division immediately adjacent to the 28th. The newly arrived 104th Division would assume responsibility for the Stolberg corridor. Initially, strategists pinpointed 2 November for the VII Corps GIs to start their offensive, aided by massive raids by the Air Corps and barrages of artillery equal to that thrown at the enemy to kick off the Saint-Lô breakout.

The 28th was not virgin to battle. It had engaged in some strenuous combat in Normandy and sprinted across France. After the victory parade through Paris, it was among those who first tested the Westwall. Still, their impressions of their new battleground must have been disquieting. The weeks of shelling and the consequent treetop bursts had cut away the uppermost branches, leaving the forest looking much like a graveyard of discarded telephone poles, some reaching like fingers into the sky and others like decapitated torsos. Timber, boughs and branches, and military equipment littered the ground. The men of the 9th, whom they relieved, were dirty, their clothing torn and their faces often etched with a thousand-yard stare as they left their foxholes without much conversation. It did not take long for the place to depress its newest inhabitants. The ground was saturated with water, and keeping dry was near impossible. The constant problem of supply showed in the absence of overshoes or wet weather gear. The gray days could not muster enough light to dissipate the natural gloom of the area.

Captain Harry Kemp, who led M Company of the 109th Infantry, said of recently promoted Maj. Howard Topping, his battalion CO, upon his return from a six-hour reconnaissance of the sector committed to his organizations, "His company commanders and staff had never seen him so concerned or explicit about conditions in the new area. Topping described the new positions as heavily forested, shell-shattered, gloomy, and pillbox-infested. It was served by narrow, muddy roads and footpaths bordered by wood-encased [to escape metal detectors] antipersonnel mines. . . . He strongly stressed that all soldiers and vehicles must stay on defined roads and trails. Future operations were unknown and not mentioned. But it appeared the Old Gray Mare Regiment was heading for trouble."

Sergeant Al Burghardt, a mortar squad leader, recalled mixed impressions upon arriving in the woods. "The Huertgen Forest, on first observation, looked like heaven. The dense forest, with its towering pine trees, looked like a place where the German artillery observers would not be able to locate us. In the hedgerows, it was a fight for each hedgerow, and the casualties were severe. The Siegfried Line, with its pillboxes, was another world. The pillboxes, for the most part, were in large open areas. They were camouflaged and had excellent fields of fire, and German artillery observers could watch our movement. It always seemed the Germans had the high ground.

"On second observation, when we got into it, the Huertgen Forest looked ominous. It was dark, and as we went to our positions, we could see some of the problems that the 9th Division faced. The pine forest, which composed 99 percent of the forest, was littered with branches, and it was difficult to go in a straight line because of all the debris. We noticed the trees were scarred from shrapnel, and many trees were down from direct artillery hits. In general, the forest floor was a mess. This was caused by what we learned to fear—the tree burst. The 9th Division and German dead were all over the area. I remember the Huertgen Forest as being dark, dreary, foreboding, sinister, close, and desolate.

"I had no idea what was involved when we relieved the 9th Division in the Huertgen Forest. We relieved them in the dead of night. We passed each other in silence. We did not have time to talk. It was a still night. They were veterans and so were we. Veterans learned long ago that you don't talk at night. Sounds carry, and we didn't need an artillery barrage to announce a change was taking place. We didn't sleep that night, and in the morning, the ever-present smell of battle was in the air, the smell of death and the odor from exploding shells."

Although most of the 9th Division GIs quietly left their foxholes for the incoming men of the 28th Division, a few remained to assist in the exchange. "The guide from the 9th Division mortar section," said Burghardt, "took our three squads to their mortar positions. They had been forced to construct an underground shelter against the tree bursts. These consisted of a dugout about four feet deep. The length and width I no longer remember, but I do know that you were always on your hands and knees. They were covered with layers of pine logs and dirt. It had one entrance. There were a number of these covered dugouts for all members of the three mortar squads.

"The position made by the 9th Division mortar section was completely surrounded by tall pine trees. The clearing did not have to be large, because of the trajectory of the 60mm mortars. This helped us from being observed by the enemy. We had telephone lines going to the three rifle platoons on the line and one forward listening post. The sergeants took turns at the forward listening post, a very lonely and scary job. Every time we changed sergeants on this post, you wondered if you would make it to the post. Because of all the debris from the trees, it [was] ideal for an ambush or a sniper. Secondly, you wondered if you were hit in this tangled mess, if anyone would ever find you. At this period of time we had more mortar ammo than I had ever seen. There were cloverleaf canisters, which held six 60mm mortar shells piled up about five and a half feet high for about fifty feet, and there were no restrictions on the use of them." The shortages that plagued artillery did not apply to smaller arms.

Platoon leader Bill Peña, with Company I of the 109th Infantry, in a party that reconnoitered by vehicle the area where the units were to relieve the 9th Division GIs, returned to an assembly point on the night of 26 October. In the dark, he placed his weapon and other equipment within easy reach of his foxhole. "When we awoke [before dawn], conditions were much worse than I had anticipated. The effect was that of being completely blind with the eyes wide open. I groped around for my gear and rifle. The order was given to fall in on the road. We were no more than thirty yards from the road. Some men had difficulty finding their gear and weapons at the time squad leaders began calling them. Complete frustration set in. In their blindness, men would fall into someone's slit trench or run into trees. After a few turns in this serious game of blind man's bluff, all sense of direction was lost. Leaders kept calling their unit designations cautiously trying to avoid extra loud sound while providing directions toward themselves.

"The time schedule had not allowed for this hour lost in forming the column on the road, which would have taken only a matter of ten minutes during daylight, if this had been possible. The black, tall forest, hugging the road closely, broke overhead, revealing a slightly less dark, starless, overcast sky. This view was the only way one could tell he was on the road."

When the battalion finally assembled and moved out in a long column of twos, apparently to make up for the delay, the lead company took off at a fast pace. Said Peña, "Soon the accordion effect began—the running to catch up with the man in front and then the sudden stop after running into him in the black void. One couldn't see his hand in front of his face, much less his feet on the uneven road. Men stumbled and fell with their equipment. They cursed this rat race openly and loudly."

Inevitably, the trailing soldiers lost contact with the faster moving lead company. A brief conference among officers from the rear elements nominated Peña, who had the day before made the trip to their destination, to guide the three lost companies, although he had only a vague idea of the route.

"I found myself at a Y in the road, which I could distinguish only by looking overhead at the sky. I decided to lead down the right fork. I established a slower pace commensurate to [that] of men carrying heavy machine guns now immediately behind me. If these men could take the pace so could the rest. At another fork in the road, I again took the one toward the right. There were no signposts to be seen; no flashlights could be used if there had been any. I was going by half-remembered impressions, trusting to luck.

"I heard the rippling of a stream to our right. Yes, I remembered the stream. I remembered crossing it. Now to find the bridge. Still looking up, I now saw two breaks in the forest; one led right toward the water but no bridge; the other, to the left ran parallel to the stream. I chose the left road in the sky, hoping to find the bridge further upstream. It took me twenty yards to confirm my doubt that I had mistaken a firebreak for the road. The ground underfoot felt different. I halted and started to double back. Just then I heard a jeep coming from the opposite side of the stream. It came across a submerged bridge." The crossing was a concrete slab, ankle deep under water, which Peña failed to notice while making his previous trip in a truck. The battalion CP was only a quarter of a mile off.

In the jeep was Major Topping, who, Peña recalled, loudly shattered the mandated combat zone silence. "Lieutenant Peña, we were supposed to complete our relief by 6 o'clock under the cover of darkness. We're way behind schedule. If there is one man killed during this relief, I'll hold *you* to blame! I'll have you court-martialed and sent back to the States!"

Peña was stunned. "Me to blame? The man didn't know the whole story. Perhaps I should have refused to take the lead. Perhaps I should have charted the route myself but that hadn't been included in my orders. As we began to see daylight, I started to worry about the consequences. My prayer was answered by a thick fog, which did not lift until 11 o'clock, long after the relief had been safely accomplished."

Kemp observed, "The sights . . . viewed en route to and at [the] new positions were also not conducive to high morale. Shattered trees from artillery and mortar shelling were everywhere, along with numerous shell craters. Discarded equipment of all sorts littered the sides of the muddy, rutted vehicle trails and footpaths. The bodies of friend and foe alike were still being removed. The fighting had not spared noncombatant wildlife, and an occasional bloated deer carcass was seen. The evidence of tough fighting was abundant. Fortunately, both the weather and the enemy cooperated during the exchange. A thick fog developed the night of 25–26 October and provided concealment of the exchange [with the 9th Division soldiers] until late morning of the 26th."

Peña and his comrades relieved parts of the 39th Infantry in Germeter, a village with twelve to fourteen houses that lined both sides of the road, which ran north and then northeast to Huertgen, a somewhat larger settlement two miles off. East and southeast of Germeter, barely a mile away, was Vossenack, still bigger than the other two hamlets in the forest. Peña's outfit protected the road toward Huertgen while facing toward Vossenack. His weapons platoon occupied a house and barn on the highway's east side. They settled in, awaiting orders to attack.

John Chernitsky, son of a Depression-era butcher who became a manager for a steel company in the Pennsylvania coal country, enlisted after high school in the National Guard for the six dollars a month. In February 1941, the 28th was federalized. It was make-believe time for the U.S. military and Chernitsky's antitank company, which dragged a piece of pipe mounted on a truck axle to simulate a 37mm cannon. "When we got to Indiantown Gap [in Pennsylvania] with these three dummy guns, the rest of the 110th Regiment tagged us 'Captain Scott and his Clang-Glangs.'"

The antitank company soon traded in its ersatz weapons for the genuine article, and when Chernitsky reached Omaha Beach, a few days after the invasion, the puny 37mms had been replaced by the only slightly more puissant 57mm, still unsuitable for the heavy German armor. He remembered the bitter combat in the Normandy hedgerows and near Percy, France. There was a brief celebratory moment as the 28th marched through Paris, but, recalled Chernitsky, "At the end of the parade route we ran into German resistance. We reorganized to resist the German attacks. The Germans retreated ahead of us, and we would run into skirmishes until we hit the Luxembourg border. To show you how fast we were moving, the antitank men slept on the trucks as we were moving along. A couple would be awake for lookout."

During this odyssey, Chernitsky recalls, "The only men I had lost were six before we got to the Huertgen, when a lieutenant insisted on taking a gun up front in the open. We had four KIA and two WIA as a result. It was a helluva shock." He also had personal contact with Omar Bradley, whom he recognized when the general commanded the 28th back in the States before he became the 12th Army Group head. "He came forward in a jeep with his aide, a captain. We were pinned down by snipers, and I started walking toward him."

Bradley apparently expected Chernitsky to deliver a smart salute and demanded, "Don't you know who I am?"

"I said, 'If I salute you, we're both going to be dead.' Just then a bullet hit his captain in the shoulder." Bradley left the scene, rapidly.

Chernitsky's outfit moved into the forest on 2 November. "It didn't snow until we had been there three or four days, and we got a chance to dig in. We could fortify our foxholes and slit trenches with all of the logs from trees knocked down." He did not need to worry about a visit from the likes of Bradley. "None of the brass ever came forward to our position. We were too far up front for them."

To fill out its thinned ranks for the offensive, the 28th absorbed hundreds of replacements, including GIs from other branches as well as those with little more than basic training to qualify them as combat infantrymen. Jerry Alexis, a twenty-year-old native of Johnsonburg, Pennsylvania, had completed four academic quarters at Drexel Institute of Technology in Philadelphia when he was called up with the Enlisted Reserve Corps in April 1943. He had finished his basic, served briefly as cadre, and then lost an opportunity to be an Air Corps flight crewman when the army washed out thousands of such candidates as "surplus."

At the end of October, Alexis reached the headquarters of the 28th Division in Rott, where he was assigned to B Company of the 110th Infantry. "After the other replacements and I had been interviewed by the commanding officer (and we had some personal talk after he found that I came from western Pennsylvania, the home of the 110th in its National Guard days), I was told to get some sleep in one of the nearby foxholes before we were taken up to the front-line platoons after nightfall. In the one I picked, I discovered a GI apparently already asleep. I shook him without rousing him, and when I drew back my hand it was covered with blood. He had been killed by artillery shrapnel from a tree burst, despite the log covering that we always tried to use in the Huertgen Forest to protect ourselves from this hazard."

Along with the batch consigned to B Company, which included Alexis, was the Chicago newspaper feature writer Ed Uzemack. At twenty-nine, he was old enough for the eighteen-year-olds drafted along with him to be referred to as "Pop," had he not been gifted with a boyish face. He entered the service in July 1943, leaving behind a pregnant wife. "I didn't see my son until he was seven months old, and I didn't see him again for another eleven months." Initially trained as a radar technician, Uzemack received reassignment to the infantry to meet the demand for riflemen.

"The packet I came up with was dumped about midnight on Halloween in the Huertgen Forest. We slept on our shelter halves that night as ordered. When roused at dawn, I found I had placed the head part of my shelter half on a pile of feces. There were bodies of Germans killed in action scattered throughout the area we temporarily occupied. I learned that the division had enemy on three sides; we came darn near being completely surrounded."

As part of the plan to strengthen the 28th's attacks, the 707th

Tank Battalion moved into the general vicinity of Hahn to add its firepower to the attack of the 112th Infantry against Vossenack. Originally an element in the 5th Armored Division, the 707th split off in September 1943 to become one of many independent tank battalions that would be shuffled about among the infantry divisions. The 707th had three tank companies, A, B, and C, each with fifteen Sherman medium tanks armed with 75mm guns. The short-barreled 75mm cannons of the Shermans lacked the muzzle velocity to penetrate the heavily shielded German Mark IVs, Tigers, and King Tigers. Only a shell through an aperture could damage the massive pillboxes. A fourth element, Company D, operated light tanks equipped with a 37mm cannon that was only useful against soldiers in an exposed position or nonarmored vehicles. All of the companies possessed recovery and maintenance equipment. Headquarters company fielded four assault guns, 75mm short-barreled howitzers mounted on M4 tank chassis. In addition, the command unit had a couple of tanks. Because the 707th had no amphibious instruction, it did not participate in the D-Day Normandy Beach landings. Except for some shelling of enemy Siegfried Line positions in mid-October, the 707th, commanded by Lt. Col. Richard W. Ripple, and which disembarked in France on 1 September, had no combat experience.

Howard Thomsen, a Nebraska farmer drafted in June 1941, went through basic training at Fort Knox, Kentucky. During this period, he signed up for the tank mechanic class, and although after graduation he was qualified to be an instructor who would never leave the States, Thomsen preferred to soldier in a line company. He started with the 81st Armored Regiment in the 5th Armored, undergoing many months stationed in California's Mojave Desert before reaching England in February 1944. In addition to his duties as a mechanic in B Company, Thomsen also served on an 81mm mortar crew.

As a maintenance man, Thomsen rode a tank retriever on the LST that ferried his unit across the Channel at the end of August. "What a feeling when they let the door down on the LST and you start moving out, not knowing how deep the water was. For luck it was only three or four feet deep."

"When we landed in France," said Jack W. Goldman, who was a radio operator and loader with B Company in the 707th, "Patton had run out of maps, gas, and tank treads. Our immediate job was to piggyback tank treads for Patton's medium tanks by attaching them to the back decks of our tanks. This arrangement made our vehicles fishtail, and at least one tank had a fatality. [A snapped chain lashed Thomsen above the eye, and he had to see the medics to repair the damage.]

"We had a successful trip, including a quick view of Paris," said Goldman. "When we reached our destination, we delivered Patton's supplies and were quickly ushered into the Huertgen Forest. Things were quiet at first, and B Company was busy setting up for a future indirect fire mission by working with division artillery. A few of us began to wonder what was going on up at the 'front,' and we decided to take a peep [the armored forces name for a jeep] and see for ourselves what to expect. We took the only road until we spotted an infantryman in a foxhole situated about fifty yards from the road. We innocently drove toward him, but he shouted, 'Get the hell out of here! The Krauts are just across the valley!' By this time we realized that we were just stupid and were risking our lives. We turned the vehicle around and gunned the engine just as a mortar shell landed right in the same spot we had just occupied."

John Marshall, from the small town of Lincoln Park, New Jersey, had worked in a defense plant but nevertheless his draft board summoned him. He remembered, "Eddie's father drove Eddie and me along with four other guys to the draft board eight miles away in Boonton, New Jersey. The war was to deal a cruel hand to us six inductees in that car; four were killed, Eddie was injured and lost an eye, and I beat the odds."

Shipped to Camp Hood, Texas, Marshall discovered he was in a tank destroyer outfit only when they issued the shoulder patches. "For the next twelve weeks I learned about the blind sides and the unmaneuverability of a tank and how one man could knock out a tank single-handed. In short, a tank, I learned, is an iron coffin. The training was rough, and we had quite a few fatalities through negligence of the cadre. Cadre are a special brand of loudmouths that train and teach you how to kill in combat, but they never get to go themselves, because they are so good at shouting they have to stay behind where it is safe."

Marshall and some eighty others, plucked from a group of 2,000 recruits, boarded a train. "I had gotten good marks on my army induction aptitude tests and the other guys with me didn't look like a bunch of klutzes, so I assumed we were being sent to officer training school or some special instruction." Instead, he found himself a member of the 707th, at Pine Camp, New York, a few miles from the Canadian border. Furthermore, he discovered that he was now a tank crewman. In Company B, 2d Platoon, he became an assistant driver. An independent type, Marshall pulled more than his share of company punishments, but he paid attention to the duties of a tanker and could handle any of the tasks.

Although not overly impressed with many of the officers and noncoms, Marshall noted, "We had maintenance Technical Sergeant Howard Thomsen that knew tanks and any vehicle in the battalion from end to end. He was so knowledgeable that he was able to adjust the tank motors in B Company to go five miles faster than the tanks in other companies, for which he was almost busted by the battalion CO. Five miles an hour faster doesn't seem like much, but in combat, if a Kraut shell explodes in front of you and the next one in back of your tank, you better move the tank quickly, as your tank has been bracketed and the third shell is probably on its way already and is going to hit you.

"Halfway through France, our tank motor conked out on us while in convoy, and unlike a car, you don't roll over to the side. The rest of the convoy went around us. Thomsen pulled up with his crew and pulled the old motor out and replaced it with a new one in less than two and a half hours!" Indeed, the only way that Thomsen had been able to keep pace with the outfit in his slow-moving tank retriever was by disregarding the rules and overriding a governor set to limit its speed.

While the 707th rolled across Europe toward its destiny in the Huertgen Forest, the battalion detached Marshall for a special task. Driven all the way back to the French beaches, he saw "thousands of vehicles of all descriptions and what looked like a sea of tanks stretching from the water's edge to the foot of the cliffs. We were told we were to drive thirty command cars and forty-nine tanks to the front lines. A sergeant said, 'Take whatever one you feel like driving.' I could see some tanks were a newer model, so I hurried down to the beach and climbed into the nearest tank. It was a dream compared to the M4 our crew had. Ours had a radial airplane engine; the clutch brakes and steering demanded raw strength to operate. This tank [an M4A1] had a Ford engine; power brakes, clutch, and steering; and a better, bigger gun.

"This trip was going to be a picnic. Just start the motor and move out. We formed a convoy and started back. We were told to stay fifty yards apart, but on the second day it rained, and I found by staying just a few yards behind the tank in front of me that his exhaust would keep me warm and dry. I was to pay for this disobedience. When we stopped for the night, I became very sick and could hardly gas up the tank and add the oil. I felt that I was going to die. I have never been that sick in my life, including to this day. Later, I realized it was carbon monoxide poisoning.

"I looked at the tank and it was a formidable, unclimbable mountain. I did not have the strength to lift my feet, my eyes burning in my head. I thought if I just lie down and rest I may feel better so I laid down in an L-shaped furrow, placed my head on the high part, and closed my eyes. It seemed like only minutes later I heard someone shouting, 'Mount up, prepare to move out.' I opened my eyes, it was daylight and raining. It had rained all night, my furrow was full. I was completely underwater except for my head. I had slept through a thunderstorm and missed breakfast." Muddy and soaked, Marshall climbed into the tank and took his place in the convoy, carefully maintaining the prescribed fifty-yard interval.

"When we got to the front lines, six or seven of us had to drive our tanks to a further location. Within an hour, we came to the Siegfried Line, the dragon's teeth. The engineers were blasting a lane through these concrete spears. When we arrived the Germans were shooting at the engineers from a pillbox. They sneaked back somehow after being ousted the day before. There were no heavy guns available. Our tanks had no ammo and no one to fire the guns if they did. It was a stalemate and vehicles behind us began to pile up.

"Then an engineer private started creeping from tooth to tooth toward the pillbox, while pulling a heavy amount of explosives. He crawled right up the vision slit; the Krauts couldn't depress their guns to get him. All they had to do was roll a grenade out, but they didn't. He brazenly stood up as he walked to the aperture and placed his explosives. When he came away he decided the safest place for him would be on top of the pillbox. He scrambled up, and when the charge went off it flipped him face down among the teeth like a wet sack of rags. A moment later, he stood up apparently unharmed and waved his arm in a gesture as though saying, 'Come on, roll 'em.'"

The 707th initiated itself into battle starting in mid-October, acting as artillery to harass enemy soldiers and perhaps damage Westwall emplacements. Both John Marshall and Jack Goldman recall an unusual deployment to carry out the mission. Marshall explained, "The company set up for indirect firing, seventeen tanks side by side about 100 feet apart from tank number one to tank number seventeen, a total distance of about a third of a mile. We had dug a trench about three feet wide and six feet long and then backed our tank over it. We would take turns, two men at a time, sleeping in it, as it was a luxury to sleep stretched out prone. The tank would protect us from shell bursts. Gilbert Burgess, a driver from another tank, asked us if he could have a log lying close to our tank. We were tired of stumbling over it and told him to take it. As he leaned over and picked one end up, he detonated a German pressure mine placed under the log, tearing up his legs and stomach. John Alyea [an Indiana farm boy and the driver of Marshall's tank] and I were standing within ten or twelve feet from the log and never even got a scratch."

Goldman noted, "Suddenly mortar fire tore through the whole company from one end to another. No one was hurt, but our duffle bags, containing all our clothes, et cetera, had been severely shot up. They had been stacked on the back decks of each tank. This was not serious, but it indicated that the enemy knew exactly where we were and our bodies were next. Most men now stayed inside the tanks for protection. We were learning how to survive."

Unlike the situation with the 1st and 9th Divisions, where the foot soldiers and attached armor had learned to rely on one another, the 707th joined the 28th Division only a few days before they would be required to work in concert. Alyea, an original member of the 707th who was drafted in November 1942, had qualified to drive a tank. In the crew as assistant driver and loader was John Marshall. "Not too much happened before we went into combat in the Huertgen," said Alyea, noting that in concert with the 229th Field Artillery and his outfit's assault guns, they shelled enemy positions east of Krinkelt in mid-October. "On October 12th, the first platoon, the one I was part of, moved back to receive assault training with the 110th Infantry Regiment for two or three days."

Lieutenant Raymond Fleig, a platoon leader in Company A, remarked, "You'd never know we were in the same army. We married up with the infantry on the run. There was little or no coordination of communication, routes of attack, et cetera. Even though each tank had an external telephone for ground forces to [use], the infantry didn't know that. The phone was in a box at the rear of the tank and painted the same color as the tank. The usual method of communication was to bang on the side of the tank until you got the tank commander's attention and then point to the target. Often the infantry would not approach the tank because they feared that it would draw artillery and mortar fire."

American tankers labored under a severe communications handicap. Aside from the unfamiliarity of their partners with the external phone, the armor relied upon SCR506 [or later versions] line-of-sight radios that depended on a clear path for transmissions. Mountains, hills, and thick stands of trees interfered with the signal. "If the antenna touched a branch of a tree," said Fleig, "it grounded it." Furthermore, the external aerial, necessary for any distance, often was damaged by enemy fire or from simply plowing through obstacles. According to John Alyea, the radios in most tanks could only receive orders and lacked ability to call back. Only the tanks carrying a platoon leader or a platoon sergeant had two-way radios.

Originally, the attack by the 28th, in a strategy dictated by V Corps and the First Army, was due to begin on the last day of October, but rain, fog, and poor visibility postponed the offensive for two days. Although conditions continued to be dismal, there could be no further delay because of the timetable for subsequent attack of VII Corps forces.

Elements of the 28th had begun to press forward as early as 29 October, according to Bill Peña, to secure a line of departure for the advance to Schmidt. "The entire battalion attacked through the forest early in the morning. We were to move to the high ground half a mile north of Germeter. During the attack a single American fighter plane, a sleek P-47, made a couple of low passes coming from our rear. I was in a firebreak lane, otherwise it would have been difficult to see it from within the thick forest. I wondered if he knew whom he was striking on the first pass. On the second pass we all ducked when he dropped a big object we expected to explode within our line—since it didn't explode, we guessed it was an empty gasoline pod.

"The German outposts had already been spotted by reconnaissance patrols and were easily overcome. When I came up to one of them, the fighting was over. What was left in the wake was a pitiful sight. The bodies of three dead Germans didn't bother me; it was the sight of a wounded German boy, looking not over seventeen years old, crying for his mother. This was war. I shouldn't allow myself the luxury of compassion. Traska, our medic, came up in his easy manner and began taking care of him. He stopped crying, but I couldn't erase the picture of his poor frightened face for a long time."

The wounded youth probably lived in one of a couple of houses located by a sawmill on a hill. One of the buildings became an observation post for the mortar section, with the tubes near the crest of the slope. An enemy gun that the mortars could not silence covered an open area between platoons. Peña and his associates detoured through a wooded area when traveling between the units. "I was coming back from the 2d platoon," said Peña, "walking leisurely through the woods. Suddenly I came up to a uniformed German man sitting against a tree. I almost shot him before I realized he was dead—from the fracas a few days ago. I would have felt ridiculous shooting a dead man. This wasn't the first time I'd walked through these woods; I was surprised I hadn't run into him before." Peña did not realize at the time just how difficult it was to see anyone or anything more than a few feet off in the forest.

Although most of the American cast of characters changed for the November offensive, the Germans could not afford to rotate their troops. Hubert Gees, the runner for the Fusilier Battalion of the 275th Infantry Division, still defended against the GIs in the Huertgen and recalled, "At the end of October, there was another change of position from the right wing in the valley to the left wing of the Fusilier Battalion, bounding here at the Haptstrasse to the edge of the forest before the Wittscheidt sawmill. Americans held the main road Germeter-Richelskaul-Raffelsbrand-Peterberg after heavy fighting since mid-October."

The battle plan for the offensive assigned the 707th Companies A and C for direct support of the 112th Infantry. In reserve, B Company, attached to the 28th Division artillery, would supplement the big guns with its own indirect fire. Headquarters company would work with the 28th's recon units and preserve the right or south flank. Meanwhile, the 110th Infantry would move on Saltonstall, while the 109th placed itself short of the village of Huertgen. After assessing the horrific injury to the 9th Division during its days in the Huertgen, the staff issued a five-page report dated 31 October. Titled "Notes on Woods Fighting," the paper said, "It is strongly recommended that units . . . be given previous training in this type of fighting. . . . Woods fighting is radically different from ordinary operations, and a knowledge of its basic requirements will save lives and insure success." The document pointed out the difficulty of protecting an individual against the frequent tree bursts with ordinary foxholes, slit trenches, or assuming a prone position. The authors labeled night operations as physically impossible. "Unless a route has definitely been established, do not travel in the woods at night without a compass." Quite emphatically it warned, "Never send replacements to a company in the heat of battle. . . . Replacements should not be sent forward during hours when enemy barrages are likely." Whether any of this was read by the officers of the 28th is unknown, but the evidence indicates the men from the

Keystone Division were not tutored in the lessons learned through the painful experiences of their predecessors. Certainly, the cautionary note about replacements was ignored.

Following the delays of weather, the attack was definitely on for 2 November.

7

TURNS FOR THE WORST AT SCHMIDT

Major General Norman "Dutch" Cota, who owed his command to his effectiveness as assistant division commander for the 29th Division when it became hung up on Omaha Beach, had little input into the strategy that pitted his 28th Division against the enemy entrenched in the forest. The plan, including the deployment of the regiments in their specific sectors, emanated from V Corps headquarters, which in turn bowed to the dictates of First Army and 12th Army Group leaders.

High hopes pervaded the First Army chieftains. Diarist Sylvan reported on 1 November, "General Gerow came to see the general [Hodges] for final discussion of V Corps' attack tomorrow morning and with him the general left for a visit to the 28th Division, which was to spearhead the attack. He found them in fine fettle, raring to go, optimistic over their chances of giving the Boche a fine drubbing. The general said their plan was excellent. The feinting toward the north in hopes of fooling the Boche into belief this was the main effort and then whacking him with everything in the direction of the town of Schmidt. General [George] Davis [an old friend of Hodges] was chiefly responsible for the plan, and the general said he had never looked in better shape. Weather report for tomorrow still uncertain, two groups of fighter bombers were to support the attack."

In his book *The Regiment,* Harry Kemp remarked, "There is little evidence that officers who drew the plan were knowledgeable of the conditions existing in the battle area (enemy, terrain, weather). Perhaps they were overly optimistic after almost three months of pursuing an obviously defeated foe. A current phrase for such detailed direction would be 'micro-managed.' In any event, Cota and his subordinate commanders were told what to do and how to do it down to battalion and separate company level."

In fact, after the war, Cota admitted that the 28th's attack had, in his words, "a gambler's chance" of succeeding. Under the best of circumstances, those making the wager were at most risking their commands or their reputations; the chips on the table were the bodies of soldiers.

Whatever the source of the plans, the 28th appeared a winner for only a few hours before it became obvious the outfit held a losing hand. At 0800, sixty minutes before H hour, the first artillery shells whistled through the air and exploded in the Huertgen Forest. Salvo after salvo shattered the air as the guns of both the V and VII Corps artillery launched more than 4,000 rounds, while the 28th Division's own pieces poured forth 7,313. At the appointed moment, 0900, the riflemen from Companies F and G, 2d Battalion of the 112th, along with tanks from C Company of the 707th, passed through the outposts around Germeter. As they did, the U.S. howitzers and cannons elevated their barrels to shift their barrages to more distant targets, beyond the areas being attacked by the GIs. The German guns promptly laid down heavy fire on the advancing Americans, inflicting a number of casualties. But with the 707th's armor as a spearhead, the foot soldiers, carefully staying within the paths marked by the tank tracks to avoid mines, advanced on the objective of Vossenack, clearly marked by its shell-scarred church tower, which undoubtedly served the enemy as an observation post.

As historian for the 707th, A Company platoon leader Ray Fleig described the efforts of the combined attack by foot soldiers and armor. "Two gaps had been cleared in the friendly minefield in the left sector. The assault platoons moved through the gaps in the wake of the seven tanks. Within a short distance of the line of departure, the driver of T/Sgt. Audney Brown's tank misread the minefield markings and strayed out of the cleared gap. The tank hit a mine, which blew the track off. When the six remaining tanks moved forward, the platoon leader's tank became mired in the sponge-like ground. The tank company commander, Capt. George S. West, came forward in his command tank and picked up Second Lieutenant Quarrie and took his position on the line of advancing tanks.

"At the approach of the coordinated tank-infantry assault, supported by artillery fire, many of the defending Germans in Vossenack fled north, east, or southeast. En route, a soldier stepped on one of the numerous mines sown along the road from Germeter to Huertgen. When a machine gunner attempted to aid the wounded GI, he triggered another mine that killed him and set off an additional batch. Company G pressed ahead, leaving a dozen killed or wounded from the minefield. Past outlying farms and open fields north of Vossenack, the tanks of Company C and the infantrymen of Company G pushed on quickly and soon reached the objective, the nose of the ridge northeast of Vossenack, pointing toward the dominating Brandenberg and Bergstein ridge. In an attack for which the planners had allowed three hours, the tank-led assault force had taken only one hour and five minutes, gaining the objective shortly after 1000 hours."

The offensive on the right side encountered much stiffer opposition. Fleig reported that the first three tanks from Company C of the 707th led off with the 112th's Company F platoon so closely behind that the platoon leader had his hand to the rear of Lt. James Leming's Sherman. Only sporadic mortar fire fell until the column cut across the main Vossenack road. From a wooded draw, a well-concealed *panzerfaust* knocked out one tank. The remaining armor lumbered on while blazing away at suspected enemy positions hidden among the trees. Some 300 yards farther, Lieutenant Leming's guns jammed from overheating. A radio message brought up a section of three tanks from the reserve.

Other elements from Company C of the 707th moved forward to assist infantrymen taking fire from Germans in a house at a crossroads near Vossenack. Two 75mm shells blasted the building, enabling the GIs to charge into it and capture seven soldiers with a pair of officers. After the platoon leader's tank was disabled by a mine, two Shermans rattled down the main street, pouring shells into each building while their partners on foot then stormed inside to seize any surviving enemy. The initial achievements of the offensive in this area may have fooled the upper echelons into believing their strategy correct. The ground in front of the Vossenack ridge was relatively open terrain, allowing tanks to maneuver more easily.

In the main arena of the Huertgen, the possibilities would be far more limited.

While their brother companies, aided by the 707th tanks, occupied Vossenack, other elements of the 2d Battalion, at the insistence of Gerow, Cota, and Brig. Gen. George Davis, the assistant commander of the 28th, moved to the eastern edge of the ridge overlooking the town.

The accounts filed with the First Army were summarized by Sylvan: "Nov. 2 at 9 o'clock, the 28th Division launched the V Corps attack to the east with the 109th and 112th Infantry after an artillery preparation by almost 25 battalions participating. The attack progressed well in the morning but slowed up in the afternoon [because of] increased fortifications and heavy mines. The 1st and 3d battalions of the 109th reached their immediate objectives, advancing over a mile southeast of Huertgen. The 2d Bn. of the 112 Inf. advanced 1-1/2 miles to the town of Vossenack, its initial objective. The 110th Infantry jumped off at noon but made only a slight advance. 350 prisoners were taken during the day and the Gen. pronounced himself 'well satisfied' with the progress made. The air had only a slight opportunity to aid in the attack because of the bad weather, on one occasion dropping the bombs in the midst of our troops causing, according to preliminary reports, 15 casualties."

The first night in possession of the Vossenack ridge passed fairly quietly but, recalled then-Lt. Preston Jackson, the 112th liaison officer with its three battalions, "The Germans were on the high ground looking down on us." In full view of German artillery observers during the daylight hours of 3 November, the riflemen could not leave their foxholes even to relieve themselves, such was the fury of the mortars and artillery rounds that burst upon them.

On the left flank of the 112th, the 109th Infantry proceeded according to the plans issued from on high. Captain Wilfred Dulac, CO of I Company, explained the mission to platoon leader Bill Peña. He described the operation as partly a feint but also a deployment to protect the Germeter-Huertgen road while the 112th did the heavy lifting.

Said Peña, "At nine o'clock our rifle platoons began the movement forward. The sounds of the initial volleys of rifle fire were evidence of the resistance. Our mortars were busy firing according to plan. The artillery fire was lifted to more advanced targets."

The tactics called for I Company mortars to cover the front of the lead platoons with a flare gun signal to cue them for a barrage. Although the troops had walkie-talkies, they did not depend on them but relied instead on a field telephone line back of the mortars from an observation post in a house, a distance of only seventy-five yards. It was Peña's job to see the flare and then relay the order to fire to the mortar squads.

"The enemy artillery started firing at our sawmill position—an obvious location for some of our activity. I jumped into the hole in which I had located the rear field phone. Jamison and Reger, regularly ammunition carriers, were in charge of the phone. The hole itself was some seven by twelve feet in size and six feet deep—originally it had been dug by the sawmill people as a dry trash pit. When we heard the whistling of incoming artillery, we crouched low against the earthen walls. It was almost as if the Germans knew exactly where the trash pit was located. In quick succession, the rounds came in; one, ear-ringing noise; two, closer even with our fingers to our ears; three, close enough to splatter us with dirt; four, earth-shaking and more dirt. The deafening noise was enough to leave us in shock. The thought of one of them landing in the hole was completely unnerving.

"I looked at Jamison and Reger. They were visibly shaking. I grabbed the phone and turned the handle. 'This is Item, this is Item. Can you hear me?'

"Again, again. No response. The wire could be broken, I thought, or else the two observers were out of action at the house. I turned the phone over to Reger. 'Here, you try it.'

"Reger couldn't say the words nor go through the motions. I took it and gave it to Jamison. 'Try it.'

"Jamison had difficulty with the ritual. He stuttered at first. Then he said it loud and clear, 'This is Item. This is Item. Can you hear me?'

"Back to Reger. 'Try it again.' He began quavering but effective enough. 'This is Item. This is Item. . . .'

"I left them saying, 'Keep taking turns. I'll check the wire. We must be in touch with the observation post.' I was hoping to keep them busy. I didn't know what else to do.

"I ran to the sawmill. I found one of the observers there. 'They're shooting 88s at the house.' [88s were different from other artillery in that they did not have the warning whistle.] Stroud got hurt. I brought him back here. He's now on his way to the aid station.' It was almost time for the flare signal. We had to be there to see it."

Franklin (the other soldier who had been in the observation post) and Peña ran to the house, which had been battered. "Franklin and I took cautious positions by windows and waited for the flare signal. The phone was dead—I'd forgotten to check the line. It'd be easy enough to run back when the signal came. The approximate time came and passed without a flare signal in sight. I hadn't known Franklin well, but I knew that he wasn't afraid. An unexpected round came in. It hit another part of the house. Franklin joked about the way they were destroying German property. Later a whistler came in and hit in front of the house. We both held our places, trusting the thick stone walls.

"We talked about the situation—the sputtering machine gun across from us, still active, meant that our men had not reached that point. But why no flare? We were putting too much importance on this signal." After what seemed like an hour had passed, Peña decided to check back with the sawmill outpost and send up another GI to stay with Franklin.

"Dulac came to the sawmill. He'd just come from the 1st Platoon area. That platoon had advanced up to a point where they were stopped by a barbed-wire barricade and a minefield covered by machine gun fire—in fact, several barricades and minefields.

"Dulac said he wanted to go to the 2d and 3d Platoon area to our left. I told him to take the rear route, because the machine gun was covering the open space which he wanted to cross. He calmly ignored my warning. With him were 'Pop' Johnstone, our acting first sergeant, and Dallas Elwood, our communication sergeant. All three started walking leisurely across the open space.

"When they were halfway across, the machine gun opened fire with a burst. All three fell to the ground. Someone was hit. The other two were helping him back to the sawmill. It was Captain Dulac. Johnstone and Elwood were carrying him between them. Once at the sawmill, they laid him down on the ground, and our medic took Dulac's shoe off. 'You've got a million dollar wound, Captain Dulac. A clean hole through the meaty part of the heel,' our medic said smiling.

"Dulac didn't feel like joking—quite the opposite. His eyes flooded with tears. He turned to me and said, 'I hate like hell to leave the company in such a mess. Johnstone can fill you in on the situation at the 1st Platoon. You're the senior officer here—you're in command now.'"

Major Howard Topping, the battalion commander who had reamed Peña out during his misguided effort to lead the outfit to its position, appeared and declared the first order of business to be the elimination of the machine gun. Private Joseph Clark, a robust soldier with a history of disciplinary infractions volunteered to take a BAR and destroy the threat.

Clark crammed extra magazines inside his shirt and then snaked his way along the edge of the woods into enemy-controlled ground until he came within sight of the gun emplacement. Peña said, "We heard the distinct sluggish bursts of his automatic rifle, putt-putt-putt-putt. The machine gun answered his fire with rapid spry bursts—purrrp-purrrp. Now they were both firing. Weapon for weapon. He was one man against a team of two to five men. The two firing sounds alternated, then only Clark's fire continued. He'd known well to take plenty of ammunition. The machine gun was silenced!"

The elated Topping announced he would nominate Clark for a Silver Star, and the hero returned unscathed. But now Peña attempted to find the platoons pinned down by the enemy fire, barbed wire, and mines. With Johnstone and Elwood, the platoon leader searched for the men, finding a handful but not the main group, even as they worked their way so far into the forest that they came upon another outfit. Peña noticed the men digging in a position that left their rear exposed to the enemy. He spoke to the company commander, but the officer insisted that battalion orders directed his unit to face southwest. Only later that night did his superiors require him to turn about. The fog of war had begun to envelop the 28th, with the officers and men blindly groping to establish rational, effective action.

When Peña returned to the sawmill, the total number of able-bodied men added up to about twenty-four from the eighty or so who jumped off for the attack. One platoon leader, winner of a battlefield commission earlier, recalled Peña, "had left the scene dazed. He had drifted to the aid station. The doctor had diagnosed his case as acute combat fatigue. This documented diagnosis saved him later from the charge of desertion at a court-martial. He served with distinction in another company the rest of the war. The 2d Platoon leader had been wounded and evacuated.

"Among the many casualties was a man who had been recently hospitalized and who shot himself in the toe with no witnesses to his 'accident.' The number of casualties was frightening—most of them wounded, few dead. With the key officers and sergeants on our left gone, the remaining few men had wandered aimlessly, although the worst was over." For the moment.

Harry Kemp also observed some skittish reaction to intense enemy fire that fell on his heavy machine gun platoon. "Staff Sergeant Raymond J. Barber, the platoon sergeant and acting platoon leader, seeing that some of his men were becoming increasingly perturbed and slacking off in firing their mission, took immediate action to reassure them. He moved from gun to gun, demonstrating by his example that accomplishment of the mission came first. Barber was later awarded the Silver Star medal as a result of his leadership in this instance."

The 1st Battalion of the 109th achieved more success, albeit at a cost of the operations officer, two company commanders, and a number of enlisted men before the opposition fire slackened. The poor visibility in the dense woods, which defied efforts to exert command and control, caused the battalion CO, Maj. James C. Ford, Jr., to growl, "If anyone from a private right on up to myself said that he knew where he was at any one time, he was a damned liar!" Nevertheless, stumbling, fumbling, and firing through the darkness, the infantrymen evicted the defenders from a critical position while capturing about 100 soldiers. The GIs dug in at the edge of the forest overlooking the key town of Huertgen.

As part of the offensive, the 1st Battalion of the 110th Infantry was assigned to guard the left or northern flank of the 112th as it struck out toward Schmidt. In the ranks of the 110th's Company B, Jerry Alexis and Ed Uzemack were among the replacements who had reached the scene the night before the unit would jump off.

Uzemack recalled, "As we moved out on some prearranged schedule, I soon got into the habit of watching for snipers in the treetops, as did the combat veterans guiding us. At one point I slipped on the wet ground and fell to my knees. I felt somebody reach under my arm to help me up and heard him ask, 'Are you all right, soldier?' As I turned to answer, I saw a general's stars on the man's helmet and was amazed to see the cigar in his mouth as he grinned. He was Gen. Norman Cota, the division commander. Later I would see him in combat areas several times."

On 3 November, the 3d Battalion of the 112th, in coordination with the armor of Company A, 707th Tank Battalion, would make a daylight assault on Schmidt. With the temperature hovering around the freezing mark, the first Americans walked through the wreckage of Vossenack, southeast toward Kommerscheidt and the final objective. Ray Fleig reported the weather as "typical of a late fall day, with a heavy mist hanging over the forest, and a cold, drizzling rain added to the discomfort of the troops. The spongy soil was saturated; the bomb craters and shell holes were pools of water; mud clung to the leggings covering shoes [there was a critical absence of overshoes in the 28th Division]. Tank tracks and suspension systems were choked with the viscous mire."

The frigid Kall River posed a natural obstacle, but the GIs hauled themselves up the steep east bank by grabbing at the trees along the narrow stream's edge. At Kommerscheidt, the tank fire from beyond the Kall dispersed any real resistance and a handful of Germans surrendered. The soldiers were pleasantly surprised by the lack of significant enemy forces a mile farther south in Schmidt, and by nightfall the battalion held the town. The 1st Battalion, under orders to reinforce its brethren in Schmidt, had moved out of Germeter around noon, but the regimental commander, Lt. Col. Carl Petersen, halted the troops at Kommerscheidt, apparently fearing he might lose both of his outfits if the Germans threw a major counterattack at Schmidt.

At Dutch Cota's command post in the town of Rott, though the staff knew this was only the opening round, the mood was celebratory. Unit leaders sent messages that stressed successes without accurately reporting the precarious states of their positions and their troops. Corps and other division leaders proffered congratulations to the 28th Division boss, whose assistant bragged that the offensive to this point had been "extremely successful."

The reports to Hodges continued to augur well. For the day, Sylvan wrote, "The 28th Division this morning resumed the attack with the 109th and the 112th Infantry on the offensive with heavy attacks. The enemy artillery and mortar fire [made] it difficult for our troops to approach and place demolition charges for pillboxes with considerable small arms fire. Barbed wire in eight foot concertina rolls. 3d Bn. 112th to the outskirts of Schmidt at 4 o'clock after advancing about 5,000 yards. The bn was followed by the 1st Bn. about a mile southwest of Schmidt. The 2d Bn. continued toward its objective, Vossenack. All buildings there were destroyed by our artillery, but the basements were fortified and led to hand-to-hand fighting to clear out the enemy of this point. The Gen. is extremely satisfied tonight with the progress made."

Although the brass shone with elation, the major concerns for the 3d Battalion of the 112th were the lack of an adequate supply route and the absence of tanks. Engineers deemed passable a stone bridge over the Kall and narrow muddy trail through the Kall River valley, which was barely able to accommodate a wagon, much less a thirty-two-ton tank. During the afternoon of 3 November, the A Company tanks attempted to reinforce the foot soldiers in Schmidt. Captain Bruce Hostrup, the company commander, led the column forward until he reached a narrow passage with rock outcroppings on one side and a gorge on the other. The side of the cart path crumbled under the weight of his tank, and Hostrup narrowly avoided being pitched into the canyon.

The 20th Engineer Combat Battalion, after being held up by interdicting enemy artillery, arrived with mine detectors but no heavy equipment for widening and solidifying the trail. It was not until early on the morning of 4 November that a bulldozer started to move earth, and it soon broke down. The engineers continued to labor with picks and shovels. The enemy steadily showered the 707th's vehicles with mortars and artillery rounds that wrecked periscope heads, antennas, headlights, and any personal equipment strapped outside. Meanwhile, the GIs in Schmidt battened down for the night without orders for reconnaissance patrols to discover any German activity, although the enemy habitually counterattacked whenever it lost any ground. Lookouts thought they discerned movement at dusk but no one thought to investigate. Under cover of night, German strategists shifted units into an array designed to obliterate the American advance.

A convoy of three M29 Weasels, small vehicles on tracks, navigated the pathway to Schmidt bearing ammunition, rations, and antitank mines. But the tired GIs, instead of burying them, simply spread them across the road without any camouflage. Before daylight broke, with only a partial reconstruction of the pathway, the Company A tanks began to move forward, with Ray Fleig at the head of his 1st Platoon. As he sought to negotiate one of the more narrow spots, Fleig said a Teller mine blew off his M4's track. Although no one was injured, the disabled vehicle totally blocked the trail. Some suggest that Fleig's tank did not strike a mine, but because of the darkness and with no one out front to guide the driver, he slipped off the trail. The cause of the breakdown, however, was far less significant than the obstacle created.

Staff Sergeant Anthony Spooner, commander of the following tank, improvised with cables attached to Fleig's tank, to maneuver around the blockage. Although the remainder of the platoon followed suit, Fleig boarded Spooner's Sherman with his precious command radio and instructed Spooner to bring the other tanks after him for a meeting in Kommerscheidt. When Fleig reached the stone bridge, the lieutenant climbed out and guided the tank across using a blackout flashlight.

The trail followed a series of hairpin turns, a difficulty exacerbated by the mechanisms of an M4. Drivers steered by applying brake pressure to one track while the opposite track continued to churn. The operation requires manipulation of a pair of three-foot-long, lateral levers extending between the driver's toes. Without any power boosters, the technique relied on sheer muscle strength, particularly in low gear at low speeds.

Sunrise signaled the dawn of disaster. German shells crashed into Schmidt, walking back and forth through the town for perhaps thirty minutes. The intense barrage hammered at the besieged GIs from almost every direction. Those hunkered down along the perimeter spotted enemy soldiers assembling for an attack. The Americans in Schmidt called for their own artillery, but, mysteriously, there was no response.

German infantry accompanied by tanks began to strike from a number of areas. The armor moved along the road on which the Americans had placed antitank mines. But the panzers easily detoured around the visible explosives. The tanks, which shrugged off hits from bazookas, fired rounds point-blank into foxholes with devastating results.

When a machine gun opened up on the outskirts of the town, SSgt. Frank Ripperdam led a couple of men against the emplacement. As they wriggled near the gun, they were astonished to see five enemy soldiers jump up, yelling in English, "Don't shoot." Ripperdam and the others held their fire and stood, expecting a full surrender. But the quintet suddenly leaped back to their gun and resumed banging away. Ripperdam hit the ground and a GI launched a rifle grenade. Two of the crew were wounded but the gun continued to fire. A soldier tried to sneak to the side with his rifle but he was cut down. The Americans withdrew and so did their antagonists.

American artillery now sought to turn the tide with furious concentrations. Nevertheless, the situation deteriorated rapidly. The Germans were coming from all sides except along the Kommerscheidt-Vossenack route to the northwest. Driven from the perimeter foxholes, the embattled Americans first fell back to refuge in buildings. As the torrent of shot and shell swept over the area, they abandoned their posts and fled, sometimes in their bewilderment heading deeper into enemy territory. Flight became the only imperative. Ray Fleig wrote, "Many historians and self-appointed experts have written of this battle, and they universally deride the conduct of the American infantrymen, but they were not there. A wool shirt and a field jacket are no defense against tank cannon [at least ten Mark IV behemoths led the Germans] and machine guns or 15.0 cm mortars, and no sane man will confront these fearsome weapons with his M1 rifle."

As the rout deepened, the dead and even the wounded were left behind. By 10 A.M., the soldiers, largely on their own, had abandoned Schmidt. Battalion headquarters advised company headquarters that it was disconnecting the switchboard and all should withdraw. Shortly after noon, in recognition of the abandonment of Schmidt, the Air Corps dispatched a squadron of P-47s, the dreaded Jabos to strike the usurpers.

A frantic effort to rescue those in trouble and halt the debacle gripped the 28th Division. Lieutenant Colonel Albert Flood, commander of the men who had been trapped in Schmidt, sent an urgent message to the aid station, directing it to move forward from Germeter to Vossenack to receive the influx of casualties. In an underground log bunker beside the Kall River, the medical personnel directed by an administrative officer, 2d Lt. Alfred J. Muglia, set up shop, dispatching litter bearers to scour the area for wounded. Captain Michael DeMarco tended the men there, while Capt. Paschal A. Linguiti, another battalion surgeon, treated casualties in a Vossenack house converted into an aid station.

To repel the German armor, elements of the 893d Tank Destroyer Battalion moved into Vossenack shortly before noon. Almost immediately, all four TDs from the 1st Platoon of Company B had been hit. Company A of the 20th Engineers, working to improve the supply route, also came under heavy fire. They threw aside their shovels, pick axes, and mine detectors and picked up M1s to defend themselves. Several perished as mortars and artillery blasted their area. In the dark of night, packs of German infantrymen moved by, only a few feet from the engineers, who felt themselves too far outnumbered to confront the enemy.

An attempt to furnish ammunition to those trying to make a

stand against the onslaught was blocked when the same three Weasels that had made the journey to Schmidt the night before, then returned to Germeter with wounded, were frustrated by Fleig's detracked tank blocking the route.

That obstacle loomed larger when more armor from the 707th tried to make their way toward Schmidt. Company A's 2d Platoon, reduced to a trio of Shermans and ignorant of the winch method of safely bypassing Fleig's abandoned tank, sought to squeeze past. The lead tank slipped over the edge of the incline, and the slippery slope prevented it from regaining the road. When the crew dismounted to investigate, enemy shells killed the tank commander and an officer riding with him. The surviving armor negotiated this section but came a cropper at another juncture. The score for the 707th showed Fleig in one tank at Kommerscheidt with two more from his platoon about to join him, while five disabled Shermans littered the trail behind.

Fleig checked in with Maj. Robert Hazlett, CO of the 1st Battalion in Kommerscheidt, who ordered him to "Get out there and stop those tanks." Nearby infantrymen advised Fleig that there were "lots of Germans with tanks over that hill."

The trio of Shermans led by Fleig advanced toward the enemy. As they crested a slight rise, the M4s opened fire. Fleig believed his gunner accounted for two of the attackers while one of his associates knocked out a third with a high explosive shell that slammed into the breech of a 75mm cannon.

On the outskirts of Kommerscheidt, the tank commander saw a German Mark IV Panther using an orchard to screen its movement. He called instructions on the range and location to the gunner. Fleig says he saw "a bright splash of light on the turret of the Mark IV." He called for another round. Another fiery eruption on the Mark IV signified a hit. Two crewman leaped from the tank.

Fleig realized his gunner was using high explosive shells rather than armor piercing (AP). The thick skin of the Panther protected it, and the Germans who abandoned the tank were not hurt but only frightened. Fleig's crew scrambled to retrieve their armor-piercing shells stowed on a sponson rack on the exterior of the Sherman. The Germans seized the time to reenter their Mark IV and throw a round at him, but they missed. The Americans' first round of AP sliced the enemy gun barrel. Three more shells then pierced the thinner side of the Panther's hull, setting the tank ablaze and killing all of its crew.

Two other panzers poked toward the GIs trying to mount a defense. P-47s suddenly dove down, and two bombs from one halted the lead tank. Sergeant Tony Kudiak then delivered the coup de grâce with a bazooka. The rocket struck the Panther in its vulnerable side and ignited a fire. In the German positions in Kommerscheidt, the sustained hammering of mortars and small arms and almost incessant U.S. artillery exacted a fearsome toll. Temporarily, the counterattack by the Germans halted. However, the worsening weather would limit the ability of the Air Corps to help.

Although the main thrust of the 28th Division by the 112th Regiment had temporarily achieved its objective, it had been hurled back. On 3 November, the 109th Regiment on the left flank expected to begin a limited attack. But at 0730, the Germans interrupted the schedule when their attack sought to drive the 1st Battalion from its positions. Lieutenant Charles E. Porter, the S-2, said, "The trees in this place were so thick that it was impossible to see more than thirty yards in any one direction. In many places they were not over four feet apart. The artillery had been knocking the tops out of them, and they were piling up and making it more difficult to move and to see any distance from the positions. This attack had been preceded by a ten-minute artillery preparation and we lost some men from . . . tree bursts. These tree bursts were the worst thing we had to contend with. In this morning attack the machine guns did not open fire until the Germans were right on top of them. By this waiting they killed many more than usual, as the Germans were unable to see our positions and walked right into the face of the guns. Some fell within six feet of the position and the gun crew had to remove them to continue firing. The forward observer brought down the artillery about 100 yards in front of the positions and the attack was broken up." The troops claimed to have captured about 100 men, although the assault overran the 1st Battalion observation post, killing or seizing a number of Americans.

The 3d Battalion, now led by Howard Topping, had been about to start a move east toward the Huertgen-Germeter road when a regimental radio order directed the outfit to "continue the attack to the west." The language puzzled Topping, but because the directive passed through the tight security of the command radio net, he obeyed, particularly because the battalion heard the sounds of battle in the west.

The outfit fought its way toward the other battalion, encountering substantial pockets of Germans. Bill Peña recalled the trek through the poorly charted forest. "I had the map of the area, and I was in charge of leading the column to the position of the 1st Battalion, marked on the map as somewhere in the forest southwest of Huertgen. At the start I recognized some landmarks."

The column passed through the foxholes being dug by F Company of the 2d Battalion. "Once we left F Company's area, we were in unknown territory. The character of the forest was changing. There was more underbrush, shorter views—at times we were hemmed in to a trail with walls of underbrush. [Communications Sergeant Dallas] Elwood chose one of these times to test his backpack radio in a full voice. 'This is Item. This is Item. Do you hear me? Over.' If we were looking for an ambush, this was one way of inviting it. And then, 'This is Item. I hear you loud and clear. I hear you loud and clear. Over and out.'

"This was too much! I turned to Elwood and said in a low tone that if he wanted to test that damn radio again, he'd have to go toward the rear of the column.

"By now, one tree, one bush looked like any other. Looking for the green moss on the north side of tree trunks was futile in this thick forest. I didn't think we were lost yet, I told [company commander Bruce] Paul. I thought we were going generally in the right direction, but it had gotten more difficult to tell on the map where we were. Major Topping was right up there with us, behind the 1st Platoon. From time to time he'd come up, we'd pause, and I'd point out our approximate location on the map. But we had only the approximate location. Somehow we'd have to find it without attracting the enemy's attention. We were not deployed for action.

"As it turned out, the Germans themselves led us to the 'lost battalion.' We heard the fire of German burp guns nearby to our right and then the answering rifle shots from the 1st Battalion. The light intensity of the fire indicated that only a small German patrol was involved." They had reached their objective and dug in. The regimental commander later demanded of Topping why he had abandoned his originally assigned mission. When the latter mentioned the radioed order, his superior denied ever sending such a message. No one ever determined whether the radioman garbled the directive or who sent it.

Ironically, with the roles of attacker and defender reversed, the GIs in this sector temporarily enjoyed an advantage. Unfortunately, as in other instances during the Huertgen campaign, First Army leaders and the corps commanders never realized the import of such events, and the futile life-consuming strategy continued unaltered.

Although the counterattack was ultimately rebuffed after the 3d Battalion arrived to reinforce its brother unit, when the day ended, the 109th held an uneasy, fragile line. Nor was there substantial progress by the 110th Infantry operating in the woods to the south. Ed Uzemack said, "We spent the night in previously dug foxholes after being instructed to prepare to move out at dawn with only light combat packs. It was still fairly dark when we moved into an orchard and spread out. Despite orders not to, we lit cigarettes and smoked them with cupped hands to shield the glow. Suddenly, all hell broke loose. The Jerries had zeroed in on the orchard and were lobbing mortar shells and artillery fire in a continuous barrage that lasted about forty-five minutes.

"The green replacements suffered the heaviest casualties. More than half were killed or wounded. The veterans were calling to the men to keep their heads down and follow as they crawled toward the direction from which most of the shellfire originated. Although my newshawk instinct was to look and see what was going on, my many weeks of infantry training, some of it under live ammunition fire, reminded me to do as the veterans commanded. Unfortunately, not all of the replacements had similar training before being shipped overseas.

"A GI crawling ahead of me had both his legs blown off by a shell that landed on his limbs. Another shell hit so close to me that I could feel the heat on one side of me as it exploded and my ear buzzed. I kept crawling toward where I thought the shells were coming from and eventually left the orchard with the survivors, mostly combat vets. A sergeant told me to round up the guys who had come with me as replacements. I told him I didn't even know who the hell they were, but I would do my best. Somehow I managed to find about half a dozen totally frightened replacements, and suddenly I realized I was just as scared as they were. But that morning we became combat vets."

Jerry Alexis explained, "Company A and C led the attack astride the road toward Simonskall, and we followed in reserve. We immediately came under artillery fire from the vicinity of Schmidt as we double-timed down the open road between farmers' fields. Company A had the mission of knocking out pillboxes 764 a and b [so designated on a map], but casualties were so heavy, not only from the bunkers, but also from small-arms fire from the dense woods on either side of the road, that the attack failed the first day. We spent the night there until the attack continued the next morning. It took another day before Company A captured the pillboxes and continued down the road to Simonskall, with still more pillboxes to neutralize. Company C moved south along the Raffelsbrand ridge, while my Company B peeled off north at the horseshoe bend and dug in."

Over the next few days, the 28th Division infantrymen maintained a largely static front, digging in so close to the enemy at times both could hear the other's entrenching tools crunching into the dirt and even exchanged words that would be followed in a few hours by grenades and small-arms fire. Confined to their soggy foxholes, wet and cold, the GIs, protected only by ponchos and lacking blankets, shivered in the frigid weather. Unable to move about freely because of the risk from snipers, artillery, or mortars, their shoes soaking up water, they could not practice the hygiene of clean, dry socks and massage of toes, and the World War I malady of trench foot began to afflict the troops.

On the night of 4–5 November, Alexis recalled, "My partner and I were assigned to the extreme left flank as an outpost there. By now it was dark and we took turns on watch.

"When the dawn arrived, we discovered that we and the GIs in the adjacent hole had been left alone—evidently the company had moved out and forgotten us. Replacements meant so little that we were never really integrated into the unit with the rapid turnover in squads and platoons from the terrific casualties being sustained in the Huertgen. The only smart thing to do, it seemed to us, was to go back in the direction from which we had come the day before.

"Scared almost out of our wits, not knowing where the enemy was, and bewitched by the foreboding woods, we carefully made our way back by following some phone lines we had found. Eventually, we reached the forward command post of the regiment, where we were drafted by the intelligence and reconnaissance platoon leader, Lieutenant Lacey. He took me on as one of his bodyguards, while he cruised around the lines trying to find out what was going on. The others became part of Task Force Lacey—his platoon and other stragglers—which had been assigned to take over the position Company B had left."

While Cota ordered the 110th's 1st Battalion to move to Vossenack, the 3d Battalion, with mortar squad leader Al Burghardt, remained in the woods facing a road that ran from Richelskaul to Raffelsbrand, an area infested with pillboxes. Burghardt recalled, "K Company was to advance 1,000 yards, hold, and dig in. I was to follow with the mortar section. The attack gained a hundred yards or so and was stopped cold by hidden pillboxes and German artillery. There were many casualties and the objective was not gained. The mortar section didn't move."

The Wehrmacht juggernaut retired to regroup around 1600 hours. Astonishingly, only an hour earlier, division headquarters blithely ordered the GIs, frantically digging in to preserve themselves and stop the counterattack, to retake Schmidt. That absurdity occurred even though the assistant division commander, Brigadier General Davis, had come to the command post for the battle at Kommerscheidt to confer with the regimental leader, Lt. Col. Carl Petersen, and his battalion heads. Davis saw the conditions firsthand—the state of the troops and their equipment—before advising division headquarters. He remained overnight in a cellar before returning to Cota's CP.

At First Army, the grim news pricked the bubble of anticipated success. "The Gen. did not leave his CP today," wrote Sylvan, "but spent most of his time in the war room and also in G-3, following the corps attack closely. Things did not go very well. The 3d Bn. of 112th was counterattacked, and at 10 o'clock withdrew almost a mile to the vicinity of Kommerscheidt. Early yesterday afternoon after a heavy art. concentration and air bombardment was placed on Schmidt, the 3d Bn. attempted to regain the village, but this attack was met by a counterattack of a bn of infantry with a dozen tanks. Our progress toward Schmidt at nightfall was only about 300 yards. Reports from Gen. Gerow to Gen. Hodges this evening are to the effect that the 3d Bn. suffered very heavy casualties. Some progress was made by 109th Inf. 2d and 3d Bn. toward village of Huertgen area. Progress was slow because of numerous mines and accurate art. fire."

A critical problem remained the single torturous route from Germeter to Vossenack that bedeviled Fleig's tankers. Repair crews struggled to fix the damaged Shermans, while engineers, hampered by the presence of the armor, labored to improve the trail. Not only did the besieged troops at the front desperately need the armor, they also required fresh infusions of ammunition, food, and other supplies, all of which were blocked by the disabled tanks. Sporadic German artillery rounds disrupted the work.

Five Weasels, towing quarter-ton trailers loaded with the necessities for continuing the fight, reached the impasse shortly after dark. Only by pushing several of the damaged tanks into the gorge could the Weasels, which encountered their own problems of lost tracks, maneuver forward. They arrived in Vossenack at dawn.

John Marshall, a crewman on the Sherman named *Bea Wain* (a popular singer of the 1940s), remembered moving deeper into the Huertgen. "It was late afternoon [on 4 November and] through the trees we could see the hilly countryside and buildings. We dug our trench. As we were going to back our tank over it, Mike Kozlowski, our tank commander, was summoned to a meeting of all tank commanders and officers. We waited for Mike to return.

"We had just dug a trench wide enough for two men to sleep in, side by side. We would then drive our tank so that the tracks would straddle it—giving protection to whoever may be in it. All of us then would get a chance to stretch our legs as we rotated sleeping under the tank. However, we decided to leave the tank where it was and spent the night in the tank. Two soldiers asked us if they could have the trench, which we gladly said they could.

"When Mike returned he seemed upset and told us, 'We move out tomorrow.' We asked him, 'Out to where? What are we to expect? How far away are the Krauts?' Unknown to us, the Krauts were already among us. 'Will we be fighting with others? If so, who are they?' Mike was embarrassed and frustrated because he could not tell us more. 'That's all they [the officers] told me.' We thought what a senseless way to lay out lives on the line not being informed.

"Mac [Leonard McKnight, the gunner] said he was going to fix something to eat and pulled out a Bunsen burner to light and heat some food for all of us. The sly fox did not bury all the bread, jelly, soup, and cheese as we had been ordered yesterday. He had squirreled some of it from sight in a 75mm shell cavity. Mike reminded us it was against regulations to light one of those up inside a tank, especially one carrying 125 gallons of gasoline. Mac looked at Mike and smiled, 'If I'm going to get killed tomorrow, at least for tonight I'm not going to be cold and hungry."

Members of the crew climbed out of the tank, unfolded a large canvas tarpaulin, and tied the corners to trees just over the tank. It acted as a roof to keep out rain, while the hatch remained open for ventilation without shedding light for German observers.

"We had just come back into the tank when, about 2300, the Germans saturated the area with heavy shelling, aerial bursts that exploded at treetop height to send shrapnel down into tank hatches and foxholes. After a tremendous explosion rocked the tank, we ate in silence, knowing a shell had killed those two 110th infantrymen. It had landed directly in the trench, leaving nothing but a few body parts and a shredded overcoat."

Earlier, in Kommerscheidt, the area of the 112th Infantry's 1st Battalion aid station had become a center for supply deposits and assembly of troops. German artillery observers from their elevated perch spotted the activity and soon blanketed the site, hitting not only the combat-potential equipment and GIs but also injuring patients and killing medics. Battalion surgeon Linguiti, disturbed by the concentration of materials that brought shelling on his aid station, abandoned the site and transferred the work to the log bunker chosen by Lieutenant Muglieti.

During the evening, many Germans infiltrated the area. At three in the morning, a German private banged on the entrance to the dugout and summoned a noncom. One of the American personnel spoke German and explained that they were treating the wounded. The Germans asked if they had enough food and promised to bring more rations and German medics. However, the GIs were not to leave the dugout and a guard was posted on the door. Throughout the night, German patrols passed nearby, but at daylight the sentry at the entrance disappeared.

Preston Jackson had been busy, scurrying between the battalions of the 112th in the vicinity of Schmidt and Kommerscheidt. "There was no way we could hold onto Schmidt. Because of that narrow Kall Valley, we couldn't bring up enough armor to support the men when they counterattacked. An infantry soldier just can't beat a tank. We took a lickin' every day we were there."

8

Defeat Deepens

That first week of November, the demarcation between "them" and "us" could only be described as fluid, changing so swiftly that combatants, unaware of who occupied what and where, frequently blundered into one another, as exemplified by events at the aid station in a dugout near the Kall River.

"Mass confusion" is how Alexis described the situation of the 28th. "Its commanders and staff tried to learn what was happening to the units in the hell that was Huertgen. When we tried to move down the fire lanes in the woods, we discovered they had become machine gun fire lanes for the Germans. When we tried to go directly through the thick evergreen and deciduous woods, we either got lost or artillery tree bursts took their toll. The rain and snow made mudholes of our foxholes and that, combined with the cold and our lack of adequate footwear, began a rising tide of evacuees from trench foot and respiratory illnesses. The dirt roads became foot-deep in mud, which made them virtually impassable to all vehicles except the full-track, M29 Weasels, which also served as ambulances. The steep hillsides wore us out both going up and coming down as we tried to advance. It isn't any wonder that combat fatigue resulted in many of those exposed to all these horrible conditions."

At First Army headquarters, on 5 November, the lack of success prompted Hodges to "tour the front," in Sylvan's words. "Beyond CP of 28th at Rott met Gen. Cota . . . to see the tough time the bloody bucketeers were having." The 28th Division, with its keystone shoulder patch, because of its high number of casualties, had already earned the nickname, "the bloody bucket." Cota apprised Hodges of limited progress, a 300-yard gain by the 110th over heavily wired defenses and a few pillboxes cracked. Although the 112th bulked up with fourteen tanks and fourteen TDs, it could move no closer to Schmidt and struggled to hold its ground. The 109th maintained the position that it achieved two days earlier. The village of Huertgen itself was heavily attacked by bombers after enemy tanks were spotted in the area. The brief summary of the situation gives no hint of the savagery endured by both sides around Kommerscheidt. Cota ordered the 112th to renew that attack toward Schmidt without delay, seemingly oblivious to the fact that it was the Americans who were barely hanging on in the face of almost incessant attacks by the Germans.

Fleig, with three tanks and a handful of tank destroyers that managed to move up on one of the narrow muddy roads through the forest, dueled with the enemy armor. The morning ended with the attempt to oust the GIs from the town denied, but the bodies continued to pile up. In the afternoon, five more tanks from Company A of the 707th joined Fleig and his trio to defend the flanks of Kommerscheidt. The thin line of defenders in their foxholes and in the crumbled buildings feared most the advance of enemy armor. A flight of P-47s caught one enemy tank in the open and demolished it. Even with the additional Shermans on hand and the 893d tank destroyers, positions around Kommerscheidt remained static.

Prospects around Vossenack appeared equally dismal. The 112th, 2d Battalion, clung to the exposed high ground of the ridge and cringed under intensive enemy shelling. It was difficult to believe that the foe suffered from any shortage of ordnance. Self-propelled guns and tanks hurled as many as twenty to thirty rounds at a single foxhole before focusing their attention on another target. Enemy patrols, which the GIs believed presaged a new attack, frequently sifted through the woodsy cover. One company commander, Lt. Melvin R. Barrileaux, just returned from a pass to Paris, visited his platoons after dark and found the men so distraught that he felt all should be evacuated for combat fatigue. Some had to be ordered by a platoon leader to eat. The members of the other companies were in no better shape. The battalion commander, Lt. Col. Theodore Hatzfield, officially was still in charge, but his emotional state was such that his executive officer carried out the major command functions.

At 5:45 in the morning, 6 November, B Company tanks of the 707th trundled toward Vossenack to relieve C Company, reduced to only seven functioning Shermans. In *Bea Wain*, driver John Alyea remembered moving slowly toward the town with infantrymen alongside. "We fired one round of high explosives at a building. I was taking orders from the tank commander and the bow gunner, assistant driver John Marshall was firing rounds of .30 caliber toward enemy positions. Noise was at a high level. We were buttoned down, the hatch closed. I had a small periscope to see through, two inches by six inches when raised, and could mainly see only straight ahead. In one instant, I was seeing all the action, infantry moving toward the enemy and then seeing them fall from mortar shrapnel and small-arms fire by the Germans. This lasted maybe fifteen minutes, and then the [tank commander] got orders to withdraw."

Said Marshall, "It wasn't quite daylight yet, and we traveled several hundred feet, when Mike leaned out of the turret to ask two infantrymen from the 110th a question. With my hatch closed I watched the men's expressions through my periscope. They were less than two feet away. They were dirty, tired, scared—I did not realize that they had been there for over a week before we arrived, clean and fed. At this moment, there was a tremendous explosion as a heavy mortar hit our tank between the two front hatches. I was crushed with a strange numbness from the concussion. Although I had blood in my mouth, my nose was bleeding, and I was temporarily deaf, I was not wounded. I was alive. I looked over at our driver, John Alyea, and he was staring straight ahead as in a trance, but I concluded that he was not hurt either. I removed the shattered periscope and replaced it with a spare and peered out. All that remained of the two soldiers was a leg with the shoe still on, a head bared to the skull, and a shredded overcoat. I tried to believe this was a bad dream, until I heard someone faintly calling me as though he were miles away in a cave. It was Mac, Leonard McKnight, our gunner, telling me, 'Mike got it and needs help.' I crawled back to him in the turret. As I tried to make him comfortable, I could see that his chest was torn from his body. I dumped all the [sulfa] powder we had on his wound. His last words to me were, 'Don't kid me, how bad am I?' I answered, 'You won't be able to write for a while but you will be okay.' He died before I finished the sentence."

Alyea believed, "When Mike got word to withdraw, he raised too far out of the turret, according to our gunner McKnight, to try to get the infantry to withdraw. It was then a piece of shrapnel hit him. I did not see Mike again. The tank driver stayed with the tank, and the rest of the crew tried to get him out of the turret and on the ground for the medics."

"The shelling continued," said Marshall, "exploding so close that mud came into the tank like rain but no direct hits. We turned the tank around and went back to the aid station. It was a pitiful scene, two men carrying a dead man; a couple of severely wounded men helping each other. They say, 'Men don't cry,' but they do, whether it's from frustration, hopelessness, or pain—men do cry.

"Mac jumped out of the tank and stopped a medic running to help someone and asked him to come to the tank, hoping beyond hope that maybe something could be done for Mike. The medic refused, as he was swamped with work and we were several hundred feet away from the aid station. Because of all the vehicles and ambulances, we couldn't get closer. Mac pointed his gun at the medic and he came to the tank, not that he feared Mac's gun but he was a tolerant and understanding man. He climbed up on the tank and looked in the turret, and said, 'Bring him in.' We turned Mike over to the medics. They examined him and placed him with the others that had been killed. The bodies were stacked [in rows] three or four high and forty to fifty feet long—there may have been many more but I saw two such 'stacks.'"

Marshall's tank was now operating with a four-man crew. McKnight assumed the role of commander, Marshall became the gunner, Jim Spencer continued as loader, and Alyea was the driver. The tank rolled toward a church in the village of Vossenack.

Alyea recalled, "Later in the day, we moved out in an open area and were able to inflict some 75mm rounds of high explosive on enemy positions, but no forward progress was attained. The Germans remained dug in, and what few tanks they had were well camouflaged. To knock out a German tank took more than one of ours to do the job. The tank commander was given orders to move forward slowly. As we came up a slight rise in the terrain, a large German artillery shell exploded near the tank, digging a large hole in the ground. Part of the track was in the hole; we were unable to move and were out of action. We got orders to leave. In the meantime, we were pinned down by the enemy but out of range of 88mm fire, so that helped."

Marshall saw it slightly differently. "We received a direct hit in the rear of the tank," reported Marshall. "It went forward for fifteen or twenty feet down a swale and into a tremendous burst of exploding mortars. The now-trackless side of the tank dropped into some of these craters, rendering it immobile. We discovered the turret could not traverse; the shell that killed Mike had jammed the gears. The 75mm gun was useless but we were alive and for the moment 'safe,' because the tank now was lower than the grassy mound on our left.

"The Germans, knowing we were there, kept shooting at us many times with heavy guns. The shells would slam into the mound, tear through the earth like a giant mole, and then glance upward with a sickening whirring sound, raining dirt, rocks, and grass into our tank. It seemed like forever, but the shelling directed at us finally stopped. The tank was a mess with blood mixed with mud and debris. Since the gun was not working, we decided to abandon the tank. I was for jumping out while it was still daylight, but John and Mac thought it would be unwise; we should wait until dark. John then suggested we set up a machine gun outside the tank and take turns on guard. We decided against that move. John often wished he had an M1 of his own. The field to our right was littered with dead Americans lying near M1 rifles. Just to hear myself talk, I said to John, 'There's your chance to pick up an M1 rifle for yourself.' John thought a moment and then opened his hatch, unseen by the Krauts because it was much lower than the turret. Nothing happened until he ventured a short distance from the tank to pick up the rifle and was now in view of the Krauts. Again all hell broke loose, prompting John to throw the rifle down and run like mad back to the tank.

"Darkness comes early this time of the year, but there was still daylight left when we decided our evacuation procedure. One man at a time would exit the tank and run, diving from shell hole to shell hole for forty or fifty yards, then run again when the second man exited. We were to repeat this procedure so that we would all be heading toward the command post forty or fifty yards apart.

"When I got about 300 feet from the tank, I realized we had no blankets, actually nothing but the clothes on our backs. I turned and went back for my bedroll. From the explosions on and near the tank all day, the rods [of the rack with the gear] were twisted and knotted around the bedrolls like ordinary rope. I pulled and tugged but couldn't dislodge my bedroll. It was now dark, and I was angry with myself for not sticking to our escape plan. I really started to worry when I heard someone sloughing their way toward the tank for I had no gun. I slid off the tank and crouched against it in the shell hole. I heard someone ask, 'Marshall?' It was Alyea. Although he had almost reached the company area, he had come back to see what had happened to me!

"Together we each pulled a bedroll free and in the fog and darkness made our way back, in imminent danger of being shot by our own outposts. We found Jim and Mac lying under a tank on blankets. Mac knew there would be bedrolls lying all over the forest floor, just for the taking. Their owners didn't care; they were in the fields, dead. I later learned that Sgt. Jack Goldman of Company B would risk being killed by the Germans or our own guards and enter this forbidden forest under cover of darkness to gather up these idle bedrolls and distribute them to men that lost all their possessions, as we had."

The forlorn quartet from the tank *Bea Wain* accepted an offer from the cooks to use their tents. As Marshall tried to relax on a cot, he realized, "We had lost our tank commander, the first man in the platoon to be killed, and all of our possessions. We had lost our tank with thousands of rounds of ammunition. I nudged John. 'Do you realize we never fired a shot?' Exhausted, sleep came quickly. So ended our first day in the Huertgen Forest."

As darkness fell on Vossenack, a concentration of shells obliterated several two-man foxholes, shattering the bodies of the occupants. Their comrades, traumatized by seeing their friends mangled beyond recognition, retreated to the false security of buildings, leaving a gap in the defensive line. Ordered back to their foxholes, they sneaked back into the houses in the darkness. There could be no relief because the division no longer had any reserves. Astonishingly, the regimental situation report for the day listed the combat state of its forces as "excellent."

The damage to *Bea Wain* had forced its tankers to flee, but there was hope the Sherman could be salvaged. "During the night," said Marshall, "Howard Thomsen and his crew undertook a daring task. They were to go into Vossenack and retrieve our tank, knowing the Germans had infiltrated back in the town and taken positions in it as well as around our tank. Somehow in the darkness they were able to 'steal' the tank from under their noses and bring it back to our company area."

According to Thomsen, "The retriever crew—an officer, driver, assistant driver, and myself—went in the evening to get some of the tanks back. I got the engines to go again except for one. We had to pull that one through the churchyard and out into the street. After we were on the road the tow cable broke. I was in the act of putting another one on when I heard a shell coming in. I dove to the ground and landed in an old shell hole. The dirt hit my face, and I couldn't tell if I was bleeding or not. There was a Tiger tank firing off to our right. The shells kept coming in on the right side of us, and shrapnel would fly on ahead. But we got the tanks back to the company area. The company commander asked why we stayed, as they had word there was a Tiger tank in Vossenack. After we checked, we found our radio was not receiving the order to pull back." For his efforts, Thomsen was awarded a Bronze Star.

Marshall said, "We were up before daylight cleaning the inside of the tank—the ammo, guns, and instruments were covered with mud, flesh, and blood. The maintenance crew worked on tracks, turret, gas, and oil. Except for the inability of the turret to turn 360 degrees, the new *Bea Wain* was ready to roll again. However, when we climbed out in daylight and faced one another, the first time actually in twenty-four hours, our facial features had changed so much that Mac remarked, 'Lord, do you guys look different!' I said, 'Wait'll you look at yourself,' for he had changed also. Several days later, when Mac took his tanker's helmet off, all the hair from his head was in it. He was bald."

While John Marshall and the crew of *Bea Wain* had been so occupied, a platoon of B Company tanks worked with troops from the 112th Infantry on the northeast side of Vossenack. From the woods came heavy small-arms fire, to which the tankers responded. The foot soldiers started a withdrawal as the enemy added heavy mortar and artillery, preparatory to another attack. Jack Goldman as a loader and radio operator in the B Company command tank of Capt. George Grainger could see very little from his position in the turret with a radio. He did observe the 1st Platoon already heading down the valley and approaching the town. "Suddenly, a tank appeared and took a position quite close to our command tank. I couldn't see exactly what took place, but Captain Grainger was talking to Captain [George S., Jr.] West [C Company commander], when suddenly an enemy mortar shell hit the turret of Captain West's tank. He was killed instantly. His head had been severed from his body. Captain Grainger dropped to the floor of our tank. I did not hesitate. I ducked under the gun and grabbed the captain. I cradled his head in one hand and passed my other hand before his eyes. He was stunned but, thank God, not hurt. He stood up and I returned to my position.

"He tried to send a radio command to other tanks of our company. Once again I ducked under the gun, and I grabbed his pant leg and began to tug until I got his attention. I pointed to the intercom switch. It was on 'Intercom' not 'Radio.' He slowly realized his error and made the switch. He gave his commands and the battle went on as before, with casualties on both sides. We killed a great number of German infantrymen and they shot up many of our tanks with their 88mm guns, which had a superior muzzle velocity, entering the front of our tanks and piercing out the rear. We were under fire-powered. Our armor-piercing shells would bounce off the German tanks, doing no damage. Our men did a great job, like they had been trained to do, but it was not good for morale."

According to Goldman, "As daylight began to fade, the tanks withdrew toward the aid station, so they could provide for their own safety out of reach of enemy infantry, who would throw a grenade into a turret or anything to disable a tank. The captain ordered me and the gunner out of the tank, so he could confer with the platoon leaders. I started toward one of our tanks, where I could duck into the turret out of mortar fire. I was walking along a road which crossed another when I heard 'incoming mail,' a mortar shell at tree level. I froze with fear and held my arms above my head. I did not drop to the ground. I heard the shrapnel all around me in a circle, but once again, thank God, I was not hurt.

"Suddenly all shelling stopped and a strange silence took over. I heard from others that a medical truce had taken place. It was now that the bravest men in the world, the battlefield medics, went forth to tend the wounded and to gather the dead and their severed parts. I saw a peep loaded with legs, feet in boots, arms, and bodies. I try now to block it out of my mind. I don't want to see it anymore. Yes, Captain West was there with the rest of the dead."

At First Army headquarters, a crisis atmosphere developed. During the day, Hodges never left his command post, reported Sylvan, as word came of no less than four separate counterattacks being made against the 28th Division. The messages spoke of heavy artillery fire and in the 112th sector at Vossenack, the 2nd Battalion was forced back, dislodged from town by an enemy assault of 500 infantry supported by ten tanks. However, the front seemed to stabilize when the GI squashed a second counterattack without further loss of ground. Still, there was no progress toward Schmidt. Bad weather coupled with uncertain smoke markings made the air support of little value.

The situation for the 112th and its associates approximated disaster. The increasingly frigid, wet conditions sorely afflicted the troops, who lacked proper winter gear. There was a shortage of ammunition, particularly mortar rounds that were so effective in the terrain. Command was elusive. Communications verged on a total breakdown. Telephone facilities, dependent upon wires, were almost nonexistent as the rain of shrapnel and ground explosions destroyed lines. Radio signals were plagued by the interference of the trees and other natural obstacles. Casualties among company and battalion officers reduced effective leadership. Those seeking to determine the true facts had to depend upon hearsay, the statements of the wounded, stragglers, and individuals with a narrow vantage point. It was difficult to organize the soldiers because the battle scattered men until they lost contact with their own units.

Perhaps under pressure from his superiors, not fully aware of the plight of his soldiers after hearing the 112th's headquarters declare the combat condition as "excellent," Cota and Davis doggedly directed another venture against Schmidt. He created Task Force Ripple, an assault team led by the 707th's commander, Lt. Col. Richard Ripple, to be composed of the nine surviving tanks from Company A, the entire complement of Company D, which fielded light tanks, a handful of tank destroyers from the 893d, and foot soldiers from the 3d Battalion of the 110th Infantry, approximately 300 battered infantrymen.

Task Force Ripple was doomed from the start. The light tanks never arrived. The strategy called for the 110th Infantry's 3d Battalion to shift from their sector on the right flank of the 112th to meet up with the armor at Kommerscheidt and pass through the depleted ranks of that organization and capture Schmidt. However, the Germans vigorously protected their interests on the trail across the Kall Valley. The toll exacted reduced the short-strength battalion by two officers and fifteen men before the battalion reached the woods north of Kommerscheidt.

Al Burghardt, the mortar squad sergeant of Company K in the 110th's 3d Battalion recalled, "On the way to join the 112th Regiment, we went through Vossenack, a village in flames. It was late at night or early in the morning. It was just like you see in a war movie, smoke and fire all over. The smell of burning buildings, gun powder, gasoline, and oil from burning tanks and the ever-present smell of death were very evident. The eerie light from the fires showed damaged buildings everywhere, and when a shell exploded, you could see a church steeple in the distance. It was during one of these flashes of light that I saw what was left of a GI who had been run over lengthwise by a tank. I could tell it was a GI because of his clothing, web belt, steel helmet—a sad sight to see. There were many bodies in the village, both German and American.

"We went down into the Kall Valley and across a stone bridge wide enough for one vehicle. This part of the march had less shelling, because the Germans did not know where we were at the time. A light but steady, cold rain was falling. After we crossed the bridge, we started up the Kall Trail. It was very narrow in spots. There were no vehicles with us, and we had to carry our 60mm mortar and ammo, which was very difficult because of the steep terrain. The Germans finally found us and the shelling picked up.

"It was starting to get light enough to see. A shell hit somewhere ahead, very close. When I got to the area, a shell apparently had hit the top of a tree. There were five men hit. Four of them were dead. They looked like rag dolls that were carelessly thrown around. Their arms and legs were not in normal positions, and medics had not arrived on the scene. As I came up to one of the men, he was in a sitting position, looking in sort of a stupor. I don't know if he was watching the water from the rain, along with his blood, which had turned the little stream red. As I passed him, I looked at his face, but I'm thankful that I didn't recognize him. It had to be one of the fellows I knew. I was able to look down inside of him, because of the large wound in his shoulder. I am quite sure that by the time I passed him, he was dead due to the depth of the wound. This all took place in a matter of seconds, but at the time it seemed like hours."

Task Force Ripple's commanders and Lt. Col. Carl Peterson, heading the 112th, quickly recognized the weakness of the newly arrived foot soldiers of the 110th Infantry. They had struggled for three hours to overcome the enemy fire before digging in along a tree line. They were pitifully short of manpower. Their morale suffered from awareness that associates from the 112th in foxholes along their proposed route could not even leave their cover to relieve themselves. Because the area was new to the 110th's officers, Peterson arranged for a reconnaissance of the terrain.

Lieutenant Colonel William Tait, the battalion leader, his S-2, and an intelligence sergeant attempted to advance stealthily toward the positions of the 112th, but enemy riflemen spotted them and opened up. Bullets seriously wounded Tait and the S-2, who, unable to crawl to safety, died from a shot to the head. A tank destroyer, commanded by Sgt. Marshall Pritts, saved the two other Americans when it blasted the location of the German soldiers. The shell killed one, while his two companions emerged hands over their heads. One of them cried that he had not been the killer of the S-2.

Peterson and Ripple concluded that they could not possibly succeed without more armor. As Task Force Ripple waited for reinforcements, the Panzers again maneuvered into range to kill and harass the skittish GIs. To prevent a panicky withdrawal, Peterson and Ripple summoned their own armor to take on the Germans.

Ray Fleig, acknowledging the weakness of his 75mm cannons against the Panzers gunning for the Americans from a distance of 800 yards, hastily plotted with Lt. Turney Leonard, platoon leader for the tank destroyers, to close with their more effective 90mm guns. Leonard had already distinguished himself by leading his platoon in the face of heavy fire, and on one occasion, while dismounted, personally silenced a machine gun with a grenade.

Fleig and two other Shermans moved up toward the crest of a hill to attract the notice of the Germans, while Leonard's TD and others using the wooded area as cover would sneak up for a flanking attack. The Panzers enthusiastically snapped at the bait and exchanged fire with Fleig's group. But the American tank destroyers never got in place. While moving forward, they became hung up on hidden stumps from a hedgerow, cut down to several feet by the battles around it.

Leonard had dismounted in an effort to discover the problem, and Fleig said he caught sight of a frustrated Leonard flogging a bellied up TD with a riding crop. "His left arm looked like it had been mangled by artillery, and his uniform was covered with blood." Hits on turrets of two U.S. tanks left them useful only as armored machine gun platforms for the defense of Kommerscheidt, but the engagement persuaded the enemy tanks to temporarily back off. Leonard was observed on his way to the aid station. He did not survive the slaughter in the forest and received a posthumous Medal of Honor.

Further efforts to reconnoiter the proposed line of departure only brought more casualties, including a KIA company commander. Peterson refused to commit Task Force Ripple to its assigned mission. Instead, he instructed the 110th's 1st Battalion to consolidate its positions with those of the 112th until more armor, supplies, and troops could come forward.

The onslaughts of the Germans, with guns and armor that overmatched the best the tankers and TDs could offer, and the inadequate defenses against the deadly missiles eroded soldierly discipline. Shermans, the tank destroyers, and bazookas disabled some of the enemy armor, but the Panzers methodically destroyed the

American vehicles, some of which also shut down after throwing tracks or were hooked on the ever-present stumps. The GIs began to melt away from their posts.

The 28th Division commander, unhappy with the performance of the battered 112th, decided to replace regimental commander Carl Peterson. The colonel, who, with several other officers, had frantically striven to prevent a total rout, received a radio message summoning him to the division command post. Peterson set off with a jeep driver and an enlisted man, leaving Colonel Ripple in charge of the sagging Kommerscheidt defenses, which continued to deteriorate.

On 7 November, German Panzers and infantry attacked from Schmidt. GIs in forward positions knocked out a pair of tanks. Sergeant John Ostrowski, after felling three of the foot soldiers with his M1, lobbed a bazooka rocket at an oncoming tank. Black smoke poured from the Panther and it reversed course. Captain Clifford Hackard, a company commander, blasted a second tank with a bazooka shell. Lieutenant Richard Payne of the 707th's Company A attempted to cut off an enemy tank seeking to outflank the Americans. On the previous day, shell fragments rendered Payne's 75mm gun's elevating mechanism inoperable, but Payne still scored a pair of hits on the Mark V turret. It charged on, however, and only the timely intervention of tank destroyers with their 90mms halted the Mark V. One Panzer clanked to within thirty yards of a TD before it succumbed to rounds from the tank destroyers, which claimed three additional victims.

Ray Fleig reported that he and the sole other survivor from his platoon engaged a trio of enemy tanks and put down all three of them. But in the fight, a shell killed Fleig's driver and assistant driver while setting the Sherman afire. The lieutenant and his turret crew boarded the tank commanded by Staff Sergeant Spooner.

Peterson welcomed an opportunity to inform headquarters on the truly desperate state of the 112th while aware of rumors indicating that he would be relieved. As Peterson sought to find a safe route to the rear, Ripple tried to rally his forces for reinforcement of the soldiers still in Kommerscheidt. But the company commander whom he approached and his men did not respond, even when Ripple personally attempted to lead them forward. The 707th commander could only direct them to hold their positions.

German tanks resumed their advance, wreaking physical and emotional havoc. Efforts to stop their rampage by the remaining American tanks and TDs petered out, as the enemy shells and the terrain reduced the armor to a single Sherman and two tank destroyers. The infantrymen of the 112th withdrew from Kommerscheidt under orders, but many refused to stop at the point where the officers tried to organize new lines.

Peterson and his two companions encountered heavy fire along the Kall trail as they drove toward the rear. The enemy fusillades obliged them to abandon the jeep and continue on foot, passing other wrecked vehicles, some of which contained the corpses of GIs. Hoping to dodge the enemy patrols, Peterson and the enlisted men plunged into the woods in search of a way to cross the Kall upstream. But even when they reached the west bank, they found themselves subject to more shots.

A brief firefight ended with the two Germans dead, but a rain of mortars inflicted a shrapnel wound in the colonel's left leg. One of the men with him insisted on going ahead alone, against Peterson's orders, to get help. He disappeared. As Peterson and the remaining GI, Pfc. Gus Seiler, crept forward, a burst from a machine pistol ripped into Seiler's body, killing him. Another mortar round disabled the colonel's right leg. He dragged himself on, fording the river to its east bank with the vague hope of discovering a more secure route to his destination. A trio of passing Germans saw him, but Peterson drove them off with a blast from his submachine gun.

Peterson crossed and recrossed the river again and entered the woods, where he saw two Americans capture a pair of Germans. He called out to them but they left the scene. Later, in delirium from his wounds, he cried out, "General Cota, Colonel Peterson." GIs came to investigate and brought him to a site where he could receive medical attention.

Peterson's replacement, Col. Gustin M. Nelson, a recruit from the 5th Armored Division, started forward to his command of the 112th in Kommerscheidt. He tried four separate times but was frustrated, once because the guide could not locate the unit to accompany him, and on three occasions he turned back because of enemy shelling.

The only success of the day came in Vossenack. There, the 146th Engineer Combat Battalion, a component of the 1171st Engineer Combat Group, took up the weapons of battle. During the morning of 7 November, under Lt. Col. Carl J. Isley, backed by artillery and mortars and supported with tanks from Company B of the 707th, the 146th people attacked with the objective of seizing the portions held by the enemy. The mission developed so hastily that the engineers operated without radios or telephone lines for communication. The only case of hand grenades brought forward lacked fuses. When the B Company Shermans reached Vossenack, they assisted the foot soldiers in a systematic, building-by-building assault. As they proceeded, self-propelled guns and perhaps tanks opened up on them. Captain Grainger, the commander of the B Company armor, requested an air strike against the enemy gun positions. The smoke from fires and the uncertain weather hindered visibility.

John Marshall and *Bea Wain* were on the scene, and he remembered a communications officer whose precombat behavior marked him as a stickler for proper use of codes, by-the-book messages, and radio discipline. “In the Huertgen, he saw German tanks but while they were far out of the range of our guns, we were not out of range of their superior 88s. When his tank slid off the road into a ditch and a few German shells exploded near his tank, he started screaming for aerial support. ‘Tell them to bomb where my smoke shells hit; I’m seventy-five yards from the only church in town.’ He kept broadcasting that message. There were disabled tanks all over the area, abandoned by their crews, some now probably occupied by Germans listening to every transmission. When the P-47s and P-51s arrived about two hours later, we were enveloped in smoke. The Krauts were smoking us and our own planes were bombing our tanks and killing infantrymen. We finally waved them off by exposing ourselves to cover our tanks with identification panels. The communications officer abandoned his tank and men, ran back to an aid station, where a medic classified him as suffering from battle trauma, hung a tag on his neck, and shipped him back to a rest area. He never did come back to the company but probably got the Purple Heart and Bronze Star for heroism."

Most of the P-47s correctly spotted the target, but a pair of them bombed and strafed Vossenack itself. Guido Orlando had been in a Sherman that apparently struck a mine. He and his driver fled the tank and sought shelter inside a house. A 500-pounder struck the house, and Orlando grabbed his driver and dragged him down the stairs, only to discover the man was dead from wounds. Orlando, however, escaped injury. Several of the combat engineers were wounded by the errant aerial strikes.

Despite their handicaps, the engineers killed, captured, and drove off the enemy, except for a stronghold at the extreme eastern end of the town, which would become known as "the rubbish pile."

During this period, Glen Vannatta, the executive officer of heavy weapons Company D in the 110th said, "I generally was ordered to send a machine gun section or two with the advancing rifle company, while I stayed with the battalion command group to control mortar fire. Lieutenant Harry Mason was a machine gun platoon leader in D Company. He took his platoon along with the rifle company that was attacking in the Huertgen and came back like a beaten man, since he lost about half of the platoon in a futile effort.

"On one occasion I was ordered to go to the CP of the front rifle company with a radioman and a mortar section leader and runner before dawn in preparation for a local attack to take a pillbox in the woods. A little snow was on the ground. We, a group of four, walked up a path in the woods toward the front and were prepared to be stopped by the CP guard. We were not halted, and in the first light of dawn unknowingly passed the CP, where the guard was asleep or not alert. I was second in line and the first man tripped a wire for a grenade from our rifle company attached to a tree at ankle height.

"We saw the pop-flash and dived to the other side of the path. Luckily none of us got a wound. This alerted the rifle company men, and I raised hell with the CO for what it was worth. Then we prepared for an advance of the rifle squads. I was in a foxhole with my radioman, ready to direct mortar fire when needed. Immediately, on the first move, German machine gun fire along fire lanes made movement impossible, and I could do nothing about our own mortars. The attack stalled before it got started. I huddled in the foxhole for several hours while intermittent enemy fire made movement suicidal. I joked to my radioman that by putting my little finger above the foxhole and daring the Germans to shoot it off, I could get out of the Huertgen hell. Finally, I was able to get back to D Company and Capt. Andrew Carter, the CO, said we four were lucky we all made it back."

The destruction of the 3d Battalion of the 112th Infantry unnerved its commander, Lt. Col. Albert Flood, whom a subordinate described as "pretty well exhausted." Regimental commander Peterson, Flood's superior, with his wounds treated, requested an opportunity to speak to Cota. The latter astounded the colonel, telling him he had never ordered Peterson to report to the CP. In fact, he believed that the 112th's commander had deserted his troops. Subsequently, Cota accepted that someone had indeed sent the message to Peterson. The traumatized Peterson could only relate in rather incoherent fashion the situation at Kommerscheidt, but Cota and Davis, digesting the news from Ripple, hearing firsthand what Peterson had eyewitnessed, and the frustrations of Nelson, finally recognized the appalling state of affairs for their men. They recommended to V Corps that all Americans withdraw west of the Kall River, leaving Kommerscheidt totally in German hands, while holding onto the Vossenack ridge west of the stream.

During the final day of the debacle, Hodges traveled to Luxembourg to testify before the Joint Chiefs of Staff on reorganization of U.S. forces for the national defense. Upon his return, Sylvan noted, he found "the 28th Division situation going from bad to worse. The 112th Inf. completely relieved the 109th, while the 109th moved down to assist the 2nd Bn. of the 112th in vicinity of Vossenack, which the enemy is now in possession of. The remainder of the 112th and the 3d Bn. of 110th were forced back 500 yards to the high ground northeast of Kommerscheidt." In his clipped reporting, Sylvan spoke of "very heavy pressure and continual counterattacks." He also wrote, "Reports from the 28th indicate that never has enemy artillery along our front been so heavy. The Gen. insists the battalions cannot be properly deployed or dug in. He said that no matter how heavy enemy art. was, casualties would not be high nor ground be lost. He is rather worried tonight about the general situation since full employment of his other divisions in the drive toward the Rhine rest to a certain extent upon the success of the 28th. A possibility some personnel changes may be made."

The strategists now accepted that they could not break through the Huertgen with the forces committed and started to commit additional units. The 9th Division, less the 47th Infantry, still stubbornly entrenched at Schevenhutte, was to be completely relieved by the 4th Division, another regular army unit, which had first cleared Utah Beach and fought in the Cotentin Peninsula before reaching the Westwall.

The changes specifically detailed the 12th Infantry of the 4th Division to relieve the 109th. Although the badly battered survivors savored a brief respite that brought hot meals and resupply of rations and ammunition, they soon moved out to what were essentially defensive positions. The 2d Battalion checked in at Vossenack to replace the GIs of the 112th and the 146th Engineer Battalion. The 3d Battalion assumed responsibility for securing the Kall River trail, protecting the retreat of what was left of the 112th. Some rear echelon strategist consigned the 1st Battalion to Task Force Davis, a paper operation, for another assault on Schmidt.

Even as the decision was being made to replace the 109th with the 4th Division's 12th, the former organization received infusions of men. James Reed, who at age twenty-nine had enlisted in 1942 in Texas and graduated from OCS, held a slot as an infantry training officer until shipped to Europe. "I was assigned to I Company, 109th Infantry [Bill Peña's outfit] on the 8th of November. Myself and other replacement officers were trucked to regiment, where we were addressed by Colonel Gibney. He stressed to us that when we were with our troops, we were to set an example by behaving in a courageous manner. The example he gave was that if enemy artillery came into our area, we were to remain cool and not show any signs of fear. After this inspiring talk, we all noticed how carefully Colonel Gibney managed to stay safely within the entrance of the pillbox from which he addressed us."

On the drive to battalion headquarters, Reed saw a small truck loaded with steel helmets, mute testimony that the wounded and dead no longer needed protective headgear. Howard Topping provided a brief orientation about the general situation as well as some comments about his lost units.

When they left for I Company, Topping accompanied the party. "We soon left the road and entered the forest. Every once in a while Major Topping would stop and cut one of the many wires that seemed to be everywhere. I inquired why he was doing this. He explained the [lines were] German telephone wire, and he was cutting it just in case it was still active. Later on, he signaled for us to halt. He said he had spotted a German soldier. We were to lay down and be quiet while he reduced the German army by one. Like an Indian, he crept forward, took careful aim, squeezed the trigger, and fired. He missed. He was not at all pleased. We found ourselves following a cart path in some sort of a valley. Later I realized it must have been the Kall River valley."

Darkness began to smother the woods. Reed and his companion replacements took refuge with engineers fighting as infantrymen, while Topping returned to his battalion headquarters. "The training I had received at Fort Benning in no way prepared me for the night that lay ahead. My first night in a combat area was a lonely feeling, although all around me there were other GIs in their holes. Although I was tired and hungry, the newness of the situation kept me wide awake. I had a strange feeling this was all a bad dream, that soon I would awake. After I had been there a few hours, the Germans began an artillery barrage. It was the most terrifying night of my life. The Germans seemed right on target, the noise was unbelievable. I was ashamed of myself and of my behavior as I cried, prayed, and cringed in the bottom of my hole. I was grateful there was no one to witness my shame. I tried to remind myself that I was an officer, supposedly a leader, and it was my duty to set an example for those who served under me.

"The firing seemed to go on forever. It would stop and then after a short time it would begin again. Some of the people in the holes around me were wounded and in severe pain. They were calling for help, and I lacked the courage to leave my hole to help them.

"As time went on, bit by bit, my common sense began to assert itself. I began to observe and analyze the German fire. I soon realized they were firing a pattern and not every round would hit close to my area. After a while, I was able to predict when a shell would hit somewhere close. With my new confidence, I finally relaxed enough that I was able to fall asleep and slept as well as could be expected." When dawn broke and the artillery ceased, Reed left his foxhole and learned that an officer who had come up with him, along with several of the engineers, had been wounded.

Shells began to fall as a Company I patrol led him on a dead run to the unit's position. Bruce Paul, the company commander in a foxhole, directed the newcomer, "Get the hell over to that hole and join the man in it." Reed settled down for the night with a nervous noncom. "The following morning, the sergeant [with him] said in an emotional voice that he was tired of relieving himself in a ration carton and throwing it out [of] the foxhole. He said he was going to get out and take care of his needs on the outside. I tried to convince him that it was too dangerous but he insisted. Once outside, he unbuckled his trousers, squatted. As soon as he did this, the Jerry gunner opened fire. I heard the shell explode and the sergeant scream. I came flying out of the hole to find him in shock and pain. His trousers were down around his ankles, his buttocks were bare, and on the side facing me was a large, bloody, gaping hole. It appeared to go through to the other side. I managed to get a medic, and in short order he had treated the wound and started the evacuation of the sergeant to our aid station." Forward observers for the enemy constantly pinpointed such targets.

On the day that Reed joined the 109th, the First Army chief lunched at the V Corps and held a brief "chat" with Collins. Eisenhower, Bradley, and Gerow visited with Cota. "Pleasantries were passed until the official party left," wrote the diarist Sylvan, "then Gen. Hodges drew Gen. Cota aside for a short, sharp conference on the lack of progress made by the 28th Div. The Gen.'s chief complaint seemed to be that the Division HQ had no precise knowledge of the location of their units and was doing nothing to obtain it. Since 8 o'clock that morning they had no word of Gen. Davis, and two armored cars that had set out for Kommerscheidt to lead back and disengage from action the 1st and 3d bns of the 112th and the 3d bn of the 110th. Gen. Hodges is extremely disappointed over the

28th Div. showing. His feelings were shared by Gen. Thorson and Gen. Keith, both of whom served a long time with this division."

Hodges apparently also chewed out Gerow. In his postwar interview, VII Corps commander Collins, critiquing the attack on Schmidt, remarked, "Hodges is usually pictured as a man who lacked toughness. That is not quite correct. In my presence, which was unusual, he bawled the hell out of Gerow for not taking Schmidt. . . . He was very tough on Gerow, tougher than I had ever heard him before. He didn't relieve Gerow because it was terribly difficult fighting. But he was pushing Gerow awfully hard. My personal judgment was that the reason for not taking Schmidt was they didn't use their artillery fire as well as it could have been used.

"The tanks they tried to send into Schmidt got bogged down on a narrow road in the forest. It was just not the place to use tanks. The Germans, recognizing their interest in the [Roer] dams, counterattacked and drove out the leading troops of the V Corps, which had already gotten into Schmidt." In contrast to Preston Jackson's comments about the absence of tanks defeating efforts to hold Schmidt, Collins ignored the advantage of the enemy with its armor. Again, the accounts of the strategizing in November 1944 suggest his reference to the dams is hindsight.

Sylvan made no mention of a scolding by Hodges but wrote that Gerow received instructions to "keep close watch over the division efforts and to recommend any personnel changes thought necessary." He concluded his day's entry with the ominous remark, "Drove back through a blinding snowstorm."

Later that evening, Gerow telephoned with word that Davis had successfully withdrawn three battalions to the assembly area, approximately five kilometers to the rear of Kommerscheidt. However, the underreporting of the casualties and the erosion of the situation continued. Davis apparently spoke of "some twenty-five walking wounded," twenty-five litter cases among the three battalions, which hardly described the toll. Davis focused on the minor successes, advising that the 2d Battalion of the 109th held despite enemy pressure, while the 1st and 2nd Battalions of the 110th registered small gains.

9

The Grand Disaster

Although the first strikes into the Huertgen bought little ground at great cost, the American strategists never faltered in their obsession with the forest. Instead of reassessing the military value of the Huertgen, the planners now plotted on a grander scale. A conference at Ninth Air Force headquarters on 7 November approved a plan known as Operation Queen. It envisioned a broad-front lunge by the First and Ninth Armies toward the Roer, backed by a massive amount of air power that would include everything—four-engine heavies, mediums, and fighter-bombers. The offensive that included the Huertgen Forest was part of a much larger scheme.

Sylvan's diary reported, "Nov. 9 we had a conference for the big show today at V Corps HQ with Gen. Hodges, Gen. Gerow, Gen. Collins in attendance. Long-range weather reports for the period of 11–16 Nov. do not look too promising at the present time. Gen. Hodges told the press the attack would exceed in magnitude anything thrown at the Boche since D Day. The entire 8th and 9th AF plus heavy bombers from the RAF will precede the attack." Sylvan also wrote of a huge artillery preparation that would include rockets. Smoke rockets would delineate the American lines to forestall errant drops by aircraft. He remarked that if the weather prevented air support, the attack would still start no later than 16 November.

According to Hodges's aide, "Careful planning into this attack, unceasing efforts to obtain more ammunition. As is customary, Gen. Collins extremely optimistic about its success. Gen. Hodges, although he sees hard fighting ahead does not think the Boche can long stand up to such a coordinated, concentrated blow. Dined that night on plover."

Although the First Army mess provided such delicacies, more replacements filtered into the remnants of the units still hunkered down in the Huertgen. Tom Myers, whose job as an overseer at a food processing plant provided a deferment, had been inclined to enlist immediately after Pearl Harbor. But his manager convinced Myers that he could contribute more to the war effort by remaining at his job. After a change in employment, however, Myers's draft board shipped him to the army. Qualified as an infantryman, Myers reached Europe in September 1944 and south of Aachen joined the 5th Armored Division on detached, or temporary, assignment.

"It was at this time that I came under fire for the first time and saw casualties. The first man that I saw killed was a young officer, who did not have his helmet on when an 88 shell landed in the street." Myers's stay with the 5th Armored accustomed him as much as is possible to artillery barrages. After reporting back to the replacement depot on 8 November, he traveled by truck to the Huertgen Forest, joining the 110th Infantry and Company I.

"We assembled at kitchen tents of Company I and were fed. The cooks and KPs filled us in on what had happened the past few days. They said that the company was pinned down up there, a short distance away, but a guide would be there to guide us up to the 'line.'

"While we were waiting, we saw two men emerge from the forest, trudging along with no rifles or packs, their heads down. They were dirty, unshaven, and looked as if they could hardly put one foot in front of the other. They did not seem to see us. Another fellow and I went up to one of them and asked him where he was going and where he had been. We got no response. One man briefly looked at me, but his face was like a zombie, with no expression. He just kept walking west on the trail. I guess he had seen too much war. It wasn't until later that we heard about the huge numbers from another unit of the 28th Division that gave way to fear and panic and did just what these men were doing.

"When we went up to the line—if you could call it that—the guide told us to keep under cover at all times, because we were in sight of the Germans a short distance across the canyon. Of course, I didn't have to be told, as I had learned many lessons while on the line with the 5th Armored. His warning was brought home to us, though, as a new replacement, next to Wayne Newman, my foxhole buddy, and I, straightened up to remove his pack before getting in a foxhole. As he did, a well-placed rifle bullet from across the way felled him. His war ended before it started."

Myers and Newman found a previously constructed foxhole with a log cover and moved in. "Wayne had remarked that he would like to have a pair of the new two-strap combat boots that we had seen some of the men wearing. When we got into our foxhole, I could feel a lot of clothing, blankets, et cetera, in the bottom. As I was cleaning some of it out, because it was blood-stained, I picked up a boot that seemed too heavy. Upon examining it closer, I could see that it still contained a severed foot. I told Wayne I had found a pair of boots for him, handing him the boot without telling him what was in it. When he saw what was in the boot, he heaved it as far as he could. He didn't appreciate my little joke. These bits of humor, though [they] may sound very grim, helped a little to keep our minds from cracking under the strain.

"There seemed to be a certain lack of respect for replacements by some of the older 'regulars.' However, as the situation was so serious, we were generally accepted as a necessity during the Huertgen battle."

On 8 November, the tanks from the 1st Platoon of the 707th's B Company rumbled out of Germeter and into Vossenack. An hour or so after the Shermans dispersed to outposts, six German tanks, operating in the vicinity of Schmidt, opened up at a distance of nearly 2,000 yards. The Americans responded, possibly scoring significant hits on one of the enemy, but the fire from the Panzers continued. U.S. artillery shells were fired into the woods, in the hope of discouraging, if not destroying, the armor. When the heavy fire continued to fall on Vossenack, the 707th's tanks withdrew to the relative safety of Germeter under instructions to charge forward in the event of an infantry attack.

Although the battles and exchanges of ordnance raged, the aid station set up by the 112th Regiment between Vossenack and Kommerscheidt remained in a no-man's-land. American wounded accumulated while German patrols frequently inspected the premises. Despite their hazardous state, some of the walking wounded sifted through the combat zone to reach the American lines. Cascades of enemy shells, however, thwarted attempts to reach the site with Weasels and remove more seriously hurt soldiers. More and more GIs staggered, limped, or were carried to the aid station. The overwhelmed medics could only suggest to those still on their feet that they try to walk to safety. With no more room inside their bunker, the aid men placed newly arrived patients on litters alongside the Kall trail, posting men without weapons and bearing Red Cross flags to guard the wounded. Two more convoys of unarmed vehicles that tried to rescue the wounded turned back after the Germans opened up with small arms, killing one medic. However, some personnel at the log bunker discovered a shot-up but still functioning Weasel, and on their own managed to remove a number of the casualties.

The 112th regimental surgeon, Maj. Albert Berndt, recommended that the division open negotiations with the Germans for a brief truce to allow removal of the dead and wounded from both sides. Berndt volunteered to seek a cease-fire, division headquarters authorized him only to determine the attitude of the enemy to a proposal for such a truce. Under a white flag, Berndt and an interpreter, Sgt. Wheeler Wolters, journeyed to the aid station on the west side of the Kall.

Because the enemy occupied the ground just across the narrow stream, Berndt and Wolters paused at a shattered bridge to figure how to cross and parley with the Germans. Suddenly, a German soldier confronted them from the other side. When the Americans shouted the purpose of their mission, he ran off and soon six Germans including a lieutenant appeared. After some discussion, the German agreed to permit evacuation vehicles to come forward without interference from his troops. But, he warned, because of problems with communications with the rear, he could not guarantee the reaction of the artillery behind him. Over the next several days, under intermittent fire from units that did not get the word, both sides removed wounded and dead. Howard Thomsen recalled a message that requested that no tanks approach Vossenack, to avoid any suspicion of violations of the brief armistice. At some point, a different German officer accompanied by soldiers to enforce the edict declared he would not permit any more walking wounded or medical personnel to leave. The confinement order included the chaplains.

Platoon leader James Reed, a thirty-one-year-old "ancient" and a replacement, remembered his three or four days in the Kall River as "pretty much routine. From time to time we received harassing artillery and sniper fire. Also we had a few firefights with German patrols and sent out a few of our own.

"During this period I was able to get acquainted with the men of the 1st Platoon. They respected my rank and gave me no trouble. But I had a very strong feeling they had not accepted me as their platoon leader." On one occasion, a machine gun crew notified him of the approach of a German patrol and asked for his instructions. "I told the gunner to be prepared to fire when I gave the order. When I felt the patrol was close enough, I gave the order to fire. I waited for the gun to start shooting. Nothing happened. I turned to see what the problem was and saw the gunner pushing and pulling at various parts of the weapon. It seemed obvious he knew nothing about firing a machine gun. By this time the patrol was very close. I told the crew to be quiet, that I would take care of the situation. I lined my sights on the man who appeared to be the leader and squeezed off a round. My target went down but so did the rest of the patrol. We were behind a small embankment, so I moved left and right, firing as I went. After about six or seven rounds, I stopped. We watched and listened for quite a while. Nothing happened so I went out and checked the area. I was unable to find any signs of the patrol.

"When I returned to the gun crew, I gave the gunner a chewing until he informed me that he had not fired a machine gun since basic training. He had forgotten all that he had learned. When he joined I Company [as a replacement], he was assigned to a machine gun. No one asked him if he could fire it. I spent a few minutes showing him how to get a round in the chamber and what action to take in case of a jam. After that I felt a difference in the attitude of the platoon and that they now accepted me."

Aware of the imminent collapse of the entire effort by the 28th Division, Hodges directed the 4th Infantry Division to attach its 12th Regiment to the 28th and assume responsibility for the sector held by the 109th Infantry. While the latter would move to Germeter, the 12th's 2d and 3d Battalions would relieve soldiers stationed near the huge Wilde Sau minefield and overlooking the Weisser Wehe Valley. The hastily scheduled substitutions began the night of 6 November and continued over several days.

James Reed recalled, "We accomplished the transfer of troops without incident. It was very dark and our vision was zero. It was impossible to see the man in front, so we maintained contact by holding onto his belt. The sight of trucks waiting for us was a welcome sight."

Among those replaced by the 12th Infantry was weapons platoon leader Bill Peña's I Company. "Five days in this surrounded position plus the previous day's experience [an enemy barrage just as the troops assembled, suggesting a sharp-eyed German observer] had made us cautious. We talked in low tones and made some attempt at camouflaging our foxholes. The new outfit came with a different attitude, which made me nervous and anxious to leave them. Their loud talk and their setting out of blankets and shelter halves to dry as so much laundry was most disturbing. Either they were a brand new outfit or we had become overly cautious." The 12th Infantry, which had made the D-Day Utah Beach landing, was hardly virgin to combat, although five months of hard combat meant the ranks contained a fair number of newcomers.

Lieutenant Jack Crawford, an infantry replacement, joined the 12th Regiment after being busted from private first class to private for punching a first sergeant while at an embarkation camp in the States. At Mortain, France, where the 12th's battalion strength fell from 860 to 196 soldiers and 14 officers by end of the third day's fighting, Crawford earned a Silver Star and was slightly wounded. He also received a battlefield commission from General Barton for his heroism. "After Mortain," recalled Crawford, "the 2d Battalion was reorganized and many replacements were brought in to get us up to full strength. When we went into the Huertgen Forest, I was in charge of an intelligence and recon platoon for the regiment. I had two jeeps and we led the column.

"When we relieved the 28th Division, the lieutenant in our sector was so anxious to leave that in his haste to show us where his mines had been put along a trail he set one off. It killed him, blew the arms off my sergeant, and temporarily blinded me. I was evacuated to a hospital."

South Carolinean Marcus Dillard, still six weeks shy of his nineteenth birthday, and a mortar gunner with the 12th Infantry's Company M, had stepped onto Utah Beach on D Day. As a member of the 4th Division, he participated in the campaigns that carried him across France—Cherbourg, Saint-Lô, Mortain—through Paris until the outfit bedded down in the steep hills, swift flowing streams, narrow ravines, and woodsy area known as the Schnee Eifel, along the Germany-Belgium border.

"We were alerted to move at once on the 6th of November," recalled Dillard. "We were told to cover our division insignia on our helmets, remove or cover our shoulder patches and all markings on our vehicles. At about 1800 hours, we started moving north. It was cold, miserable, and raining. We arrived and started detrucking about 0200 in the morning of the 7th.

"It was dark, and I mean dark, raining, cold, wind blowing. We all wondered, 'Where are we?' This was a secret move and no one except the top brass knew where we were. I looked up, trying to see something, and all I could make out were the tops of trees swaying and hear the wind whistling through them.

"We were told to move out and to follow the man in front as close as possible. We didn't want anyone to get lost. We were told to leave our 81mm mortars behind. We would take the ones left by the unit we were relieving and they would get ours.

"We walked, stumbled, and slipped for the next couple of hours, barely able to see where we were going. We finally halted and were to stay in place. Wet and miserable as I was, I dropped off to sleep. I don't know for how long, but then we were told we would take the foxholes and positions of the soldiers we were to replace. It was starting to get daylight and we could see the shoulder patches of the 28th Division. They didn't say much. They just moved out and looked tired and exhausted.

"As it got brighter, what I saw scared me. Shell holes all over, the trees, most of them looked like shredded match sticks with points. Half of the trees standing, the bark was torn off by shrapnel. Just utter devastation. It was cold, rainy, foggy. Just plain miserable. No hot food, just K rations.

"Our positions must have been the only open area around, because we had to have clearance overhead in order to fire our 81s. The Germans had to know our positions because of that. We could not see our targets but were told what they were. The forest was so dense in places you couldn't see ahead. And you would have to stoop down to see through the fog in front.

"The artillery fire on us was very intense. My platoon sergeant, Gerald Fields, was standing next to me talking when the Germans started a barrage that lasted over three hours. He jumped in my small bunker with me. We had cut logs and put them over the slit trenches that had mounds of dirt around them. We could not even get out to our mortar positions, which were about twenty to thirty feet out in the clearing. The telephone line to the company CP was cut by the barrage, and we had no communication. We could not give supporting fire until we fixed the cut lines."

A day after their arrival, the 4th Division troops had commenced an attack designed to eliminate a salient that extended into the Weisser Wehe Valley. Dillard remembered, "As we started through a firebreak there was a minefield and barbed wire. The company commander stepped on a mine. Then the Germans started shelling us. They must have had an observer in the woods. Almost all our supplies had to be hand-carried over trails and paths barely wide enough to walk [on] and past fallen trees and shell holes. We had never encountered terrain like this to fight in. We had done no prior recon of the Huertgen. We just moved in during the dead of night and then started the attack."

After initial success, a barrier of booby-trapped obstacles covered by automatic weapons halted progress and Regimental CO Col. James Luckett pulled the GIs back to their original positions. "When the regiment renewed its drive 9 November," according to Dillard, "Company I and K were designated as the main assault units, but a 500-yard-wide minefield separated them. Company I had to withdraw from its front-line position, and a support platoon from Company L replaced it."

"Company K moved rapidly until it reached a booby-trapped concertina wire covered by machine gun fire. All this time, we in Company M were laying down a mortar barrage in front of K. Company I, which circled around the minefield, came up in the rear of K, then swung to the left. They too caught intense small arms fire. Both of our infantry companies were calling for our 81mm mortars, but the Germans were well dug in. K and I had to dig in for the night, all the time under intense artillery and mortar fire."

The German gunners, mines, and soldiers with small arms effectively broke up the attack, inflicting severe losses. When some GIs tried to return to their old foxholes, they found Germans in residence. Command and control broke down; shortages of food and ammunition plagued the Americans. The broken-up regiment reverted to the 4th Division. Only three days after being committed, it was a shambles, counting 562 casualties among its complement of 2,300. Lieutenant Colonel Franklin Sibert, the 2d Battalion commander recalled, "God, it was cold. We were hungry and thirsty. . . . That night we really prayed. . . . In the morning we found that God had answered all our prayers. It snowed during the night, and the whole area was covered with fog—perfect for getting out. . . . The supply line was littered with dead. The men that came out with me were so damned tired that they stepped on the bodies—they were too tired to step over them."

The GIs of the 109th that the 12th relieved approached the area near the besieged aid station. Bill Peña remarked, "Across the stream, half-hidden in the woods, we could see a hunting lodge flying a Red Cross flag." Some historians have faulted Howard Topping, Peña's battalion commander, for not have aggressively protected the medical station in his sector. But the major had incurred a sniper's wound in the arm shortly after he himself spotted a German and hit him with his M1. "He was the only one I knew," said Peña, "to notch the wood stock of his rifle, and he had about a dozen notches."

After Topping reluctantly left for treatment but remained at battalion headquarters, General Davis appeared in Peña's area. "His mission was to cross the bridge and to contact the 112th Regiment at Kommerscheidt with verbal orders to withdraw across the bridge to our side. The general was told that although our side of the bridge was fairly secure, German units covered it from the other side. He said he'd give it a try and asked for a platoon reinforced by a light machine gun.

"[First Lieutenant Bruce] Paul [Item's commander] asked me to organize such a platoon from our company and to take my orders from the general. The platoon turned out to be our whole company less a dozen men. Before we started, the general asked me a question, which I was expected to answer with pride, 'Is that your platoon, lieutenant?' Of course I was proud of our men, but my answer disturbed the general: 'Yes, sir, but it is also nearly my whole company.' I wondered if division headquarters realized how decimated we were." Common speech uses the word *decimated* to indicate a huge loss, but in fact the word literally is defined as a 10 percent shrinkage, and Peña obviously meant much more severe casualties.

Peña continued, "We started through the woods toward the bridge. Halfway there, we were spotted and we began receiving light mortar fire. Immediately we scattered and threw ourselves to the ground. When the volley was over and I found that no one was hurt, I also found smiles on everyone's faces—the men could now say that a general could hit the ground as quickly as anybody.

"We continued and reached the bridge. I pointed out that we would have to run across the bridge, since we knew it would be covered by fire from the opposite side. The general decided that the crossing would be difficult in broad daylight. He would go back and recommend another solution to the problem. We went back to the battalion area and delivered the general to his escort patrol."

The Germans apparently believed the Americans in the forest had lost their ability and will to fight. A startled Peña was suddenly confronted by an American officer, who walked into his area from the direction of the territory controlled by the enemy. "He introduced himself as Father [Alan P.] Madden, Catholic chaplain of the 112th. He had been ordered to tell us to surrender since we were surrounded. Paul radioed the demand to Major Topping. [His] answer was 'Hell no, you're not surrounded. We'll answer the demand with artillery fire.'"

Madden told Peña that his agreement with the Germans, which allowed ambulances to take out American wounded, required him to return to the aid station. He disappeared back toward the enemy lines. Shortly after, an artillery forward observer appeared and spotted the location of the German troops across the stream from Peña and company.

Peña said, "He radioed his orders back and placed one round in enemy territory. He adjusted his range and ordered, 'Fire for effect.' The barrage started going out. Unfortunately, he had not accounted for the height of the trees in our area and had not called for high angle fire. The low angle fire caused tree bursts in our area! Many of our men were out of their holes to watch the fireworks. The order to cease firing was quickly radioed back, but the damage had been done. A couple of the men were wounded; one man was killed instantly." The dead GI had tumbled into the hole shared by a pair of soldiers, both of whom broke from the stress. One was laughing "completely out of control," while the other was sobbing. The two were sent to an aid station for treatment for combat fatigue.

On the following day, the Item Company position welcomed four Americans stumbling toward their location. Among them was Father Madden, who, after the Germans refused to allow any more ambulance evacuations, on the grounds that those who remained were all walking wounded, escaped with some companions.

Hubert Gees, the young German soldier in the German 275th Division, was among those who fought off the GIs of the 12th Infantry. He recounted an ordeal as severe as that which befell the Americans, noting, "The battles swung in continual bitterness back and forth. It is raining, wet snatches of fog or snow clouds sweep over the softened land beset with puddles. The fighting infantrymen, wading, lying, and fighting in mud are close to complete exhaustion. The reported battle strengths are sinking at an alarming rate. Continually the artillery battle rolls on.

"In the forest itself it looks completely crazy. The trees are leaning on one another through continual fire, and the roads are completely soaked, and everywhere stands water a foot high. The infantrymen look like swine. No rest for over a week and not a dry thread on their bodies. . . . Man against man with enormous efforts for the individual man. . . . Infantry of the division is completely finished. There are only staffs there and very few men. Even men who cannot be brought forward except at the point of a pistol, are also there.

"Two of our machine gun crew securing the mine-free path were shot through the head by American sharpshooters, who had infiltrated and were encircling us. We had another enemy: vermin—lice! For weeks we had gone without washing and being able to change our undergarments in the damp foxholes. When I discovered a white band of lice eggs, I threw the pullover immediately away, although I had a second urgent need because of the wet cold, severe weather.

"On 12 November, after the soldiers of the U.S. 12th Infantry Regiment had again captured the Forester's House in a night attack and during the morning lost it again, our company received a heavy blow. During the early morning an obviously wounded American soldier was crying pitifully for help. He lay in the middle of the minefield Wilde Sau, at the edge of the embankment in No Man's Land. My company commander, Lieutenant [Friedrich] Lengfeld sent me with the order to the machine gun that was guarding the mine-free path that in no case should it shoot if American first-aid men should come to rescue the severely wounded soldier. When the heartrending cries for help continued for hours, Lieutenant Lengfeld ordered our medical aid men to form a rescue troop. It may have been about 10:30 A.M.

"Lieutenant Lengfeld went at the point of our rescue troop on our side of the street, itself secured with antitank mines whose location was relatively easy to recognize. As Lieutenant Lengfeld was on the point of crossing the street, directly over to where the severely wounded American was lying, an exploding antipersonnel mine threw him to the ground. In haste, he was carried back to our company CP for first aid. Two deep holes in his back implied there were severe internal injuries. Lieutenant Lengfeld groaned under deep pain. Under the leadership of a lightly wounded NCO, he was carried to the medical aid station at Lucasmuble. Yet, during the evening he died of his severe wounds.

"I had lost my best supervisor. He meant much to me in the difficult weeks lying behind us, and he had given me much inner strength. He was an exemplary company commander who never asked us to do more than he himself was ready to give. . . . When American infantry ammunition exploded in the trees overhead and gave us the impression that the enemy had broken through, he did not order, 'Go at once!' but rather, 'Come with me!'

"On 13 November, the attack against the surrounded Americans commenced. Most of the Americans escaped to their own lines. Only twenty-seven prisoners were brought in. . . . On the evening of 13 November, Field Marshal Model visited the staff of the 116th Panzer Division in a bunker near Grosshau. Relief for the division was finally ordered. On 14 November, we linked up with the German unit to the north. The U.S. 12th Regiment had withdrawn some 300 meters to the northwest corner of the minefield Wilde Sau. The retreat had been very hasty. They had to leave behind weapons, machine guns, bazookas, and even their dead. Our first interest lay in the rations which had been left behind, cans and packets, C and K rations."

Compiled the first week of December, the after-action report of the 707th Tank Battalion, which covers the month of November, exemplifies the reality gap that pervaded the understanding of the rear and upper echelons. The document says that from 2 to 7 November, the battalion, while incurring one KIA, a total of nine casualties, including four missing in action, it lost only four tanks, while "estimated damage to the enemy registered 115 killed, 500 captured, and two Mark VI tanks knocked out." The overall tone conveys a sense of victory. However, since C Company's leader, Capt. George West; B Company tank commander Mike Kozlowski; and Louis Livingston, a crewman for a C Company tank, were all KIA, the figures were obviously in error. The outfit's complement of armor was significantly more damaged than indicated. The destruction wrought upon the enemy is also wildly inflated.

John Marshall scoffed, "This was all show for the little boys that wanted medals and to become generals. We knew different. When the shooting finally stopped, the count was one for one. For every German we killed or wounded, they killed or wounded one of us." Throughout the Huertgen campaign, exaggerated body counts pervaded the reports with underestimation of the strength of the Germans in the number of soldiers, the quality they fielded, and their armament. In fact, it was because the tankers and the American foot soldiers had absorbed so much punishment that the proposed Task Force Davis, designed to renew the quest for Schmidt on 8 November, never went beyond the planning stage. Davis had been misled by the sunny description of the 707th's achievements in cooperation with infantrymen.

John Alyea, as the driver for the *Bea Wain* in Company B, described a desperate situation. "From the time we went into combat through our entire stay in this area, the weather was bad, no letup on the rain. Any foxholes dug by infantry were filled with water. Our final position was outpost duty in Vossenack, with the tanks in a line position at a clearing in the forest, where we were under periodic mortar and artillery shelling. We were not supplied with any gasoline or ammo for the tanks, as the road was impassable and we had to wait until the weather improved a little, maybe by the 17th of November. The roads and ground had become a quagmire of mud and the ability to maneuver the tanks was almost nil."

During the period the 707th tanks stayed in Germeter, Howard Thomsen busied himself with maintenance and repair chores. "One day I was replacing the spark plugs in the tank engines. One of the tank commanders yelled, 'Look out, Tommy!' I grabbed my carbine, raised up, and hit my head on the armor of the engine compartment. I thought a Jerry had come in but nothing was there. He pulled the trick twice, and then I told [the tank commander], 'Do that again and I will be tempted to shoot.'

"Captain Grainger came up and asked if the tank was ready to go. I said, 'Yes,' and he crawled up on the back deck and asked [the tank commander] if his crew was ready and [the tank commander] started to cry. They called the medics and put a tag on him 'combat fatigue.' It was the first time I'd seen that. I found out later, after the war was over, he just stayed in Paris."

Jack Goldman, the radio operator for Captain Grainger's command tank, recalled his exhaustion. "I was summoned by my captain. He had two German prisoners for me to guard until the MPs would arrive and take them for questioning. I herded them into the aid station, a huge dugout with a tarp over it. When the dead and wounded arrived, they would put out the lamps, roll back the tarp, bring in the wounded, reset the tarp, and then light the lamps. I found a spot where I indicated to the prisoners they should sit with their backs to the wall. I sat to their left with my gun on my left, away from them.

"I felt exhaustion coming on. I covered my head with a blanket and passed out. I don't know how long I dozed, but when I suddenly awoke I quickly remembered who was with me. I looked but they were so happy to be out of the war, I could not have lost them. Once again, God was looking out for me. The MPs arrived and the prisoners were taken.

"It was then that Captain Grainger had the unpleasant job of trying to remove a gunner from one of the tanks. The man had shot so many of the enemy that day with the machine gun that he was out of his head. He would not dismount from the tank. Grainger tried to reason with him, but he pulled the captain into the tank with him. The gunner was a good soldier, but he had been through too much." He was eventually persuaded to be evacuated.

As the time for relief of the 707th by another armored unit drew near, Goldman became aware that those still manning positions were shivering from the low temperatures. "It was cold, very cold. There was one tent with a heater, and the men would take turns getting warm and then leave. They would sleep three or four in one pup tent. They would pool their blankets. I noticed that when the 28th went into battle, they would drop their blankets in one pile in the woods and then go to fight. Of course, most never returned, at least during their battle. I got permission from the first sergeant to take a truck and go through the woods gathering blankets. I had a driver and one helper who refused to get out of the truck for fear of booby traps. I did not have time to pull rank, because I did not have much rank. I jumped to the ground, threw the blankets up on the truck. We returned and gave them out. Once again, God had looked after me."

The misery did not except rank. Goldman recalled, "I met my captain, who had been summoned to battalion headquarters. He stopped to talk to me, and he was shivering. I had an overcoat in my shot-up duffel bag. It had shrapnel holes in the sleeves and the body. But it was a coat with corporal stripes. I gave it to Captain

Grainger, because I could not stand to see him shivering. I really loved the guy."

Replacement Tom Myers described his foxhole existence. "Imagine if you will, crouched in a cold wet hole, four feet square and three feet deep. You have covered all of the hole, except an opening large enough to crawl out, with broken pieces of trees and limbs. There is not a shortage of those here in the forest, because the tree bursts have mowed the tops of the trees off, like a giant scythe. Your clothes are sopping wet, including your socks. You have brought extra socks with you, but those have been changed several times in an effort to avoid the dreaded trench foot. You have dehydrated coffee and some water to make coffee for a while, but you don't dare build a fire to heat the water. The K rations carton is coated with an almost smokeless wax, so when you have them, you can burn one under your canteen cup to heat the coffee. But now your K rations are gone, and you have only some crackers and chocolate D bars.

"When the artillery stops, the silence there in the forest is eerie. Those once beautiful conifers are now broken and torn, and the ground is a tangled mass of bushes and broken treetops. But then the shells start coming in again, and you wonder if one of them today might have your name on it. I did not waste a lot of time worrying about it though. By this time I was convinced that I was leading a charmed (or rather guided) life. I don't mean to say that I wasn't afraid. I just didn't let my mind dwell on it too much."

Myers and his foxhole buddy, Wayne Newman, depended in part on the heavy log over their foxhole, which protected them, except in the event of a direct or close hit by a shell. On one occasion, that dire possibility surfaced. "The Germans were giving us their daily raking. That is, put one round near the top of the hill we were dug in on and then another directly below, et cetera. Then they would move over a few yards and repeat it. In the course of time, your foxhole had a fair chance of being hit. Wayne and I heard one explode directly above us and knew that the one that would come in a split second would probably hit our hole or near it. Sure enough, there was a dull thud outside our hole. As the ground shook, we both waited a long time before either of us spoke the two words 'a dud.'

The next day we would see where the shell had buried itself in the edge of our foxhole but failed to explode. I'm not sure what the odds of that happening was, but I was more convinced than ever that I was under divine guidance.

"Unfortunately, there were many, many of our buddies that were not as lucky as Wayne and I. The screams and moans of the wounded in that dark, eerie forest is hard to wipe out of your mind. Usually there was so little that we could do for them, except give them comfort and some minor first aid until the medics took care of them."

For all of their travail, the 110th Infantry GIs could do little to carry out the strategy dictated by V Corps. "During the next eight or nine days we were there in the forest," said Myers, "we were not able to move very far. The Germans had us pinned down with their small-arms and machine gun fire, but the worst of it was the constant fire from the mortars and artillery, with the devastating tree bursts that chewed up the men, and I suppose kept the battalion off guard and not able to fight our way out. We made some night patrols, and at least once during that time, we were supposed to go on the attack, but they couldn't muster enough able-bodied men in the company to make the attack. Most of the time, it was sit in your foxhole and watch for the Germans to attack, when the tree bursts were not too close to you.

"When we replacements left the assembly area, we were taken by huge piles of K rations and boxes of M1 bandoliers. We were told they had no idea how long we would be up there without more supplies, so we should take all we cared to carry. I filled my musette bag with K rations and hung several bandoliers of ammo over my shoulder.

"My buddy and I ran out of K rations before we were relieved. I don't remember how long we were without food but well remember when we got some. It was well past midnight. Newman was asleep while it was my turn to keep watch. I heard a loud whisper, 'Hey, Mack, where is your hole?' It was one of our company KPs. He crawled to our hole and handed me two thick sandwiches of corned beef—the best sandwich I had ever eaten.

"I was quite disappointed in a certain officer and a couple of noncoms. One night we were under a heavy artillery attack. A foxhole some fifty yards or more from ours received a direct or near-direct hit. A man was screaming for the medic. I waited as long as I could stand it, then told Wayne that I was going to see if I could find a medic for him. It was a totally dark night, but I had no trouble finding the wounded man. His leg was badly severed. I could only bind it with his belt and went after the medic. In a large, log-covered foxhole, I found not only the medic but an officer and two noncoms huddled there. The hole was closer to the screaming, injured man than ours. I asked the medic, 'Couldn't you hear his screaming?' He reluctantly went with me to aid the man."

Al Burghardt, the mortar squad sergeant in the 110th, spent his final days in the forest on the reverse slopes outside of Kommerscheidt. "With what was left of the 3d Battalion, we dug in and waited for the word to renew the attack on Schmidt, but because of the problems that the Kall trail presented, the attack was delayed. No tanks or supplies were getting through. The Germans could not shell our position with their regular artillery because of the reverse slope, but they were able to use mortars, due to the higher trajectory. We hadn't eaten in three days, except for a roll of Lifesavers, which I shared with a friend. There wasn't any part of me that wasn't cold, wet, or damp. While in this position outside of Kommerscheidt, the wounded increased at an alarming rate, and they could not get proper treatment. Our medics negotiated a temporary truce. I was told by our medics that the Germans checked each stretcher to make sure that only the most seriously wounded were being evacuated.

"Sometime on the 8th of November, word was radioed that we were trapped and our troops would not be able to break through to us. We were to abandon our position and all our machine guns and mortars were to be destroyed. We were to break up into small groups and get back to our original areas. Since I was in charge of a 60mm mortar, I destroyed the mortar sight with the butt of my rifle and buried the base plate, bipod, and the mortar tube in different spots and camouflaged the area.

"When the group I was with took off late that night, we went down the Kall trail and across the stone bridge over the Kall River.

It was guarded by troops. We came upon it very quickly, and it was very dark and raining. My platoon sergeant and I, discussing this years later, are sure the troops were Germans, but since our group was larger than theirs, and this happened fast, no action resulted. After crossing the bridge, we went cross-country out of the Kall Valley, up some very steep slopes suitable only for mountain goats. Everyone was very quiet and we received no incoming fire. The Germans apparently had no idea that we had left our position. During this time, someone lost his helmet. It went crashing down the rocky slope to the bottom of the valley, making a tremendous amount of noise.

"When we arrived at the top of this valley, we came to a flat area, where we were challenged in English by a sentry. Whoever was leading us satisfied the outpost that we were GIs, and we passed through to our company area. We were too tired to dig in. We just laid down and went to sleep. At first light, when I awoke, I was covered with the first snow of the season. The medics arrived and were checking everyone. When they came to me, they asked how I was, and I said, other than being cold, wet, and hungry, I was okay. They asked how my feet were. I said okay and proceeded to take my M1 and hit my left foot with the butt of my rifle. I felt nothing. They had me take my boots off and examined my feet. They were as white as the new snow.

The medics wrote out a casualty tag and put it on me. They brought up a stretcher and told me to get on it, which I thought was great, until the circulation started to try to get back into my legs and feet. When they took my M1, I saw for the first time that six inches of the barrel were missing, probably removed by shrapnel. I had no idea when this happened because my rifle was always within my reach. This started me on my way to the States, through numerous hospitals in France and England and onto a hospital ship to the States.

"I never did find out who led us out of the trap. Whoever did was one hell of a soldier. The night was so dark that you couldn't see four feet in any direction. In my group there were eighteen of us. We were lucky. Some groups didn't make it, but we did.

"At a regimental reunion, many years later, I asked my platoon sergeant who the hell lost his helmet that night. His face turned red, and he confessed that it was him. We had a good laugh."

Although Burghardt was one of hundreds of soldiers disabled by trench foot, VII Corps commander J. Lawton Collins insisted that the malady was never a serious problem.

During this rather static but deadly period, John Chernitsky's antitank platoon manned a position that covered the bridge over the Kall River, which had been blown up to prevent an attack by the enemy. "Our targets were German engineers who tried to repair the bridge or put up a pontoon bridge. We only fired twice. There were no enemy tanks and ours could not move around the bend. Engineers tried to widen the roads, which were made of stone. We laughed at the maps, which showed roads—they were cow trails without cows.

"None of the brass ever came forward to our position; we were too far up front for them. I had the distinction of bringing up replacements. They'd call me and say we've got twelve men for E Company and G Company, which were about a quarter of a mile ahead of us. The replacements had no discipline, couldn't keep their mouths shut. We had to try to get word to the companies to meet us. Very few of the replacements survived.

"I had never seen such destruction to forest land. The German artillery kept firing at the tops of trees and artillery bursts hit the trees—the shrapnel fell just like rain and the artillery was constant—day and night. The casualties in the 110th were heavy. Very noticeable in the Huertgen Forest was the movement of medics and ambulances. When they had a chance they picked up the dead. The German losses were heavy also, but we never could figure out what happened to the Germans who were wounded or dead."

Replacement Jerry Alexis, dragooned into an intelligence and reconnaissance platoon after his Company B had departed their positions without notifying him, was released back to the company around 8 or 9 November near the settlement of Simonskall. "Day and night we got direct fire from the German 88s anytime we moved in or out of our foxholes. On November 11 we moved a few hundred yards to join what was left of the battalion to go into another attack down into the Kall Valley, about a mile south of Simonskall.

We were so understrength however, that the battalion commander received permission to abort the attack.

"Early on the 11th, a sergeant assigned me and another GI to the outpost line [OPL] about fifty yards in front of the main line of resistance [MLR], where what was left of the 1st Battalion was digging in. The sergeant showed us the spot where he wanted us to put our foxhole. I immediately protested, because it was several hundred yards behind the military crest of the hill on which we were located, which meant it dropped off at that point. We wouldn't be able to see anyone coming up the hill until they were practically looking down our throats. My arguments were to no avail, since he insisted we were already further forward than he wanted us to be anyhow. Right then I knew we were probably on a suicide mission if the Germans decided to attack, because there was little or no cover between us and the MLR to hide our movement to the rear. The role of the combat outpost is to give an early warning of the enemy's approach, laying down as much fire as possible to deceive him of the actual position of the MLR, and then get back and reinforce the rest of the unit.

"We started to dig in. Fortunately, the ground wasn't very hard, so we made good progress, despite the many roots and stones we encountered. The availability of logs for cover against tree bursts was limited, so we made do with smaller branches, which served more as camouflage than as any real protection.

"We spent the night there, and the next day continued to do what we could to improve our hole. About noon, we settled down to await what the Germans might have in store for us. It wasn't long in coming.

"About three o'clock in the afternoon, I could hear guttural voices in front of us, and the coal-scuttle helmets popped over the military crest. As was customary in attacks by the Germans, each of the half dozen or so point men were armed with machine pistols, burp guns, as they were known for their staccato bursts of rapid fire. I began to fire my M1 rifle as rapidly as I could squeeze the shots off, but I noticed that my partner was huddled down in the bottom of the hole. I swore at him to get going or at least hand me his loaded rifle when my clip was exhausted. He didn't move, so I was left to try to change clips as quickly as possible, while the attackers ran from tree to tree over the last few yards, firing bursts as they ran.

"Then it was all over. From the side of the hole there appeared over us a German with his gun pointed down at us, shouting, *'Raus mit du!'* [Get out!] As my partner came up from the bottom of the hole, I noticed he had been nicked by a shot across the forehead, just enough to draw blood, but apparently not too serious. By this time, several other GIs on the OPL had been captured and lined up by two guards. As the firefight had now moved toward the MLR, we were getting stray shots around us and things were pretty hairy. Then, whether from an aimed shot or a ricochet or a stray, the guard standing about two yards from me was hit squarely in the stomach and went down screaming. I could just see us getting mowed down in retaliation, but the only reaction of the other guard was to shout something unintelligible to us, which we interpreted to mean, 'Let's get the hell out of here!' We ran pell-mell over the hill, but in a column so he wouldn't have any excuse for thinking we were trying to escape. We quickly arrived at a huge concrete bunker at the bottom of the hill, which was evidently serving as a command post for the attackers.

"An English-speaking noncom there wisecracked to us that there really wasn't any need to interrogate us, because they knew we were the 1st Battalion of the 110th Infantry, 28th Division, and that fifty or so who were still fighting at the top of the hill would soon join us as *kriegsgefangener,* my introduction to a word that would soon be a part of daily life—prisoner of war.

"We were relieved of what few items we had in our wallets. In my case, my social security card, some family pictures, and military scrip money. Surprisingly, we were allowed to keep our watches and rings. It wasn't long before another noncom came into the room, and after a short conversation with the interpreter, announced that we would carry some litter patients back to an aid station. We went to another bunker, where some medics were cleaning wounds and bandaging wounded Germans.

"We picked up two patients, one of who was in especially bad shape. His back had been made into hamburger by shrapnel and his bandages were blood-soaked. As we lifted him and started to carry him outside, he was alternately screaming in pain or crying. We went just a few yards down a path, which led to the Kall River, really just a small stream at this point. There was a swinging bridge across it, but it was too narrow for us to use with the stretcher. We were ready to move down the riverbank and into the water when suddenly an artillery round roared in and exploded not more than twenty yards away, followed by others in the immediate vicinity. Our litter case nearly went wild as he screamed for us to put him down. As soon as he was on the ground, he began to crawl as quickly as possible to a nearby depression in the ground. The rest of us jumped for whatever little protection we could find around the bases of the trees and in previous shell holes.

"As quickly and as abruptly as the barrage started, it ended. The German NCO had us get our patients back on litters, and we took off through the river. We nearly went into shock ourselves as the swift, icy water rose up to our waists. It was a job to keep our litter above the water and our feet from slipping, but we made it to the opposite side and onto a fairly decent road that soon led to another pillbox, where the evacuation station was located."

Alexis and about a dozen other prisoners ate a small amount of food given to them and then began a hike to the rear. "It wasn't long before the combination of the cold night air and our wet clothes had us in agony with every step we took. For a while we were going up a steep road, and we began to retch from the exertion, our dry mouths, and the mental trauma of captivity. Day one of my POW experience came to an end as we arrived around midnight at a small village, where we were herded into a one-room schoolhouse along with some GIs already lying with their coats wrapped around themselves. Those nearest the two stoves made room for us to get warmed. Most of the group immediately began to take off their shoes and socks to reveal badly swollen feet, which they put close to the stoves.

"Somewhere in the back of my mind I recalled a medic's lecture in training camp warning about the danger of this, so I kept my boots on despite my pain. This was one of the smartest things I did in my POW days, because by the next morning those who had put their uncovered feet near the stoves woke up to find them ballooned to twice their normal size. Some had already begun to turn all shades of red, black, and blue. I could walk with a great deal of pain, which was more than most could do. The Germans sent in some medics, but all they could do was shake their heads and mutter something that must have meant 'Too bad!'" Within a few days Alexis joined a growing number of GIs in the stalags.

While the enemy destroyed the 28th and its attached units, the 3d Battalion of the 9th Division's 47th Infantry continued to maintain its grasp of Schevenhutte. Chester Jordan, as a platoon leader in K Company, survived two full months in the hills overlooking the town. He and his colleagues had taken up residence about 16 September.

"Our new positions were well established just inside the woods facing a cutover area. The Germans were just as well established in the woods on the other side of the clearing. There was a fringe of woods on the east side of this clearing that connected the warring parties.

"After hearing about the vicarious thrill of watching your enemy doing exactly what you are doing, I decided I had better have a look. I went alone. I was crawling through the needles when I saw right in front of my nose a Luger pistol. It was lying on the top of its barrel with the grip pointing straight up. It surely had to be placed like that, but why. Was it a booby trap? It had to be, but it was too damn intriguing to pass up, so I started lifting needles one at a time to expose the area around the gun. The gun had absolutely no rust on it, so it could not have been there very long. I finally got down to bare earth and there was no trip wire. It evidently had just fallen from the pocket of a careless Kraut. I crawled on and spent some time watching a couple of soldiers shooting the breeze, but this was anticlimactic. After the Luger incident, I could have shot them easily but who wants to stir up the hornets.

"My CP was in a crude hut made of rocks stacked in the bottom of a quarry. Although it was not tall enough to stand in, it made a snug little hole to sleep in. One day, I was lounging in the hut, talking to a sergeant standing in the door. A mortar shell landed right on top of him, and he was blown all over me. This period in Schevenhutte sticks in my mind as a period of relative inaction, but the company was replaced over twice while we were there.

"The 39th and 60th Regiments of the 9th plus several other divisions were getting the shit kicked out of them just southwest of us in the same Huertgen Forest. They were fighting for the same woods we had walked through. I don't know what the rest of the 47th was doing, I just know they were not in our village. Schevenhutte remained the deepest Allied penetration into Germany for over two months, but, to my knowledge, no one said as much as 'Good job.'"

The substitution of the 4th Division for the ill-fated 28th continued during the first two weeks of November. The 8th and 22d Infantry Regiments traveled north to take their places in the forest and prepare to participate in the great offensive that would include the 1st Infantry Division. Theoretically, it had recovered from its first encounter with the Siegfried Line and the edges of the Huertgen. On the left flank of the endeavor, the 104th Division would assume responsibility for the Stolberg corridor, and the 90th Division would in turn carry the First Army offensive beyond there.

During this period, the flow of replacements continued. Bill Kull, married and a father, recalled moving up a road toward the forest around 9 or 10 November with others to fill the depleted ranks of the 12th Infantry. "We had two or three truckloads of about twenty guys each. A stupid officer I didn't know at the time, who was just back from a hospital, Captain S__, was in charge of Company C, had landed on D Day, and been wounded later."

On foot, the replacements followed their captain. "He takes off at a quick place and, man, this road was littered with bodies, most likely from the 28th Division, and the mud halfway up to your knees. There's a head sticking up out of the mud here, a hand there. S__ just takes off and all of a sudden the shells start coming in. These poor recruits are getting shelled, and they didn't know whether to run back or run ahead, and they're getting knocked off, and they didn't even know where they were yet. I was with some kid I had never seen before, Pvt. Rocco S. La Fauci, and I said, 'This is crazy walking up this stupid road. We may as well at least go up the side through the trees. Maybe they won't see us.'

"Eventually, we got to a foxhole, and we didn't know where it was in relationship to the line. We ducked into it, hunkered down, and a couple hours later, a guy with some experience crawled up and said, 'Hey, you're new guys, aren't you? Got any water?' We didn't have much, because in our shock and exhaustion we had drank half a canteen each and didn't know where we were or where the next water would come from. We told him, 'no.' He said, 'You're new. You must have some water. You just came up.' We said, 'Yeah, well, we drank it all.' So he crawled on. During the night the shells pounded in and nobody else came by.

"The next morning, I told Rocco, 'I'm going back where we started from' [possibly near Zweifall, which was the 12th Regiment's headquarters about a mile or two back], and find out where we're supposed to be, and maybe not ever come back again. We went to the motor pool area and were moseying around there. An officer came up and asked, 'Where are you guys from?' We told him we were recruits from the day before. On the way up we came under heavy fire, people got killed, people got wounded, and the officer we were with took off, and we have no idea where he went. We don't think we want to go back.

"After a day, the officer says, 'You have a choice. You either go back with the next group that comes in or you get court-martialed. And,' he says, 'if you get court-martialed, you probably get shot, and if you get shot you lose all your benefits [the GI insurance paid to survivors]. So if you're gonna get killed anyway, you may as well go up there and at least protect your families.'

"I said I would think it over, and during the night I talked to Rocco. I said, 'You know that really makes sense. I'd sooner get shot up there and have everybody think you're a hero, rather than die here and have everybody know you're a coward.' I wrote a letter to my wife, Ethel, and made the officer promise to mail it.

"That day a couple more truckloads of guys came. I said to Rocco, 'The problem is carrying all this crap. It's not ours anyway. Take your personal items, like I have a picture of mother and of the two kids, and maybe an extra pair of socks. Take your gun, some ammo, some food and water, and leave the rest. If anyone questions us, we can say we were up there before and our gear is all up there.'"

To avoid the problem they encountered during their first day under fire, Kull said he suggested to La Fauci, "When they start off, they're gonna be like us the other day. When the shelling begins, I'm gonna take off up that road, leave everyone behind, and get on the other side of the shelling. Then maybe we'll find somebody up there."

The two followed this script, and Kull recalled, "We got to a place where a sergeant said, 'You guys, where ya goin?' We said to your foxhole, hunkered down, and moved over to him. He said, 'Get down! Get down! Don't let them know where I am!' He said, 'Where are you supposed to be?'

"'Beats us. We don't know. They just told us to come up this road.' 'This is C Company.' 'That sounds like a good company to me. We don't have to look further.' 'Okay, you're in C Company. I'll get a sergeant to find you a foxhole that's empty.'"

Another noncom crawled over to them and then led them to a vacant position. "He said, 'You just stay here, now.' I said, 'Yeah, but when do we get to eat?' He answered, 'Whenever they can, they bring up food, water, and ammunition. All you can do is stay put, but just be ready when we pass the word down the line. We're finally going on the attack in a couple of hours.'

"We never saw anybody again, and the shells are raining like water. You can only go up on the ridge of the foxhole to go to the bathroom, when you really had to, and usually at night. Meanwhile, we just stayed there. I don't remember how long, several days, maybe more. We heard battles going on but nobody ever told us anything except we're going to attack, or something like that, but nobody ever said when. We just stayed there."

The near-standstill in the forest incited spasms among those charged with masterminding the Siegfried Line campaign. Any combat unit available was summoned to play a part. The 2d Ranger Battalion, an elite organization that played a critical part in neutralizing the Omaha Beach defenses and then spearheaded subsequent operations across France, moved to the Belgian border under attachment to CCA of the 5th Armored Division.

Wounded on D Day but having recovered sufficiently to win a DSC during the battle for Brest, Lt. Bob Edlin, a Ranger A Company platoon leader who had been wounded on Omaha Beach, relished a month-long sojourn at a rest camp before trucking to the Huertgen area. "You could always tell when it was getting time to go into combat. Good things started happening. We were visited by General Eisenhower. The whole battalion gathered around, and he just flat out asked if anybody could tell him why we didn't have the new boot packs. One of the men yelled out, 'Hell, everybody back at headquarters has got them,' which was true. Back in army headquarters and corps headquarters and division headquarters, everyone was wearing boot packs, parkas, and warm clothes. Up in the front lines [that gear] never leaked down. We were still wearing summer clothing, and the temperature was now down in the low thirties, high twenties. General Eisenhower said that [it would] be taken care of and, God rest his soul, it was. A few days later, we received boot packs and even wristwatches. He must have raided the whole damn headquarters to get enough for one Ranger battalion."

The table of organization for a Ranger battalion listed 500 soldiers in six companies of sixty-two men each with three officers. Each company carried its own aid men, and headquarters company fielded communications specialists, the requisite clerks, and supply people. The Rangers operated with abundant small-arms firepower but lacked any heavy weapons. Their original mission was to strike quickly and hard, then turn over the position to larger units. But as the Allied armies had moved across France, the Rangers had been employed more and more, as if they were an ordinary infantry battalion. The resultant casualties and the absence of Ranger-trained replacements meant an infusion of GIs with neither the physical nor psychological screening or extended training that had previously marked the outfit.

Sid Salomon, a Ranger captain who participated in the capture of the strategically vital Pointe du Raz Percée overlooking Omaha Beach, noted, "Cold weather and a driving rain did not help the morale of the inexperienced American troops. Trench foot and casualties helped to add to the confusion that was rampant. After one month of fighting, the Americans had barely advanced twelve miles into Germany. The Rangers of Baker Company were amazed to see the GI equipment, clothing, and even weapons that had been discarded by the division troops who had previously held this area."

Frank South, a medic and an original among those who stormed the heights during the Normandy invasion, said, "We were placed on repeated alerts for various attack missions on the 4th, 8th, and 11th, each of which was called off. Finally, on the 14th we were detached from the 5th Armored and assigned to relieve the 112th Infantry Regiment. We moved by convoy to the wooded area near Germeter, where temporary battalion headquarters and the aid station were set up. The line companies were placed either in perimeter or reserve positions. On the way in, the convoy came to a crossroad and received direction from a combat MP who suddenly emerged from the trees. Our motor pool driver, who had to go to a rear depot for supplies during the following month, was amused that the MP became harder to see or find. He was no longer hidden in the trees but would emerge briefly from a foxhole, which became deeper and deeper each time they passed, precisely as in a Bill Mauldin cartoon. He was justified since the crossroad received a fair amount of artillery fire." Like the others during the forest's November, South remarked on the deepening cold, the freezing rain. The Rangers of the line companies began to use quarter-pound charges to break the frozen surface before they dug.

"The entire battalion," noted South, "came under artillery of varying intensities. We dug in, as it became apparent that we might be held there for a day or two and were even able to cover our entrenchments where the medics slept with logs that had been felled. I caught a shell fragment in the arm. The wound was too light to warrant anything but cleansing, a few sutures, and bandaging. Until then, I had been becoming convinced that I would be one of the few to make it through the war with impunity."

During this period, the Rangers operated patrols to ensure contact among their companies and to gain intelligence on the enemy. One four-man patrol, led by Bob Edlin, poked through the woods to the outskirts of Schmidt and saw few signs of activity in the town. The patrol team agreed that this might be staged to lull the Americans into a trap, and Col. James Rudder, the 2d Ranger Battalion CO, concurred. In any event, after several days in the Germeter-Vossenack sector, the 28th Division relinquished its responsibilities in favor of the 8th Division. The Rangers passed into the status of a reserve for that organization.

It was not until 18 November that the last of the Keystone Division soldiers, the men from Bill Peña's 109th Regiment, left the area bound for Luxembourg. The 28th at this point was in tatters, no longer an effective organization. Cecil B. Currey, a former member of the 28th, wrote in his book *Follow Me and Die* of the 110th: "By 13 November all officers in the A, B, C rifle companies were listed as KIA, MIA, or WIA or evacuated with trench foot or combat exhaustion.

"Not only did Able Company have no remaining officers, neither were any NCOs left. Baker Company consisted of only four men, three privates, and a sergeant. Charlie Company had twenty-three men but only one NCO. In Dog Company, only two officers and six privates were still carried on the roster. Their MIA statistics were high; Able Company lost thirty-eight, Baker lost forty-four, Charlie counted thirty-nine, Dog suffered eight.

"These figures become even more poignant in light of the fact that the 1st Battalion began with 871 men and received nearly 100 replacements [like Alexis] during the fighting. When its remnants returned to the battalion assembly area on 13 November, only fifty-seven men stood there. Medics immediately evacuated thirty-seven of these because of trench foot, wounds, combat exhaustion, or a combination of all three. Only twenty-five out of nearly 1,000 men could still function as infantry. In the next two days, perhaps fifty men straggled back from the front. Most of them were evacuated because of trench foot."

The entire 28th incurred 5,684 battle and nonbattle casualties. Attached units added another 500 soldiers to the totals. (German losses were estimated at 2,900.) Along with horrific figures for dead, missing, wounded, and otherwise disabled, the organization also suffered the loss of an incalculable amount of savvy, highly trained men whose ranks would only be replaced in numbers rather than quality.

Dutch Cota later told the survivors, "I am *very, very* proud of the fight that you men have put up and of the results you have accomplished. It cost us heavily in killed and wounded. You who have come through this fight know full well the hardships and heartaches that the soldier must endure during battle. It has been rough and tough. History will record you men of the 28th Infantry Division can take it and hand it out. I congratulate you on a job WELL DONE!"

His comments must have seemed small comfort to men of the 28th. At all high levels of command, from division up through the First Army, there was no talk of "a job well done." Cota and his closest advisors talked about "certain weak links in the training of the division, both tactical and command and staff." Gerow blamed, among other things, the failure of the division artillery commander to keep close contact with battalion artillery. Everyone at the top agreed that they had been misled by status reports from the combat units. No patrols attempted to gather intelligence on the defenses in front of Vossenack and Schmidt. The maps left out such important items as the huge minefield Hubert Gees knew as Wilde Sau. Missing from these critiques was any question of the basic strategy—head-on assaults on the redoubts of the forest.

Lt. Gen. Courtney H. Hodges, a West Point dropout, veteran of the American Expeditionary forces during World War I commanded more than 250,000 soldiers in his First Army.

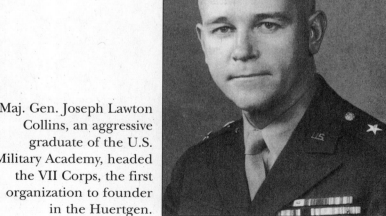

Maj. Gen. Joseph Lawton Collins, an aggressive graduate of the U.S. Military Academy, headed the VII Corps, the first organization to founder in the Huertgen.

Maj. Gen. Leonard Gerow, a planning specialist, led the V Corps during its forays into the Huertgen and his inability to achieve the objectives brought a tongue lashing from Hodges.

The first GIs from the 110th Infantry, members of the 28th Division, entered the woods 2 November while the trees still had branches. It is believed that few of these riflemen survived the blizzard of shot and shell that followed.

The narrow, twisty Kall Trail prevented tanks from readily moving forward to support the embattled soldiers of the 28th Division.

Medics tended a pair of wounded on the slopes of a hill early during the Huertgen campaign.

Flooded roads denied easy passage to U.S. vehicles like this jeep crawling through the woods.

Infantrymen from the 8th Division occupied the badly battered town of Huertgen during the final days of November.

Incessant bombardment by mortars, artillery, planes and small arms denuded the once lush green forest to stands of scarred tree trunks.

Pfc. Thomas W. Gilmore, Company 1, 121 Infantry, weary of combat as the campaign dragged into December, clutched his bazooka.

The mighty Schwammenauel Dam resisted both Allied efforts to destroy it from the air and feeble attempts by the Germans to open its gates. It was captured by the 1st Battalion, 309th Infantry and engineers of the 78th Division.

A tank from the 5th Armored Division prowled the streets of the village of Huertgen after it fell to the Americans.

M-10 tank destroyers from the 893d Tank Destroyer Battalion traveled along a forest road to aid the besieged soldiers of the 28th Division.

On snow-covered ground a bazooka team blasted one of the huge pillboxes that confronted the GIs.

Temporarily out of harm's way, men from the 121st Infantry trudged out of the forest after their ordeal.

During a respite from the action, a soldier cleaned the mud encrusted tracks of an armored vehicle.

From behind a low wall, a mortar man attempted to register on a target.

As night approached, soldiers stood watch at the edge of a wooded area.

A jeep plowed through the innundated streets of Huertgen while the shattered buildings testified to the fury of the fighting.

Engineers used fallen trees to create corduroy roads but the mud frequently claimed the repairs.

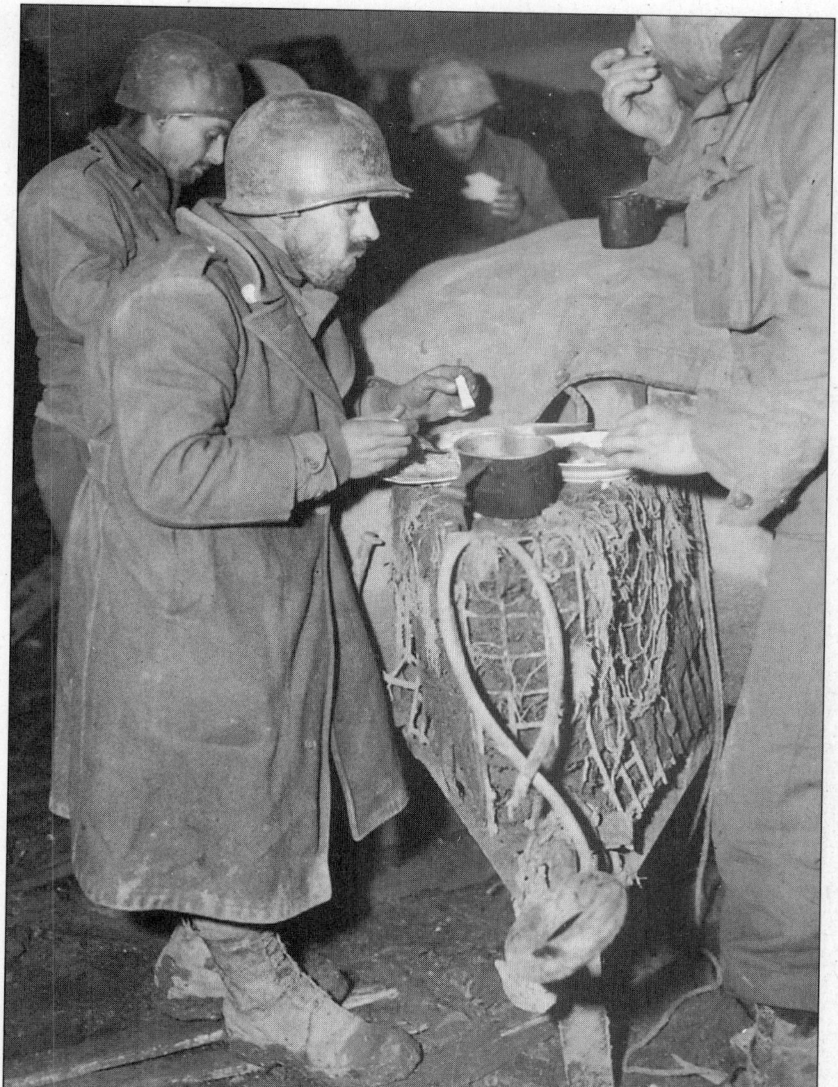

The china platters seem out of place as American infantrymen eat their first hot meal after fifteen days of siege in Huertgen, Germany, 5 December 1944.

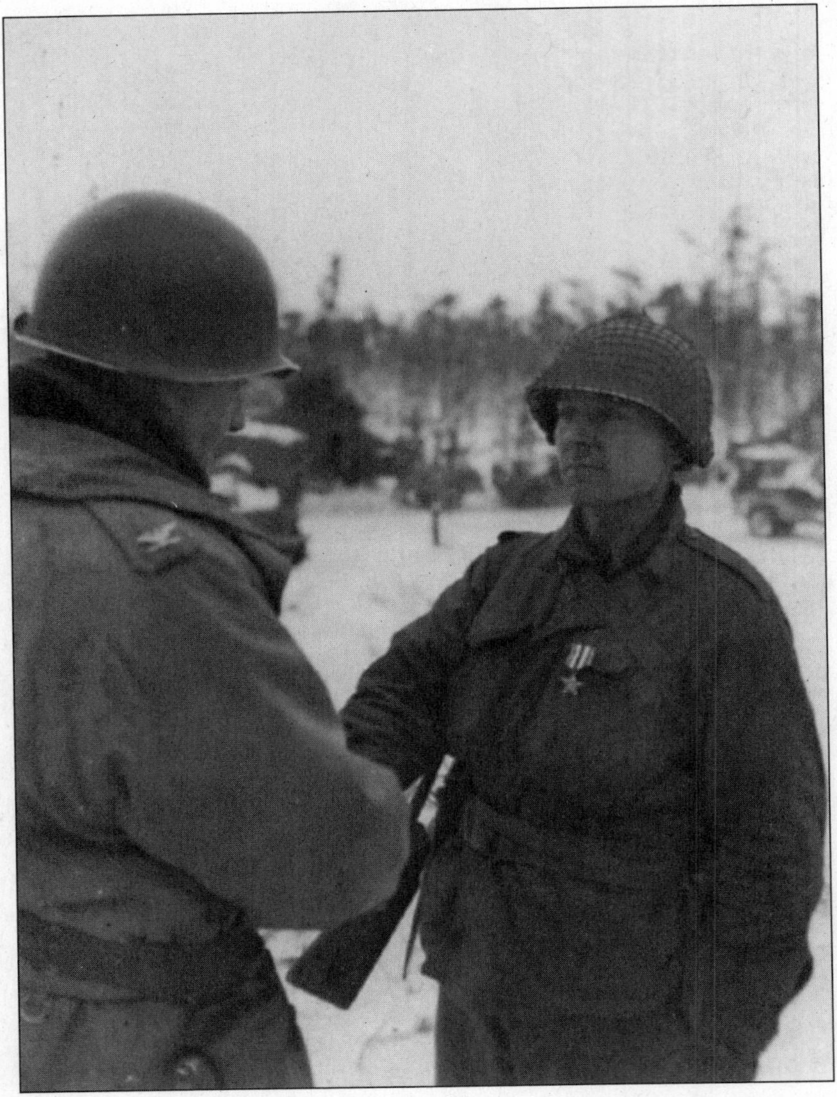

Technical sergeant Harry A. Burroughs, 8th Infantry Division, is awarded the Silver Star by Col. Thomas J. Cross, commander, 121st Infantry Regiment.

10

The Start of the Great November Offensive

Originally, the plan called for the new offensive to start as early as 10 November, but through the 13th, the weather refused to cooperate. Heavily overcast skies, frequently punctuated by outbursts of rain or even snow, canceled air missions. And while the strategists vainly waited for more benign skies, the ordeal for some American tenants in the forest continued. On 10 November, while the men of the 28th Division and the 707th Tank Battalion vainly struggled to maintain the semblance of an organized armed force, at First Army, Sylvan summarized: "Situation was more or less status quo. The need to hold Vossenack; 1st Bn. of 109th in north and 2d Bn. of 109th and 3d Bn. of 112th made astonishing progress to within 1,000 yards of Huertgen." What is truly astounding is the credence the First Army granted to any indication of success, for it was obvious to anyone except perhaps those at Hodges's headquarters that the 28th Division soldiers were themselves under siege. The first reinforcements, the troops of the 12th Infantry, had already been repulsed with such tremendous damage that the outfit could not play any immediate role in the coming offensive.

The appalling conditions soon seemed to blast the unwarranted optimism and hopes. Sylvan noted the next day: "Gen. Gerow was closeted in Gen. [Hodges] office this afternoon from 2 until almost 5:30. The Gen. is still far from satisfied with the situation and the relief of 28th Div. Concerned with what steps to take to enhance the military situation. Main question of the day was about the weather, and preliminary reports gave no cause for hope and the final report telephoned shortly before 12 o'clock being no."

With the First Army still grounded by the atmospheric conditions on 12 November, Sylvan deadpanned, "After lunch Gen. left for the VII Corps, where Gen. Collins tried unsuccessfully to woo away from

Gen. Gerow most of the latter's troops. It was snowing." Again, the meteorologists advised Hodges of weather problems, with the comment, "There was a one in 1,000 chance of sun tomorrow."

Regardless of the visibility, whether the First Army counted on an element of surprise or not, it cloaked Operation Queen under the darkness of top secret. But the Germans were well aware not only of the coming offensive but also who would be involved.

Platoon leader George Wilson, who joined E Company of the 4th Division's 22d Infantry just before the Saint-Lô breakout, was at the Elsenborn ridge area during the first week of the month. "Long after darkness on [9–10 November], the 4th Division leapfrogged some thirty miles farther north along the German-Belgian border. This was to be a highly secret maneuver, so elaborate pains were taken to erase all signs of our identity. Divisional and regimental numbers were blocked out on all vehicles, and the green four-leafed ivy shoulder patches of which we were so proud were removed from our uniforms. All personal letters bearing the division number were burned.

"Our blacked-out trucks took long, confusing detours to the rear to mislead local enemy agents, and we arrived at our new post before dawn, sleepless and miserable. It was something of a shock early that morning to pick up the English-language propaganda broadcast of Berlin Sally, welcoming the 4th Division to its new position in the Huertgen Forest." No one determined the sources of information for German intelligence, but, as Wilson pointed out, the disappearance of a known organization from one sector and the arrival of an outfit with its identity hidden a short distance off could hardly be a coincidence in the eyes of a watchful enemy. Furthermore, the long delay because of weather problems between the inception of Operation Queen and its actual start enabled the Germans to acquire an accurate picture of what they faced.

Perhaps because word of the enormous damage done to the 12th Regiment might dampen morale of the other elements of the 4th Division, on 16 November, its commander, Gen. Ralph O. Barton, visited the command post of the 22d to state, as written in that organization's journal, "that the 12th Infantry has made a remarkable recovery." Five days later, however, Barton relieved the 12th's commander. Lieutenant Colonel James Luckett moved to another division, while the unit itself, in the words of the historian Edward Miller, "was in no condition to do anything more than secure its own position."

As part of the offensive forces, the 1st Division marched from their sites in the Aachen area to the toeholds held by Americans in the Huertgen Forest. Warren Eames, a replacement, caught up with G Company in the division's 18th Regiment outside of Aachen, where he endured his baptism by fire in the grim contest for the heights labeled Crucifix Hill.

"We left our positions on Crucifix Hill," said Eames, "between 7–10 November. Up front we lost track of time, never really knew what day it was. Instead, it seems as though, like Indians, we judged the season by the increasing cold and bitter weather." To shield his body against the lowering temperatures, Eames donned an extra olive drab shirt and a sweater. "We started out in the darkness on what proved to be a very long march to the south and at double time also. After an hour or so, in which there was no respite or slowing down, I became so overheated that I thought I could not stand it any longer. I thought I would pass out. In the midst of this long and arduous march, I began trying to peel off some of my excess clothing, no mean task, since I was loaded down with rifle, sixty pounds of pack, entrenching tools, blankets, canteen, and two extra bandoliers of M1 cartridges, which I wore crisscrossed over my shoulders. The bandoliers were the first to go. I pulled them off and threw them away. Then I tried to take off my combat jacket, one half at a time, in order to tear off the sweater and extra shirt underneath. Somehow I succeeded in slipping off half my pack straps, getting shirt and sweater undone and ripped off my left side. After much effort I got [them] off my right side and threw them away in the dark." He would soon regret the loss of the extra garments.

"Sometime before dawn, we reached our destination, a bivouac area in the deep woods. There, in the dawn, we tried to pitch our pup tents in the pouring rain. The ground was very sodden, and we were completely exhausted from the prolonged march." To his dismay, there were no further orders despite their forced march. Instead, they waited out day after day under seemingly endless cold mists and rain that inundated their encampment. The prolonged inactivity stemmed from the delay of the attack and the 18th's initial role as the reserve troops.

"Walking through these woods in the daylight was a fascinating sight. The whole 1st Division had moved there, and there were thousands and thousands of men in pup tents, sprawled up and down the hillsides of the western part of the forest. The 1st Division had a reputation for being nonconformist, and they certainly were in their dress. Soldiers were everywhere 'out-of-uniform,' wearing all kinds of miscellaneous captured clothing; many of them had camouflage scarves made from parachutes and crazy hats. I found [that] up front anything went. Officers, too, were totally changed in their behavior from stateside. They were considerate, easy to get along with, and did not shout at us. The prime reason was that with so many bullets flying around, it was absolutely certain that any unpopular officer would end up dead of a stray bullet.

"While we were in bivouac, they handed out a large number of citations and medals for valor in the Aachen battle [contrary to the remarks of Sylvan on commendations]. We had a large contingent of boys from Tennessee and Kentucky, and they just loved to fight. As a matter of fact, it soon became too quiet for them there. They could not stand a few days rest, and soon bad fights broke out among them. If they couldn't be fighting Germans, then they had to fight among themselves, and officers would have to stop them.

"J and I talked a lot in the pup tent [which they shared] to pass the rainy days. J was a little runty guy, and he hated the war with a passion. He told me repeatedly that he planned to surrender to the Germans the first chance he got and he meant it. I was disgusted with him. J had a best friend in the company, E. J., a bespectacled little intellectual who had the same ideas. They spent a lot of time trying to figure out a safe way to safely defect to the Germans. Most everyone wanted to get out of the war, but this was cowardice."

Although Eames and his associates languished in reserve, the 16th Infantry drew the assignment of exploiting the 47th Infantry's tenuous grip on Schevenhutte to gain the objective of Hamich. The 9th Division organization, temporarily attached to the 1st Division, would operate on the left flank. The 1st Division's 26th Infantry, meanwhile striking from the right flank of the 16th, would threaten Langerwehe and Merode.

The outpost established by the 47th Infantry's 3d Battalion at Schevenhutte acted as an assembly area for the 1st Division soldiers. During their prolonged stay, frequently under artillery and mortar fire, the GIs in the Schevenhutte area had nestled in the remains of buildings and created reasonably well-protected bunkers. Henry Phillips, who commanded the heavy weapons company for the 47th's 3d Battalion remarked, "In their more permanent and improved positions, troops of the 3d Battalion shared their improvised stoves and shelter with the less fortunate newly arrived, and all troop leaders moved among their men inspecting the conduct of foot massage exercises and daily sock changing prescribed to minimize the danger of trench foot."

While waiting for the clouds to vanish, Hodges toured his combat divisions. Sylvan noted, "Today, preliminary for the big show, he went to 1st Div. CP on the top of a hill in captured German bunker, personal HQ of Gen. [Clarence] Huebner. Aside from telling Gen. Hodges that everyone in the 1st Div. says they fight differently than the rest of the army, Gen. Huebner was perturbed about decorations for 1st Div., although it is the most dec. [decorated] div. in the 1st Army. Gen. Huebner still insists that his div. should receive more, since 12th Army Group has now put a quota on the number of decorations that may be given out in a month per outfit. Gen. Huebner's wishes will in all probability not be granted.

"From the 1st Div. the Gen. went to the 4th Div. In the absence of Gen. Barton, he had a brief chat with Col. Roddwell, the assist. div. commander. A long talk with Gen. Davis at the 28th Div. followed. Gen. Davis [explained] the failure of the 28th to hold Schmidt, and bad showing afterwards [occurred because they] did not get armor up forward quickly enough, because of the terrain." The post-mortem served more as a distraction than as a valuable lesson for the immediate future. The November offensive, with its enormous preparatory aerial and artillery bombardment, and the infusion of elements of three infantry divisions were expected to rout even the most stubborn enemy from the Huertgen.

As 13 November passed without an opportunity for the Air Corps to blast the enemy, a new window on 14–16 November automatically appeared. However, Hodges insisted that even if the weather remained unfavorable, the attack would begin on the 16th. On that day, Bradley sat at the breakfast table with Hodges, and, according to Karl Wolf, the executive officer for K Company of the 16th Regiment, the First Army commander glanced out the window and remarked, "Just look at that ball of fire—that's the sun." His audience laughed but Hodges then warned them not to stare too intensely, "or you'll wear it out and chase it away."

Operation Queen commenced shortly after 11 A.M. with broken clouds at 1,500 feet and a light fog that permitted two miles of visibility at an altitude of 8,000 feet. To avoid incidents of friendly fire, antiaircraft batteries lofted red smoke shells to indicate the American positions, while the troops set out orange-colored panels marking their front lines, and the RAF contributed eleven barrage balloons as additional markers. From Eighth Air Force fields in England, 1,204 four-engine bombers dropped 4,120 tons of fragmentation bombs, designed chiefly to kill and wound soldiers. A thousand heavyweights from the RAF dumped more than 5,400 tons on rail lines, roads, marshaling yards, and other installations in Düren, Heinsberg, and Jülich, which might act as hubs to feed reinforcements and supplies into the Huertgen defenders. Fighter-bombers from the Ninth Air Force also smashed at known enemy emplacements and any armor or artillery caught in the open.

Henry Phillips reported, "Following the heavy and medium bombing deep in the enemy's rear, screaming P-47 Thunderbolts dived in to drop their destruction on Gressenich and Hamich and other towns up the Wehe Valley. Many of the dive-bombers, deceived by the smoke and dust of earlier bombings, dropped their loads too far to the enemy's rear to be of the best ground support. The single tactical air control party in the vicinity of Schevenhutte was incapable of correcting this to any great extent."

As the aerial assault faded, a TOT (time on target) synchronized artillery barrage thundered into the village of Gressenich, less than two miles from Schevenhutte and the objective designated for the 1st Battalion of the 47th Infantry. Fearsome as the combined weight of a five battalion artillery fusillade was, the German defenders rallied sufficiently to greet the GIs rushing from the woods with deadly small arms. Nevertheless, the Americans doggedly advanced. The defenders, perceiving themselves threatened by encirclement because of the 3d Armored Division gains to the north and the thrust by the 1st Division in the east, abandoned Gressenich to soldiers from the 47th Infantry, for the first achievement of the November offensive.

About a mile northeast of Gressenich was the objective of the 1st Division's 16th Infantry, the village of Hamich. Two companies of German soldiers held Hamich and the woods in front of the attackers from the 1st Battalion of the 16th Regiment. The platoon leader, Lt. John Beach with C Company of the regiment, recalled, "From the first to the eighth of November, we remained in the rear preparing for our next attack toward Hamich. For several days, we occupied the woods near the town of Schevenhutte, a few thousand yards from Stolberg. The weather was the worst we had experienced since Normandy. Trench foot attacked many. Provision was made to move one platoon at a time into the town to dry out. Inclement weather delayed our attack for several days until the 16th of November. In the many artillery barrages while staying in the woods, we lost four men. One was killed, one wounded, two were cases of combat fatigue who had to be sent to the rear. In addition, three were victims of trench foot."

"The platoon was down to thirty-six men. Two squads of machine gunners from D Company were attached to me for the attack. I therefore had fifty-six men under my command at the jump-off line. To my left was Jim Wood [a fellow platoon leader]. Our orders were to move out at 0830 no matter what happened." Beach said his orders directed him to attack "regardless of casualties. . . . If we were hit by artillery shells, we should leave our casualties where they lay and keep on moving." Toting a Thompson submachine gun, he followed instructions after the enemy began to fire artillery, killing one man and wounding another. "We left him behind to be picked up by the medics. Harassed constantly by artillery, we moved forward; the shriek of shells and the loud crack as they exploded over our heads acted as a sort of devil's serenade. My squad leader fell, his shoulder pierced by a fragment. The compass I was carrying to guide me through the woods was knocked from my hand. I called the assistant squad leader forward and told him to take charge of the men. Having nothing to guide me, I moved forward, by dead reckoning, attempting to follow the edge of the forest to my right.

"The shells rained down like hail and two more men fell. I could do nothing for them other than discerning they were still alive. I had to continue. Then, Kuhn, who had been in the rear with the supporting squad, came up and reported he was the sole survivor. The rest of his squad had either been killed or wounded by shell fire. Dyer, with the other front squad to my left, had been lucky so far, having not lost a single man so far. We came to the enemy's barbed wire entanglements. A machine gun fired on us, hitting a man in the throat. The fire came from a small gorge to the right. I saw an earthen emplacement from which the machine gun was spitting death at us. Woody could not bring his platoon forward unless the gun was knocked out.

"I fired into the slit from which the machine gun protruded, while Strickland, now acting leader of the right squad, fired some antitank grenades. A few well-placed grenades fell into the open top of the emplacement, killing most of the crew. The two surviving Germans immediately jumped up with their hands in the air. We disarmed them and sent them to the rear, making sure the machine gun could not be used again. A second machine gun emplacement met us as we moved forward and effectively stopped us. By a direct assault, we killed one man and wounded another, taking the remaining prisoner. We were now coming out of the woods to a group of buildings—Woody's objective.

"Woody came up with his platoon and we conferred briefly. 'All right, Beach, here's where I leave you,' he said. 'I'll see you later.' We didn't expect that our next meeting would not take place until three months later, in a German prisoner of war camp.

"I swung over to the right and counted my men before continuing the advance. They added up to fourteen left out of the fifty that I had started with a few hours before. I was studying the map when Dyer interrupted. 'There's a Heinie,' he observed. A German was rushing toward us with fixed bayonet. Dyer stood up and one of the men already taking aim behind us shot the enemy down within two feet of us. I looked down at the map again. We had to cross an open ditch to reach the final area, and I posted the fourteen men there as best I could before being called back to company headquarters.

"No sooner had I arrived there than I received a frantic call that the Germans were counterattacking. I rushed back to my position. The Germans had pushed back one squad, killing four men and taking the area they were holding. Strickland was out there wounded. Dyer was holding up the remaining eight men. A particularly heavy enemy burst came from one direction. I yelled, 'Dyer,' but there was no answer.

"A German in front of me began waving a white flag. A moment later, German medics ran out from cover, turning over the green-clad bodies to determine who survived, dragging the living out of the firing area. I carefully relaxed the finger with which I had taken up the slack on the trigger of my tommy gun.

"I was no medic, but there were some of my men out there, too. If only those who were wounded could be given first aid, perhaps carried to the rear, their lives might be saved. Deciding to take a chance, I laid down my submachine gun, stood up empty-handed and walked quickly but carefully toward the spot where several motionless olive-drab figures lay. Suddenly, I heard the enemy machine gun open up again. Simultaneously, I saw flashes of fire from beneath and alongside the white flag and felt sharp stabs of pain in both legs. I felt paralyzed.

"I could see the German medics ignoring the Americans but hurriedly caring for their own wounded. Having dragged the last of them away, they scurried back to the safety of their own positions. Around me I could see the bodies of my own men, but I could not tell whether they lived or not.

"A few yards away, I began to make out the shadowy shapes of silent soldiers moving in; in the distance, an occasional rifle spat, the bullet crackling overhead. The darkness grew rapidly, and I commenced to shiver uncontrollably in the gathering coolness. The underbrush rustled. In a moment, I stared at the downy cheeks of a boy perhaps eighteen years of age, a determined look on his face. He was preparing to pull the trigger of a vicious-looking machine pistol pointed straight at my nose. In despair, I raised my hands and in what little I knew of the German language told him I was helpless. He pointed the muzzle of the gun away from me, nodded, and moved on down the slope. The sudden rattle of an American machine gun yammered briefly, and the German boy fell flat on his face a few feet away moaning. In a few minutes he was still."

Beach suddenly remembered a German pistol in his pocket. He quickly pulled it out and tossed it as far as possible. Later that night, several German soldiers discovered him. Using a blanket from the combat pack of an American casualty, they improvised a stretcher to carry him to a building with a large room filled with the Huertgen fallen. He watched a priest give last rites to a number of men, while medics gave injections to the wounded and changed bandages, occasionally signaling to two men with a litter, who would move quickly and remove the body of someone who had died. The place just vacated would be occupied by another man brought in from outside. Beach was subsequently removed by ambulance and taken to a hospital to receive treatment for his wounds before entering a POW camp.

The Germans counterattacked seven times on 16 November but were beaten off each time. Months later, in a prisoner of war camp, Jim Wood related to Beach what happened to him while his platoon was engaged alongside Beach's. "I got what was left of your platoon, Beach. But there were only four men left. My own platoon was down to six, while the 3d Platoon had seven. The machine gunners had been wiped out and the mortar section badly hit by artillery fire. I had dug a foxhole for myself under a fallen tree, and it wasn't long before shell fragments had chopped away most of the log.

"Youngman was a casualty. He had gone down in a blaze of glory, his hands tightly clutched around the throat of an enemy he had killed with his bare hands. Then the artillery let up, and the German tanks started to move in on us. The men I had placed on the left flank pulled out of their holes and came to my command post. One of them cried, 'Lieutenant Wood, there are five tanks coming up the road. They will wipe us out! We're getting out of here before they kill us! What are you going to do?'

"What could I tell him, Beach? My orders were to stick. I was just as scared as he was. I could see the tanks moving up. They had started to shell us. We didn't have a bazooka to fight back with. I couldn't think of anything to say and finally managed to answer, 'I'm going to stay right here.' It must have been the right answer. No one wanted to be called a coward and desert one's post in the face of the enemy. It was a pretty serious thing, and they all looked unhappy about it. Staying there seemed like nothing but suicide, but they knew they had to. Finally, one of them spoke. 'Well, if you're sticking, I guess I will, too.' They got back into their holes. Beach, we held those bastards. We got a hold of a few rifle grenades. We knocked out the lead tank. We held them. I don't know how ten men held off five Jerry tanks.

"[Jake] Lindsey, my platoon sergeant, was with me in my hole during a particularly heavy part of the barrage. Lindsey said to me, 'Seeing you tremble like that makes me realize I'm not the only one who is scared.' 'Scared,' I answered him, 'I am scared silly. I don't know when I have been so scared.' We both laughed and felt better."

The account by Wood does not describe heroic acts by any of the soldiers under him. More than a month later, Sgt. Jake Lindsey was credited with single-handedly destroying a pair of enemy machine gun nests, forcing the withdrawal of two tanks, and driving off marauding enemy patrols. While wounded, he allegedly engaged eight German soldiers in hand-to-hand combat, killing three and capturing another trio while two fled. As a result, he received a Medal of Honor. However, his purported deeds would become a matter of controversy after Beach and Wood were liberated from a stalag.

Wood reported to Beach, "Naturally, during those days there was no way of bringing up supplies, and it wasn't long before there were only a few cartridges left. During the last few days, I had only half a can of C ration to eat, and my canteen was dry." Still, by late afternoon of 19 November, the 16th Infantry occupied Hamich.

At its headquarters in Verviers, the First Army staff digested the messages from those in direct communications with the legions engaged in the November offensive. While the troops in the Huertgen Forest were a major part of the overall plan, equal attention focused on the renewed effort to blast through the Stolberg corridor to the northwest. The diarist Sylvan described the great effort: "The attack for which Gen. Hodges had waited impatiently, and Gen. Bradley believed would bring the last big offensive necessary to bring the

Germans to their knees, started at 12:45 Nov. 16 with a coordinated attack by 104th, 3d Armored, 1st Div., and 4th Div. started with use of unprecedented number of heavy bombers; 1,100 in number saturated the area in the vicinity of Eschweiler and Langerwehe, started at 11:15 and from 1:30 to 3:30, 700 of our bombers struck at eight other sites and targets. The RAF wound up the afternoon by sending over 1,150 Lancasters. Although we could hear the American heavies, we could not see them [and they couldn't see the targets]. It was not until the overcast cleared into spotty sunlight in the late afternoon that we could see the British Lancasters flying low over the CP. Rockets were used in preparations for the attacks, very important in that [for the] first time there were no shorts [bombs or shells falling on friendlies]. So effective was the counterbattery and bombing that during the first four hours only seven shell reps [enemy responses] were reported. However, the enemy troops dug in close to our line were not affected by the bombing and aided by the heavy minefields and barbed wire, considerable arms and mortar fire at our troops as they started out. The Gen. said you can't tell anything about an attack of this nature until passage [of] forty-eight hours. At midnight, the main progress was made by the 3d Armored Task Force Mills, 1st Bn., 33d Armed Inf. advancing outskirts of Hostenreid. Task Force Lovelady, 2d Bn., 33d Armored captured Werth. 1st Div., 1st Bn. of 47th Infantry to outskirts Gressenich, where bitter house-to-house fighting. 4th Div. made very little progress in the dark against camouflaged positions. Impenetrable woods. 104th Div. limited gains up to 500 yards. Ninth Army's gains were more considerable."

At best, Bradley and Hodges could draw satisfaction from the progress in the Stolberg corridor by the 3d Armored and the lesser successes of the 104th Division and Simpson's Ninth Army troops to the north of them. The Huertgen nut hardly cracked that opening day. On 17 November, the 3d Armored Division again gained its objectives, while headquarters groused about the failings of the 104th Division. Although there was little evidence of significant advances in the woods, when Hodges visited VII Corps he found, in Sylvan's words, "Gen. Collins optimistic despite the limited gains thus far reported. Gen. Collins stressed he had told the 104th Div. in no uncertain terms to get moving and moving fast. At the VII Corps the Gen. met with Gen. Barton [whose 4th Division had been inserted into the Huertgen campaign], with whom he had not talked for a long time. The Gen. said it was the worst topography he had seen in a long time, but he was under the impression they were going about the attack in the wrong way, running down a road as far as they could, instead of advancing through the woods tightly buttoned up yard by yard. Gen. Barton said the resistance was fanatical. One platoon, which had tried to infiltrate into our lines, was killed to the last man." The critique by Hodges indicates an absolute ignorance of the terrain. As those on the line testified over and over, no one was "running down a road," and the belief that the men could travel through the dense stands of trees "tightly buttoned up" was nonsense, in light of the skillful placement of German defenses.

The cheery optimism continued at the upper echelons. Though recognizing that the enemy was putting up a fierce fight, Sylvan mentioned that the 104th began to pick up its pace as the Germans abandoned their positions. "Gen. Collins told Gen. Hodges that with two more days of good weather, the enemy crust could be smashed. Today, he said there were signs it was giving due to the 1st Division's strong pressure. Tomorrow and the day after will bring excellent results."

That was hardly the experience of the 1st Division soldiers, like George Wallace. Born in 1914 and raised in Buffalo, New York, he struggled through the Depression and entered the University of Pennsylvania in 1931; he dropped out for several years to earn his annual $400 tuition before he finally graduated in 1939. He worked as a page boy and then in sales for NBC, and the navy refused him for poor eyesight. He failed his first draft exam, but in 1942 he was deemed fit for duty. Through a friend of his wife's father and with his educational background, he received an appointment to OCS, where he memorized the eye chart in order to qualify.

As a replacement officer, he crossed the Channel on D Day plus six for his assignment to A Company in the 1st Division's 16th Regiment. "I was so green, I couldn't tell the difference between incoming and outgoing. I learned on the job." By the time he reached the Huertgen, however, he had gone through the hedgerow fighting and been treated by medics for injuries from butterfly antipersonnel bombs dropped by German aircraft.

"In the Huertgen, we held a more or less defensive position. The Germans had a way of holding a line, then pulling back, and you would occupy their holes. But they had [by artillery and mortars] registered those holes. My foxhole was half full of water. We must have had 30 percent of our men disabled by trench foot. I kept my radio in a tree, and I got cut across the face by splinters caused by our own artillery. You always smelled the cordite [from explosives], it was constant."

While Wood and a handful of survivors of the 1st Battalion had been pinned down without conquering the objective of Hamich, and Wallace with the 3d Battalion held a static line, on the morning of 18 November, the 16th Regiment dispatched the 3d Battalion to seize Hamich. Karl Wolf, executive officer for K Company, recalled that along with L Company his outfit led off. "By noon, they got into town, where there were German soldiers and three German Tiger tanks, as well as six more German tanks with infantry coming down the ridge from the northeast. The Germans put up a fierce defense and continued to counterattack. Our planes dive-bombed the German tanks, hitting some, but two of our planes were shot down.

"I set up K Company's command post in the basement of a house about a half block from the cross street in the town that had a row of houses, which K Company had been able to reach before holding up and digging in. The town had not been cleared of all Germans. That night we were in for some excitement." During the earlier engagement, the duels with enemy armor and antitank weapons disabled five of the accompanying Shermans and tank destroyers, leaving only two tank destroyers and a single tank to repel a counterattack.

"The enemy came down on K Company from the northeast to reenter Hamich," said Wolf. "Five German tanks and 200 infantry got into town. In our command post about 2200 hours, I got a telephone message that a German tank had gotten through the platoon lines and was headed down the road toward our command post location. I made the men turn off all the lights and be quiet. Sure enough, the German tank rolled up and stopped outside our house while we were in the basement. I was afraid they would put a round through the basement window, and we could become a statistic.

"After waiting about fifteen minutes, there was suddenly a big explosion and flames outside. Next, a German officer came running down the stairs screaming. Private First Class Carmen Tucharelli, a bazooka man, had worked his way back from his front line position and fired his bazooka from a second-story window across the street into the German Mark VI tank. This caused the gas tank to explode as well as the ammunition in it. It lit up the sky and caused the German tank officer to be severely burned. This was what he had been screaming about. He was our prisoner in the basement until he could be evacuated after things settled down.

"During this night, some posts of our platoons that were in foxholes or buildings were overrun by Germans, both foot soldiers as well as tanks. The platoon leader would radio back the situation, and we, in turn, at the company command post would advise the battalion headquarters. When we were certain we could pinpoint on the map the exact position of the Germans, I would radio back to battalion to get artillery fire on that position. Several times that night I had to call down artillery fire on our own positions to prevent being further overrun. This action was pretty extreme, and I had a difficult time convincing battalion that I had not made a mistake on map coordinates, because they knew we had previously reported being in position at those coordinates. I figured that our soldiers were well dug into defensive position, and we might well catch the Germans moving in the open. Finally, I told them on the radio that I knew the location was correct and that we did have our troops located there, but we needed the fire desperately. They finally ordered the shoot and it worked. I didn't hear of any casualties among our men, and it had driven off the Germans. Sometimes in battle, risks must be taken, and this was one of them."

According to an American summary made well after the great offensive, the attackers captured 114 German defenders of Gressenich and Hamich on the opening day of the November deployment. During the penetration of Hamich by the 3d Battalion of the 16th, the report insisted, "Enemy losses were very high, but the enemy had no intention of permitting our occupation of his critical block without dispute. . . . Hill 232, that constant thorn, was finally reduced in the afternoon by the 2d Battalion, 16th U.S. Infantry, following an artillery barrage, which can best be described as stunning. Fifteen battalions laid on an area no more than 500 yards square and included a high percentage of heavy artillery. When it was over, the 2d Battalion took the hill without a conspicuous struggle. Many prisoners were taken, most of them from the 12th Fusilier Battalion and all of them in a dazed condition." Exploring their new turf, the GIs found a honeycomb of dugouts and tunnels under construction with the obvious intent of further strengthening the natural defenses.

Determined to restore their positions, the Germans plotted a massive counterattack, spearheaded by a large number of tanks. But, said the analysts after the fact, the tremendous artillery that fell on the Wehrmacht troops and the difficulty of relieving the most badly battered organization with fresh units created considerable confusion. To confound matters further, the lieutenant chosen to lead one group of tanks accompanied by foot soldiers in the dark over rugged terrain was unfamiliar with the area. He set off in the night and soon lost his way in the woods. He strayed straight into positions held by C Company of the 16th, and the GIs leveled heavy fire on the armor. The German officer reversed course only to track again in the wrong direction, where U.S. forces rained down artillery on the column, killing the tank guides and many of the soldiers with the armor. The tank with the lieutenant now clattered down the main street of Hamich, and it was this Mark VI that fell victim to the second-story bazooka round with its hapless officer, seriously burned and seized by the GIs under Karl Wolf.

Desperate to retake the most advantageous terrain sites, the Germans continued to hurl counterattacks that originated from Langerwehe. A German general declared, "All guns will fire to the last shell, and once the last shell is expended, the gun crews will fight as infantry. Only when there is no longer ammunition for the infantry weapons will an order be given to destroy the guns." Entire companies that numbered something less than 100 men were annihilated along with five Mark V tanks, a couple of self-propelled assault guns, and other vehicles.

But the defenders stubbornly refused to yield, extracting their own substantial toll. Colonel Frederick W. Gibb, the 16th's commander, sent a message to division headquarters three days after the attack: "I will need 500 more replacements. We had 491 evacuated, between 120 and 125 killed. I am hurt for leaders. In B Company we have only two officers and thirty-two men left. C Company has three officers and thirty-five men."

Oswaldo Ramirez, an 81mm mortar section leader for the 16th Infantry when it first touched Omaha Beach, became the 3d Battalion's liaison officer with regimental headquarters in an effort to improve coordination. As dead and wounded from the battle for Hamich piled up, a shortage of line officers limited effectiveness. Regimental Commander Gibb, after debriefing Ramirez on the situation, dispatched him to serve as a line officer under Capt. Everett Booth, CO of K Company and the shards of the 3d Battalion.

Said Ramirez, "Commanding remnants of the 3d Battalion [Captain Booth] had led an attack on an enemy position on the high ground north of Hamich, captured the hill, and was holding out in the basement of a shattered castle. By requesting artillery fire on his own position, he had managed to repulse a number of counterattacks by enemy tanks. However, he was uncertain as to how long he could hold out.

"I arrived at this place early in the evening, after a long and perilous trek punctuated by constant enemy artillery fire. I found the basement crowded with wounded soldiers, all strangely silent, nursing their own wounds and gashes. Captain Booth promptly gave me my specific assignment. I was to take charge of the men surrounding the approaches to the position. The men were deployed in foxholes guarding against possible enemy counterattacks. This was exactly the same charge that Lieutenant Lazo had when he was hit by a direct mortar shell a few days before.

"Captain Booth [said] I should move out and assume charge right away, and that an artillery observer, already familiar with the ground, would accompany me in case I needed to call for artillery support. As he and I started to climb out of the basement, an enemy artillery shell exploded right over our heads, striking the artillery man and blasting me from the top of the ladder to the floor of the basement, where I remained unconscious for a while. Upon regaining consciousness, Captain Booth suggested that I wait until morning.

"By morning the situation had changed. Elements of the 2d and 1st Battalions had cleared the woods in our immediate area, and the enemy seemed to be pulling out altogether. Captain Booth and I reconnoitered the grounds and identified the bodies of 2d Battalion men killed during the assault on that hill. This was a required operation for Graves Registration purposes. It was heartrending to find bodies of comrades with bandaged lacerations, men who had stayed with the attack despite their wounded conditions."

The third leg of the 1st Division, the 26th Infantry, attempted to advance along an extremely narrow front east of Schevenhutte, with the eventual mission to wheel right toward the town of Merode, just beyond the forest. Once the 18th Infantry entered the battle, the 26th also provided immediate protection for that organization from hostile action originating in hills to the northwest.

Colonel John Seitz, the 26th's commander, assigned his 2d Battalion to gain enough space for a wider attack. But, as elsewhere, the Germans refused to cooperate, restricting the breadth of the front. The pace of progress, measured in yards, incited General Collins's anger. The VII Corps chief upbraided Huebner, who in turn heckled Seitz, "Got to take a few chances and get going." The regiment sent both its remaining battalions into the thick woods amid a near avalanche of small-arms, mortar, and artillery fire. Wet weather reduced the forest trails to muddy sloughs, impenetrable for American armor.

The hard-pressed 2d Battalion paid a stiff price for the mile of real estate obtained in three days of grueling combat. The inevitable counterattack ensued. Following the artillery barrage, Pfc. Francis X. McGraw of Company H emptied his machine gun at the oncoming soldiers until they halted. When the enemy tried to set up a machine gun, McGraw rose far enough out of his foxhole using a BAR to eliminate the weapon. A nearby explosion knocked the automatic rifle from his grasp, but he retrieved it and destroyed another machine gun. He continued shooting even when wounded, and when the BAR ran out of ammunition, he tried to hold off the charging

Germans with a carbine. A burst from a machine pistol killed him. A posthumous Medal of Honor went to his survivors.

The casualties mounted, and medics such as Paul Treatman of Company C, 1st Medical Battalion, assigned to the 26th, sought to lend succor. "I was 4-F," said Treatman, "because of poor vision. General [Lewis B.] Hershey [head of Selective Service] issued a directive that those with minor disabilities could volunteer for the draft. I was a replacement until assigned to the 1st Division, which I joined on D plus eight. I was a member of a medical collecting company, sent out to relieve those at an aid station."

He recalled that on 20 November, "as our jeep, plowing through the slimy mud, approached an infantry company aid station [a large dugout, roofed with fallen timber, that could shelter perhaps six men], we saw scores of dead GIs lined up like cordwood alongside the gluey trail that passed for a road. The men's feet were perpendicular to the path, waiting for the Graves Registration men to collect their butchered and punctured corpses when conditions would permit. [Clifton] Thibodeaux and I dug a hole, a double-width slit trench close to the aid station, and completed our two-man bunker by covering it with the remnants of shattered trees. We crawled in and simply waited for calls to pick up wounded. Charlie, a Company C veteran of the African and Sicilian campaigns, and Clyde Weeces were holed up a few yards away. Litter bearers from other units were also dug in.

"It wasn't long before our squad was dispatched to retrieve a wounded man from a castle—one of several dotting the forest—half obscured by stands of trees where infantry were poised in defensive positions, their M1s aimed at unseeable enemies. The castle was about 200 yards off. A tank covered us as we scudded through the gate in the castle wall. The casualty was sheltered in what looked like a small storage room at ground level. He needed blood plasma, and it was Charlie who volunteered to return alone across the killing ground to the aid station and secure the container, an act for which he was subsequently awarded the Silver Star. A medic attached to the infantry company administered the plasma.

"Just as our squad was carrying the wounded man beyond the castle wall, an incoming mortar shell burst nearby. It hit too close for

Weeces's comfort, and in a panic he dropped his litter handle and hit the dirt. Thibodeaux, Charlie, and I somehow managed to steady the litter and prevent its occupant from falling out. An infantry lieutenant observing the scene some forty feet away screamed at Weeces, 'Get back to that litter, you yellow son-of-a-bitch!' Weeces did, and we raced the infantryman back to the aid station. I do not believe Weeces was cowardly. It was the one time he panicked. When weeks later he transferred to an artillery unit, I bade him farewell with a twinge of envy in my heart.

"The day after the rescue from the castle, while Thibodeaux and I lay shivering in the damp of our hole, waiting for the next call, a lone mortar shell struck a tree just a few yards away, killing instantly a medic who at the split second of his death was peering into our hole, asking us to come out, impatient for us to come out, and help him find some casualty he had heard about.

"Tremors of fear and pangs of guilt—should we have emerged when he asked us to?—instantly shook my body and chattered my teeth as I lay supine on the carpet of damp leaves matted underneath me. Contemplating this sudden brush with extinction, I asked Thibodeaux for the only cigarette I ever smoked during my time in service. The dead man, nameless to us, was one of thousands of callow replacements, as I myself had been, who were fed into the maws of the Huertgen and became dead meat almost immediately. The new man never knew what hit him, but I did. When I finally mustered enough courage to creep out and inspect, I noted that shrapnel had pierced or severed his spine. Our squad was relieved after six days in a struggle that would last six months. I became twenty years old that week, and miraculous survival was my birthday present. It was a gift of time."

Although Americans occupied both Gressenich and Hamich, the slow advances and the inability to smash through the German defensive lines continued to dismay Hodges and Collins, who advised Huebner of their displeasure. He quickly committed his reserve outfit, the 18th Infantry.

"We moved up to the front," said Warren Eames of G Company, "and took positions in foxholes. The Germans sent a lot of special shells in our direction, 'screaming meemies,' because [they] let out a screaming sound as [they] came at you. No matter where you might be, the shell sounded as though it was going to land right on top of you and was obviously a method of psychological warfare.

"Even worse, the Germans started sending over V-1 rockets, called 'buzz bombs' from the sound of their engines. Most of this was at night and deprived us of sleep. The engines were very erratic and would seemingly conk out from time to time, giving you the impression that it was then going to crash onto us, but after a few moments lapse, it would start up again and go on over, much to everyone's relief.

"At this time, we had some new replacements come into our company to replace men lost in the battle at Aachen. One of these new men was a tall, gaunt, and slightly stooped man with a dark complexion who looked a great deal like Abraham Lincoln. I never did get to know his name, and he was killed a couple of days later. Our platoon medic was killed by a shell. This came as a shock, as we always took some comfort in the medics who were with us, knowing they were there in case we were wounded.

"It was the middle of November now and very cold and miserable all of the time. Our foxholes, burrowed into shale rock, filled with seeping water, which soaked us through as we sat in them. German shelling was sporadic; about every few minutes, there would be a shell going over somewhere. Up front, a little ahead of us, there was heavy fighting going on. Our days and nights were spent listening to screaming meemies. I was in a foxhole on the side of a hill sloping toward the German positions, but I couldn't see much of anything at night because of the dense forest cover. It was totally different from our situation in Aachen, where everything was exposed.

"The Germans had buried what were called 'shoe' [*schu*] mines. These were small mines that were encased in wood, and therefore our mine detectors were of no use in locating them, and they were big enough to blow a man's foot off. There were many casualties from them.

"Another thing we had not experienced before were tree bursts—mortar and artillery shells exploded high up when they hit the trees, showering down shrapnel in every direction. Tree bursts were one of the first causes of battle casualties here. Because of all this, most everyone stayed in their foxholes as much as possible. There were a lot of jokes about the multipurpose use of our helmets. Under heavy fire it was often just too dangerous to leave your foxhole, so the helmets were used to shave in, bathe in, cook in, and even shit in, because you could then throw it out of your hole without exposing yourself.

"I began getting paranoid about taking all this shelling without being able to dish it back. Along with the water, earthworms would be wiggling all around the edge of the foxhole when you awoke in the morning. They began to weigh on my mind. I had the feeling that I might be killed and they would eat my body, so I methodically smashed them with my rifle butt.

"The afternoon of November 20, word was passed down that we were going to 'kick off' in a frontal attack on the German positions at 0630 the following day. The objective was ultimately the town of Langerwehe, located to the northeast of us. We waited in silent anticipation."

After the Rangers reverted to the control of the 8th Division, four companies, C, D, E, and F, withdrew behind the front, although still within range of enemy mortars. Able and Baker Companies remained in the Germeter vicinity, with the latter unit deployed on the extreme right flank of the 121st Infantry.

Frank South, a medic with the 2d Ranger Battalion, was located to the rear of the line companies. "It became obvious to the aid station personnel and our medical officer, Capt. Walter Block, that we were too far away from the companies to be fully effective. We moved to what had been a German troop shelter at a crossroads near Vossenack. Here we could keep our litter jeep close by; the ambulance was left back in the woods because it was too conspicuous.

"When we entered the troop shelter, we medics were shocked to find several wounded Americans there. In addition to abandoning equipment and supplies along the road, the 112th Infantry Regiment deserted some of their own wounded in their haste to retreat. Of course, we took care of their injuries and immediately evacuated them. We wondered if they had been left behind in the expectation that the Germans would overrun the position and tend to these wounded.

"Artillery and mortar fire varied from desultory to intense. The line companies were widely spread as they continued to probe the enemy. Although other activity was largely confined to the night, because the Germans could see almost every movement we made, the medics had little choice. They invariably moved to a wounded Ranger regardless of when or where he was hurt, and the need for evacuation was radioed back to the battalion aid station. Because of the severe cold, we had to take every means to evacuate our wounded rapidly.

"As soon as word was received, Charley Korb [another medic] and I would rush to the always ready litter jeep. We paused to let it warm up—we couldn't afford to have it stall on the road because of artillery fire—and sped as fast as possible to the closest point to the company. We carried litters, plasma, temporary splints, and anything else that might be needed to supplement whatever the company aid man might be able to do. Usually, we were guided to the casualties, and one or two Rangers would help us get him to the jeep and strapped onto a litter if necessary. In daylight, we were always fired upon by artillery, mortars, and small arms during these trips, which were roughly parallel to the German positions. Consequently, we never tarried, and Charley was expert at the art of dodging pot[holes] and shell holes. Back at the aid station, the wounded was given whatever treatment available under supervision of Captain Block. Then the man either returned to his company or rode in an ambulance to a field hospital."

The First Army remained more than content about the November offensive. On 19 November, Sylvan wrote, "The 104th Division prodded into action by Gen. Hodges, and Gen. Collins made excellent advances on the left flank of the [1st Division] and gained up to six kilometers. Other elements west of Stolberg advanced 2,000 yards. House-to-house fighting on the outskirts of Eschweiler. 1st Division likewise continued to move ahead against stiff resistance. Story was told today that Gen. Collins had given Gen. Huebner hell when the latter protested that the 1st Division was holding the enemy in check. 'Hold the enemy in check,' protested Gen. Collins. 'I don't need you to do that, I want you to advance. This is an offensive.' The 1st Division advanced in some places more than a mile, while the 1st Bn. of the 47th Inf. led the way to advance to Hill 187 north of Nothberg. The 18th Inf. entering between the 26th and 16th advanced the 3d Bn. to the edges of Wenau. The 4th Div. continued to meet extensive wire entanglements and mines with little change in the front line. Tonight the 3d Bn. took an enemy strong point capturing 40 PWs and inflicting heavy casualties. Today the 8th Div. officially assumed responsibility for the 28th Div. Sector, and the 1st Bn. of the 109, the last remaining element of the 28th, began its march."

The diary laconically records the entry of still another American infantry division in the Huertgen, the 8th. Like its predecessors, all of the outfit's previous combat experience would not save it from the hell of the Huertgen. Now attached to the 8th Division was the 2d Ranger Battalion, which was previously listed as assigned to the 28th Division.

11

We Were There to Be Killed

When the attack of the 28th Division crumbled, the first outfit hurled into the breach came from the 12th Infantry Regiment, part of the 4th Infantry Division, with its distinctive shoulder patch of ivy leaves. That attempt to regain the advantage ended with a badly depleted 12th withdrawn to a defensive position.

On 16 November, early in the afternoon on the same day the 1st Division soldiers began their assault toward Hamich, GIs from the 4th Division's 22d Infantry, following the massive artillery barrage, left their assembly point at Zweifall and entered the forest. The objective was Grosshau, a village to the east between Hamich and Germeter. In addition to the three battalions of foot soldiers, the attackers included armor from the 70th Tank Battalion and the 803d Tank Destroyer Battalion, a 4.2-chemical-mortar unit, assorted engineers, and medics.

Only light resistance cropped up, until, just short of a mile beyond the line of departure, the Germans greeted the leading 2d Battalion with a torrent of mortar and artillery blasts that forced the men to halt and dig in. The other pair of battalions swung north and south to cover the flanks of their comrades ahead of them. Everyone settled in for the night and prepared to renew the drive in the morning.

Dr. Bill Boice, a chaplain, wrote in his *History of the 22d U.S. Infantry in World War II:* "As each battalion dug in for the night, new orders for the next day arrived. It was almost impossible for plans to be set forth more than twenty-four hours in advance. As reconnaissance patrols were never able to extend more than a few hundred yards in front of the lines, troop leaders rarely knew the exact disposition of hostile firepower until they actually exposed themselves." Indeed, the inability to operate on little more than an ad hoc basis and without effective intelligence about the defenses doomed the soldiers of the 4th Division to blindly grope toward their objectives at an exorbitant cost in blood.

George Wilson, a platoon leader in F Company, while placing his men in a perimeter defense, suddenly fell into a hole and for several minutes lay stunned at the bottom. When he recovered, he completed his rounds and then with his runner sought to find the foxhole as their home for the night. In the darkness, it could not be located, and the two men were obliged to dig for themselves. When morning came, some of his soldiers explored the void into which Wilson had dropped. They discovered that it actually led to a dugout in which four frightened Germans quickly surrendered. "I couldn't help thinking," recalled Wilson, "how lucky I had been they weren't fanatics who would have finished me off as I lay stunned at their feet."

The battalion resumed its progress, with F Company trailing in reserve, but the lead companies met strong opposition from soldiers ensconced in log bunkers with the backing of machine guns, mortars, and artillery. "Our casualties were prohibitive," said Wilson, "and the wounded had to be carried out on stretchers in a continuous stream, since not even a jeep could find a path through the dense forest.

"The front line companies frequently were held up for long periods, and during those times F Company was caught without foxholes. We also picked up more shelling than we would have if we had been able to keep moving forward. Once, when we were in a thick grove of thirty-foot-tall reforestation pines, a shell hit a tree only twenty yards ahead, and we all dove for cover. Almost instantly, another shell took the top of the tree right over my head and I was knocked silly.

"I got up and ran like a madman. I must have covered 75 to 100 yards before a glint of consciousness got through. My head was reeling and my hearing was gone, but I turned around and made it back to the platoon. Five or six of the men had been hit, three very seriously. One had a grapefruit-sized hole in his back, and air sucked through his punctured lung."

Minutes later, a messenger informed Wilson that he now commanded F Company. Although the day started with six officers in the outfit, only he and another second lieutenant remained. Company commander Flanigan was a KIA, and the others were all evacuated for wounds. A shell struck battalion headquarters, wiping out the 2d's CO and two of his staff. When the executive officer moved up to take charge, he, too, was wounded and his S-3 killed.

"A little before dark," continued Wilson, "I received orders to move F Company up to the front and dig in to the right of G Company. As I was doing this, an officer appeared and pronounced himself our new company commander. He took over and began by ordering me to have the men dig in along the edge of a gully to our right rear. My experience told me this was a dangerous position, so I suggested he have us move up the hill, because gullies usually were natural targets for German artillery. He refused the advice and insisted we dig in where he'd said at once.

"We had barely started our foxholes when, to my disgust, the enemy artillery plastered our gully, one terrible shell after another. I immediately stood and flattened myself against the thick trunk of a big beech tree and yelled at the men to get up and find trees. A few of them had time, but many were hit before they could move.

"Our new commander broke down in tears, blubbering about how it was all his fault. He kept at it, and when I realized he was completely out of control, I called battalion to report the situation and was told to send him back to the aid station.

"Very soon, another officer was sent to take command of the company. He was a good man, a combat veteran who had been wounded earlier. Though not yet fully recovered, he was being rushed back into a special hell called Huertgen.

"He was just not ready. On a cold November day, beads of sweat plastered his forehead; his fingers trembled so much he couldn't manage to light his cigarette. Next day, he went back to battalion headquarters and was sent on to the rear. It must have been hellish to come back to the front lines after a serious wound.

"Since headquarters apparently had no one else to send up, I was left in command of F Company once more. I felt totally inadequate. I was sure I could handle a platoon of forty-some men in combat, but I was overwhelmed by the responsibility for a whole company with its four platoons and a headquarters section."

The devastation that befell the 2d Battalion shattered the other elements of the 22d. Don Warner of Company A, like so many of his contemporaries who entered the Huertgen as a platoon leader and emerged as company commander, told the historian Edward G. Miller, "We were there to be killed, and the sooner you realized it, the better. Lord knows, they were dropping like flies."

On the first day, the 1st Battalion commander, Maj. Hubert L. Drake, was killed, and the 3d Battalion commander, Lt. Col. Arthur S. Teague, was wounded. So many of the officers had been cut down that the regimental commander, Col. Charles "Buck" Lanham, instructed the replacement for Drake not to share a foxhole with his executive officer. The drain on experienced company leaders further impaired combat effectiveness.

Bill Boice, a chaplain with the 22d, like the other clergymen, threw himself into the desperate efforts to treat the wounded. "Perhaps they had been patched up after a fashion by the forward aid man, but the casualties were too great and the wounds too many for him to be able to see all of them, and so back they came in an ever-increasing stream, some on litters having to be carried through mud, setting their teeth at every jar, or crying out in pain as the litter bearer slipped and perhaps dropped his end of the litter. Streams had to be forded, and, indeed, it seemed as if nature and God himself had turned his face away from this embittered and tragic regiment.

"At 0200, a railroad gun had fired from Düren, some five miles away, and had hit upon a dugout occupied by three officers. The dugout had a heavy roof of two layers of six-inch logs, but the shell, having landed beyond the dugout, blew back in. One officer was killed outright. Another, a TD officer, was wounded in the chest. The third, an infantry officer, had his right leg broken in a compound fracture, the shrapnel passing on through his left ankle, leaving a hole the size of an egg. Strangely enough, the pain came from the broken leg, and in the dark the officer put a tourniquet on the broken right leg, not even knowing his left foot was injured. And so he lay through the hours of the night—long, bitter, terrifying hours—while he constantly bled, growing weaker and weaker, and feeling the great grayness approaching closer and closer. Nothing could be done, for in the hell of the inferno of artillery which continued minute after minute and hour after hour, no creature could move with impunity, and it would have been sheer suicide to attempt evacuation under these conditions. Indeed, the evacuation could not be effected until eight o'clock the following morning, when a litter party had to remove the two layers of logs in order to evacuate the two living officers to the aid station.

"In the aid station, the battalion surgeons, working under strain, loss of sleep, and the pressure of increasing casualties, still continued to work quickly and effectively. Blood plasma, priceless life-giving fluid, was quickly rigged and administered. The wounded officer was given four bottles, and now for the first time some semblance of life began to appear in his ashen cheeks, but with it, stupefying and heartbreaking pain.

"They were placed in the ambulance, these wounded, two litter cases, carefully slung in racks, with the wounded sitting on the floor and on the seat along the side. Then the ambulance started down the makeshift road toward the safety of the collecting station. A man with an arm off at the shoulder tried to sit erect. The ambulance lurched as it headed for the ravine and the bridge, which had been thrice blown out by enemy artillery. The driver increased his speed, for he knew there was intermittent fire on this bridge and that it was by luck and a prayer that any vehicle got across without being hit. Ambulances, like any other vehicles, were fair prey for artillery. The increased speed over the rough roads, pockmarked by shell and mortar, had the effect of a medieval torture rack on the broken men within.

"The collection station, set up in a German farmhouse, was busily working, since the wounded from the entire combat team were collected here. Every wound was quickly examined, and the wounded sorted into categories. The walking wounded sat in one room on the floor or on chairs or simply stood, staring vacantly at one another.

"In the next room, the litters lay on the floor so close to one another that the doctors and the aid men frequently had to step on the litter itself. Aid men quickly and efficiently appraised wounds and brought into play their first and most efficient weapon, a pair of scissors, which they carried tied to their wrists or waists by a piece of Carlisle bandage. A sergeant took a quick look at the wounded captain's feet and, grabbing his scissors, began cutting the clothing from the knee down.

"The amount of clothing which the soldier wore was appalling, but he wore everything he could get his hands on in an effort to keep warm, since there were no blankets. The scissors cut through a pair of fatigues; beneath the fatigues, a pair of ODs [olive drabs]; beneath the ODs, long underwear and long socks. Now the sergeant saw the condition of the leg. He cut the clothing completely open to the shoe, but the foot lay twisted in an odd and somehow horrible position. The slightest movement of the shoe or the litter caused the soldier to grit his teeth with the pain. The sergeant took a razor blade and began to cut the laces of the shoe and the pain became excruciating. It was necessary to remove the shoe from the broken foot, and the soldier fainted from the pain.

"The sergeant had called sharply for plasma, and from a wire run across the center of the room between two windows, a T/5 had already hung a bottle and, with another stretch of bandage had twisted the tubing and had tried to insert the needle into the veins of the forearm, but the soldier had been through too much, and from lack of blood, the veins had almost collapsed. The T/5 appraised the situation and called sharply, 'Captain!' A tired, hollow-eyed surgeon raised his eyes and, without a word, immediately saw the situation. He came at once and, calling for a scalpel, he slit the skin inside the elbow, exposed a vein and expertly slipped the needle into the vein itself. Then he stood and rested his back as he watched the plasma drop by drop giving life to the almost empty veins of the captain."

During his time at the medical facilities, Boice, who bandaged wounds and even helped administer plasma transfusions, also observed a steady flow of men in emotional collapse. "The standard treatment upon the arrival of an exhaustion or combat fatigue case was to give the man narco-therapy. This consisted of enough sodium amytal to keep the man sleeping constantly for three days.

He awoke only long enough to go to the latrine, and, in most cases, he had to be helped even for this. Frequently, he was given saline intravenous injections in lieu of feeding. During this time his subconscious condition was horrible to behold, and he lived over and over again his most terrifying events of combat. When he awoke he was hollow-eyed, cheeks drawn—the shock upon both his physical and nervous system had been tremendous. He was taken to the showers, where he enjoyed a hot, invigorating shower, perhaps for the first time in weeks.

"Subsequently, it was a matter of care, perhaps of psychoanalysis, which at best was but fleeting, due to the number of men and the scarcity of psychiatrists. An attempt was made to rehabilitate him for use in the front lines—which never worked. Having once found he could be evacuated with combat fatigue, the soldier instinctively knew that the medical tag reading 'combat fatigue' represented safety for him and surcease from danger. Frequently, some soldiers made the circuit from the rest center to the front lines three or even four times. It was another one of the hells of war. The psychiatrists had no choice, for there was no other place to send the man unless he was physically disqualified or mentally unstable. If he were simply and truly exhausted, he went back to the front lines.

"It was pitiful to observe the genuine fatigue cases in the tent wards of the rest center. It was time for chow and hot chow was being served. An artillery observation plane flew overhead. The effect was amazing and pitiful. One soldier poured a cup of hot coffee over his head. Another turned his mess kit of C rations over in his lap. Still a third made an effort to dive in the latrine and had to be forcibly restrained. Some of the others crawled underneath canvas cots for instinctive protection. The wards with shattered and missing legs and arms were bad, but the hospitals with vacant and missing minds were worse."

Entering the forest at the right flank of the 1st Division's 26th Infantry was the 4th Division's 8th Infantry Regiment. Harper Coleman, a draftee out of Shippensburg, Pennsylvania, and a machine gun squad member in the heavy weapons company, had landed without incident on Utah Beach on 6 June 1944, where he saw the assistant division commander, Brig. Gen. Theodore Roosevelt, Jr., waving a cane as he urged the troops inland. As Coleman trekked into the morass of the forest, he recalled, "We had no idea what it was, or where. We knew we relieved the 28th and I had an uncle in that outfit. I remember thinking, maybe we passed in the dark as they went back through our line.

"We stayed in a number of captured bunkers, which we used to dry out and get in out of the rain. The fire going in the bunker and smoke was about as bad as being outside. It was difficult to move, but more so for vehicles and tanks. I don't recall seeing much of either. There was artillery fire, and much of it was treetop explosions with wood splinters much of a problem.

"At one point, we were in a sort of retreat through hedgerows. We were with the rifle company and had moved across a field two to three hundred yards wide with a small stream at the far end, a ditch or canal through the middle. We were under heavy artillery and machine gun fire when word started for everyone to get out as best they could. This was later said to have been said in error, but we lost several machine guns and equipment at the time.

"Several of our people in a land mine area were hurt and could not move. One of our officers convinced a group of prisoners who happened to be on hand that it would be good if they brought them out. They kept saying, '*nein*,' but in the end they do go and carry them out. Elsewhere, we were moving past a group of buildings, and a wounded German lying in a ditch asked for '*vasser.*' He kept repeating this, asking for water, and a lieutenant said, '*vasser,* hell' and shot him.

"There was a group of Germans in a sort of fortification to our left front who waved a white flag of surrender. A captain of one of the rifle companies took several men with him and went forward to accept their surrender. When he was maybe fifty yards or so from them, they opened fire, killing him and those with him. I often thought later that this was not a smart thing to do. He should have let them come to him.

"Sometime early in November, I was hit in the right arm by what I always presumed to be shrapnel, but it may have been wood. It did not draw blood but tore my clothes and caused quite an infection. My arm swelled and I was evacuated." It was not quite a million-dollar wound, because Coleman was returned for active duty about five weeks later during the Battle of the Bulge. About a week later, he developed trench foot and then left the combat area permanently.

While their comrades from the 22d butted against the stalwart enemy defenses guarding the approaches to Grosshau, the 8th Regiment jumped off in pursuit of its major objective, the Roer crossing near Düren. Deep in the forest, about a mile and a half from Schevenhutte, was the initial objective, a ruined monastery called Gut Schwarzenbroich. To reach the place, the GIs would embark on a frontal assault through a two-mile thick belt of enemy defenses. The men from the 4th Division would pass through the sector maintained by the 9th Division's 47th Infantry at Schevenhutte. Lieutenant Colonel Langdon A. Jackson, Jr., the commander of the 2d Battalion, along with his executive officer, Maj. George L. Mabry, Jr., visited the command post of the 47th to learn what his troops faced.

According to James Haley, initially with the 1st Battalion but subsequently executive officer of the 2d, "Information of the enemy defenses was very limited," although they included "barbed wire entanglements of unknown extent or type and log bunkers, whose exact locations were unknown. No information on minefields was available except that the road running east from Schevenhutte was mined and blocked." Jackson requested his hosts at the 47th CP to send out reconnaissance patrols to gain additional intelligence. Jackson was not permitted to use his own soldiers for this purpose because of security reasons. The insertion of the 4th Division and the forthcoming attack were supposed to be a surprise, and, should any man from the 2d Battalion be captured on a patrol, the game would be given away.

Unfortunately, the 47th Regiment leader denied the request on the grounds that, with his people so thinly spread over the front, he could not afford to assign anyone to the task. Jackson, Mabry, and some of their staff attempted to reconnoiter the front but the results were meager. "Observation was very limited," noted Haley, "because of the thick woods and because the commanding ground was in the hands of the enemy. No locations of enemy positions were obtained except for that of a machine gun that fired on the party. The opportunity to study the terrain over which the battalion was to attack proved of great benefit. Especially noted were the two rock quarries located about halfway up the slope of the ravine, one in the center of the sector and one on the left flank, and the two trails leading up to them." Both of these quarries were just inside the 47th's domain.

As 16 November dawned, the plans had been drawn, and while the soldiers recognized a difficult time lay ahead, according to Haley, "spirits were high, morale was excellent. The possibility that within a few days they would be out of the cold, wet, and depressing forest brought some little comfort to the men. Little did they know how long it was to be before this possibility was to materialize."

All along the forest front, the air support pounded the area with tons of deadly ordnance, but, as Haley remarked, "the enemy positions close in front of the 4th Infantry Division went untouched [because] no clearly defined bomb line close in could be defined."

The artillery that followed the aircraft, however, struck much nearer. Haley continued, "The shells could be heard whining overhead and crashing into the trees showering the area with fragments. The forest was literally being chewed to pieces by the exploding shells. Trees were shot off and fell across each other, making large areas absolutely impenetrable. However, as it was soon to be evident, the Germans were so well dug in that they suffered only slight casualties."

South Carolinean and, Clemson graduate Capt. John Swearingen, the battalion S-3, said, "We moved out, proceeded approximately 1,000 yards without opposition until all hell broke loose. The Germans had prepared and occupied a massive defensive position. They had concertina wire stacked three high, two on the ground and one on top. The enemy machine guns were spaced every fifty feet with fields of fire placed between trees. In front of the wire were mines, almost solid, with mortars zeroed in front of them."

Still, by stretching the interval between men slogging over a muddy road to conserve strength rather than attempting to cross rough, but more concealing, terrain, the forward part of the column reached positions that put them close enough for a final assault. Of necessity, the friendly artillery and mortars shifted their attention, and, no longer forced to seek cover, the enemy drenched the GIs with devastating fire from a variety of weapons. The well-camouflaged guns defied efforts to pinpoint their locations.

The Americans doggedly pressed their case, gaining perhaps 200 yards before a barbed wire entanglement, higher than a man's head, spanned the entire front. *Schu* mines blew off the feet of the first to venture close to the triple layer of concertina snarls. The Germans, hidden from sight, could target every man from E and F Companies, leading the assault.

"It also became evident," said Haley, "that E and F Companies were caught in an area on which the Germans had previously registered their artillery and mortars. In spite of all efforts, the advance was halted and E and F Companies were pinned to the ground by deadly machine gun fire from the front and flanks. Friendly artillery and mortar fire was brought in as close as possible, but still the enemy fire continued. By this time [it] had reached a crescendo. Experienced officers who had fought all through Normandy and across France, later stated that they had never before seen the Germans mass so much artillery fire on one area.

"Men trying to dig in were blown to pieces where they lay. If a man rose from the ground, he was almost certain to be hit by the machine gun fire, even if he escaped the artillery and mortars. The support platoons of both E and F Companies were committed but were stopped as soon as they hit the minefield and barbed wire. Officers and noncommissioned officers, exhibiting the highest order of bravery and leadership, moved along the line encouraging the men and trying to find some way forward until there were few left who had not been killed or wounded. Still, neither company could advance. No bangalore torpedoes or other means of blowing gaps through the mines and wire had been provided, since the information available prior to the attack had not revealed the presence of these obstacles."

At the hillside battalion headquarters, 400 yards behind the killing field, the long-range weapons of the Germans blasted the slope, putting in peril any individual not in a bunker. Jackson talked to Regimental Commander McKee by field telephone, explained the dire situation, and advised that his people had been so hard hit they could not advance. McKee ordered him to renew the effort.

Jackson summoned the G Company Commander to the CP for instructions to commit his unit. As he made his way toward Jackson, his opposite number at F Company also worked his way back in order to give a first-hand report. Before either reached the destination, a concentration of artillery shells seriously wounded both. The company commander of E Company had already been killed. The insertion of G Company only added more dead and wounded without a breakthrough in the deadly barbed wire barrier.

As night fell, Jackson could only direct the survivors to withdraw under the cover of darkness and dig in at the original line of departure. The battalion commander spoke again to his regimental leader and reported the loss of all rifle company commanders and most of the platoon leaders and noncoms. He requested his battalion be taken off the line. McKee not only refused but ordered the shaken survivors to attack in the morning.

According to Swearingen, who overheard one side of the conversation, McKee apparently accused Jackson and his men of being "yellow." The battalion commander, said Swearingen, replied, "I am not yellow and neither are my men."

Haley described an awful night. While staff officers hurriedly formulated plans and orders, he noted, "Food, water, and ammunition had to be brought forward and, the largest job of all, the wounded had to be evacuated. Furthermore, the depleted rifle companies had to undertake some kind of reorganization. The night became miserably cold and wet, but blanket rolls were out of the question. Everything had to be hand-carried up the steep slope of the ravine, and too many items took priority over the rolls. The ammunition and pioneer platoon worked unceasingly through the night, carrying supplies up the hill and bringing casualties down. The night was pitch black, and the wounded could only be found by their cries of pain. A round-trip for a litter team required from one and one-half to two hours, and many of the wounded died from exposure before they could be evacuated. The number of wounded officers and enlisted men who passed through the aid station during the night, plus those who had been killed, totaled approximately 135 men." He remarked that Jackson stayed up the entire night, drafting the script for the following day and trying to comfort the wounded.

"The battalion plan of attack for 17 November," said Haley, "was essentially the same as that for the previous day, and for this reason was doomed to failure before it began. E and F Companies were again to attack abreast in this area, in which they had been slaughtered the day before." The only two changes were a supply of bangalore torpedoes to cope with the barbed wire and the assignment of tanks to mash a pathway through the minefield and breach the barbed wire.

The noise of the armor clambering up the trail to the rock quarry alerted the Germans, who scoured the area with artillery and mortar fire, while the foot soldiers burrowed deeper into their foxholes as they awaited H hour. At 0900, zero hour, the GIs obediently left their refuges, only to discover that just one tank out of the five had made it to the line of departure. Mud and the steep slope balked the others. The sole tank gallantly led, breaking a path through the mines, but could not penetrate the wire, even though it slammed into the obstruction several times. Again, the GIs cowered on the ground, unable to move without being picked off and vulnerable to the rain of shells.

First Lieutenant Bernard Ray, platoon leader from Company F, loaded his pockets with blasting caps, wrapped primer cord about his body, and charged the barrier. As he placed the charges, mortar shells crashed down nearby, wounding him. Instead of unraveling the primer cord from his body, he simply connected it to the explosives, blowing a gap in the wire, killing himself in the process. For his act he received a posthumous Medal of Honor, but it was a futile sacrifice. Several other men, mostly noncoms, crawled close enough to place more bangalores, but the fuse igniters, damaged by exposure to mud and water, failed. The continued shot and shell from the Germans remained too deadly for any advance.

Jackson again pleaded with McKee for relief. Instead, he was ordered to hold the present positions and prepare for a third assault on 18 November. Jackson replied that such a venture was impossible in light of the condition of his forces. The regiment finally agreed to replace the 2d Battalion with the 3d for the next round.

Officially, Jackson repaired to regimental headquarters to confer with McKee. After the war, George Mabry told his son, Benjamin

Mabry, that when ordered to attack a third time, Jackson "quit." He followed the telephone wires back to the rear and was relieved of his post. Mabry, a 1940 graduate of Presbyterian College in South Carolina who went on active duty in 1940 and for his exploits on D Day earned a Distinguished Service Cross, took over the battalion with Haley as his exec.

Mabry said he was chagrined to hear McKee announce that he would write off the 2d Battalion and offered to reorganize the outfit and mount another attack. McKee then gave Mabry a day to prepare his new command for its role. About 200 replacements checked in to fill the depleted ranks, but even with these additions, the 2d Battalion mustered only about 60 percent of its complement, and the line companies carried only an average of two officers.

Meanwhile, McKee ordered the 1st Battalion, buttressed by tanks and tank destroyers, to smash through on the third day. The enemy refused to yield any significant ground. If anything, the toll on the 4th Division soldiers only worsened. Company C, committed to the fray from 18 to 21 November, managed to gain 1,800 yards before it withdrew with only one officer and thirty-five men from the 184th, who began the attack still fit for duty.

As the disintegrated 2d Battalion assembled in the village of Bend, Mabry scrounged for officers and noncoms, even cajoling a victim of battle fatigue to leave a rear echelon post and return to the front. On the morning of 19 November, the reborn 2d Battalion started out from their brief interlude in Bend. In the hope of surprising the defenders in the chosen sector, the American artillery remained silent. The strategists believed the Germans might be focused on the ongoing effort by the 3d Battalion on the 2d's left flank. Charles Haley, executive officer, watched the men en route to the line of departure. "The old men [veterans] appeared to be still suffering from the effects of the attacks of 16–17 November, and the new men appeared to be dejected and low in spirits due to the weather, the mud, and the thought of their first taste of action. Only grim fortitude and determination seemed to be pushing the wet, muddy feet of the battalion." At least one individual found the prospect too daunting. A veteran of much action, and formerly a highly effective sergeant, shot himself in the foot.

As the troops climbed a steep ravine, a machine gun on a nearby hill locked on them, and any try to evade the withering fire drove the GIs into one of the ubiquitous minefields. The scouts and others leading the battalion sought cover and refused to advance. Mabry, who with his staff had been following in the footsteps of the lead company, moved to the head of the column.

"We received heavy artillery and mortar fire," recalled Swearingen. "We heard the shrapnel zinging through the air. My radio operator was hit in the shoulder by a large piece. It severed his arm about three or four inches from the shoulder."

Arriving at the mine-seeded turf, Mabry conducted a hasty personal reconnaissance and then directed his people to detour around the hill with the machine gun emplacement, rather than try to go through the infestation of *schus* and up the slope. The functioning elements of the battalion succeeded in bypassing these obstacles, only to encounter an even more extensive minefield. Several soldiers went down, and when an aid man started to work his way toward the wounded, he, too, incurred serious injury.

In conversations years later with his son, Benjamin, Mabry said he needed to figure a way to clear a path in the minefield. Looking over the snow-covered ground, he noticed indentations in specific places, which he reasoned indicated the presence of mines. On his own, using his trench knife, the battalion commander crawled into the field and dug out the devices to clear a safe route.

Beyond this danger zone were enemy bunkers. Mabry, as he had done when he landed on Utah Beach, physically led the soldiers, with several scouts trailing him. He approached the first emplacement, kicked open the door, and it was deserted. He proceeded to a second dugout and again smashed through the entrance. Nine German soldiers came at him. He knocked down the first with his rifle butt and bayoneted the second. The GIs behind him rushed up and subdued the remainder.

The small party of Americans, with their battalion commander still in front, charged a third bunker, despite the vigorous small-arms fire. The inhabitants also surrendered. The American forces under Mabry now rallied sufficiently to fight their way through stubborn resistance to a small stream. When the lead platoons crossed to the opposite bank, the Germans from above rolled grenades down toward them. It was now late in the day, and Mabry halted the attack to tie in for the night. For this day's work, he received a Medal of Honor.

That evening, another fifty replacements appeared, and they immediately began to act as carrying parties for supplies and the removal of wounded. During the following week, the 8th Regiment's three battalions were all committed to the fighting. Working in concert but separated at many points, the Americans coped with enemy pockets that lay behind their thin front line. On 22 November, the day before Thanksgiving, the 2d Battalion was relieved, pulled back to the Schevenhutte vicinity. At a horrific human cost, the regiment had, in six days, gained about a mile, but the objective of Gut Schwarzenbroich still remained about three-quarters of a mile distant.

The accounts of many, such as Mabry, emphasize the lack of information on the nature, location, and strength of enemy defenses. In some cases the timetables established by strategy wonks denied the men on the line an opportunity to dispatch reconnaissance patrols, but the terrain also seriously handicapped units that specialized in intelligence gathering. Bill Burke, a graduate of what was then the Oklahoma Military Academy and recipient of a commission through the reserve, became a member of the 803d Tank Destroyer Battalion, which was well trained and combat experienced. Attached to the 4th Division in the Huertgen Forest, the line companies of the 803d relied on the M10 tank destroyer, which mounted a U.S. Navy three-inch gun, more effective against German armor than the standard 75mm weapon on the Shermans. However, the M10 operated under a deadly disadvantage in the Huertgen, because its open turrets left it vulnerable to tree bursts. The crews fashioned log pallets to provide some protection over the turrets.

Burke actually commanded a mechanized company in the 803d, and, among its other duties, his outfit specialized in recon. "The Huertgen was the worst place to perform recon. Vehicular mobility was limited to the few roads, trails, and firebreaks, the majority of which were zeroed in with German 88s or mines. Conducting medium/long-range reconnaissance with mounted units was extremely limited, due to terrain and difficult or lack of avenues of approach. The designed-in mobility, tactics, and missions of my reconnaissance potential could not be fully realized in the thick forest.

"Our mechanized reconnaissance unit did not seek out direct combat, because it was not equipped with armored cars and jeeps for that purpose. Instead, it employed stealth and maneuver in seeking out or maintaining contact with the enemy and wherever possible bypassed enemy concentrations." The most useful element in Burke's command was his pioneer platoon, which had the capacity to construct bunkers, build or remove roadblocks, lay down corduroy roads from the fallen timbers, and defang minefields.

While the 8th Regiment of the 4th Division struggled east from Schevenhutte, the 22d bogged down in its first drive toward Grosshau, reorganized after catastrophic losses of enlisted men and officers as high as the battalion level. On 19 November, Lt. Col. Thomas A. Kenan appeared at the 2d Battalion CP, taking over command from Major Howard "Wild Man" Blazzard, the regimental S-2 who had temporarily taken charge when, as George Wilson related, his predecessors were either wounded or otherwise disabled.

Kenan informed his four company commanders, including Wilson, of the script for the following day. As Wilson listened to the plan, a line abreast approach for E and F Companies with the flanks open and visibility extremely restricted because of the omnipresent pines, he sensed disaster.

"As a brand new company commander at my very first meeting with experienced company commanders before a new battalion commander, did I wait to find out what the others might think or did I brashly stick out my young neck?

"'With all due respect, sir,' I heard my myself saying, 'I don't like this plan, because I think it would be a major mistake to spread out so thinly with our flanks unprotected. We're very short on officers and noncoms, and, in my opinion, control would be extremely difficult. With unprotected flanks we have to be able to move very fast.'

"The colonel looked startled. and after he'd swallowed, asked if I had any suggestions. 'Sir, why don't we hit in a column of platoons? Hit hard and quickly and punch a hole through fast. That way we have our men closer together, we can control them, and we can defend better if we get hit from a flank. If we move fast enough, we might get in ahead of a lot of shelling.'

"I was sweating a little as Colonel Kenan looked around at the other officers and asked what they thought. They quickly supported me. My hat was off to the new colonel. He would listen to suggestions and be willing to follow them. The colonel thanked me. . . . We worked out some details and returned to our company areas as the colonel wished us luck."

Wilson led his company, the first time under his command, on schedule the following morning. With his second platoon up front, Wilson entered thick woods. Checking their position on a map, Wilson realized they were off course. He radioed the head of the column to shift in the proper direction and then waited for the lead platoon to adjust.

"A few moments later, I looked up to find the lead platoon tearing headlong back to us like frightened deer. When they were near enough, I jumped in front of them, waved my arms, and ordered them to stop right there. I was mad enough to use my rifle on them, and it must have shown, because the men all hit the ground and hid behind tree trunks and stared back the way they had come.

"I walked right up close to the most senior man visible and was practically spitting in his face, as I demanded to know what he thought he was doing—trying to start a stampede? I raised my voice and told him he'd better not ever again move to the rear without permission. I had not heard any enemy action up front, so I asked just what all the running was about. He said they had run into a big German tank and were pulling back so we could hit the tank with artillery."

Wilson conferred with a Lieutenant Caldwell, his artillery observer, who agreed to take a look, and when he located the tank would call down artillery on it. Meanwhile, the company commander started to tour his other elements, only to discover the rear guard missing. "I went back to the road we had crossed earlier and whipped the men out of the shell holes they were hiding in and sent them back up to the main body of the company, which was still where I left it.

"I had been gone less than fifteen minutes but it had been costly. The fine, young, redheaded second lieutenant who led the 2d Platoon had been shot between the eyes. There he was, fresh from the hospital, his first day back on the lines, and he was dead before he even saw a German." Wilson was further dismayed when Caldwell reported that the big German tank was only a log sticking over a stump.

Company F ran into genuine trouble, well-entrenched Germans, occupying high ground, which opened up with rifles and machine guns when the Americans closed within range. "We all hit the ground at once, and now no one could move. Our position looked hopeless. I crawled forward until I got the nearest platoon leader and told him to get his men going by fire and movement. This was slow and painful, but it seemed the only way, since we were too close for artillery support."

In "fire and movement," a few men crawl or run forward toward the next available cover, while their comrades lay down heavy fire to keep the enemy buttoned up. Then, others repeat the process until the objective is reached. Although the maneuver can be successful, it also risks considerable casualties and requires uncommon courage from those engaged in "movement." It is a standard tactic taught during infantry training.

Wilson realized that the main threat was a bunker with a machine gun. He worked his way to his 60mm mortar section. "The noncoms who led this section had been wiped out and not yet replaced, so I asked a likely private if he could fire the mortar. He said he wasn't sure but would give it a try. I showed him the target in a clump of trees 150 yards ahead. He and the men fired a round." But the novice had set the weapon to fire almost straight up, and the shell fell quite close to its origins, forcing Wilson and the nearest soldiers to duck for cover. That convinced Wilson to summon the artillery observer, who brought in a few 105mm howitzer rounds. "These shells, plus a few near misses with rifle grenades, finally gave the German machine gun crew the right idea and they withdrew."

However, F Company was in a dire predicament, and Wilson contacted his battalion commander, Colonel Kenan. "I spoke very carefully on the radio as I explained to him that all my officers were gone, that we were getting loaded down with wounded needing evacuation, that our ammunition was almost gone. I said I didn't see how we could continue in this condition against such a formidable enemy defense. It seemed to me I was completely objective, simply listing the plain facts, and that my assessment was correct.

"Colonel Kenan then taught me a powerful lesson in positive thinking, one I've never forgotten. In a calm, matter-of-fact voice, he said, 'Wilson, ammo is on the way over now. I know what you're up against, and I know *you can and will* continue to advance and take that line of defense.' Without another word, he broke the connection.

"I was furious. The guy back in his CP was asking the impossible. It was crazy. Then the bearers arrived with bandoliers of ammunition, and somehow we took on new life. Lieutenant Caldwell laid down some more artillery ahead of us and we moved out again. Just before dark, we knocked out the last German breastwork and cleaned out that defensive line."

Wilson and company took up abode in abandoned foxholes or dug new ones. While they had gained about 500 yards, their foe had no intention of a cessation of mortars and artillery during the night.

In the northern reaches of the forest, the 47th Infantry, attached to the 1st Division, struck out from Gressenich, beyond Hamich toward the objectives of Nothberg and Bovenberger. Success would pinch the enemy between them and the 104th Division and 3d Armored. The 47th's 3d Battalion received the assignment to clear out a nasty patch of enemy strongholds in the Bovenbergerwald.

Having reconnoitered the turf ahead of them, on 20 November, the lead platoons of the 3d Battalion jumped off at 0800. Within minutes they entered the woods, and soon the thick canopy atop the trees shut out daylight. With visibility reduced to a few feet, the advance slowed. Two hours after the start of the journey, the Company K commanding officer, 1st Lt. Hubert A. Urban, at the end of his column of GIs, paused to kneel by his radio for the hourly position report to the battalion commander, Lt. Col. Donald C. Clayman. Urban glanced up from the radio to see a group of German soldiers standing a few feet off. He quickly grabbed his carbine and opened fire. Sharp exchanges erupted after the first shots. The enemy obviously had been surprised by the sudden appearance of the

Americans. The 9th Division men rousted the Germans, but Urban realized that he could expect artillery shells on his outfit as soon as the Germans could notify their batteries.

Company K lunged through the underbrush, and just as Urban foresaw, explosions rocked the ground behind them. The unit had hardly organized a defense against a counterattack when a column of Germans, unaware of their presence, marched into them. A firefight, accentuated by a well-placed machine gun, scattered the enemy, and more than 100 of them surrendered. Urban, concerned that the hasty, but necessary, rush of his K Company left the unit isolated, obtained permission for his people to dig in for the night.

Patrols probed the adjacent territory, seeking to pinpoint the locations of friends or foes. One party from Company L attempted to reach Heistern, reportedly in the hands of the 16th Infantry. Instead, shells from tanks and self-propelled guns signaled the place either surrounded or occupied by Germans.

The battalion A&P platoon swept the road to locate mines. To save time, instead of disarming them, the A&P men covered the mines with mess kits. Even in the dark these could be seen, and vehicles drove around them while bringing up supplies. Other soldiers laid field telephone wire along the road and by an alternate route through the woods. Sporadic mortar fire interrupted this activity, wounding the battalion communications officer and several of the linesmen. The loss of these specialists, plus the persistent rain, hampered communications throughout the remainder of the operation.

During the night, orders from regiment directed Clayman to march north and seize the town of Hucheln. The 3d Battalion commander requested artillery fire to suppress resistance in the Heistern area. He was denied on the grounds that with men from the 1st Division's 16th Regiment occupying the town, the barrage would endanger them. Having seen his people fired on from the locations claimed by the 16th Regiment, Clayman was dubious but unable to protest.

At 0600, a patrol from Company L investigated the territory ahead and brought back valuable intelligence on the presence of enemy soldiers and vehicles. Artillery struck these defenders, and L

Company overcame the resistance, nabbing some 200 prisoners. With Company I right behind, the Americans advanced, breaking out of the woods to a meadow that stretched 300 yards in front of the dairy known as Bovenberg Farm. It consisted of a collection of buildings mostly enclosed by an eight-foot-high stone wall with the main structure a two-and-a-half-story stone house. A shallow stream and a wire fence encased in brush crossed the meadow.

The lead platoon, under SSgt. Raymond W. King, cautiously advanced into the open ground. Shots rang out from behind the fence, and the GIs hit the dirt to return fire. At the edge of the woods, a machine gun platoon from Company M doused the buildings with bullets while King's men charged the fence line, routing the German squad posted there. But mortar fire fell upon the Company M emplacements, shutting down the machine guns even as the infantrymen rushed toward the stone wall. Furious ambuscades from those hidden in the buildings forced the Americans to retreat to the positions formerly held by the enemy at the fence line. They left about twenty dead just shy of the stone wall.

The company commander advised Clayman of the situation and requested tanks. Although the armor platoon leader feared problems with mines embedded in the road and the thick mud of adjacent fields, he guided forward the Shermans. When they reached a point where they could see the action, enemy tanks in the woods by Heistern opened up, knocking out the lead pair of American tanks. Their companions scuttled back to the safety of the forest.

A massive artillery concentration crashed down upon the woods, where the GIs of Company I frantically sought cover. Almost every round was a tree burst, hurling jagged slivers and fragments on the hapless troops huddled below. Chester Jordan, as a platoon leader with the unit, recalled, "We were walking through open woods and just walked smack dab into the Krauts. One of my BAR men fell almost immediately, and I grabbed his gun, gave the ammo to my runner, and started shooting up the woods. I really ran amok. I shot up Germans, trees, bushes, and anything that looked like it might hold a Kraut. I ran away from my ammunition, and when I finally noticed the fact, I discovered I was the only one shooting and I was all by myself.

"Before I could run around to search for the platoon, artillery shells started falling all around. There was nothing to get under, so I lay down next to a small fir tree. I was lying on my back, looking at the treetops and praying. A shell hit the ground about fifty feet away, and it seemed like a minute after the explosion when a piece of shrapnel came whizzing through the air and struck the fir tree just above my body. The whole thing appeared to happen in slow motion. The eight-inch tree was cut almost half and started leaning slowly toward me and then rested on the ground. The butt of the tree stayed on the stump and I was not touched. It was a comfort to me to have anything over me during the rest of the shelling.

"When the shells stopped falling, I slid out of my fir lean-to and started to walk back to where I had last seen a friendly face. I came to a cutover area and was about to go around it when a squad of Germans emerged from the other side of the clearing. They moved in single file, carrying their weapons behind their necks, as they were wont to do. As soon as they were in the clearing, they cut to my left and all came into my view. I put the BAR up against a tree, ready to shoot. Then a stroke of sanity hit me. The odds were against me getting all of them, but the odds of them getting all of me looked formidable. I didn't put the safety on, but I stood very quiet."

During this period, Capt. Ralph E. Manuel, CO of I Company, observed less intensive fire in the meadow. He worked his way forward and organized a charge toward the buildings. From behind the walls of the dairy main house, barn, and other structures, machine guns and rifles slashed through the ranks, inflicting heavy casualties. Manuel split his forces, sending some to the rear of the German positions. From all sides, German tanks and antitank guns blasted those in the forest and the Americans trapped in the meadow. As the I Company captain neared the main building, Sergeant King was wounded. Manuel ordered him to report to Colonel Clayman and ask for artillery to shell the tanks and defenders, protected by a nearby railroad embankment.

Manuel and a group of GIs sprinted forward until they enjoyed temporary safety in the lea of the cement wall around the buildings. While protected against small-arms fire, they soon contended with grenades tossed over the wall. In a last gasp assault, Manuel led a charge around to the rear of the enclosure and smacked head-on into a counterattack. The GIs, led by Manuel, burst past, plunged through a door in the wall, only to be taken prisoner by a much larger force.

From his observation post, Clayman pleaded for the big guns to relieve his pinned-down troops, but 1st Division Artillery refused, insisting the target was too close to 16th Infantry soldiers. Clayman tried to raise Company L on the radio, and only after several tries did an operator respond with the news that Captain Manuel had either been killed or captured. A huge German railway gun rolled down the nearby track and heaped further misery onto the 3d Battalion's rapidly diminishing numbers. It departed after ten minutes, and later in the day American planes destroyed the piece.

Lieutenant Gael Frazier, the exec of Company L, arrived at the dugout serving as the battalion observation post. He told Clayman he was the only officer left, and the company itself was down to forty men. With the artillery forward observer missing and his mortar counterpart dead, Frazier suggested another effort by American tanks. Clayman summoned the leader of the attached tank platoon, who, according to the battalion commander, was "completely shaken and incoherent." When ordered to take his tanks to the farm, "the officer became hysterical," and within a few minutes he was wounded.

Clayman personally went in search of Company I and found the unit badly damaged by the constant tree bursts and shells from tanks. He radioed regiment, which agreed to a disengagement of what remained from the two companies. The battalion executive officer, Maj. William L. Tanner, brought forward the armored half-track prime movers for an antitank platoon, and a crew of cooks and clerks worked to evacuate the wounded behind smoke concentration under the guidance of Tanner. On the battlefield, the litter bearers encountered German medics picking up wounded GIs. The Americans relieved the enemy of their burdens and both sides retired to their own lines.

Clayman dispatched Red Phillips, the heavy weapons company commander, to explore the right flank and find the reason so much fire issued from the direction. Phillips, who had the palm of his hand torn off during the day by a shell from a high velocity gun while he rode in a jeep, could not locate Americans where the plan specified. When he dropped back to the rear, he discovered the adjacent battalion. Its commander explained that he never received an order to attack, but instead had been shifted south to reinforce the 1st Division soldiers still battling for Heistern. Unfortunately, word of the changes in the script never went to the unlucky 3d Battalion of the 47th, whose casualty list numbered twenty officers and 335 enlisted men killed, wounded, or missing. The total exceeded that of the regiment throughout all its campaigns that began in North Africa.

Intelligence specialists, men from the A&P platoon, and antitank crewmen manned a weak but organized line against an expected counterattack. Apparently, the day's action had also exhausted the enemy, for their expected response never happened. Subsequently, when he analyzed what had happened, Red Phillips credited the leadership and reactions of Company K for staving off disaster. However, he attributed the failures at Bovenberg Farm to poor coordination between the 1st Infantry Division and the 47th Regimental Combat Team. In addition, he noted a common weakness, the lack of experience among tankers and foot soldiers working with one another.

While still in reserve for the Huertgen campaign, the 18th Regiment of the 1st Division played host to a major and several other Rangers. "They had lost a lot of men," said Eames, "and they had come to our company for replacements (like a press gang in the days of the old sailing ships). After conferences with our company commander, we were all called out and lined up. As we stood in ranks, the Ranger commander went down and said, 'You, and you, and you and you,' to every other man in the front row. I was the odd man out, the men on either side of me were picked to join the Rangers, even though they had no knowledge of demolitions. The Rangers were an interesting bunch; they all had packet charges of high explosives hanging around their waists, while on their helmets, they had detonator charges all taped on, with lengths of fuses wrapped around the helmets. They were a very 'edgy' bunch and couldn't sit still. I was glad I wasn't shanghaied into that outfit."

Eames had escaped the hazards of the Rangers, but his regiment deployed toward Langerwehe, north of the fighting for Hamich. He recalled, "The afternoon of 20 November, word was passed down that we were going to 'kick off' in a frontal attack on the German positions at 0630 the following day. We waited in silent anticipation. That night, E. J. smashed his glasses so that he would not have to go. He was dutifully sent back to the rear for new ones, as he could not see well. Here and there, a soldier would shoot himself in the foot, so that he would not have to go. Foot wounds were highly suspect when they were inflicted with a bullet, and the threat of court-martial hung over the recipient. However, there were many such cases anyway."

At dawn the following day, following a bombardment into the woods, Eames and his squad, still shy two of the normal complement, gained a hilltop position looking northeast toward Langerwehe. "Beyond us was a ridge, and our orders were to take it in a frontal attack. Beyond that ridge was another one where the German front line was dug in. The Germans were anticipating us, and the ridge we were ordered to capture was being heavily pounded by German mortar and artillery fire. I had never seen such concentrated fire on one position before. We stood and watched the firs go up in shell fire. There was just no way that hill could be captured; it was living death to go out there. Ignoring the order to attack it, our outfit just stayed where they were. I wondered what in the world would happen, and where we could go from here.

"The squad leaders called for a conference to decide what to do. They and members of the platoon huddled in a forest clearing debating the next move. I stood on the outside edge of this, having no voice in what was to be done anyway. I suddenly was overcome with the feeling that something terrible was going to happen, and since I wasn't needed, I headed for a depression in the ground about fifty feet away to take cover. I had just reached it and was starting to squat down when there was a terrific explosion behind me. I was knocked flat on my face. At the same moment, I felt a burning piece of red hot shrapnel tear a hole in my upper left arm. It felt like a burning brand. Another piece of shrapnel grazed the right side of my helmet, and I was hit a blow by something on the right side of my combat boot.

"Looking back, I saw chaos in the platoon huddle. The shell had exploded right where I had been standing a few moments before. Most of the group was scattered about on the ground, screaming and yelling and covered with blood. Some of them had been killed outright. Duane Corbin had been in the middle of the men. His new ammunition carrier, who had been assigned to him only three days, absorbed the blast and was killed instantly. Duane was hit above the left knee by a large piece of shrapnel and in both arms as well. The wounded were yelling for medics. 'Ole Moe,' the squad leader, was unhurt. He came running up to me and said, 'Eames, you've got to follow me out of here; the platoon is all shot up, and we will need everybody we can get to hold the line.' So I followed him past the wounded. Men, all covered with blood, lying on the ground, cried out to me and clutched my pant legs as I went by. In this split instant, I was faced with multiple factors. Moe didn't know that I had been struck in the arm, and I could have gone back to the hospital for treatment. I decided to follow his orders and left the wounded behind.

"Not being able to help those screaming, bleeding men gave me a sense of guilt that took many years to overcome, as I elected to put my duty first. Out of all this, the Germans had decided for us what we were going to do next. Our plans to attack that ridge were ended. Duane was carried out on a stretcher, and the other men were eventually evacuated. Moe and I and my second scout, Patrick McBride, were joined by Lieutenant Stephenson in a position more to the east of where the shell blast had occurred. We all started digging slit trenches. This was a terrible task, as there was shale rock right under the surface, and we literally had to pick our way through it in order to get any shelter.

"Moe scattered sulfa powder on my arm wound and tied a bandage around it. Then we waited for night. When things finally quieted down, I wearily took my pack out and pulled out a can of cold C-rations hash. I looked at it and looked again. It had a large shrapnel hole in it from that morning's shell blast. That can of hash had stopped that big piece of shrapnel. If it hadn't, I could have ended up a paraplegic, as it would have hit me in the spine. A lowly can of C rations, which I hated to the extreme, had saved my life.

"Stevie [the lieutenant] spent much of the night with me in the slit trench. Somehow, he looked to me a lot like our new commanding general, Clift Andrus, who had been the brigadier in charge of artillery for the division. Stevie and I talked about the war for a long time. Water was seeping rapidly into the trench. I finally fell asleep with my arms over the rifle, which lay crossway across the top of the trench. In the morning, when I awoke, I found myself frozen in with a sheet of ice across my chest, which I had to break off and throw out of the hole. We had to stay in our holes because of the constant tree bursts caused by the constant German artillery fire. So we sat there, cold, frozen, and miserable."

Into the maw of the Huertgen moved other elements of the 8th Division. Arthur Wagenseil, a radio operator assigned to the 56th Field Artillery, was the son of a German immigrant. He had an uncle who wrote letters with the greeting "Heil, Hitler," which considerably angered Wagenseil's father. Wagenseil had started his career through the Citizens Military Training Program, working with French 75s that used World War I shells. He had arrived in France on 3 July and commented, "The roads were slippery, very muddy, very slick. Several times we had to manhandle the guns around the turns until we reached our position near midnight. It was pitch black, you couldn't see a thing. We unlimbered the guns and started to lay them for action. Word got out, 'Watch for mines,' as though you could see anything. Luckily, we managed to follow in the other guys' footsteps and suffered no casualties.

"We started to dig holes but there were many slit trenches already. My first one had someone in it, but at another hole it was empty and I fell into it. When daylight came we found many GIs; they were already tagged but apparently Graves Registration had not picked them up."

12

THANKSGIVING CELEBRATIONS

On the day after he was wounded but elected to remain with his G Company, Warren Eames of the 18th Infantry Regiment, along with his colleagues, was assigned to the second wave in a frontal attack, as they approached a village. "Shelling was fierce everywhere. We moved forward onto a hillside position, and the Germans were dug in on the next ridge beyond us. Off to the right flank, our Tennessee boys had made a wild attack on that section of the rough ridge, and using only entrenching tools—small picks and shovels—they were 'braining' the Germans and pulling them out of their holes by the hair. A lot of the German troops there were young fellows from the Hitler Youth and were too scared to shoot straight. I remember not being bothered by any rifle or machine gun fire from them, but the shelling was terrific.

"Down in the gully ahead of us, our old platoon sergeant was coolly directing the attack, pointing out which area was to be charged next and looking for all the world like an old farmer, his hands in his suspender straps and chewing on a piece of straw. Our group was lying on the ground about 100 feet behind all this, about as useless as we could be. Although we were the immediate reserve, we were far enough away from the Germans, so that they could shell us without hitting their own men, and we had no place to go, as we were out of our foxholes and lying on the frozen ground. All we could do was wait. One of our men appeared from the line ahead, carrying a carbine and with a German prisoner in front of him. [The German] still had his steel helmet on and was wearing the characteristic gray uniform. He had a terrible look on his face as he crossed right in front of me.

"Then what we dreaded started to happen, traversing mortar fire. Over to our right flank, there was a distant explosion, followed in a short while by another and then another nearer one. They were systematically trying to wipe [out] our second line, which was what we were. I lay on the ground and could determine the plot they were following, and it was coming right at us. A few more shells and they would be on top of us. I remember lying there waiting for death to arrive, since we could not move from the position without orders.

"Then I heard a tiny whirring whistle sound, the sound of a mortar shell coming in right on our position. There was a terrible explosion no more than a few feet from the right side of my head. This blast was nearly on top of me, and I instinctively knew that I must have been hit, but I did not feel a thing. Further back, twenty to forty feet away from me, almost all the men were wounded, and the scene of screaming wounded men was repeated from the day before.

"Mortar shells explode in an upward arc, and then the shrapnel rains down again. Since this shell hit the frozen ground, instead of being a tree burst, the men farther away from me were showered with shrapnel." Something similar happened to Eames near Aachen, where, although closest to the burst, he was uninjured, while those more distant were wounded or killed. "I felt the rim of my helmet and the left side of my head and in my fingers were a little water and a slight trace of blood. I put my hand back to my left ear, and this time it was covered with blood. The third time my hand was soaked with blood, and I knew this was bad. Still, I had no pain. What upset me then was Izzy Cohen, who was lying on the ground facing me. Izzy's face was contorted in a look of horror, and as he looked at me, he cried out, 'Isn't there anything anyone can do for him?' Then I knew I was hit bad.

"By this time blood was running down all over the front of my combat jacket. I got up and hastened back toward the rear, struggling at the same time to take off my pack, which was impeding me. I threw it away and also my rifle. About seventy-five yards to the rear were three medical aid men. They had to pry my helmet off my head, as there was a large hole in the left side of it, and the sharp edges of the steel were sticking into my head and ear. The medics worked carefully and fast, and they put a large compress bandage over the whole left side of my head, although they were so scared their hands were shaking as they did it.

"Sergeant MacAulay was there, too, his face also a bloody mess. His jaw had been smashed in the shell burst. Back there on the ground lay our new replacement who looked like Abe Lincoln. He was lying on his back with his eyes closed, and he seemed to be completely at peace. I believe he had been killed outright in this, his first action."

The medics instructed the walking wounded, Sergeant MacAulay and Eames, to hike down a fire lane to the battalion aid station in the rear. "We reached a spot where the lane forked. MacAulay thought battalion aid was over to the right; I thought it was to the left. We decided to go my way and I was wrong. We got lost and wandered through the forest. We were both groggy from loss of blood and head wounds. Meanwhile, the shelling from the Germans got more and more intense. Finally, hopelessly lost, we took shelter in a large shell crater in the dense woods. We lay there awhile, trying to decide what to do next. Suddenly, a second lieutenant with a carbine, followed by a radioman carrying a large field radio on his back, appeared. The lieutenant, a platoon leader, saw us from a distance and raised his carbine to fire at us. We stood right up with our hands way up, and he could see we were both wounded with bandages wrapped around our heads.

"He approached us warily and exclaimed, 'What are you doing here?' We told him we were from G Company and lost. 'You certainly are lost,' he said. 'Do you know you are behind the German lines? I am the point man leading an attack. Don't you know they are shooting all the prisoners out here?'"

The officer directed the pair to the correct route to battalion aid. After treatment there, Eames boarded an ambulance that carried him to a field hospital at the edge of the Huertgen. "We disembarked from the ambulance and walked down a muddy lane to the entrance. Lined up on both sides of the entrance were about a dozen German prisoners, who rushed forward to assist us walking wounded. Several anxiously ran up to me and tried to support me. But I couldn't stand to have them touch me. I flung them away. I wanted to walk in by myself and I did so."

Although the offensive faltered, the First Army expected the 8th Infantry Division, commanded by Maj. Gen. Donald A. Stroh, to capture the villages of Huertgen and Kleinhau, along with a ridge that ran from Brandenberg to Bergstein. This area, formerly the objective of the 28th Division, was southeast of the battlefields that engaged the 1st and adjacent to the 4th Division's drive toward Grosshau.

The situation on 20 November, according to Sylvan's diary, seemed promising. He noted, "Substantial progress was reported all along the First Army front with the exception of the 4th Div. area. 104th Div. occupied Stolberg and . . . was sitting on the outskirts of Eschweiler. 1st Div. had stiffer going against heavy mortar and artillery fire, but 1st Bn. of 47th attacked and took Hill 187. 3d Bn. advanced almost a mile, Heistern was cleared by the 18th Inf. 4th Division again made little progress over rugged terrain stubbornly defended by the enemy. 1st Bn. of the 8th however made almost a mile, closed the gap between the 2d Bn. and the 26th Inf. and 2d Bn. of the 28th Inf. 121st Infantry of 8th Div. last night . . . moved into assembly area preparatory to its attack this morning. Gen. Hodges motored to see Gen. Stroh during the afternoon, came back extremely well pleased with the tactical planning which had evolved. Gen. Hodges especially noted that Gen. Stroh thought he was being particularly well supported by a remarkable amount, 18 bn of artillery, and was confident of success.

"Attack was to jump off at 9 o'clock. I heard Gen. Hodges say, wait until 11, it will be more favorable. . . . He was pinning much hope on the success of the 8th Div. attack tomorrow. If the attack should fail, advance of VII Corps to the north could be seriously hampered. Paid greatest compliment to Gen. Stroh's tactical ability. With a halfway break in the weather, we could push the Boche back a good piece."

The 8th Division's chief of staff, Col. Tom Cross, a native of upstate New York, had served on the Mexican border before World War I. He graduated from OCS in 1918 and with the 3d Division was shipped to France as a member of the American Expeditionary Forces. With the 8th Division, having fought from Normandy to the Siegfried Line, Cross had been at a newly opened recreation center for officers in Luxembourg when, around midnight of 13 November, he heard of a possible move north to relieve the 28th Division. In his diary, he noted that the 13th Regimental Combat Team (part of the 8th) moved at 0700 into the V Corps sector to relieve the 110th Infantry. "Reports indicate that our new sector is a tough one and has been the graveyard of two other divisions."

Subsequently, he listed the mission of the division's 121st Infantry Regiment as an attack supported by division artillery and rocket guns to capture Huertgen and Kleinhau. "Then [it would] protect against counterattacks for the north, east, and southeast. Then the 22d and 12th Regiments to capture the woods north and east plus attack by CCR of the 5th Armored division, which will make the main effort followed by the 121st."

But because the brutal introduction of the 4th Division's 12th Infantry to the Huertgen had left that unit palpably damaged, instead of an orderly transition, the First Army hastily dispatched the 8th Division's 121st Infantry from its base in Luxembourg, 107 miles away. From his command post, General Stroh issued urgent instructions to the 121st commander, Col. John R. Jeter, telling him to move his men "at the earliest practicable time."

Jeter's battalions, beginning on 19 November, traveled through rain, sleet, and snow in largely uncovered trucks, and for some men the journey lasted throughout the night. They had little time to orient themselves to the peculiarities of the forest when they passed through the lines of the tattered 12th Infantry to take their places for the 21 November offensive.

Cross remarked, "Only one battalion [the 3d] of the 121st arrived in time for a good night's rest and to make essential dispositions for the attack. The 1st and 2d Battalions arrived late. The last one was not in position until 0330. Men had not slept in two nights. The attack should have been postponed for twenty-four hours and time devoted to resting the men and for company and platoon commanders to make reconnaissance. The battalion commanders of the 121st so recommended, which I passed onto the commanding general without gaining approval."

Among the veterans of the 121st was Stephen "Roddy" Wofford, a student at Texas A&M at the time of Pearl Harbor. He signed up with the enlisted reserve in June 1942, which enabled him to continue his education for another nine months before being called to active duty. He completed the OCS program at Fort Benning. "I thought our training was top notch. I feel my ROTC experience at A&M gave me a real edge in understanding what leadership really was and how to get along with people. I believe I would have been better prepared for combat had we been given more 'live fire' exercises."

Assigned to a rifle company as a platoon leader with the 80th Division, he was dispatched with many other second lieutenants shipped overseas as replacements. He landed on Utah Beach on 16 July. "A couple of days later, I joined A Company, 121st Regiment, and was in my first combat. That first day, even though I was in reserve, I lost every NCO except one. That was my baptism of combat, and I was mortally terrified. My brain seemed to function independently of my body. I saw my first casualties.

"I had absolutely no idea of what was involved in our movement to the Huertgen. I had no personal contact with anyone from the 28th but saw many of them in trucks as they were being evacuated. I didn't think they looked any better or worse than any other troops who had been in combat. I heard 'You'll be sorry' several times while we were passing, but that was normal for combat troops.

"I think our Company A was at about full strength on going into the Huertgen. We had been in a quiet sector in Luxembourg and had been able to build gradually to full strength. We had no opportunity to reconnoiter the position we were to occupy. We went into it at night, taking the same position as the company we relieved. I suppose this was done at night because of the urgency, and also because this position was in a fire lane in the forest and the Germans could see us in the daytime.

"I'll never forget the flash of the artillery that night. It was continuous and gave us some light to see the foxholes that the 28th had been using. What disheartened and demoralized some of our men was finding corpses in the holes they were trying to occupy. It was a terrible way to start any operation. To be truthful, I never knew where the artillery was coming from. I assumed it was German, and it was dangerous because of the tree bursts. My main impression was that we were 'fresh fodder,' and it didn't seem we had much choice about anything."

Norris K. Maxwell, a Texan, like Wofford, attended the Texas College of Mines and Metallurgy for two years, before he went on active duty through mobilization of his National Guard unit. "I graduated in the first OCS class at Fort Benning, 27 September 1941, and the commissions were presented by an unknown brigadier named Omar Bradley."

Maxwell became a captain specializing in communications. He was working in the replacement system in England when he volunteered to substitute for a captain stricken with "foxhole fever." Assigned to the 8th Division, which he joined before the Saint-Lô breakout, he took over A Company of the 121st, an outfit temporarily under command of Roddy Wofford, then a second lieutenant. Maxwell remarked, "I had never taken a field exercise with a rifle company. My first infantry exercise was against the German army at Brest. We took our objective and captured prisoners; it's what's known as on-the-job-training."

His memory of the trip to the Huertgen is similar to that of Wofford. "We detrucked in a cold, driving rain and attempted to feed a hot meal. It got dark and a guide from the 12th Infantry came to lead us forward. It was a nightmare. You couldn't see, just hold onto the pack of the man in front. We finally stopped to get some rest. I had the impression I was sleeping in a creek, cold running water. Daylight and we took over the foxholes of the 12th, who got the hell out of there fast."

Paul Boesch, a first lieutenant and executive officer of Company E in the 121st's 2d Battalion, recalled the words of an officer from the 28th Division's 109th Regiment when he arrived to arrange quarters for the troops being pulled back to the 121st bivouac and was asked about conditions in the forest. "It's hell. Pure, unadulterated hell. That's the only word for it. It's hell. You haven't heard anything about it, because they're afraid to talk about it. That's it, they're afraid to talk about it. The Germans tore up our division. Tore it up. They kicked the crap out of a lot of other good outfits too. I've been with this division since we landed in France, and I never saw anything like it. It's artillery, tanks, mines. Everywhere mines. God-almighty, the mines. And Jerries. Everywhere stubborn, stubborn Jerries." The sight of the defeated soldiers of the 28th conveyed to Boesch, a 220-pound, former professional wrestler and free spirit, an ominous foreboding of the coming combat.

Boesch's battalion entered the forest and the positions of the 12th Infantry in the dead of night. The executive officer could hardly believe his company commander when he told him the attack would begin at 9 A.M., without any opportunity to study the terrain or mount intelligence patrols.

As a member of the 56th Field Artillery for the 8th Division, Arthur Wagenseil discovered how difficult it would be to carry out missions. "We were amazed how little space there was for our gun positions. At the same time, we noticed a small reconnaissance tank on the perimeter of the woods, where a downed ME-109 was still smoldering. I went over to look and saw two boots with feet still in them up to the shinbones. The rest of the body, what was left, was covered with dirt. The tankers started up, turned their radio on, and left. Within several minutes, the 88s came zipping in and everyone hit the dirt, crawling to the foxholes."

Troops from all three battalions of the 121st slogged forward after the opening salvos of artillery, which continued to thunder overhead as the foot soldiers and their associates in armored units, according to the division and corps blueprints, closed on the enemy defenses.

Maxwell scoffed at the notion of a carefully plotted operation. "Briefing before Huertgen? None! We knew nothing about the forest or what was facing us, intelligence on the enemy, and the fortifications. There was no formal meeting of company commanders with a briefing by the staff and orders from the battalion commander. The only words were 'go, go, go!' Reconnaissance? That happens only at service schools. Orders were to attack straight ahead, exact orders, 'Follow those tanks.' The tanks bogged down way back of the front. No trucks, jeeps, or any other vehicles, just mud and riflemen. No boundaries were designated. My flanks were wide open. I could see the Huertgen-Germeter road on our right. B Company, 121, was on our left but there was no contact. There was no fire support—no heavy machine guns or 81mm mortars from D Company.

No forward observer from the artillery. The only artillery was incoming, and it was accurate and heavy."

All three elements of the 121st encountered the same obdurate Wehrmacht defenders, deadly minefields, tangled masses of barbed wire, machine gun nests, and a wicked rain from artillery pieces and mortars. Net gains for a day in the killing fields were registered in figures such as fifty yards. Efforts to bring forward tanks failed, either because of the morass of wire and mines or skilled use of the *panzerfaust*.

Boesch, supervising the 60mm mortar squad, watched Companies E and F jump off on schedule. "They took two pillboxes; that was all. It quickly became apparent that this hastily mounted attack was stopped cold and would make no further progress through the day. Artillery fire plastered the two companies unmercifully, and a whole rifle platoon of Company F, along with part of a weapons platoon, became lost from the main body and presumably was captured."

At 8th Division headquarters, Cross noted, "Attack made little progress, except Company I, which quickly gained its objective but with whom contact was lost early. The 1st Bn., 28th Regiment, sent patrols to gain contact with Company I of the 121 but ran into a German company and captured or killed all of them. At nightfall, the situation had improved somewhat but decidedly not satisfactory. Rain and terrific mud added to problem. Heavy mortar fire caused many casualties. Horses and carts used to haul supplies, and men had lost offensive punch."

Sylvan seemed to be describing events from another war when he summarized the action on 21 November. "The Gen. ordered the attack of 121st Inf. toward Huertgen. Gen. instructed Gen. Stroh to assault buttoned up to avoid if possible mine casualties. Consequently, he was not disappointed that limited advances of 400 yards or so made by the 3rd Bn. with lesser advances by the 1st and 2nd Bn. Gen. Hodges reported he had talked with Gen. [Charles] Canham, asst. div. CO, and said he was extremely pleased with the advance. No one but the most optimistic skygazers expected you to crack the line within 24 hours, dash to the Rhine in the manner of the Saint-Lô breakthrough. There's been nothing but the stiffest kind of fighting and opposition all along our front, and the gains recorded consequently have satisfied everybody."

Cross wrote in his diary that as of 22 November, the 121st again attacked at 0900, "but with no success. Each time they attempted to move, a rain of mortar and antitank shells dropped on them. All firebreaks in the woods were mined, and apparently communications from forward positions to gun and mortar positions were perfect. The fighting is in heavily forested areas, difficult to see anything, and the Germans are protected by dugouts and wooded bunkers. Everything is mined. Morale of the troops very poor. Other regiments have been chewed to pieces in this area, and this regiment did not gain anything by listening to the harrowing tales of how tough it was from the 109th Infantry when relieved by the 121st."

Cross attended a conference of the VII and V Corps commanding generals at 1400 "to determine next scheme of attack. Much argument and Gen. Collins's dominating personality finally gained an unwilling consent to scheme of attack that was based on optimistic view of how our dispositions would be 23 November, the day selected for attack."

Sylvan sounded a more somber note: "Heavy resistance to the 121st Infantry, gains measured in terms of yards. The 8th inf. and 22d Inf. made small gains over possibly the worst terrain perhaps that the 1st Army has ever faced, not excluding the hedgerow country in Normandy."

Despite the awful toll and the lack of success, orders directed the 121st to continue to press forward. After several days, according to Norris Maxwell, "My company simply melted away. I could not find anybody. The American soldier can smell disaster and they just disappeared. In my judgment, it was an impossible situation." Maxwell sought out his battalion commander, Lt. Col. Robert Jones, whom he found in a bunker. The discussion about the conditions led Jones to relieve Maxwell, and, subsequently, charges of disobedience were leveled at him. While awaiting a court-martial, he was sent to the rear.

Roddy Wofford took over A Company. He, too, used the phrase "melted away" to describe what happened to the soldiers of A Company. "I never knew officially that Maxwell was to be disciplined. As I recall, early on 23 November [Thanksgiving], another attack order came over the phone. At that point, Captain Maxwell came over to my foxhole and said something like, 'I can't take any more of this and I am going back.' After a short period of time, I got a call from the battalion commander. He wanted to know what was going on 'up there,' because Maxwell had reached his headquarters by that time. I told the battalion commander that nothing was going on, and we still had not been able to move forward from our original line of departure. He responded that our orders to attack were the same and we needed to get to it. I told him not to expect too much, that I thought we were down to about forty men. He said he was sorry, but he had his orders and now I had mine. I don't think what Maxwell did had any effect on my behavior or that of the men that remained. Since I was executive officer, I was used to taking over when something happened to the company commander. I thought Maxwell did a courageous thing by going back. It seemed like nobody was paying any attention to the slaughter that was going on, and what better way to get attention than by going back and risking a court-martial."

As he had been instructed, Wofford tried to organize his meager forces. "I took off a Luger pistol I was carrying [a weapon he had captured earlier] and gave it Paul Yergeau [his radio operator, with whom he shared a foxhole] for safekeeping. I certainly did not want to be carrying a German pistol if I were captured. Then I got in the fire lane and tried to 'rally' the troops for another attack.

"As I was walking the fire lane, I noticed another lieutenant from another battalion doing the same thing as I. We discovered we knew each other; both [of us] had gone to A&M at the same time. His name was Joe Stalcup. We shook hands and commiserated with each other very briefly. He asked me if we were going [attacking], and I said we were going to try but not expecting to get very far. I sensed both of us were very pessimistic. We both then turned and went back to our companies. I never saw him again but heard later he had survived the war.

"We started our attack, laying down what small-arms fire we had available. There was an immediate response from the Germans with small-arms fire, and we could hear the bullets zipping past and ricocheting off the trees. At this point, I felt a terrific blow to my chest, and I believe I temporarily blacked out. When I came to, the first thing I noticed was my helmet had a hole in it. I assumed I had been hit in the head, and I had some pain in my chest. My greatest feeling was of relief. Whatever my condition, I was getting out of that miserable place. From there my memory is rather hazy. I believe I remember Yergeau doing all he could to get me evacuated.

"I believe my wounds were caused by a mortar shell bursting in a shattered tree. I had my helmet stuffed with two packets of toilet paper. I believe this saved me from a serious head wound. I just had a scalp wound. However, the fragment that hit my chest entered at the sternum and exited my right scapula. As I was hit, I felt the blood spurt and then cease. I remember the medics speculating that since I was wearing so many layers of clothing—four I think—the blood and clothing made a very effective compress to stanch the flow.

"The only thing done immediately was to evacuate me by stretcher. This was hindered by intermittent shelling, and the bearers would drop me and seek cover. This was very painful, but I couldn't blame them. They reached an area where there was a tracked vehicle—a Weasel. I was strapped on and taken to the battalion aid station, which was in a bunker. Since there wasn't much room in the bunker, a lieutenant medic looked me over and determined that I could wait outside in the rain. I took this to be a good sign. Since I had had a shot for pain, I really didn't care whether I was in the rain or not. I was soaking wet anyway.

"Before I was taken by ambulance to the regiment, the good lieutenant relieved me of my GI watch. He said I didn't need it and they really did there. I was most affable to anything by this time. The ambulance ride to regiment was very rough. I was checked through quickly, taken to an evacuation hospital in an old school building to start my long [nine months] recovery."

As part of its deployment, the 121st Regiment front included B Company of the 2d Ranger Battalion. When the GIs from the 121st wilted, the situation for the Ranger unit also deteriorated severely. The medic Frank South recalled, "On one occasion, the already weakened B Company was ordered to take a position directly in front of three enemy strong points in a densely wooded area, which was protected by a minefield. As they moved forward, a mine detonated, killing one, wounding six, three of them seriously. The aid man, Bill Clark, walking carefully in their tracks, immediately went to them, gave what aid he could, and remained through the night to comfort and guard them. B Company continued to receive extremely heavy casualties from the increasing artillery and small-arms fire; their numbers were becoming so low that their effectiveness might have become compromised. Battalion headquarters decided to have Company A relieve them the following night." However, the fluid battlefield made any transition difficult. Before the Rangers could exchange places, Rudder, the battalion commander, needed precise information on the location of his people.

Bob Edlin's A Company had exchanged places with units from the 28th Division's 112th Infantry. He encountered Capt. Preston Jackson, a friend from OCS, who said, "Bob, this is the meanest son of a bitch that you've ever seen in your life up there. I wish you wouldn't go. I wish you'd just flat tell them you're not going any further." Edlin said, "He told me that there were men up there that you wouldn't believe would ever lose their nerve but have gone completely blank. They absolutely can't hold out any longer. I thought—you know how you are as a Ranger—we'll calm things down. How in the hell I thought 500 men could do what four infantry divisions couldn't, I don't know. When I left Jack he was actually crying and told me not to do anymore than I had to."

According to Edlin, amid drifting snow, through ankle-deep mud, his platoon climbed a trail up a steep hill to the village of Germeter. As the Rangers appeared, the 112th Infantry emptied from the houses so precipitously that their tubs of charcoal still burned. "The infantry outfit that had been up there was actually almost running in retreat just to get away." Advised that they would be there only a few days, warmed by a charcoal fire and with a roof overhead, Edlin decided that maybe it was not such a bad situation. "Suddenly, the artillery starts coming. It's the purest hell I've ever been through. It was just round after round of crashing and smashing, beating on your head till you think there is no way you can stand it.

I was lying on my back on the floor, and the only way I can keep my sanity was by joking with the men on the floor around me. Most of them didn't take it as a joke and got pretty upset that I was calling direction for artillery fire on the place, hollering 'up 100,' 'right 100,' 'up.' In several hours, they literally shot the house down around us."

Still in the basement of a house, Edlin, with only about twenty left to his platoon, endured "another hellacious shelling," including one round that penetrated the cellar. "I heard Sergeant Fronzek moan. When I got to him it was the most terrible looking wound I had ever seen. Shrapnel had torn across his chest. I think his lungs were exposed. He had a pack of cigarettes in his pocket. I could see the tobacco shreds being sucked into his body as he struggled to breathe. I yelled at Sergeant Bill Klaus to get a jeep in here and get him out. In minutes, we had a medic. They carried him to the jeep, and he was gone. We heard from Doctor Block he would make it and he did."

Headquarters now summoned Edlin, who assumed his paltry few were about to be relieved. "I went down that son-of-a-bitch fire trail, past Purple Heart Corner, artillery fire on our asses all the way [his runner accompanied him]. The trail was frozen. New snow lay ass-deep to a tall Indian. We were slipping and sliding; hell, they could have heard us in Berlin. It was early evening but darker than the inside of a black cat. At headquarters, someone told me Rudder wanted to see me. I knew we're not being relieved. I don't need to see the colonel for that.

"Rudder was billeted in a small building, like a hunting shelter about the size of a small bathroom. There was a little kerosene stove, a table, a couple of chairs, a double bunk bed. Colonel Rudder was huddled by the stove. Big Jim, as we called him, was only thirty-five years old, but he looked like a tired, worn-out old man. I had never seen him that way."

The Ranger's CO dispensed with military formality and invited Edlin to sit. "He handed me a cup of hot coffee, looked at me for a minute, and said, '[Robert] Arman [A company commander] is here to make arrangements to relieve B Company. But we've got a problem. I heard from Sid Salomon [the B Company CO]. A short time ago, B Company was pinned down in a minefield. They were under heavy artillery and machine gun fire with a lot of casualties. I need a volunteer to take a patrol in, find a way to get to them, arrange to relieve them, and try and bring out some of the wounded. The patrol needs to go in now. A will relieve B tomorrow night. I'm not going to ask you to go, but that's the situation.'

"The picture runs through my mind like a kaleidoscope. I can't stand to take anymore of this. I'm tired and scared. This will be pure hell, and I can't stand any more of my platoon getting slaughtered. But then I can see B Company suffering up there. We've been through a lot together. Shit, I've got to go. I looked at Arman and back to Jim. There's no rank here, just Rangers. 'God, Jim, I hate to ask my guys to go. They're pretty beat up, and I don't know if they'll make it or not.' The Colonel just nodded and said, 'Yeah, I know.' 'Okay, we'll be on the way. It'll take me an hour to get back to the platoon. We should be in B's position in a couple of hours.' Rudder said, 'There will be a medical jeep at your CP when you get back. Good luck.' The son of a gun knew I would go."

After another, but uneventful, trek up the snowy trail, navigating the always dangerous Purple Heart Corner, Edlin asked for volunteers. He chose Bill Courtney and Bill Dreher. They would travel without helmets, packs, or even weapons. Accompanied by a driver and medic from battalion headquarters, they passed slowly along a hardtop road, aware that at any moment shells might fall on them. At the point where the remainder of the trip would be on foot, Edlin told the driver, whom he did not know, to stay with the jeep. He said, 'Lieutenant, they ain't nobody gonna steal it. Let me go with you. I can help carry the wounded out. The medic handed the driver a litter, took another on his shoulder, and said they were ready. I said, 'Let's spread out in single file. Keep as much interval as you can without getting lost. We don't want one round to get us all."

The would-be rescuers slid through ice and snow, aware of a potential mine at every step. "It was so dark, it was almost impossible to move. The trees are down as if a mad woodcutter had been through with a giant buzz saw. Shit, I forgot the marking tape. Courtney sensed the problem and said 'I've got it and we're marking the path.' I prayed, Lord, just give me the strength and guts to make a few more yards, then we can rest a minute. A shell landed thirty yards off; damn, that was close. A few more yards I could hear German machine gun fire; a German flare lights up the scene. The snow is almost blizzard conditions. The flare shows trees uprooted, dead American and German soldiers, twisted bushes. No satanic artist could dream up such a sight."

Edlin faltered, feeling he could not continue. Dreher's hand clutched his shoulder, and the sergeant said, "I'll get it [the lead] for awhile." Courtney, ten yards behind, called out, "What's the matter, lieutenant? You volunteered for the Rangers, didn't you?" Bullets rustled through the underbrush from unseen gunmen, and then a quiet voice from a B Company outpost challenged the patrol. Nobody knew the password, but when questioned on the first name of Lieutenant Fitzsimmons, Courtney answered "Bob," and they were welcomed.

"I'm led to Captain Salomon's CP," recalled Edlin. "It's under a small bridge by a woodcutter's trail. I talk with Sid a few minutes, and he tells me to go to Fitzsimmons, who's got the worst wounded. I inform Sid we've marked the path and A Company will be in at 8 P.M. tomorrow night, November 23. He thanked us for coming and said the B Company medic would meet us at Fitzsimmons's position. Artillery was still coming in and there was occasional machine gun fire. We found Fitzsimmons and decided we would carry out two wounded at a time. The jeep driver and Courtney started back with the first litter. The two medics loaded another litter. I took the front end and told the battalion medic to stay with B Company. He was at the other end of the litter. As he stepped back to let Dreher replace him, he stepped on a mine, which went off. I learned later this heroic man lost a foot. Fitzsimmons was hit in the face. I saw the Ranger on the litter bounce into the air. The blast of shrapnel knocked me into a tree. I must have been unconscious. For a moment I'm completely blind and deaf. My left hand hurts. I reach over and can't feel my hand. It must be gone at the wrist. I'm going to die right here in this damn German woods. Strong arms picked me up. Dreher throws me over his shoulder. I can't see or hear. They were carrying me through the woods to the jeep.

"I woke up, lying on a stretcher. I'm not blind; there is a dim light. I heard Doc Block's voice, 'Wash his eyes with boric acid [to remove dirt and mud].' I have some hearing in one ear. I hear Doc say, 'Take him back to a hospital.' 'Wait a minute, Doc. How bad is it?' 'You ain't hurt, you goldbrick, a little shrapnel in your hand and face. They'll fix you up back at a field hospital. It's mostly shock and mud.' I asked someone else about the others, and all they tell me is that everyone will be okay."

Loaded into an ambulance, Edlin lay next to the medic whose foot had been destroyed. "I don't know what route we took, but German artillery chased us a good ways. It ought to be against the rules to shoot at you when you're leaving."

At a field hospital, Edlin quickly recovered his aplomb and his temper. He demanded an audience with the head doctor, pleading for quick repairs, explaining, "Major, there's about fifty men from B Company still in that woods. About the same number of A Company are going in to relieve them. I know the path into that death trap. If you'll clean up my eyes and hearing, I'll take them up there." The surgeon argued that Edlin risked severe infection but eventually agreed to debride and stitch the wound. The doctor and several oversize aid men showed up to perform the work. Edlin learned that if he received anesthesia, it would require an overnight stay. Having abjured unconsciousness, he watched the surgeon remove the crusty, bloody bandage. "Shit, that hurt. Then I found out what the big aid men were for. One held my legs, one grabbed my right arm, the nurse had my left arm. He took a pan of hot soapy water and a scrub brush and went to work, cleaning my hand. I'm raising hell, it hurt so bad. The hell with B company and the rest of the Rangers, ain't nothing ever hurt so much.

"After this short period of torture, he took a knife and some tweezers. I remember he said, 'This is really going to hurt.' Right, Doc, it did. They counted forty-eight pieces of shrapnel, plus whatever is still in there. They put a bandage and sling on my arm, patched up my face, and the surgeon said, 'You're on your own.' I knew he would catch hell about the paperwork, but he just answered, 'Get a couple of Krauts for us.' I gave him some real German marks one of the Krauts had loaned me. He was quite a man and one hell of a doctor.

"I knew if I went back to battalion headquarters, Block would kick my ass, so I took off up that damn Germeter trail again. It hadn't changed—slick, slippery, slimy. It's one dark, cold, snowy night. My ass is dragging when I get past Purple Heart Corner. I go into our beat-up old house and it's empty. The charcoal fires are out and the platoon is gone. I realize they have gone to relieve B Company without me. It's twenty-four hours since I left. My hand and face hurt and I still can't hear. I've had about all of this bullshit I need."

Edlin staggered back to battalion headquarters, where he learned Rudder had left for a meeting with higher-ups. Someone took pity on the exhausted platoon leader and told him to take the colonel's bunk for the night. Another Samaritan brought some hot food from the mess, even cutting bite-size pieces and offered to feed him. Surgeon Block inspected his hand and face, then chewed him out for not remaining in the rear. When Edlin asked for a painkiller that would enable him to rejoin his men, Block ordered him to remain in the bunk, where he drifted off to sleep.

"When I woke it was still dark, but it was twenty-four hours later. Colonel Rudder was dozing in a chair while I was using his bunk. They just don't make colonels like that."

While the 8th Division's 121st Regiment endured a frightful bloodletting, the two brother organizations, the 13th and 28th Infantry Regiments, pursued somewhat less onerous paths, assuming holding missions. The 13th moved to a static line facing a ridge where the embattled town of Schmidt was still in German hands. The 28th Regiment occupied the Vossenack area, site of the 28th Division's reversal of fortune. During the first days of the offensive that the 121st began on 21 November, these regiments coped mainly with the steady downfall of artillery and mortars—the 28th reported 5,000 incoming on 20 November—and mines that threatened any movement and the menace of trench foot.

While the 8th Division challenged the German defenders south of him, George Wilson, as the CO of Company F, along with the other men of the 22d Regiment, endured frightful days in the forest before the objective of Grosshau. German mortar bursts relentlessly maimed or killed, with a sliver of shrapnel penetrating an inch into Wilson's arm. He yanked it out himself, and after a medic sprinkled sulfa powder and bandaged him, he continued his duties. After one of their sorties toward the objective, the rifle companies began to dig in, only to suddenly receive automatic fire from the rear.

Wilson said, "The men on the rear line were only partly dug in, and they dove for the ground. These were mostly replacements, and they were shocked and nearly paralyzed by the suddenness and fierceness of their first action. Very few of them even attempted to fire back.

"Lieutenant Caldwell and I began firing our rifles and yelling at the men to start shooting. Then I told Caldwell to keep trying to get them to shoot while I went up to the front—actually back to the front—to get more men.

"Bullets cut through the branches and zipped all around me as I ran back. Every damned man I came upon was trying to hide in his foxhole or under a tree, making no attempt at all to fight back. I rousted a bunch of them out and got them to follow me, running as low as possible under the whizzing bullets.

"It was easy to tell where the Krauts were from all their firing, and I led the dozen or so of my men out to the side and killed a couple of them [Germans], wounded three, and took a prisoner. A few managed to get away." The raiders had been a small but heavily armed combat patrol. Although routed, they had killed a newly arrived replacement lieutenant and severely wounded others, including a man who died later from his wounds.

The flow of fresh fodder continued; Wilson's company absorbed 100 enlisted men and one officer, bringing the complement up to 150. Among the raw, superficially trained recruits, Wilson chose a pair who claimed some civilian experience to serve as radio operators. To his dismay, both tried to fake the symptoms of battle fatigue. "Instead of seeing the humor or allowing for circumstances, all I felt was a sickening shock. I knew that everyone had a breaking point, but I had just assumed that everyone naturally was doing his best up to that point. This may seem a bit naive, but I do think it was the way most of us felt. Most of the men I knew in World War II seemed to accept their role to fight for home and country without complaint. I don't recall a single person who questioned our involvement. We were not gung ho but quietly went about our duties. Perhaps that is why the occasional shirker stood out.

"I have witnessed real emotional breakdown under enormous physical and mental pressure of combat, and for those cases, I have the most heartfelt sympathy. It is awful to see men go into convulsions, froth at the mouth, gibber incoherently. Many later responded to rest and treatment, and some were returned to the front—time after time. Some of the poor guys never did make it back to normalcy, even long after the war. But I knew of only two men who ever made a completely successful return to the battlefield.

"Our Thanksgiving dinner [23 November] was hand-carried up to us by men from the service company. Our cooks had put together giant turkey sandwiches, and they were a treat compared to K-ration Spam, even though we, of course, received none of the usual trimmings. It wasn't all celebration, however, for we learned that some of the food-carrying party had been hit on the way up. Though this happened all of the time, we never quite learned to accept it."

Ernest C. Carlson, inducted in 1943, originally trained with the 78th Infantry Division, but the demands for replacements shipped him to D Company, 1st Battalion, 28th Regiment, 8th Division, as a radio operator for the 81mm mortars in a heavy weapons platoon. He first saw combat on 8 July 1944. On 17 November, his outfit relieved GIs from the 28th Division outside the town of Huertgen near Vossenack. "They did not ever retrieve their base plates or tubes for their mortars. The base plates were buried in mud and half frozen in place."

Less than a week later, the men celebrated the November holiday. "On Thanksgiving Day our group was brought a hot meal. The kitchen help that brought the meal parked their jeep next to the mines piled at the base of a tree. Engineers had placed white tape around the mines. The food was served, and the first sergeant ordered men to carry the containers back to the jeep and trailer. One of them was a person who never got out of his foxhole since we took up our position. He, along with the sergeant, two cooks, the jeep driver, and two other GIs from our platoon, were loading food containers into the jeep and trailer, when this man who never got out of his hole set one container he was carrying on top of those mines at the base of the tree. The very large blast knocked people twenty yards away off their feet. From the carrying party of seven, two survived, the first sergeant and one pfc. All that was left of the soldier who caused the blast was his belt, part of his pants, and rear pocket, with wallet enclosed, which landed in a tree branch above me. I don't think the soldier who put the container on the mines ever knew they were there, because he never got out of his hole long enough to know better."

In the 8th Division's 22d Regiment, Paul Boesch, dealing with his company commander, who had broken under the stress, was incredulous when advised by field phone that he would need to send out carrying parties to bring up a semblance of the traditional big dinner. He pleaded with his battalion commander to postpone the meal, but the division headquarters insisted. As the food arrived and the troops reluctantly left their foxholes to receive it, a tank destroyer chose to demolish a nearby abandoned tank that may have provided cover for German infiltrators. The fiery explosion alerted German gunners, who promptly brought down shells upon the GIs. Men died and others incurred painful, disabling wounds because of the misguided notion of a morale-building portion of turkey. However, Edward Miller, in his book *A Dark and Bloody Ground*, calls the modest Thanksgiving feast "a stunning failure of senior commanders to understand the conditions at the front."

Hodges celebrated the holiday with a tour of the front. Sylvan wrote, "The Gen., accompanied by Gen. King, started early this morning with the 8th Div., where he met Gen. Collins and Gen. Gerow and Gen. Stroh. To the latter he said he was not satisfied with the progress being made. The minefields had not proven to be as much an obstacle as people feared. Progress or rather the lack of it made by the division showed lack of confidence and drive. He made it quite clear he expected better results tomorrow. As if to prove his point that the division was not going ahead as it should, one battalion had captured ninety prisoners.

"From the 8th Div. both generals went to the 4th Div., where they joined Gen. Barton for a conference and Thanksgiving dinner. None of the generals attended a Red Cross party, which they had promised to attend, but the chefs put on a magnificent spread at the homes, in addition to decorating the house and the cake. The Gen. consented to relax and see the gay movie *Jeanie*."

The news stories about the Huertgen campaign, which passed through army censors, spoke of "toe-to-toe slugfests with German infantry and armor" and "German counterattacks and last-ditch resistance." One account said, "When the full story is told of its cost in men and materials, the name of these woodlands probably will rank alongside the Argonne Forest in the First World War and the Battle of the Wilderness in the Civil War." But the people at home heard little of the details of the ordeal and the terrible casualties while the campaign raged, even though the country's most celebrated writer, Ernest Hemingway, accompanying the 22d Regiment, could have observed and written from a foxhole seat. The novelist-turned-war correspondent for the magazine *Colliers* had become friendly with the 22d Regiment CO, Buck Lanham, a West Pointer with a reputation as a poet and occasional writer on military affairs.

Jack Crawford, who held a battlefield commission and was leader of an intelligence and recon unit for the 12th Regiment, briefly encountered Hemingway. "I had been in the hospital for treatment of my eye and had been put in a ward filled with head wound cases. It was too much and I decided to leave, even though I still had an IV. I disconnected it, put on my uniform, and left. I bummed a ride to Spa and walked into a bar there.

"I saw Hemingway with Colonel Lanham sitting at a table. Lanham knew of me and he invited me for a drink. I was very excited meeting Hemingway. I had read all his books. But when we started to talk, he turned out to be a horse's ass. I felt he was full of it and this really wasn't his war. He was telling tales of high jinks in Paris. I got pissed off and said something like, 'If you want to see combat, come up with me to the Huertgen.' Lanham said, 'You're out of line, lieutenant.' I answered, 'Yes sir,' and 'Fuck you' to Hemingway."

Crawford rejoined the 12th still stuck in the Germeter-Vossenack sector. "We went on a patrol to get some prisoners. We met with six Germans. We killed four, wounded one, and captured one. My sergeant killed the wounded man, which pissed me off. Then they started firing on us and we hit the ground. The sergeant hit a Bouncing Betty [mine], which killed him and wounded me in the leg, blew off the stock of my weapon, and left me with only hand grenades. I was sure they would come to finish me off. But I was picked up by aid men, given a Syrette of morphine, and taken to the aid station." Treated at a series of hospitals, first in Paris and then in the States, he received his discharge in December 1945.

Robert L. French, a surveyor's assistant, enlisted early in 1942 and, because of his background, earned a commission in the engineers. Assigned to C Company of the 4th Combat Engineer Battalion, French made the D-Day landing and the subsequent Normandy campaign. While in that area, he first saw Hemingway. "I was impressed by Hemingway at first," said French, "a man with combat experience [as an ambulance driver on the Italian front during World War I], but after two weeks in Normandy, no longer. Other correspondents were unarmed and wore an armband, but Hemingway carried a .45 pistol and a cartridge belt. It was as useless as an officer's carbine but easier to carry.

"I saw Hemingway in the Huertgen Forest with the 22d Infantry Regiment and his friend, Edwin Lanham. We remarked on his appearance in a white sheepskin jacket, a most flamboyant garment, which made a mockery of any pretense at camouflage. The rest of us had to spend some time at least in places where that jacket would be fatal to the wearer, and we resented it as a reminder that its owner had no intention of sharing in the dangers of war. Hemingway ate with us in the officers' mess, but I never recall him anywhere but at the colonel's table." French compared Hemingway unfavorably with the correspondent Ernie Pyle, who visited the front lines regularly, "was obviously fearful," and spent his time among enlisted men and lieutenants rather than the brass. Hemingway filed a story on the 22d's initial encounter with the Siegfried Line but never reported on the Huertgen experiences. His description of the campaign as "Paschendale with trees" is curious, because he was not present at that battle during World War I, nor from the evidence did he witness much of the Huertgen battle.

Quite apart from his observation on the war correspondent, as a combat engineer, French recalled his responsibility to provide satchel charges for demolition of pillboxes. "C Company had an order for 3,000 pounds of TNT made up into pole and satchel charges. When everything was ready, I went back to load the trucks for the 22d Regiment. We had two or three trucks. I rode in the lead with the driver. I also carried two or three little wooden boxes, which had holes drilled inside to carry the detonators. They were more powerful than dynamite fuses because TNT is much harder to set off.

"The drivers were nervous because we had to pass through some intersections in the dirt roads through the Huertgen Forest. In retreating, the Germans had been careful to insure that they had zeroed in on each intersection. A day or two before, trucks carrying replacements for the infantry had been caught at a crossroads. Most of the soldiers were wounded and evacuated without ever seeing the units they were sent to join. I calmed [the drivers] down as best I could by assuring them that TNT is very hard to detonate and that shrapnel would not cause an explosion. The shell would have to explode on the surface of the TNT and that was unlikely in the forest. If one came that close, we wouldn't need the TNT. The only sensitive explosives were the detonators, and I was carrying them.

"We made it to regimental headquarters. I told the men to unload everything and put it in a barn across the road. I went in to tell Colonel Lanham that I had his satchel and pole charges. He asked where I had put them. 'In the barn across the road.' 'Are you crazy? Get them away from here!' He was no more comfortable with TNT than any other infantryman."

During this period, French led a five-man squad on a minesweeping expedition. All of the enlisted men were wounded and evacuated following a protracted spate of shells. Perhaps as a result of such experiences, he collapsed on Thanksgiving Day. His pulse raced at 136 beats per minute, and he showed all the signs of a cardiovascular problem. However, he was diagnosed as another victim of combat fatigue.

Jim Wood, the platoon leader in the 16th Infantry who had combined the handful of men from his unit and that of the wounded and captured John Beach during the attack toward Hamich, said, "We were relieved on Thanksgiving Day, a week after [Beach was] captured. What was left out of the company had to crawl prone out of their foxholes, creep by the dead bodies of their comrades to get far enough back to stand up. It was an awful sight. I had to crawl over the bodies of men I had drunk with, played cards with. In the trench at company headquarters, we saw fifteen dead men, including the old man [Briggs] himself. Some had been dragged there after being wounded and died because they couldn't get to the aid station."

An angry Bill Kull, who came to the 12th Regiment as a replacement, recalled, "The official history says the turkey was for breakfast and it 'boosted morale.' Some half-wit from the motor pool or some group back there sends up sliced white turkey meat on white bread. White turkey meat on cold, stale white bread and water to drink. Happy Thanksgiving. As hungry as I was, I don't know if I ate it all or not. It was hard going down. It made me angry because I reasoned that if they could bring up sandwiches, they could bring up something better."

13

Costly Successes

The first three days of engagement by the 121st Regiment resulted in about fifty killed in action and almost 600 wounded, reducing the regiment's strength by close to 20 percent. While the "repple depples" (replacement depots) fed in replacements, the offensive faltered, the ultimate objective of the banks of the Roer was three hard miles off, and the key towns of Huertgen, Kleinhau, and Bergstein were unconquered. In response to the criticisms of Hodges, heads began to roll in the 8th Division, beginning with company and battalion brass. On 25 November, Stroh stripped Col. John Jeter of his command and named Tom Cross in his stead.

A day earlier, Cross sat in on a meeting dealing with plans by the V and VII Corps for a coordinated drive that would introduce a new element, CCR (Combat Command Reserve) of the 5th Armored Division. Cross recorded in his diary, "Meeting was dominated by Gen. Collins, as usual. Col. [Glen H.] Anderson, the CCR CO did not radiate much enthusiasm for the job ahead in the morning." (While his diary entries connote a distaste for Collins, after the war Cross spoke well of the VII Corps commander to his son Dick, who served with the 11th Airborne Division in the Philippines and retired as a colonel after a career that extended into the 1960s.)

When Cross assumed his new post, he wrote in his diary, "The regiment has had a splendid reputation but has not done well in this fight. I hope I may lead it well and do my best as a leader." During the night, engineers busied themselves clearing the roadway of mines and brought up bridging materials to enable the armor to rattle over the larger craters. Cross commented, "Heavy mortar and artillery fire continuously rained on our position. Many inaccurate reports received during early morning hours, causing confusion."

Although the official journal for the day claimed that CCR rolled off on schedule, Cross said they went out late. The deployment fell behind schedule and foundered almost immediately, with four tanks victimized by mines, antitank guns, and infantrymen. They stalled at a bend in the road.

Rumors of imminent relief lifted the spirits of George Wilson with the 22d Regiment, but when he was ordered to battalion headquarters late in the afternoon of 29 November, Colonel Kenan announced, "Regiment insists we take Grosshau tonight in order to relieve B Company and also because possession of Grosshau is vital to tomorrow's attack plans.

Wilson said, "Night attacks are very difficult and usually require a lot of planning. To control and direct men so they shoot the enemy and not their own is a major concern. Exact directions and signals that are easily seen or heard must be worked out. Radios and other equipment must be secured and checked, passwords have to be assigned, the order of movement determined. With experienced men and officers who know them well, night attacks are still one of the worst assignments possible.

"We did not have any of the proper qualities and time was also against us. Our only advantage was the ability to move in the darkness. I hoped my new officers would be able to follow instructions and that I would be able to stay in contact with them." In addition, he had to gently disabuse F Company of its hope to be relieved, and in the dim illumination of twilight, he said he saw shock and dismay on faces.

The initial objective was to make contact with the 1st Battalion's B Company, hit hard, pinned down outside of Grosshau, and without radio contact. By sheer luck, Wilson's scouts stumbled into a small group of B Company walking wounded on their way back to the aid station and several stretcher cases borne by German prisoners. A wounded sergeant agreed to carry a walkie-talkie to his company commander. Within minutes, Wilson was speaking to his B Company colleague. From him came vital intelligence on the location of the main German defenses.

Wilson quickly constructed a plan of attack, showing his officers the layout on a map illuminated by a flashlight under the cover of several coats. Crouching to avoid any silhouettes against the night sky, his troops sneaked across the open fields on the southern side of Grosshau. To the company commander's delight, the leading forces reached the edge of the town without a single shot fired or any alarm. They fell upon the Germans from their rear, taking them completely by surprise. "Apparently, they were exhausted themselves," commented Wilson. "I couldn't understand why they had no defense at all on their south flank, but I was deeply grateful." So was battalion commander Kenan when apprised of the success, as he "was profuse in his congratulations."

Captain Donald L. Faulkner, a graduate of the University of Illinois and its ROTC program and already thirty-two years of age, led a 200-man packet of replacements onto the continent and reached his new command, E Company of the 22d, on the eve of the offensive against Grosshau. "I was a new man, a replacement, and I didn't know a soul. They were all my buddies, but they didn't know who the hell I was. My new trench coat was a nice dark green. I took my captain's bars off, put them in my pocket, and put mud on the captain's insignia on my helmet. I had no pack, no blankets. We had left our gas masks and our luggage back at regiment by their orders. We had our weapons and ammunition. I had a new carbine and a lot of ammunition in my pocket. I hadn't fired a shot yet. So, we sat waiting for orders." That night at the company CP, Faulkner dug in with his weapons platoon leader, Lt. Lee Lloyd, and a sergeant.

"We got replacements and one of the new squads, a BAR rifle team up front, saw a patrol come across the field in front of them, and they fired, which I don't believe they should have done. Within about a minute and a half, I could hear the incoming barrage, enemy artillery or perhaps mortar fire. There was also some other kind of shelling. It sounded like a railroad express train roaring into the woods, hitting trees. We stayed in our hole. I heard screaming and would have gone out, but Lee Lloyd said 'no,' and Sergeant Willard said, 'If you go you will never come back.'

"When morning came, I got out of the hole at first light. There was a patrol of several men that we had put north, guarding a stream draw, which would have been an entrance into our position. They had, it appeared, gotten out of their holes and run toward ours and had been cut down. The man who almost made it to our hole had been sliced in his thigh, and his whole artery was burned out by the shell fire, deader than a door nail. We lost a good deal of our company during the night's shell fire."

When the instructions arrived for E Company to move north, temporarily attached to the 1st Battalion in the attack against Grosshau, Faulkner counted seven officers, most of whom were replacements like himself, and a paltry sixty-five enlisted men, barely one-third the normal enrollment.

"We worked our way along the left side of the woods. Obviously, we were seen, because mortar fire started to come in and then the heavy stuff; 88mm shells were roaring into the woods. When we came to the stream draw, almost immediately I knew we should move out of there, but the mortar shells started dropping in and everybody hit the ground. We lost a few more men in that stream draw and got out of there.

"I led the company then on the run through the woods in the direction of Grosshau, up to a scene of terrible carnage. There were many, many wounded lying along the trail and in the woods, Krauts and American GIs. Some moaning, a lot dead.

"We moved to a piece of woods just in front of Grosshau. There was a lieutenant I had met aboard ship when we landed on Omaha Beach. He was a retread from the Coast Artillery, and he was the most scared person I had ever seen. He was yelling and shouting and I realized why. We were being fired upon by small-arms fire from the village, and this was not the place to be."

With Lieutenant Lloyd, Faulkner shifted the outfit's positions, deploying the platoons where they could dig in. The two officers discovered a well-protected hole with timbers over it and dirt piled atop the roof, where they established a command post for the night.

On the following day, Faulkner received orders to send a patrol into Grosshau. "That seemed stupid to me. We knew what the situation was. They were there and we were here. But orders are orders. We got a small patrol organized under one of the new lieutenants, and in the dark they started out toward Grosshau. It didn't take more than a few minutes, going alongside the road toward the entrance of the town, before they came galloping back like a bunch of big-tailed birds, followed by burp gun and rifle fire. They made it safely back to their holes.

"We were told replacements were coming in and to expect 100 to 120 men. They came in the dark, and Sergeant Willard and I counted noses as they arrived, and we then sent them to foxholes up front. We received ninety men. That meant we had lost twenty to thirty already as they made their way up through shell fire.

"The weather of the 29th November was sticky, intermittent fog, and chilling rain. We had no blankets, no sleeping bags. The journal of the 22d records that at 11:06 that morning, the S-3, Col. [John] Ruggles talked to Col. Kenan [battalion commander] on the radio, advising him the outfit would not attack but consolidate positions in the Grosshau vicinity, and on the following day, under a white flag with a German-speaking soldier, attempt to persuade the defenders to give up. 'Tell the commander [of the Grosshau garrison] that Huertgen and Kleinhau have fallen, they are surrounded, and the hills east and northeast of Grosshau are in our hands. Also that 150 surrendered in Huertgen.'"

Less than ten minutes later, a new order directed that Grosshau be taken immediately with infantrymen buttressed by tanks and tank destroyers. Faulkner's E Company drew the lead role. "During that morning," said Faulkner, "I looked for a good, big fellow to carry our radio, and I found one by the name of [Lawrence] Sussman. He was from the Bronx, New York. I asked him if he knew anything about a radio, and he said 'no,' so I showed him where to turn the switch on in order to talk with it and told him to stay with me. He did, all the way through the Huertgen Forest and beyond. He did a great job.

"We jumped off for the attack, and the [lead] platoon moved out of the edge of the woods through a small field toward the village. Suddenly, all kinds of fire started coming in. Automatic rifle fire, burp gun fire, artillery fire, 88mm and mortars. Sussman and myself dropped into the ditch at the edge of the woods and almost immediately an artillery shell hit the edge. The pieces went over our heads, and Sussman and myself were safe for the moment.

"Lieutenant Lloyd said later, 'I saw the shell with your name on it come over the town and land right on you. But you were not there. What made you lay down in that ditch?'

"I reported back by the radio that we were stopped. Colonel Kenan came on, and I advised him we had one platoon on the left, and they could not get out of the woods. Our front platoon was pinned down, and the same thing happened to our reserve platoon. We were stuck. I needed artillery fire. Our forward observer could not get the artillery to fire close enough to us to hit the edge of town. Colonel Kenan, whom I had only met once, said, 'You will take Grosshau, or else! Help is coming your way. Look for the big boys from the south, and you will have several tanks coming up the road on your left. Roger and out.'

"Almost immediately, I could see seven tanks crossing the field to our right, and as I watched, two of them were stopped because their treads were blown off by mines. That didn't look so good. I told Lieutenant Lloyd to take his weapons platoon around to what would be the south side of the village, and we would use two of our rifle platoons to go through the village on the left when the tanks came up.

"Almost immediately, two tanks did pull up. The front one was on fire. I could see their blanket rolls and sleeping bags tied to the tank aflame. A young lieutenant coolly got out of the turret, took the ramrod used to clean the gun, and started beating the flames with it. I got up, walked over to the tank, and started talking to the lieutenant, whose name was Yeoman, about how we were going to attack this damn town. He said, 'I can't, because this tank is going to burn up. My second tank, under my sergeant will have to lead.' It came up and off we went.

"The tank moved across the field, which was only about 100 feet from the road, and from there it was another fifty yards to the edge of town. Sergeant Ivey jumped up on the tank and spotted a strong point off in a bit of woods to the northwest of Grosshau and got the tank to fire on it. I brought my command group behind him, waving on the platoon. Almost immediately, a rifle landed on my shoulder, pointing in the direction of town, firing. It almost blew my ear off. One of the new replacements was using me as a support for his M1.

"As we moved along, I saw a group of some six new replacements standing around a GI who pulled a pin on a hand grenade. He tossed it through the window of a house and they all went in. Great, we were off to capture Grosshau! Down the street I thought I saw firing from the top of the church steeple. It would also be a beautiful observation post. To communicate with the sergeant in the tank turret, I tossed half a brick up. When it landed in the turret, he poked his head out. I pointed at the church steeple and he got the idea, swinging his .50-caliber machine gun around and spraying it from top to bottom. We moved through town. It was regular movie stuff, stopping and firing, moving again as the squads went from building to building, throwing grenades. By then it was dark. We stopped at the eastern edge of Grosshau. Lots of PWs.

"Lieutenant Lloyd and myself walked about thirty yards to the road junction that ran through the town, with one road east and another toward Gey on the edge of the Cologne Plain. We agreed we had gone far enough and better turn back to dig in for the night. When we checked the map later, we saw we were perhaps a mile further out from the Allied line from Holland all the way down through France and that was too far ahead."

Faulkner set up a command post in a house with a reinforced basement. While prowling the premises, he discovered a German nurse in a white uniform, and very dead. "I had spotted a wire running from under her body toward the front window. As far as I was concerned, she was going to explode if anyone tried to disturb her, so we put a guard at the front door.

"When I crossed the line of departure with Sussman, I prayed to the Lord. I didn't ask that He save me or us. I asked that He give me good judgment and wisdom to lead this company so that as few as possible would be killed or wounded. After that, I said He was my guide, and we were very thankful when we got to the edge of town that, although we'd had a lot of wounded, we didn't have too many killed in action. We did, however, have quite a few battle fatigue cases and that's understandable."

While Faulkner and his men occupied Grosshau, George Wilson had barely settled down for some rest when he was roused by a messenger from his artillery observer. "I found Lieutenant Caldwell quite bothered and upset. The forward observer agitatedly pointed to the ridge out front and slightly southeast of town and asked if that didn't look like Germans to me. With the help of field glasses, and in the light of what was by then a very bright moon, I clearly made out a column of what could only be enemy soldiers. They were wearing German long coats and were marching in single file toward the northeast, about 500 yards to our front.

"Caldwell complained that he had fired a couple of rounds at them, but that when he had ordered a barrage, his battery had turned him down. His commanding officer explained that his map showed that the hill was being held by Americans."

Wilson took another look through the binoculars at the troops and again by observation of the greatcoats and long-handled shovels identified the column as the enemy. He contacted Kenan and asked for his permission to open fire. The battalion head denied the request, stating that after checking the situation, he learned that the 5th Armored Division claimed their people held the ridge. When Wilson vehemently protested, Kenan told him to send out a patrol for confirmation.

While Wilson focused field glasses on them, a small band from his F Company sifted through the darkness to within fifty yards of the marchers and radioed back these were indeed Germans. Still, Kenan demanded further proof and directed Wilson to send a patrol to a 5th Armored CP. "The patrol leader returned in about an hour and reported that the CO there stated flatly that his men were dug in on that hill and he was sending more people up there. I was frustrated and disgusted; Caldwell was furious. The 5th Armored didn't know how to read its map, but absolutely nothing could be done about it. I went back to sleep."

On the following day, F and G Companies, hewing to a plan based on the assumption that the friendly forces from the 5th Armored occupied the ridge ahead, started an attack toward an objective some two miles off.

"As we headed across the open slope, I kept my men spread way out and watched the ridge line very sharply. It seemed odd to me that the American troops on the ridge were not at all visible from the rear as we approached. Our progress the first 300 yards was almost a stroll. . . . Then it happened. The sky fell in, and we were in hell. German artillery and mortars, machine guns and rifles, and the murderously direct fire of the tank-mounted 88s all hit us at once. Everyone dove to the ground and then crawled to the nearest shell hole or depression. There was no time to think; we simply reacted. Our infantrymen began to fire back with the M1s, and Lieutenant Caldwell set about to get some artillery on the Krauts, who were well dug in. Now we were paying for the inexcusable stupidity of that armored captain who couldn't read a simple map.

"This battle raged on insanely, impossible, for hours as we slowly moved forward. In my five months of considerable combat of all kinds, I had never had to endure such a heavy, mercilessly accurate barrage of shells and bullets." The enemy had very cleverly allowed the Americans to advance far enough into the open area from where in daylight they could not simply retreat to cover. Instead, they could only scramble for the limited protection of ditches and depressions created by exploding ordnance.

Wilson himself became a specific target, as the foe's forward observer could not help but notice one individual moving about the battlefield, obviously attempting to rally his forces while trailed by a radio operator bearing a telltale antenna. "It was almost a game and the German FO [forward observer] was very good at it. No sooner had I changed position and allowed twenty or thirty seconds for the range on his cannon to be adjusted, than the shells would start dropping in all around me."

Equally malevolent was a mortar unit that also zeroed in on Wilson. "Once my radioman and I plunged into a shell hole about three feet deep and six feet across, and we had hardly settled when the mortars began to explode very close to us. Even if it had been possible to hear their vertical descent, the other battle noises would have drowned them out. This became my single worst experience of the war. Because the shells came in so fast, I judged they must have had eight or ten mortars zeroing in on us. About 100 shells came down in an area that couldn't have been much more than fifty feet on a side. Why they never got a direct hit, I'll never know.

"A third man piled in on top of us, and we tried to bury ourselves in the bottom of the hole, praying out loud as we held on for dear life. Handfuls of dirt, chips of stones, and spent shell fragments kept hitting me in the back. The only thing that saved us was the softness of the plowed fields. There could be no tree bursts out there, of course, and the soft dirt let the shells penetrate before exploding and then absorbed much of the force.

"And it was on that terrible open slope beyond the hamlet of Grosshau that young Lieutenant George Wilson [himself] . . . came to the very edge of his breaking point. I had to fight with all I had to keep from going to pieces. I had seen others go, and I knew I was on the black edges. I could barely maintain the minimal control I had after fourteen or fifteen days of brutally inhuman fighting in those damned woods; I had reached the limit of my physical and emotional endurance."

Abruptly, the storm of explosives terminated and the tears and pleas of his radioman to be sent to the rear snapped Wilson back from his own imminent collapse. While accepting that the hysterical soldier had reason for his behavior, Wilson pointed his rifle at him, saying if he heard another word, he would shoot. "He stopped bawling instantly. A few minutes later in the next barrage, as a kind fate would have it, this radioman was wounded slightly in the arm, and I had to send him to the rear. I became my own radioman."

Wilson's GIs inched forward in the face of devastating fire. The cannonade of artillery, mortar, and tank shells spared no one, striking medics and litter bearers trying to rescue the wounded. Wilson could only tell casualties that their one chance lay in crawling back to an aid station on their own.

G Company lost its commander and the soldiers drifted back to the safety of Grosshau. Wilson, with F Company, continued to fight forward into the teeth of tanks nestled in the woods. Forward observer Caldwell called in some heavy artillery on them, and Wilson enlisted P-47s, whose dive-bombing drove the armor deeper into the forest where it was less effective.

"During what may have been the peak of the shelling, the man leading my left platoon went berserk and had to be sent to the rear. This forced me to call forward a young officer who had just joined me that morning before we jumped off. Since he had no chance to get acquainted with his men, I had left his platoon in reserve. Now I needed him and told him to bring his platoon. . . . He immediately began to cry, and he sobbed that he couldn't do it. Coming in fresh and going out on that hill looked to him like an execution. He might have been right. But I had no choice in the matter and had to send him to the rear."

There were no officers other than Wilson left and hardly any noncoms still on their feet. With no unit in support and highly vulnerable to a counterattack, Wilson on his own chose to withdraw to a former German trench, which the GIs quickly deepened until they dug down as much as five feet. "We had started out that morning with about 140 riflemen, a couple of medics, three noncoms, four company officers, one attached artillery officer, and one attached sergeant from H Company. We had lost all the medics, all the noncoms, three of four company officers, and the artillery observer. And we had lost ninety riflemen. This was, and still is, the most terrible day of my life. The ordeal was beyond human endurance, and I cannot understand how fifty of us survived.

"On top of the sickening pain of our losses was the nagging bitterness that it probably all could have been prevented if Lieutenant Caldwell, the best FO I ever saw, had been permitted to wipe out the Germans before they could dig in. The losses at G must have been similar to ours. If that armored infantry captain had only been able to read his map, that particular battle would never have taken place."

Don Faulkner began that day as an interested observer of the deployment of F and G Companies. "I stood behind Colonel Kenan on the south edge of town as F and G Companies moved out on this field with about 800 yards to cross. They didn't get very far, perhaps a couple of hundred yards, when all hell broke loose. I described the artillery time fire as little black guppies coming in from the sky just above the men's heads. I understood time fire because we had worked with it when I was at the artillery school at Fort Sill. It is murderous, and in this case the men were all exposed in an open field. They dug in; they went forward and apparently there were fewer and fewer of them. This could have been like Pickett's last charge at the Battle of Gettysburg.

"Colonel Kenan went back to his command post and I got a message. Be ready to attack to go to F Company's rescue. As we were getting organized, another message said it is going to be too dark for a companywide attack. Use your first platoon."

Advised that there would be tanks available, Faulkner met with the platoon in the backyard of the house. "I asked how many had ridden on a tank. Nobody. I said, here is the way you're going to do it. Stay on the offside and ride behind the turret. Hold on and when the tank slows or comes to a stop, it will turn. Then get on the blind side and proceed from there. We will let you know when to go. The tanks were pulling up when they got a message from the 2d Battalion to call off the attack because it was too dark."

Faulkner and his associates returned to the command post until new orders again directed them to aid the beleaguered F and G Companies. Vaguely certain of the location on a map, Faulkner said, "I led the company single file, through a line of tanks and TDs that were acting as artillery. We got out of the woods and headed toward the field where [the GIs] were supposed to be. I talked with them on a radio and said I couldn't find them and to send a runner. He found us. He was scared stiff but led us across the plain.

"We found Lieutenant Wilson and Lieutenant Greenlee, who said they had twelve men left, no officers and no sergeants. They didn't know where G Company was. They had a horrible, horrible day, losing well over a hundred of their men." For that matter, Faulkner's own E Company was little more than a shell. He could count no more than fifteen to twenty soldiers in each of his platoons along with three officers.

The First Army continued to feed in unbloodied troops. On the day after Thanksgiving, Frank South noted that the meager ranks of the 2d Ranger Battalion's B Company withdrew to the rear bivouac area, where a reorganization that included the reception and training of replacements began. On that same 24 November, platoon leader Jim Wood of the 16th Infantry Regiment noted the arrival of 150 replacements, "fresh from the States and had a whole week to get them ready for combat."

Mines, the omnipresent explosive devices, presented a paramount impediment to the progress of the Huertgen offensive. Responsibility for neutralizing the threat lay with such specialized units as the 8th Division's 12th Engineer Battalion. Its B Company drew the task of clearing the roadway between Germeter and Huertgen of any mines that blocked the deployment of tanks. Platoon leader Mike Cohen, an "ancient," thirty-four-year-old OCS graduate, had become an army engineer, because a clerk filling out his enlistment papers, noting a 1935 degree in English from Colby College, jotted down the abbreviation "Eng.," which subsequent classification personnel interpreted as engineer. Fortuitously, in civilian life Cohen had prospected for gold in the Mojave Desert, where he became proficient with explosives, a valuable skill in the engineer trade.

According to Cohen, the men of the 12th Combat Engineer Battalion brought uncommon skills to the task of disabling mines. "Back in Camp Forrest, somebody gave me a German field manual with pictures, descriptions, instructions on every German mine then in use. It was written in German, but we had a man named Schleiser, a German-born American who had been a cabinetmaker in civilian life. With a couple of helpers, Schleiser made wooden duplicates of every mine, right down to the igniters with safety pins. Then, with several copies of every mine we held a 'country fair' training procedure, booths set up with mines laid out for the men to handle, explore, become familiar with. The instructors behind the booths were changed over and over again, so that every man in the company was at one time or another instructing on every mine. We then moved out from our company to the others in the battalion, and when Division found out what we were doing, we went to the infantry I&R platoons and ran our dog and pony show for them.

"All the time we were in the States, all the time we were in Northern Ireland," recalled Cohen, "the infantry ignored us. This all changed as soon as we got into Normandy. They never made a move without getting the engineers in there first." From Cohen and his cohorts, the foot soldiers demanded safe passage through the ubiquitous *schus,* Bouncing Betties, Tellers, and boobys. "Sometimes," continued Cohen, "they told us where they planned to go tomorrow morning and would we clear a path for them tonight? I remember a time outside of Brest [a savage campaign] when we were passing the infantry front lines to get to a hedgerow to blast an opening so tanks could accompany the foot soldiers. It was dark and rainy, and I heard an infantryman say to his buddy, 'Boy, look at those engineers going up there in the dark. I wouldn't change places with those guys.' After we had done our job, as we came back through that same infantry front line position, I heard one of my guys say, 'Boy, look at those infantry sitting up here in those holes in the rain all night. I wouldn't change places with those guys.'"

By the time he reached the Huertgen Forest, the euphoria of a Jewish high holy day celebration in early September had faded. Cohen said, "I had a very clear notion of what was ahead of us. We replaced the 28th Division, and they moved into our positions in Luxembourg. I talked to some of their advance people when they came to Hosingen, and they, badly bloodied from Schmidt, left nothing out. Then I was part of our own advance party to Germeter, and I got more of the same. I didn't really know where I was. Sure, it was the Huertgen Forest, but where the hell was that. Of course, it didn't really matter. When I was told I would be responsible for clearing the road from Germeter to Huertgen, I assumed it was very important, and I had no doubt that the people giving the orders knew what they were doing."

On the morning of 24 November, Cohen led his people on their mission. "Everything was quiet. I ordered my first squad to clear the booby traps and antipersonnel mines off the trees the Germans had strewn across the road. The second squad was ordered to clear the hundreds and hundreds of mines off the surface of the road. The third squad was to fill in the holes in the road so vehicles could travel safely. Together, we would move the big trees off to the sides.

"The most worrisome part of the project was that the road had been subjected to many days of artillery fire. The mines—most of them antivehicular types—had taken a pounding. Some had blown. But most were still there, but not intact. Had their shear pins been partially severed? Would the touch of a man's finger set them off? We didn't have time to explode each mine in place, the field manual way. We had to take our chances.

"Thinking nobody was watching me disobey my own rules, I tested a mine, lifted it, carried it gingerly to the ditch at the side of the road. I tried another. One of the sergeants saw me, tried himself. Some of the men saw us. The sloppy technique spread. We moved up the road breaking all the rules.

"We came to the bend in the road, just before the tank ditch. Now the enemy was awake. I saw a German raising his rifle to take aim at me and heard at the same time the crack of the rifle of one of my guys, and I saw the German fall. Now, all hell broke out, and I scooted to the ditch on the far side of the road. One of my men, Bill Sobieski, was out ahead of me with a mine detector. I hollered for him to slide back past me. Mine detector men do not carry rifles because of the metallic interference. A German ran across the road to get a shot at us, but I was lying there, ready, and I shot him. A second and a third came across the road about forty feet away, and I shot them like ducks in a carnival shooting gallery. They were firing machine guns from a hiding place somewhere off to my left now. Next would be mortars. We had only our rifles. Mine-clearing exercises were over for the day. I sent the word, 'Let's go home, fellas.' Mortar fire and then howitzers followed us back. The score: German casualties at least four, ours zero.

"We had no sooner got back to the cement-ceilinged basements of Germeter than a tremendous artillery barrage began. The explosions were continuous, not just one at a time but solid, endless noise. Sitting opposite me were a couple of infantry replacements, just arrived, a couple of kids. They were weeping with uncontrollable terror. For two or three hours, we sat there in the fury and watched the two kids slowly crumble as the ground shook and powdered cement drifted down from the walls and ceilings.

"At a meeting later that afternoon, I was reminded that the Germeter-Huertgen road still belonged to me. The infantry was going to try to secure the road bend, and then I would have to finish getting it cleared. But that evening I was told that the infantry efforts had failed; they would try again tomorrow. I was told I could wait till tomorrow to do the clearing. If I waited, I would be out there with my men in the midst of a firefight in broad daylight. My men would be slaughtered and the job would not get done. I decided to take advantage of the present lull and try to sneak a squad of men out under cover of darkness and bitch it out." As an incentive, the commander of the 12th, Lt. Col. Edmond Fry, promised Cohen a pass to Paris as soon as the road was sanitized. "It was the kindest thing that gruff son of a bitch had ever said to me in the three years I'd known him.

"With about a dozen men, I moved quickly up the half mile to the place where we'd left off earlier. We came to the tank ditch, climbed across on a dead tank that straddled it. It was raining, bone-chilling cold, and eerily quiet. We groped along not knowing quite how far we were going nor what we would find when and if we got there. We came to a shattered barbed wire fence, the kind the Germans put up on their side of the minefield to keep their own people from wandering in. I assumed that this was as far as I needed to go, that the road ahead was clear.

"Just to make sure, we continued, oh so cautiously, forward. Then the clouds shifted. I saw the outlines of houses, heard German voices. If they saw us they must have assumed we were also Germans. Nothing happened. I tapped the man in front of me [Pvt. Archie Stewart] on the shoulder, told him to swing his mine detector around, and head back. There were three of us at that point in our little parade, and we walked in silence, folding back on the rest of our guys and reversing our march.

"When we reached the ditch, I asked the mine detector man if the ditch had been checked. He said he didn't know but he'd check to make sure. But the edge of the hole was not firm, as we had believed; it was soft and crumbly. He started to slide in and I tried to catch him. But I was too late. He slid onto a mine, which killed him and hit me with a scattering of shrapnel. As I fell, a second mine exploded, which blew over me and killed Pvt. Merle Mallard, the man behind me.

"Now the enemy was alerted and with machine guns zeroed in earlier, they let us have it. My right leg was broken, but I hopped on the other leg, climbed across the ditch on the tank, and then was hit in the same leg by a spray of bullets, one of which is still in there. My belly was torn open, a couple of fingers were shattered, and I had pieces of metal embedded all over my face. Sergeant Bellestri and his guys got me back to the infantry front line headquarters.

"I reported to [Captain John R.] "Bill" Terry [B Company commander] there that we would need a couple of bays of Treadway bridge [to cover the crater]. Bill had a new lieutenant beside him, and by protocol he should have inherited my platoon. But this was no place for a rookie, and besides, Captain Terry was just too jaw-gritting mad to let the opportunity get away from him and he took over himself. Bill was shot in the chest and in the leg for his troubles. Bill was awarded the Distinguished Service Cross for that action. Another DSC went to a wild young private named Potter. In addition to the medal, Potter got the pass to Paris promised to me by Colonel Fry. I had a week in a Paris hospital as part of my thirteen months of convalescence."

14

Deeper into the Woods

From Schevenhutte, elements of the 47th Infantry, 9th Division, pushed north to overrun the dairy at Bovenberg and, beyond that difficult assignment, take on the task of aiding the drive of the 104th Division through the Stolberg corridor. Buttressed by units from the 3d Armored Division, the 47th was to secure the hamlets of Hucheln, Wilhelmshohe, and a particularly prickly outpost, Frenzerburg Castle. The strategy envisioned a linkup with the 104th Division, which would cross the Inde River on the way to the Roer.

The effort that began on Thanksgiving saw a battalion from the 47th ravaged by entrenched German machine guns and bigger weapons. It was not until 24 November that Hucheln fell, and then the next day Wilhelmshohe, although in both instances, the support of tanks lagged because of soft ground, mines, and antitank guns. Attention shifted to the Frenzerburg objective, a fortified castle redolent of knighthood during the Middle Ages. It overlooked an open area and jeopardized any advance in its vicinity.

Chester Jordan, 3d Platoon leader with Company K of the 47th, and his closest associates believed that having endured the Bovenberg battle, they were to enter corps reserve "and have a few days out of sight and shot of the Germans." The expected deliverance from combat vanished almost immediately. Jordan was informed that the 2d Battalion of the regiment would be making an attack and needed his company "to go out and be a spectator on their left flank while they got the job done. It's a piece of cake, a stroll in the sun, and you'll be back for a good dinner."

Ignorant of the objective for the 2d Battalion, the eighty men of Company K entered an area marked by sugar beet fields with train tracks running through it. Jordan said he glanced over the rail line and spied a column of German soldiers, their greatcoats flapping in the wind, headed in the opposite direction. "It was the Ninth Army's sector, but I knew nothing of their troop locations. These Germans seemed to think they did. It is not encouraging to see the enemy going toward your rear, even if you have a rail line between you."

The promised piece of pastry quickly turned prickly. "Everything in the world hit us, mortar, 40mm ack-ack, MG, and some things I couldn't identify. We were in a fishbowl and everyone was looking down our throat." The troops found some refuge in a deep drainage ditch with weeds, bushes, even small saplings.

Jordan sought out Lt. Hubert Urban, his company commander, after persuading one "bona fide case of battle fatigue" to head for the aid station. "There was a copse of woods about 200 yards ahead that extended from the rail line well into the beet field. In the middle of the woods was what appeared to be a large house with towers and solid walls. I asked the CO, 'Why don't we get into that house and out of this shit?' He said, 'Go ahead, you take it and we will follow.'

"I set the platoon off as I walked back, telling each to run to the woods. By the time I had gotten the last man started, most of the platoon was lying out in that beet field at one place or another, either cowed by the MG or tripped on beets. Most had not been hit. They saw someone else drop, so they did and stuck their noses in the mud. If you can't see them, they can't see you. I felt sympathy, because running on beets is like running on loosely packed bowling balls. I was running around, kicking ass, cussing, threatening, and trying not to break my ankles at the same time. Some got going, and I am sure some were shot by the Krauts for not going."

When Jordan reached the woods, he found several German soldiers "standing in their half-dug holes, looking at me. They had guns in their hands, but they were not using them at that moment." They surrendered on his command. As he walked through the thicket, Jordan now realized the building he had seen was beyond the stand of trees and another 200 yards of open beet fields. The large, tall structure itself struck him as more Victorian than Gothic. As he studied the sight, Sgt. James Searles, from the 1st Platoon, came up behind him. Bullets continued to spew from the castle. "I told the sergeant [whom he did not know] that I was afraid if we stood around gawking, one of those bullets would find us, so we would try for the building."

Another rush, while bullets snapped about them, brought Jordan and Searles to a hedge that ran before a lower building. "There were about thirty or so German soldiers complete with rifles dug in along the hedge. The two nearest us stood up, and I shot one in the jaw, and the sergeant shooting over my head killed the other. The remainder threw their rifles down and [put] their hands up."

With the prisoners, service troops who demonstrated little expertise with their weapons and a readiness to surrender, the Company K band, enlarged to twelve by the arrival of others in the platoon, barged into the courtyard. A door in the low building led to a cellar, and Jordan stashed the captives there. Rifle fire from the castle itself forced the Americans to take cover. The platoon leader saw big, heavy, wooden double doors leading into the castle. It was approached by a stone or concrete bridge with balusters over a moat.

Jordan summoned his bazooka man. "I told [Pfc. Carl V.] Sheridan to go up to the baluster and take his best shot at the hinges of the far door. When he had fired, he was to stay put until I could determine if there was a hole big enough for us to get through. He arrived at the baluster without incident, rested his bazooka on top of it, and fired. It hit where he was firing, but there was a big dust cloud covering the whole doorway, so I waited for it to clear before making a decision. At that time, Sheridan stood up, looked around at me, and said, 'Well, are we going in?' He was shot, dead. The door had been knocked off one hinge, but it still hung in the way, so I didn't think it wise to attack. It is too bad, because at that time we probably had almost as many men as they did."

Jordan had dispersed his small group around the barn area with most of them in the southern unit. For the next two days, the castle and its environs witnessed cat-and-mouse skirmishes of Germans and GIs. "Sergeant [Clarence] Myers," said Jordan, "was having a one-man war in the east unit. They shot everything they had at him, including machine guns and *panzerfausts* without even scratching his bottle-bottom glasses. He would fire from the ground floor for a little while until it got too hot, and then he would go upstairs." Myers, a former Cadillac salesman from St. Paul, Minnesota, was about thirty years old, Jordan believed. Afflicted with a ruptured eardrum, a hernia, wearing thick eyeglasses, he was a veteran of combat dating back to North Africa, "He may have been the only fearless man I ever met, indefatigable, unflappable."

Later, when Jordan took command of the company, Myers acted as platoon leader so often that Jordan cajoled him into giving his permission to nominate him for a battlefield commission, but he flunked the physicals. At Jordan's insistence that they either promote Myers or discharge him as physically unfit, the higher powers relented. "He took a pay cut," said Jordan, "because lieutenants in combat made less than sergeants. Later, he lost a leg in combat but survived the war."

"Just before dark," said Jordan, "a kamikaze sprinted from the bridge toward a door, just north of me, where Sgt. Tom Sheldon hung out. The hobnail boots insured our attention, and he was blasted short of the door. Sheldon pulled him in and he was carrying twenty-eight hand grenades and a P38 [pistol]—a human bomb.

"About sunset on the 26th, the Germans attacked the cellar, killed our guards, and repatriated their men and captured two or more K Company men. Evan B. "Red" Thompson, the radioman, was in the cellar with Lieutenant Urban when the attack came. They had been wounded by the railroad tracks and brought in by German medics. He says that three Germans hit the door with burp guns and were about to spray the room when the medics shouted that there were only Germans and wounded Americans left.

"I undoubtedly had my head in my ass during all of this. An artillery forward observer had come into our barn with his two radiomen, and I chatted with the FO. I was sitting on a concrete feed trough, leaning against the upper half of a Dutch door, when a Schmeisser [machine pistol] was stuck in the door next to my ear and hosed down the pigpens. I fell back into the trough with my ears ringing, while bullets ricocheted around the sties like angry bees. No one received a scratch, but by the time I looked out the door, our assailant had disappeared. Obviously, this was the time of the counterattack and the reason I missed it."

The FO, after consultation with Jordan, attempted to call in fire upon the castle, but the battery refused because the Germans and the Americans shared the same coordinates. The executive officer of Company K, 1st Lt. William L. McWatters, had followed the path taken by Jordan and crawled through a hole in the wall around the buildings. He advised the platoon leader that with Urban wounded, he was now in charge. "He said he could operate better from the woods, so he was leaving me in command of the troops in the barns until further notice." Jordan reiterated his desire for artillery on the castle without results.

More than eighty German paratroop engineers reinforced the soldiers holding the castle. An American captain attempted to negotiate a surrender. The German officer refused but accepted a cease-fire to remove the wounded. Subsequently, a runner brought a message to Jordan that he and his fellow Americans could pull out. Artillery would then demolish the stronghold. Both sides slipped away. During the morning of 28 November, after an explosive outburst that included incendiary white phosphorus shells, two companies from the 47th's 2d Battalion entered the smoking ruins, and the battle for Frenzerburg Castle was over.

At 2400 on the cold, black rainy night of 24 November, the V Corps dispatched the 5th Armored Division's Combat Command R, attached to the 8th Infantry Division, into the forest with the village of Huertgen as the objective. The drive was spearheaded by Task Force Boyer (after Lt. Col. Howard Boyer), composed of elements from the 47th Armored Infantry Battalion and the 10th Tank Battalion, which left the base at Roetgen separately and were to meet on the road between Germeter and Huertgen.

After the foot soldiers left their half-tracks in the early hours of the morning, they trudged into the heavily mined forest. Weather and shells had obliterated the white tape put down by engineers to mark a safe passage, and calls for medics announced the first casualties. Enemy guns, large and small, fired into the woods. Antitank mines frustrated Task Force Boyer's armor, and three tank commanders were victims of snipers. Small arms and mortars peppered engineers who attempted to bridge the huge craters.

By early afternoon, with little or no progress achieved, only eighty of the 225 men from the 47th Infantry's B Company remained able to fight. Medics supplemented by GIs from the antitank platoon could not cope with the volume of wounded. C Company came forward to try a flank attack through the woods, but, after only fifteen minutes amid the mines and artillery blasts, fifty of its complement lay wounded or dead. Task Force Boyer retreated.

The 8th Division's commander, General Stroh, deeply disappointed at this most recent failure, directed Tom Cross to employ his 121st Infantry to seize Huertgen. After hearing his mission at division headquarters, Cross noted, "No doubt a tough job. Held a meeting of battalion commanders and issued instructions but new order came from commanding general, to send two battalions, one from the 121st and one from the 13th [Infantry], to attack across country."

Wretched intelligence spawned this fiasco. According to Paul Boesch, the assistant division commander, Brig. Gen. Charles Canham, told him, "We're getting ready to move in right now. The fact is F Company has already pushed off. I'm sure the town is empty. Air saw a long column marching away from it."

Subsequently, two prisoners offered conflicting information. One said that about 100 dispirited men had been prevented from surrender only by a handful of officers who remained in Huertgen. Another captive warned of some 400 prepared to fight to the death. Battalion commander Lt. Col. Henry B. Kunzig chose to believe the first man who appeared to confirm the information relayed by Canham.

The renewed attack by the 2d Battalion of the 121st, in the form of Company F led by Capt. John Cliett and Company G under First Lieutenant Boesch, would leave the woods to the southwest and strike at the town. Unfortunately, the supportive artillery would lay siege only to the center of Huertgen, where the remnants of the German forces would be, leaving structures on the outskirts untouched. To hit them would mean pulling back F Company, which had already advanced to positions on the road near these buildings. Cliett and Boesch protested to Kunzig, who refused to approve any withdrawal or alteration in plans. The field telephone lines ran through Boesch's bunker, and he listened in as Kunzig relayed the misgivings voiced by the two company commanders to Cross.

The latter adamantly refused the suggestion for a temporary pullback to allow artillery an opportunity to blast the nearby buildings. "Not one inch, he said," recalled Boesch. "We will not move that company nor any other company back one single inch, Kunzig. I'll hit them with every weapon we've got that will fire. We'll keep it up all night and then give them a concentrated dose in the morning just before the attack." But despite the assurances, Boesch saw the artillery fire line did not cover the suspected strong points of enemy defenses.

The scheme proceeded. Following the avalanche of ordnance on the outer reaches of Huertgen, the GIs left the cover of the trees to be greeted by a withering storm of small-arms fire from these buildings, which stopped them cold.

Cross summarized the operation: "The 1st Battalion of the 13th did not get off. The 2d Battalion, 121, got one company a few hundred yards from town but was forced to stop. Altogether too many fingers in the pie are messing with plans. This applies particularly to V Corps headquarters." Quite possibly, Cross had refused to heed the pleas of the 2d Battalion company officers because of thunder from the upper echelons. He, of course, owed his new command to the perceived failings of his predecessor, and no one in the regimental and division hierarchy could be unaware of the strident demands from corps and army for progress, seemingly regardless of the costs.

Cross resumed the siege of Huertgen. He directed the attached 1st Battalion of the 13th Regiment, minus its heavy weapons company, under the cover of the early hours of darkness, to approach the eastern edge of the town. However, he received erroneous information of the unit's exact placement, and there was further error in the location of some of his other troops. As a consequence, his plan of attack was delayed for a day.

To top off the mistakes, Kunzig advised Cross that patrols would slip into Huertgen during the night "to ascertain the presence of the Boche." Cross was agreeably surprised to hear at 9 P.M. that the town was free of Germans. "I directed E and G Companies to move in immediately and occupy the place as far as the church in the center. [I] directed the 1st Battalion of the 13th to do likewise, initially with patrols and then to send one company to the northeast side of town. This was accomplished without incident, before dawn. During the night, I was constantly advised that the town would fall like a plum, and, based on that information, I suspended the attack of the 1st Battalion but directed that it should be prepared to jump off at 0700."

Within the town, the small group of Americans exchanged a few shots with an unidentified source and someone ignited a building with a flamethrower. Paul Boesch, leading G Company, occupied a communications ditch about 100 yards from Huertgen along with some sixty riflemen in foxholes. He had dispatched one of the patrols during the night into Huertgen. It collided with the GIs of the 13th Infantry, and a firefight among Americans was narrowly avoided. Despite the assurances given by Kunzig, Boesch's patrol returned with confirmation of hostile forces still on the scene.

Cross scribbled in his journal, "I was informed by Lieutenant Colonel Kunzig that the town of Huertgen had come to life and that the battalion was back where it started from."

When morning light broke, any doubts were erased by showers of shells from Huertgen. Although the eruption produced no casualties, it blew away the telephone line. With his radio inoperative, Boesch said, "We remained out of touch with the rest of the U.S. Army. Jerry alone seemed to know or even care where we were, though we could hardly appreciate the violent way in which he reacted to us."

The members of G Company frantically tinkered with the radio to link themselves with battalion headquarters. As they repaired the apparatus, a covey of medium tanks clanked out of the woods and rumbled along the road leading into Huertgen. At that moment, the radio whispered to life, bearing orders to join the tanks in the assault.

As they readied themselves to leave, a sergeant brought word for Boesch to confer with a full colonel in a nearby house. To the captain's astonishment, the stranger identified himself as Col. P. D. Ginder from the 2d Infantry Division. The V Corps commander, Gerow, dubious apparently about the resolve of the 8th Division, had named Ginder to take over the assault upon Huertgen. To

Boesch, Ginder radiated a confidence previously absent. He directed the G Company leader, "Get with your men. Keep them moving and don't stop. We're going to take this town."

Later, the 2d Division colonel bragged, "Boys, I'm the one that took this town of Huertgen." He described the battle: "No movie script could equal the actual action in the taking of this town. Men didn't work in any formation, they worked in teams like clockwork."

His remark glossed over the awful fury that enveloped those immersed in the struggle. Boesch wrote, "It was a wild, terrible, awe-inspiring thing, this sweep through Huertgen. Never in my wildest imagination had I conceived that battle could be so incredibly impressive—awful, horrible, deadly, yet somehow thrilling, exhilarating. Now the fight for Huertgen was at its wildest. We dashed, struggled from one building to another shooting, bayoneting, clubbing. Hand grenades roared, rifles cracked—buildings to the left and right burned with acrid smoke. Dust, smoke, and powder filled our lungs, making us cough, spit. Automatic weapons chattered hoarsely, while throats of mortars and artillery disgorged deafening explosions. The wounded and the dead—men in the uniforms of both sides—lay in grotesque positions at every turn. From many the blood still flowed."

In describing the ultimate success, Cross wrote, "This was accomplished by putting platoons of tanks carrying infantry in the lead, followed by tank destroyers. After furious fighting, captured the place, including 350 prisoners. Losses were heavy. At nightfall, the 1st and 2d Battalion in town, the 1st Battalion, 13th, on its objective, and the regiment disposed for attack to the south."

As a radio operator in a forward crew for the 56th Field Artillery, supporting the 121st Infantry, Arthur Wagenseil occupied a position on the outskirts of Huertgen. "On the way up we saw many bodies, and the ground was saturated with blood. We stopped to examine some of the dead. There were two very young, younger than I—I was twenty-five. One had the top of his head blown off and you could see the entire brain. We noticed a shoulder patch on the overcoats, from the Air Corps. Those poor guys never had a chance. They didn't even have time to get the 8th Division patch on and were killed. They probably never had infantry training. I was so angry I could have cried, to think that the army threw these poor guys into the Huertgen Forest. [It is possible those with Air Corps insignia belonged to an observation team.]

"The Germans were very stubborn about the town. We were on top of a ridge and the Germans on the bottom. We tried three jump-offs and couldn't make it down to the bottom. The Germans tried three times to come up the ridge and they were repulsed. It was a stalemate for a while."

Among those from the 8th Division who moved into Huertgen was Ernest Carlson, radio operator for an 81mm mortar unit. "We got into a basement of a house. It was a blessing to be out of foxholes for awhile. The church in Huertgen was used as a first-aid station. You could not count the number of Keystone Division [28th] helmets that were stacked up in the basement. When it began to thaw, we found German bodies stuffed into basement windows for blackout purposes. It enabled them to burn candles in the basement."

While the American losses mounted at an unprecedented scale compared to previous campaigns, the offensives severely weakened the enemy. Hubert Gees, the German company runner in the 275th Division, had been fighting off the Americans from the first week of October. In his recollections of that period, he noted, "strong artillery fire surprised us once again. Bright red clouds of phosphorus shells darkened the cellar space. Infantry fire commenced from the front lines 300 meters away . . . north of the minefield Wilde Sau, a defense was made against the infantry attack. South of the minefield, a unit of the 12th Regiment had broken through our second company up the main road. The remainder of our company, consisting of only eighteen soldiers, had formed a small bridgehead before the mine-free side road around the company command post.

"With gathering darkness, our neighboring company on the east side started shooting in front of our positions toward the edge of the forest. For us, that was the agreed-upon signal to advance. . . . My comrade Brand and I reached a dugout that belonged to a machine gun position. With lightning speed we tore away the entrance curtain and extinguished the pocket lamp. However, we did not need to order, 'Hands up!' The dugout was empty.

"The Americans had withdrawn to their own lines, taken prisoners with them. But at our machine gun position, which I now with Brand took over, lay three dead, among whom were our top kick [first sergeant], who as an officer candidate had been ordered from the front ten days before."

After several more days, Gees noted that his unit was shifted into Huertgen. "Immediately upon our arrival on a side street, we had to take cover because of heavy artillery fire. With four men from the old 2d Company, all born in 1926 [eighteen years old at the time], we landed in [a cellar] where on the morning of 28 November we were taken prisoner."

As a captive, Gees could hear the sounds of battle for the next objective, marked by the on-board cannons of P-47s on a nearby ridge. "It was a major stroke of luck for us no longer to be in position there. Fate or divine providence led us down this road here into the valley and into captivity, seven men, all that was left of the 2d Company Fusilier Battalion [originally 100 soldiers]."

During this period, the 16th Infantry of the 1st Division continued to press northeast after the seizure of the hamlet of Hamich, in front of which John Beach had been severely wounded, and his friend Jim Wood, with less than a dozen GIs, staved off counterattacks. Beach reported, "We stayed back of the front lines only a week before going into the attack. Our assembly area was a few hundred yards back, the same assembly area we had used before. We moved through the woods to a clearing and received instructions that our objective was a small cluster of houses only a couple of hundred yards away. The houses were visible to us and we were visible to the Germans.

"As soon as we left the woods, the Germans opened up on us with machine guns down the fire lanes that were already prepared. It was plain murder, but we had to cross the lines of fire. We had started out with 170 men. A 100 or so reached the houses. Back of us, the clearing was littered with the dead and wounded we left behind. We had the satisfaction of getting those machine gunners. The houses weren't occupied, so I put my men in them, as we expected the Germans would try to get us out of there. There was a road running down the middle [of the village], and the German attack sent tanks and men down the road, smashing at us with machine guns. They had the place well scouted and all the windows covered.

"We didn't have a chance. A couple of tanks stopped right in front and began shooting down the street. I saw a house go up in flames. The fellows inside couldn't get out. They were burned alive. Another tank appeared back of the house I was occupying, the muzzle of its big gun directed at the rear door. It sent in a couple of shells, showering the place with fragments, killing one of the men with me. We ran down to the basement and heard the hobnailed boots of the Germans on the floor above us. The basement door opened and a grenade was hurled in among us. We dove behind a pile of rubble and it exploded. I decided it was all over and I surrendered. The first thing the Germans did was take our rings and watches. Then they herded us together and marched us many miles to a railroad stop, where we were packed into cattle cars and transported to a temporary camp on a railroad track at Limburg. That night the RAF bombed Limburg. Many of the prisoners were killed. It was awful. I remember dragging people out of blazing buildings only to discover they were dead." Wood endured several prison camps, saw other inmates shot in the back for minor infractions, and held a reunion with Beach before liberation in 1945.

While the 16th Infantry struggled for Hamich and Heistern, the 1st Division's 26th Infantry contended for wooded hills that overlooked a strategically valuable road between Schevenhutte and Langewehe and opened the way to important towns just beyond the fringe of the forest. For ten days, the 1st Division soldiers doggedly fought forward as the lines of the opposing forces faced off within hand-grenade range.

The GIs seized the village of Jungersdorf, and General Huebner requested the regimental commander, Lt. Col. John F. R. Seitz, to take a crack at the next objective, Merode, which featured a medieval castle. The plans included an air strike, concentrated artillery, and Shermans from the 745th Tank Battalion accompanying the advancing infantry.

Private First Class Alvin Bulau, a replacement assistant gunner in the platoon leader's crew was with a tank from Company C on 29

November. "Our objective is a little town called Merode. It is in the open about 600 yards down a gentle slope from the edge of the woods. We are to move along the road until we come to the edge of the woods. We then deploy along the edge and give supporting fire to the doughs.

"We move about a quarter of a mile, when suddenly we hear the staccato burst of machine gun fire. I have got my periscope going in all directions. I cannot see a thing. Finally, the lieutenant sees that it is a German machine gun nest that opened up on our doughs that rounded a curve. Gig's tank moves up closer. I take a quick look at 'Guinea.' His eyes are glued to the sights and his foot ready to press the solenoid trigger. The nest is neutralized by Gig's guns, so we relax a bit.

"We continue to move. The doughs meet an occasional sniper left behind to delay us as much as possible. Snipers are not to be taken lightly, because they have accounted for many men. By now the air is a screaming mass of shells going both ways. Jerry knows what's coming and he is throwing plenty at us. They are mostly tree bursts. That is ten times as bad as a ground hit, because the shrapnel flies straight down as well as out.

"The assaulting company is taking a beating. Men are getting hit right and left. A sergeant in front of us gets hit in the leg, and I see him drag himself to the ditch. Then a shell lands in that exact spot where he was laying. It was a direct hit. I do not like to even look at that spot because I know what is there. Nothing but odd-colored lumps. Some of them dirt and the rest torn bits of a human body. It is like that all over, men getting hit just enough to stop them and then getting torn apart by that unmerciful shrapnel. We can hear the sharp crack as fragments ricochet off our armor. I send a prayer to God, thankful that we have at least that protection.

"The men are fighting not only the enemy but fighting fatigue and fighting that almost overwhelming desire to run and hide in a hole. But no, those boys have got guts. They keep going until knocked down by flying steel."

The advance is slow and by afternoon the tanks are about 150 yards from the tree line. Another infantry company takes over the responsibility for the assault, while the tanks crawl slowly forward. "There is a sudden lurch and I find myself on the turret floor. Ammo has rolled all over. I look up and see that the tank is leaning at a crazy angle. I realize then that we have gone into the ditch. Tom is trying to drive out but we just sink deeper. Guinea presses the gun to see if we can possibly use it. It won't go down far enough. We are absolutely of no good."

Others from the platoon maneuver around the mired tank while a tank dozer comes forward to assist. "The Germans have heard all the noise, and now they are throwing more stuff than I have ever seen. I can see a squad of men moving across behind JB's tank. Good Lord! A heavy shell just hit in the middle of them. All I can see is black smoke and bits of dirt falling. The smoke's clearing. All I can see are two men. One is dead for sure, but the other is on his hands and knees. He too must be dead for he doesn't move a bit when a shell goes over.

"There is a sudden loud crash. I see fire going every way. I am on the floor and the lieutenant is on top of me. We just had a hit on the front end. My head feels like it is about to split open and I am shaking like a leaf. The lieutenant takes a quick look around and sees that everyone is okay. We hear some rapping on the side of the turret. The lieutenant opens his hatch a little and he sees that it is a dough. He is a runner from battalion and says that orders are to move into the town. As he turns to go, he is caught in the back with shrapnel. He was killed instantly. It is surely death to go outside now."

The crew with Bulau prepared to renew the thrust toward Merode, but the tank takes another hit on the rear deck. "Gasoline starts to run over the floor of the tank. The drain plugs won't work. The tank is bellied in mud. What will happen if we are hit again. [It was not for nothing that the Germans referred to Shermans as 'Ronsons.'] JB's tank slides into the ditch opposite. Both tanks are useless."

On the order to abandon the vehicle. Bulau disables the gun sights and removes the radio crystals. He takes his submachine gun and is the last to leave. Outside, he cannot see any of the others from the crew, who have disappeared back up the road. "I keep running; the mud is like glue. I run past a burning tank destroyer. There are two dead soldiers beside it."

There were American wounded scattered around. A sergeant with a boy who has lost his foot reports he is the only one left from his platoon. Darkness was falling and the shelling abated slightly. Cowering by the road, the assistant gunner heard the sound of a tank. Taking a chance, he peeped out from his cover and it was an American tank. Promising to send help for all the wounded, he jumped on top. Hauled inside, he joined thirteen others. A mile back, Bulau was able to inform his superiors of the many in need of rescue, and a Weasel was dispatched. "I couldn't help thinking about those boys out there, crying for help. I wonder if they died thinking I deserted them."

Men from the 2d Battalion of the 26th Infantry battled their way into the town but started to receive heavy fire from the east. Bombs from the planes did nothing to dampen the incoming nor did the American big guns blast the enemy from its positions. A trio of tanks summoned to aid the occupiers of Merode, slunk off after German shells struck two. A request for additional tanks was denied on the grounds that the 2d Battalion had not properly deployed those already assigned. Once again the weakness in tank-infantry coordination surfaced.

According to the historian Charles MacDonald, the 1st Division sent a message to Hodges, stating that "contact will be reestablished without too much difficulty tomorrow." Given the desperate circumstances of the men trapped in Merode and the determination of the enemy troops, the optimism is hard to understand. It certainly conveyed the impression that there was no cause to commit reserves whose weight might break down the enemy resistance.

The Germans swiftly created a wall between the small number of Americans in Merode and those in the woods hoping to "reestablish contact" with their comrades. Mud, wrecked vehicles, and a steady ambuscade from enemy weapons prevented the frustrated commanders of the 26th from reaching the beleaguered in Merode. Panzers clattered into the village, training their guns on the shrinking number of trapped soldiers. The sounds of battle died away and only four men escaped; the 26th Infantry listed 165 missing in action as Merode returned to German control.

The inability of the 8th Division to provide Gerow and Hodges with the results they demanded had exhausted its commander, Maj.

Gen. Donald Stroh. Grieving over the recent death of his son, a pilot, Stroh requested a twenty-day leave and he never returned to the 8th. Brigadier General Walter Weaver took over.

Despite the terrible toll inflicted upon it, the 5th Armored's CCR persevered. It formed Task Force Hamberg (after Lt. Col. William A. Hamberg) to strike at Kleinhau, a town northeast of Huertgen. The battle noise—artillery, dive-bombers, and lesser arms—mentioned by Hubert Gees involved the forces now struggling toward Kleinhau. Task Force Hamberg threw the 47th Armored Infantry and the 10th Tank Battalion at Kleinhau, following an awesome three-day avalanche of shelling, topped off with eighteen artillery battalion TOTs and fighter-bomber strikes. The torrent of abuse heaped on the village destroyed it but not the power of the German troops.

Mud mired some armor; erroneous word of minefields deterred infantrymen riding half-tracks. The foot soldiers dismounted only to come under punishing artillery fire and took refuge behind the tanks. Nevertheless, the attackers rallied sufficiently to bull their way into the ruins. Although Task Force Hamberg evicted the enemy, it found itself badly exposed in the rubble of Kleinhau and its immediate vicinity. German self-propelled guns pummeled the outfit until higher headquarters permitted a withdrawal to a wooded area.

Colonel Cross at the 121st headquarters tersely noted, "Tough going, all ammunition, food, water, etc., had to be carried by hand for a distance of 3,000 yards. This battalion [3d] needs a rest. 1st Battalion not too good. Needs a new commander. Job ahead looks tough, big woods to the east of Huertgen should be cleaned out. Not enough troops being employed to give the push required."

On the first day of December, Cross gloomily recounted, "Operation today started rather poorly. 3d Battalion had a tough time and was cracking its head against a group of pillboxes with poor results. One pillbox was captured with thirty-five prisoners. The German officers shot men in this area when they attempted to surrender. The 1st Battalion relieved from its terrible position in mud and water and moved into Huertgen. Later one company moved to Kleinhau, relieving the 46th AIB. Troops are in bad shape and need a rest *badly*. Should be relieved."

With Company E of the 22d Regiment, Capt. Don Faulkner and his troops burrowed into the earth in a wooded area just beyond Grosshau. "We were told we were to be relieved and that morning, the new division, a sorry-looking outfit [the 83d Infantry Division] came to relieve us. They were very jittery and of course they should have been. They were under fire when they came in and we put two men in each hole. I didn't tell them that the night before, when we had been warned of a counterattack, I started to go round and warn the men myself. I did three holes and instructed, 'One man up, bayonet fixed, one man down. Prepare for counterattack. Pass it on.' That morning in the first light I saw only three holes with the bayonet sticking up. I walked over and asked if they passed my message on. The answer was 'no.' The rest of the company was sound asleep. We would have been open season if the Krauts had actually come through with their counterattack."

While walking toward this area a few days earlier, Faulkner had seen a shovel flash in the sun from a nearby hill. Having some knowledge of artillery tactics, he had consigned to his memory the map registration number for that locale. After some enemy fire doused his positions, Faulkner requested that the regimental cannon company concentrate on that particular registration. "After they blasted that hill we had no more fire. I'm positive that the Germans had a forward observer up there, looking down our throat, and we'd knocked him out."

With the substitution of the 83d Division soldiers, Faulkner welcomed the opportunity to leave. "We sent a squad at a time over into the woods and down the road to Grosshau. I was the last one to come out in the dark. You have never seen anyone so relieved and so exhausted as I was as we walked through Grosshau, down the road to the big woods, where our company and battalion lay down in the rain and went to sleep soundly. The next day we were in trucks headed for a rest area in Luxembourg. My feet were cold. I am sure I had frozen them, the circulation was so bad. We had about sixty-three men left; the rest had gone back to the aid station."

George Wilson's F Company, fighting in the Grosshau sector, had been reduced to twelve able-bodied GIs. Dug in alongside

Faulkner's E Company, the outfit picked up sixty-six enlisted replacements plus a couple of new officers. Word came from battalion headquarters that Wilson would be recommended for the Distinguished Service Cross and a promotion to captain. Neither reward came through, but on 3 December, as it had for Faulkner's contingent, the survivors of F welcomed the 83d Division. "I toured them around my defensive position and cautioned them not to bunch up, because we probably were under observation and would draw fire. They paid no attention to the warning and continued to move around in a tight group. In less than a minute, the shells began to whistle in. One landed not far from the captain, and although he had not been hit, he claimed he couldn't get up. Some of my men had to carry him into my dugout." Like Faulkner, Wilson viewed the newcomers as undisciplined and poorly led. Nevertheless, he was delighted to depart.

When portions of the 22d Infantry Combat Team began its thrust toward Grosshau, they had collaborated with the 46th Armored Infantry, nominally an element of CCA of the 5th Armored Division. They, too, suffered cruelly because of misinformation. Troops from Companies A and C embarked on a mission in which the dismounted soldiers would attack through American positions on a bald knob near designated Hill 401. A few hundred yards from Grosshau, the heights afforded an excellent view for artillery observers in the vicinity. As the dismounted forces under Lt. Col. William H. Burton, Jr., started out, they were assured their comrades from CCR held 401.

Less certain of who owned 401, people from the 22d Infantry, who had dodged artillery and mortar fire as they tried to ascertain the disposition atop the hill, tried to warn CCR of potential trouble. Unfortunately, Burton's radio had failed, and, lacking further word or cautionary advice, the two companies from the 46 AIB emerged from wooded cover and in almost parade ground march formation began the ascent of Hill 401. A shower of small-arms fire, interspersed with thunderous artillery and mortar explosions, erupted.

Nick Tschida, rejected by the marines in 1942 because of his slight stature—five feet, eight inches, 145 pounds—had planned to enter the navy, but the draft swept him into the army in March 1942. He trained in the California desert with the 46th Armored Infantry, and it was with Company B that, as 2d platoon sergeant, he entered the Huertgen Forest. "We were shelled a lot but had no head-to-head confrontation until 29 November. I did not know at the start of the program what the mission was about, except that A Company and maybe C Company would lead an assault across 1,200 yards of open ground to reach another part of the forest. B Company was supposed to be in reserve while A led.

"When the shells started to fall, I guess A Company became disorganized and B Company received the juicy honors. Like a lot of other times it was, 'Okay, Second Platoon, take the lead.' I think I had a Lieutenant [James] Foster at that time. He called for his squad leaders and asked, 'Where will you be, Nick?' 'I will be wherever you want me to be, with you, in the middle of the platoon, or in the rear of the platoon pushing the men on and on.' Most of the time I was just behind the 2d Squad, directing and leading comrades, patching up wounded, cradling the dying. We no sooner jumped off when the shelling increased and the enemy machine guns started spraying. Lieutenant Foster and the first two rifle squads took out one or perhaps the second one.

"Captain [Robert C.] Bland [the acting S-3 of the battalion] said we had 35 to 40 percent casualties. For awhile I thought I was the platoon medic. It was quite cold; I thought it to be about 10 degrees above. It got cold enough to start freezing my feet and legs. (After the war I learned I have very small arteries and veins, which causes this.) We dug in and were motionless for at least two days, when a runner from the CP—Lieutenant Foster was acting CO—said, 'Tschida, form your platoon. Make sure all rifles are working, et cetera, go up and see what's going on.' This was about December 5 or 6. So, it was fix bayonets, check your bolts and ammunition, and be ready for action. I chose Stu Persinger as my scout. He and I would run the program. I was the platoon leader, without the promotion to lieutenant.

"We had only gone about 100 yards when the big shells started to rain down on us, taking some toll on the platoon. We were not near any foxholes, so we had to hug the ground the best we could.

Shortly, the CO called to cancel the program and move back to our original starting point. While the shells got bigger and bigger, the men got to some shelter as best they could.

"During the two days, while sitting still in foxholes most of the time, my feet and legs had become more frozen and navigating with them became impossible. Now, a huge shell landed between Sgt. Champ Montgomery and me, as well as the other 1st Squad members. It took care of Montgomery's hearing and damn near amputated my left arm at the shoulder. A large shell fragment, red hot, dug a hole two inches from my shoulder then bounded away to land sizzling in the snow.

"Trying to get about my duties, my legs failed me, and I asked Sgt. Bill Grant to take over while I trudged and crawled to the medic station a short distance behind us. Not realizing that the shell blast took a toll on my equilibrium, I kept falling down a lot. Two medics helped me into the station, sat me down right next to the pot-bellied stove, and gave me the 'Blue 88' [morphine injection] that put me out of the war right quick. A few days later, I came round to find myself in a temporary schoolhouse hospital. They would ship me to a hospital in England, and after nearly three months and almost having one leg taken off, I was released." His war was over, although it took him a year and a half to obliterate the nightmares.

Clifford Lamb served as a member of a mortar squad with Company B in the 46th AIB. He described the Huertgen as "a dark, brooding, evergreen forest. Now, in late November, the trees dripped with the incessant rains. Blanketed by fog in the short winter days, it was shrouded by blackness in the long winter nights."

Like those who had gone before him, Lamb gaped at the shredded trees, the mud-stuck vehicles, "the German and American soldiers [who] still lay where they had fallen." His column paused in the woods before Kleinhau as the half-tracks edged off the road around the corpse of a German soldier sprawled beside the pathway. "The platoon leader called out, 'Once you are on the ground, don't move around. The place is booby trapped.' Hardly had this been said [when], as one GI moved forward, a Bouncing Betty he had stepped on jumped waist high behind him. Seeing it, I yelled, 'Hit the ground!' Had the second charge exploded, yelling would have been too late. We all were yet to live for the next day's battle."

On foot, the armored infantry advanced to the edge of a firebreak that led to a clearing before Kleinhau. Said Lamb, "The firebreak had been churned into raw mud by tank treads. Teller mines removed by engineers were piled by the sides of the firebreak. Weasels, tracked ammunition carriers, now worked their way forward through the firebreak.

"Heavy barrages of U.S. artillery thundered overhead in an attempt to blast out the enemy wherever he was. The German artillery was more precise. It knew where we were. Round after round shrieked down the firebreak, bursting somewhere behind us. We hugged the ground and waited. Some medics appeared saying they needed help in evacuating wounded in the open field ahead. I, with others, went with them, but upon arriving at the edge of the woods, the medics took a look at the intense small-arms fire and decided there was not any way we could get the wounded out without getting hit ourselves. The wounded would have to wait.

"Riflemen [forward of Lamb's mortar squad] began bringing in surrendering Germans from dug-in positions in front of Kleinhau. With hands clasped behind their heads, they stumbled forward with exhaustion embedded in their dark faces, undoubtedly fearing that they might not yet survive the lethal fire erupting around them. At times like this, GIs occasionally remarked, 'They are lucky. I wish I could go back as an American prisoner too!'"

The open field in front of the town became a pitiless killing ground. Wounded from both sides, Americans and Germans unable to continue to resist, staggered, stumbled, and crawled toward the firebreak. The German artillery zeroed in on the opening, but the only chance for an injured man to survive was through that passageway to the rear.

Lamb noted, "Some didn't make it. I dove for the ground as an incoming shell exploded beside a hobbling GI heading for the firebreak entry. He twisted around and collapsed on the ground. I yelled 'Medic!' and hunched low moving quickly forward. The wounded continued to stream past us. One seemed unhurt. I asked him why he was leaving the field. He took off his helmet, showed where a bullet had gone in and out on one side, and then pointed to the long groove on the side of his head.

"Having once read that one GI survived shelling in North Africa by crawling along the ground in the several-inches-deep tank track groove, I did the same. I worked my way from shell hole to shell hole, never being willing to believe that I wouldn't make it. I could only think that this had to be a devil's football game and what could be so wrong that men had to kill each other."

A small artillery spotter plane appeared overhead and seemed to promise pinpointed artillery fire that would blast the big guns of the foe. But the Germans continued to torment the American troops with a steady rain of ordnance. The cries for medics did not slacken, and wounded steadily struggled to reach safety.

Lamb and some associates achieved the first line of houses at the edge of the village, and they huddled behind a building. "A German gunner, who perhaps really knew his field of fire, sent an artillery shell between the two houses, and it exploded beside the group. Miraculously, I was not hit. We yelled for medics. This time we lost our mortar gunner, Lou Napolitano, who had taken a shell fragment in the leg."

Jim Carnivale, a native of Fitchburg, Massachusetts, who had joined the National Guard while in high school, was a machine gunner with Company B of the 46th Armored Infantry. In the battle for Kleinhau, he recalled, "We were strictly infantry, foot sloggers. My captain told me to get another platoon up to reinforce what we had. Artillery shells were coming in like rain. I looked at him and he knew what I was thinking. I wasn't about to go out in that barrage. 'Wait till it cools off,' he said. When it did, we all moved out and that's when I got hit. I ran for a trench the Germans had dug. I knew it was there because I saw it as we went by.

"In the trench was the 2d Platoon. 'Where's the 3d?' I asked. That was the one wanted by my captain. 'Back on the road,' I was told. I followed the trench back, and as I went around a jut in it, I spotted a German soldier. I pulled back. Nothing! Gingerly, I peeked around that jut and saw a dead German who had shoveled out the side of the trench for protection. I am sure he was a victim of time fire, a shell burst above the ground.

"I started off again and the trench ended. I came up above ground and ran for the ditch alongside the road. There was a medic with no bandages or morphine, or nothing. He was trying to carry a GI wounded in both legs. We sat him on my rifle and started to carry him back across a wide open field. One of our jeep drivers saw us and brought us to the aid station.

"Mine was not a severe wound. The medics took care of the badly hurt ones first. But after they treated me, I went back to Paris and was out of action for nine weeks before I returned to my outfit in Herleen, Holland, the same place we had left to go to the forest."

Kleinhau yielded, and for the night, the GIs from Lamb's company fell back to the woods to regroup but without further harassment from enemy artillery. In the morning, B Company set out for the area beyond Kleinhau with the mortar squad formed into riflemen. They passed through the village where buildings still burned from the previous day's battle.

"On a forested hillside, through the trees, we came upon large bomb craters filled with the wounded, some with waxy faces having turned yellow [because] of the loss of blood. They were waiting for nightfall to come, so they could be safely evacuated by ambulances over the daylight-exposed roads. Alarmed by our apparent lack of caution, they yelled to us to 'keep low,' that there were snipers around.

"Here on this steep wooded hillside, we moved into shallow foxholes, apparently evacuated by some of the wounded whom we had seen shortly before. There was no enemy fire as we dug the holes deeper into the dirt and shale, fearful that the enemy fire could start any moment. None did. Nevertheless, remembering the intense artillery fire the day before, many of us continued to dig deeper through the night." Lamb did not quit excavating until his head was below ground where he sat.

The outfit was scheduled to jump off in an attack across a small valley on the following day. But the order to move out never came. "Suddenly, the hillside erupted in a rain of artillery fire with shrapnel screaming in all directions. The slope of the hill and our position on it made us the victims of plunging artillery fire, the worst. I clenched my teeth and hunched as low as I could, thankful that I had dug the hole as deep as I had.

"Finally, the barrage lifted. It had devastated our positions. The wounded began struggling up the hill to whatever help and safety they could find. Seeing some would not make it without help, some of us left the safety of our foxholes and helped the badly wounded to get to the top of the hill and on into the basement first-aid station in Kleinhau."

The battered company staggered backward, hoping to reduce their vulnerability. But the enemy renewed its fusillades, cutting them down in exposed areas. "Nearby," said Lamb, "a shell exploded in a group of five. They lay there in a heap. None got up. To the unit command, it must have become obvious that we had been cut to pieces and could no longer fight as a unit. The remnants were ordered to the rear and to find our way back to our half-tracks in the woods on the other side of Kleinhau."

Alone, or in small groups of two or three, the GIs scrambled toward the vehicles. Lamb passed a pair of soldiers who lay in a ditch where they fell. On his way through the village, he saw "Sherman tanks, standing on the road, side by side, with their 75mm guns roaring and the machine guns raking the woods in preparation for an infantry attack. One by one the exhausted remnants of B Company found their way back to their armored half-tracks in the woods from where we had started. Night came and you could hear the subdued anguishing over lost comrades. This was not the end of the fighting for us, but at this point others would do the fighting."

Michael J. DiLeo was a rifleman in the headquarters squad of Company B of the 46th AIB. He echoed the sentiments of tens of thousands of others as he entered the woods on 29 November. "I found the Huertgen Forest to be hell on earth, snow, cold temperatures, mud, dense woods, and an enemy that had all open areas zeroed in by artillery. One day I ended up digging three foxholes. The first one I finished I dug deep enough so a tank could go over. Shortly after completion, we were told to pack up, as we were being relieved by foot infantry. When we got to our next stop, we started digging again. I went down three feet and hit water. Very soon after we were told not to dig, because, come sundown, the enemy would start dropping shells on the area. So, when it got dark, we moved into the woods. There I decided to dig a slit trench instead of a foxhole, making it twelve inches deep, wide enough and long enough to sleep in. But the area was shelled all night. Every time we heard the shells coming, we stopped digging and hit the ground. When I was finished, I got in to sleep, but there wasn't more than an hour when we were told to get ready, as we were attacking the town."

Colonel Burton, as head of the force designated to occupy the high ground, erroneously believed to be in American hands, reached his pinned-down troops and rallied them sufficiently for a successful but bloody assault. The 46th AIB bagged Hill 401 but at excessive cost; nearly half the outfit was rendered unfit for duty because of the wrong information about who occupied the heights.

Having seized Hill 401, the 46th AIB continued its offensive through the thick woods beyond Kleinhau. Captain Tyler Bland, formerly the CO of B Company in the States and during its first months in combat, received a promotion to the position of S-3. When the leader of C Company went down, Bland was sent to take charge of the unit. As he attempted to organize an assault on German big guns, a shell burst amid the group he was leading. Three men died on the spot and several others were wounded, including Bland, who lost a leg.

In the same attack, DiLeo, as a member of Company B, recalled the severity of the artillery and mortars that pelted them along with withering machine gun fire after they entered a forested area on their way toward the objective. "First Lieutenant Charles Smith [a pseudonym], the executive officer, had taken over when Captain Bland was promoted. He was a very compassionate man. In training, he never yelled at anybody. I believe he was studying to be a minister. We were shelled all night long, in the dense growth of woods, big tall and short pine trees. Our casualties were very heavy. The battalion lost 40 percent of its strength during this twenty-four-hour period.

"This day, December 1, we started out behind Company C. They didn't get too far before we went in. I was in one of the last groups to go out into the open. There were five of us: the commanding officer, Lieutenant Smith; Sergeant Robinson, the radioman, had a forty-pound radio strapped on his back; I carried the spare batteries; I was with Jim Carnivali, my tentmate, and a very young boy we called 'Georgia' because that's where he was from.

"Ahead of us was a very large open area, about the size of several football fields. We came upon a fire trench about eighteen feet wide and four feet deep. We crossed it, then saw dirt kick up in front of us. We figured a sniper, and about five yards further lay a large German artillery pit. We made a run for the pit, and the front of it seemed like it was out of the sniper's sight. We were all crouched in a corner and all was quiet. Then the CO called out, 'DiLeo, go back and tell Colonel Burton [the 46th AIB CO] we need medics.'

"I was stunned. I said to myself, 'Why not use the radio? But if I don't go, I am in trouble. If I do go, the sniper will get me. If I run fast and zigzag, he might miss.' So I jumped out and zigzagged to the fire trench. I decided to head north in the trench and, right after an artillery barrage, jump out and run toward the woods we started from. But as I was walking in the trench, I ran into three or four medics walking toward me. The medical sergeant told me they were coming to take care of the wounded. I said I was on my way to tell Colonel Burton to send up medics as we had a lot of wounded. The sergeant said all of the medics are covering the area.

"I turned to go back to my unit. But they were out of the artillery pit and running toward the woods. I joined them just as a barrage started to come in. We all hit the ground. After it let up, we began to get up. The lieutenant saw me and I was about to tell him what I did. But the radio sergeant didn't get up, and when Lieutenant Smith saw the radio sergeant down, he said, 'DiLeo, take the radio off Sergeant Robinson,' who was out, unconscious, breathing very heavily. But I noticed the lieutenant didn't stop. He just kept on walking toward the woods. I yelled, 'Lieutenant, where are you going?' He didn't stop and I told Georgia to take the radio while I went after the lieutenant. I caught up with him as he entered the woods and again asked where he was going. The woods there were very dense, visibility was about five feet. Then I heard voices, and I saw a group of at least five German soldiers walking toward us.

"I said to Lieutenant Smith, 'You speak German. Tell them to surrender and put their hands up.' He did, and they were happy to do so. Now we have five prisoners. So what does the lieutenant do? He turns around and heads out of the woods toward where we had started from that morning. Two officers who recognized Lieutenant Smith came out and escorted him in the wooded area from which we had started. Nothing was said to me. I was left to wander.

"I mixed in with the troops there. A sergeant asked for volunteers to help lay down a phone line. I volunteered. After dark, we went out for a few hours, and during that time we heard one artillery shell coming pretty close. We hugged the ground. When it hit, we felt the earth shake. It turned out to be a dud. We were very lucky. The next day I rejoined my company. A major from battalion came to lead us."

On 3 December, when the 83d Division began to move into the forest to relieve the 4th Division, the Ivy Division's casualties numbered 432 known dead, 255 missing, and more than 3,300 men wounded or injured. The 22d Regiment absorbed the worst drubbing—233 killed, 750 wounded. None of the figures included those disabled by trench foot or diseases.

15

Overlooking the Roer

On 4 December, Tom Cross wrote a letter to his son Dick, then in the final stages of OCS in the States. (Another son, Tom R., serving with the 517th Parachute Regiment, had been hurt while engaged in an airborne invasion of southern France.) The senior Cross wrote, "I have command of a regiment now, a real fighting outfit, and I'm very proud of it, as the regiment has done a wonderful bit of work. I never thought that troops could be so wonderful, even fighting on with just guts and nothing else. I feel the strain of it, but so long as I get three or four hours of rest each night, I'll make out all right." He mentioned a near miss from a mortar and then devoted his comments to regrets that he could not pin a lieutenant's bars on Dick and offered advice on buying uniforms and equipment.

According to Cross's diary, conditions remained more precarious than the tone of his letter. He remarked on a German counterattack against the CCR (Combat Command Reserve of the 5th Armored Division), which looked critical. He noted that a thrust against his 8th Division's 28th Infantry Regiment was halted with large casualties for the enemy, while his own 1st Battalion dug in north of the important Brandenberg ridge. On 6 December he remarked, "5th Armored continues to get pounded by artillery and mortars. It was necessary to put in a battalion of Rangers to hold the situation as the Boche attempted counterattacks but all were beaten back. An attempt to move the two companies of the regiment to the flank of the 2d Battalion was badly handled and nothing accomplished. Miserable leadership and a sick battalion commander the main difficulties. Battalion CO relieved, sent to the hospital. Reassigned the officers of the companies that failed to move."

Contrary to the remarks to his son, he expressed unhappiness with the declining enthusiasm of the GIs. "Still having trouble with stragglers, using MPs to stop them in the main roads. Not pleasant to feel that Americans will shirk front line duty, but there are hundreds of them that will do anything to keep from fighting. I intend to handle them roughly." The official regimental histories take no note of this aspect of the Huertgen campaign.

Cross and other commanders fretted over the enemy occupation of dominant positions on high ground around the towns of Schmidt and Bergstein, from which they poured abundant artillery and mortars on anyone who sought to advance through minefields and scathing small-arms fire. The locale provided the defenders with a commanding view of any movement of U.S. troops. As Cross remarked, the CCR of the 5th Armored Division reeled from an onslaught of tanks and self-propelled guns during a defense of its tenuous grasp of Brandenberg and Bergstein. The sight of 75mm shells from M4 tank destroyers bouncing off the hulls of the enemy Panzers discouraged some crews from even challenging their Panther adversaries. The few TDs with the 76mm cannons fared better, but the ravages of sustained fighting left CCR unable to assault the linchpin for German observation and artillery fire—Castle Hill. Also known as Hill 400 because of its height in meters, it threatened anyone seeking to advance over the surrounding territory.

General Walter Weaver, Stroh's replacement, commanding the 8th Division, specifically asked Gen. Leonard Gerow, corps commander, for Rangers to assist his division's assault on Castle Hill. Chosen for the assignment were D and F Companies, with A, B, and C securing nearby ridges and providing roadblocks and supplementary mortar fire. Meanwhile, E Company would, with survivors of CCR, hold Bergstein against expected counterattacks.

One D Company veteran of the Omaha Beach assault, Len Lomell, was awarded a battlefield commission in October and, along with the other Rangers, boarded trucks that carried them from their reserve bivouac into the forest. Near Kleinhau, they dismounted and, bone-chilled, plodded on a wet, muddy, and icy trail in the darkness of night. Sporadically, flares and shell bursts briefly illuminated the scarified landscape.

At a crossroads, the men halted and morale plummeted as their revered commander, Lt. Col. James Rudder, passed among them with word he had been transferred to lead the shredded 28th Division's 109th Regiment. Lomell heard the news only after he returned from a patrol that prowled the base and lower elevations of Hill 400. A small party from F Company also reconnoitered the objective.

In the early morning hours of 7 December, the date that resonates through history but went ignored in the Huertgen Forest on its third anniversary, Rangers from D and F left their shelters of burned-out armor and ruined buildings in Bergstein and started toward their line of departure. At 0730, amidst a fearsome artillery duel, the Rangers jumped off for Hill 400.

According to eyewitness Sid Salomon from C Company, "The CO at the appropriate time gave the word 'Go!' With whooping and hollering as loud as possible, firing clips of ammo at random from their weapons in the direction of the hill, the Rangers ran as fast as they could across the approximately 100 yards of open, cleared field into the machine gun and small-arms fire of the German defenders. Crossing the field and before reaching the base of the hill, the company commander and his runner became casualties, but, undaunted, the remaining D Company Rangers charged up the hill.

"The enemy defenders immediately became alert. A red flare shot in the air from an enemy outpost, apparently a signal to their higher headquarters. Shortly thereafter, a heavy mortar and artillery barrage came down on the assaulting Rangers. Heavy small-arms and machine gun fire was directed on the rushing Rangers. Casualties on both sides now began to mount, but still the charge continued. Some Germans were giving ground. Others of the enemy forces were seemingly safe in well-prepared holes or behind log emplacements. Rifle and automatic fire filled the air. A creeping German artillery barrage behind the assaulting Rangers produced more Ranger casualties. The enemy continued to offer stiff resistance."

A similar lunge marked the advance of F Company Rangers. Said Salomon, "An enemy machine gun located at the left lower corner of the hill wounded and killed several of the F Company Rangers as they crossed the open field. The remainder of the company continued forward, some running faster than others, all firing their weapons running up the hill, with little opportunity for any semblance of order, primarily one of individualism or survival, to reach the top of the hill. The Allied barrage had lifted, but the enemy mortar gunners were now adjusting their range to follow the assaulting Rangers up the hill. Some of the Germans at the lower base of the hill either turned and ran up the hill to avoid charging Rangers or stood up and surrendered."

Private William Anderson, a seasoned Ranger broken from sergeant to the lowest rank for garrison infractions, Sgt. William "L-Rod" Petty, and Pfc. Cloise Manning, the first three F Company men who achieved the top, saw an enemy bunker and ran to the main entrance, which was guarded by a steel door. From inside came the voices of German soldiers. Petty thrust his BAR into an aperture and emptied a twenty-round magazine. Anderson shoved a couple of grenades through the flap. As both stepped back several feet to avoid the resulting explosion, an enemy shell landed nearby, instantly killing Anderson. In the meantime, the CO (Capt. Otto Masney) arrived along with some more soldiers. They entered the bunker and captured the wounded and stunned inhabitants.

Said Salomon, "Ultimately, the fast, unceasing, and determined forward momentum of the assaulting D Company Rangers stunned the German defenders, some of whom quickly moved away from the steadily advancing assaulting troops." Within an hour, the enemy had fled but it was an onerous victory.

Well aware of the importance of the high land, the foe now rained down a murderous assortment of explosives on the new kings of the hill. The rocky, tree-rooted ground defied the best efforts of entrenching tools. The only protection was beneath toppled trees or in shell holes. The battered able-bodied Rangers of D Company drew some comfort from the support of F Company, which had secured the left flank. However, that outfit was in just as deep trouble. Masney believed it required the authority of someone with his rank to obtain aid from below. He discussed with Petty which route to follow, but when he went off in a different direction than recommended by the sergeant, German soldiers captured him.

Lomell, now the sole officer of D Company—his company commander, Capt. Mort McBride, wounded during the uphill charge, had been evacuated—still on his feet, reached a concealed troop shelter at the top of the hill. He threw in a grenade, and another Ranger sprayed the interior with automatic fire. According to Lomell, "Survival was a matter of luck. We were under constant bombardment. Guys were lying all over the hill. We couldn't even give first aid. We were told we would be relieved and just to hold on. How long can you tell a guy bleeding to death to hold on. My God, he knew I was lying to him.

"I had tears in my eyes. We stopped another counterattack, but if the Germans had known how many men, or really how few we had up there, they would have kept coming." Bleeding from wounds of his hand and arm, Lomell offered a proposal to his noncoms. "If we retreat, they'll take care of our wounded. We can come back and take the hill later." They adamantly refused to consider the idea. An explosion near him caused a concussion. "I was bleeding from the anus and the mouth as a result." Under the cover of darkness, he was evacuated.

Originally informed that they would need to control Castle Hill for no more than twenty-four hours before infantrymen of the 8th Division would take over, the besieged Rangers endured more than forty hours on the heights. Of the sixty-five Rangers who started the charge, only fifteen could come down under their own power. On the morning after Lomell came off Hill 400, German artillery slammed into the Ranger positions just as the battalion surgeon Walter Block left his dugout to supervise removal of the seriously wounded. A shell fragment killed him instantly.

As one of his last acts, Block spared his medical technician Frank South the worst of the battering around Hill 400. "The day before the battalion was sent into action at Bergstein, I passed out due to dehydration and a severe gastrointestinal problem. Not knowing we were about to be committed, Block insisted that I get to a hospital. I was unaware we were in action until wounded Rangers began to arrive. I immediately went AWOL from the hospital and hitchhiked back to the battalion, only to find the Battle of Hill 400 was over, the battalion decimated, and Block dead. He was the first and last medical officer we had that deserved the name of a Ranger. I still feel both guilty and somehow cheated that I was not part of that battle."

Sid Salomon, CO of Baker Company in the 2d Ranger Battalion, who saw his GIs chewed up during the first exploratory thrusts into the Huertgen, considered his people cruelly used. "After the invasion, there was no need for a 2d Ranger Battalion. We were used as an infantry company, attached to maybe ten different divisions. The people in command did not know what the Rangers were. They would put the Rangers first and keep their own casualties down. A combat command of the 5th Armored Division [ordinarily about 3,000 men with tanks and other armored vehicles, although by the first week of December, its ranks fell far short of the table of organization] failed to take Hill 400. Three companies of Rangers [little more than 200 foot soldiers] captured it, going past burned-out tanks with GIs hanging over the sides."

The 13th Infantry Regiment of the 8th Division climbed into the foxholes of the Rangers on Castle Hill on 9 December. Casualties for the 2d Ranger Battalion during the siege amounted to twenty-three killed, eighty-six wounded, and four missing.

Replacing the 4th Division, the 83d, commanded by Maj. Gen. Robert C. Macon, had been transferred to the VII Corps under Collins. It drew the objectives of Gey and Strass, a pair of villages in the northern section of the Huertgen. These villages were within a mile of the Roer River. Success by the 83d would gain a network of roads, pathways for the tanks of the 5th Armored to clear away the German presence in the corps' zone along the river. The collaborative efforts of the 83d Division and the 5th Armored covered a line that ran parallel to the Roer for about four miles.

The approach would dovetail neatly with the V Corps during its coming push to the stream from the south. In this sector, Gerow intended to commit an untested, newly arrived outfit, the 78th Division, to the campaign. Farther south, from Monschau, the 2d Division, protected by the 99th Division on its right flank, would also push toward the Roer.

Toward the end of October, Ninth Army engineers reported that there would be devastating consequences if the enemy opened the floodgates of the river's system of dams, particularly the giant

Schwammenauel and the other major installation, the Urft. Now, in December, the possible significance of these structures became apparent to some top strategists. It had fallen to the First Army to neutralize the threat, which was within its sector. However, judging from the diary entries of Major Sylvan, the dams never generated much discussion, because the assistant to Hodges does not mention them.

In a decision that required the approval of the supreme commander, Eisenhower, the planners decided that it was an opportune moment to destroy the dams, because the floods would sweep over the Germans between the Americans and the Roer, eliminating any efforts to reinforce or supply the enemy. The RAF, which enjoyed a reputation as "dam busters" because of efforts elsewhere, agreed to missions against the Schwammenauel, Urft, and the lesser Paulushof Dams. Bad weather limited the raids, and those that did strike inflicted little damage on the massive earthen and concrete barriers. Hodges and his associates now accepted that the dams had to be captured rather than demolished.

The overall plan of the First Army envisioned the 83d Division to force its way to the western banks of the Roer on the left flank of the 78th, which would head directly toward the two biggest dams. General Macon, as CG of the 83d, delegated the task at Strass to his 330th Regiment and Gey to the 331st. On 10 December, the two outfits broke out of the cover of the woods during the predawn darkness, canceling out any opportunity for the Germans, well entrenched in basements and bunkers, to drench them with fire while they crossed open fields. Both regiments fought their way into the towns, where they engaged in fierce house-to-house exchanges.

The defenders had permeated the ground with mines, burying some so deep that while one piece of armor might grind past without damage, the tank following in its track prints would detonate the explosives. The plethora of shell fragments and metal detritus rendered conventional mine detectors useless. Engineers were forced to painstakingly probe by bayonet and hand to locate the devices. German gunners pinpointed the engineers laboring at the task. Efforts to bring forward additional armor to assist in routing the resistance from their positions foundered, as mines blew tank tracks or mud paralyzed movement.

Under cover of night, Germans infiltrated the thickets that enveloped a road out of Strass to isolate the GIs of the 330th. The 5th Armored Division units, despite the breakdown in the expected advance, adhered to a timetable for their movement forward. The tanks of the 81st Tank Battalion and half-tracks loaded with riflemen from the 15th Armored Infantry Battalion crawled through the muddy, light snow–covered trails in the forest beyond Kleinhau and toward an elevated wooded ground.

The foot soldiers dismounted as they neared the line of departure. Again, faulty intelligence betrayed the GIs. The area, supposedly secure, quickly shook with artillery and mortar rounds. Flurries of small-arms fire issued from the right flank along with *panzerfaust* blasts.

T/5 Hopkins of the 71st AFA Headquarters Battery drove an M4 tank as part of a forward observation crew and said, "Doughs of the 15th AIB started slogging down the frozen road to the jumping-off point. Most of them wore only field jackets, due to the quantity of equipment and arms that had to be carried. The tanks pulled out on the road in single file, moving forward at a very slow rate of speed. The road was under enemy observation and was plastered repeatedly by artillery and mortar fire. Despite this and innumerable other hardships, the attack pressed steadily forward.

"The going got rougher with every yard. Tankers had to fight the mud and sweat and artillery and direct fire from antitank guns. We finally reached the top of a mountain near our line of departure and had to hold up. The Krauts were looking down our throat from a still higher mountain. We tried to press forward down the steep hill, but this was useless due to minefields. Several of our tanks lost tracks due to the mines. It was decided to sit tight and wait for the units on our left to advance. The tanks took up a defensive position, and the doughs dug in for a stay that seemed almost eternity.

"We remained in this position for, I believe, three days and nights, during which time the only hot food we had was coffee prepared at great risk by lighting a gasoline stove on the floor near piles of ammunition. The only sleep we got was acquired dozing while sitting in our cramped positions with no room to stretch or turn. To answer calls of nature, we crawled out and stuck our fannies over the edge of the tank, praying always that a mortar shell didn't arrive to drive us from our sojourn.

"During our stay here, men were killed like flies, and mortar shells were falling at such an unbelievable rate of speed and accuracy that it was practically impossible for anyone to withstand the ordeal. Reinforcements poured in steadily, but they could not keep up with the terrific losses."

Every line company commander of the 15th AIB had either been killed or wounded. By the end of the third day, the outfit's three line companies, which at full strength contained eighteen officers and 735 enlisted men, reported their numbers as four officers and 170 soldiers. To add riflemen, the 15th's antitank platoon abandoned their 57mm cannons and toted M1s to take positions amid the shrinking files of infantrymen. Because trucks, jeeps, Weasels, and other thin-skinned vehicles could not withstand the intense enemy fire, light tanks loaded with rations, water, clothing, and ammunition crept forward to supply the pinned down GIs. On the return, they carried wounded stretched out on their rear decks.

The renewed attack stalled under the vicious artillery and mortar fire after an ill-advised maneuver dismounted the soldiers from the protection of their half-tracks. The armored division CO, Maj. Gen. Lunsford E. Oliver, complained about the ravages upon his supply trains, to which Macon growled, "The road is about as open as we can get it. We can't keep out the snipers."

From his headquarters, Collins impatiently demanded results. Barton dispatched his reserve regiment, the 329th, toward another hamlet, Gurzenich. Held up mainly by the dense woods, the tree bursts created by big guns, and ubiquitous mines, the outfit finally broke into Gurzenich on the afternoon of 13 December. The following day, the 329th pressed on to Birgel, where an entire battalion surrendered. As it had for so many American organizations, the campaign to control the Huertgen sapped German strength and will.

The place had barely been seized before the Germans, perceiving a dangerous bulge in their lines at the very moment when they were readying themselves for the notorious thrust through the Ardennes to the southwest, mounted a strong counterattack. Temporarily, the line in Birgel broke, with the GIs out of bazooka ammunition to cope with enemy armor. Macon directed artillery fire to be dumped on the town's approaches to prevent infantry from supporting the armor. He also scrounged four tanks from the 774th Tank Battalion to bolster the embattled infantrymen.

In the 329th Regiment, M Company Sgt. Ralph G. Neppell, as a machine gun squad leader, wiped out twenty soldiers on his own and forced an assault gun to retreat before a round severed one of his legs below the knee. Neppell dragged his wounded body into a position where he could continue to deploy his machine gun. He later received a Medal of Honor. Despite their determined attempts, the Germans could not retake Birgel.

Beyond Grosshau and Kleinhau lay the village of Bergstein, an objective consigned to the CCR of the 5th Armored Division. The major pieces of CCR consisted of the 47th Armored Infantry, the 10th Tank Battalion, and the 628th Tank Destroyer Battalion. Bob Herman, son of a Youngstown, Ohio, steelworker, had finished a year at Ohio University before being drafted. A field artillery trainee, he nevertheless went to the 628th TD Battalion, created from a former unit in the luckless 28th Division.

"I wasn't given any personal training for combat," recalled Herman, "but just listened to my sergeant tank destroyer commander. He seemed to be well trained and qualified, and most of the battalion had been training in the States for several years. In England, we were equipped with the M10 TD with a three-inch cannon. The TD also had an antiaircraft .50-caliber machine gun mounted on top of an open turret. I started as an assistant driver and then as a loader.

"Our battalion commander was the first one killed in combat, shortly after we participated in the breakout at Saint-Lô. The XO, Maj. William Gallagher, was named CO and stayed throughout the war. He was a good soldier who retired as a major general.

"I don't believe any training could have prepared you for what was to be faced in that forest. The weather was abominable, cold rain, mixed with snow some of the time. We usually had food, which we carried, mostly ten-in-one rations, so we didn't go hungry. The roads were muddy, hardly passable. The artillery, for example, was so intense, that not a tree was left with any branches on it.

"Our strength when we entered the Huertgen was nearly full, but at one time my company had only one TD operational, although a day later, seven out of fifteen were working. We had received the newer M36 with a 90mm gun just prior to the Huertgen. My own tank destroyer had a mechanical problem, and then, while we were trying to catch up with the rest of the battalion, we hit a mine, were disabled, and taken to the rear.

"However, C Company on 6 December knocked out five enemy tanks. The problem with the M36 was the open turret. Many casualties occurred from artillery air bursts or when exploding from hitting the trees. After this experience, the battalion modified all turrets, built an armored cover for them, which proved invaluable on a number of occasions. Our clothes were always wet and our socks, too. The cold wet socks were primarily responsible when I got a mild case of trench foot and went to a hospital near Liège."

Once again, the village of Merode became the locus of action. In place of the 1st Division's 26th Infantry, which lost 165 men while trying to capture the town, the 9th Division's 39th Infantry was chosen for the task. General Craig drafted a precise if somewhat unusual maneuver aimed at the Merode Castle, an eighteenth-century building whose towers provided an eagle-eyed view of the town and vicinity, making the castle a strong point of the defense. A twenty-foot-wide moat and a single entrance made the place a tough nut to crack. Craig arranged for his 60th Infantry to serve as a departure base for the 2d Battalion of the 39th. That unit, under Lt. Frank L. Gunn, a veteran of the first tentative push along the southeastern fringes of the forest and into Germany back in September, would march abreast of the 60th before jumping off at a right angle toward the castle. The arrangement was the only possible way to advance the troops through the cramped confines of forest, clogged or impassable roads, and open ground studded with mines. There would be tank support supplied by the 3d Armored Division.

To ensure a clear pathway, Gunn boarded GIs from F Company's 2d platoon along with engineers and 200 pounds of TNT on five tanks on the portion of the blacktop highway toward D'Horn, a hamlet between Jungersdorf and Merode that sat astride the railroad line from Aachen to Düren. The leader of the patrol was Lt.

Mike Wolfson. The question was whether a railroad underpass at the edge of D'Horn had been destroyed. If so, the engineers would use dynamite to blow open a route through the debris. Wolfson and his troupe found the underpass intact and took up residence in a house to await their associates.

On 10 December, with VII Corps commander Collins observing from Craig's headquarters, an intricate choreography unfolded, with elements of the 60th Regiment sweeping aside light resistance. As the Americans advanced at a better pace than anticipated, the 9th Division leader gave the signal for the forces under Gunn to start their assault. The men struck out according to the plan, and with their flank covered by the 60th Regiment soldiers, executed a right angle attack that carried them into D'Horn with little difficulty. Gunn and his riflemen buttoned down for the night in the village.

General Craig now directed Col. Van H. Bond, the CO of the 39th, to capture Merode Castle. Bond boasted that by nightfall he would have his command post set up in the castle, where Craig could visit. Bond's 1st and 2d Battalions attacked from two different angles that would cross at the objective.

Artillery and small arms hammered hard at the attackers, but, unlike the case of the 1st Division soldiers in November, the Americans packed many more men and much more firepower into the effort. The GIs rebuffed counterattacks that had been so successful against the 26th Infantry. Intensive shelling punched huge holes in the castle and tumbled some of its walls. Still, with their bodies and blood, the GIs took possession, enabling Bond to fulfill his prophecy. Securing the town required hours of house-to-house fighting, but along with many enemy dead, 190 prisoners yielded to the 39th.

Frank Randall, the platoon leader replacement who joined B Company of the 39th Infantry in the forest, recalled, "Many of our captives were fourteen to fifteen years old, which told us something. My reaction was to call down curses on Hitler. The next morning, we continued the attack to relieve pressure on another company. I had eaten some potatoes from a pile in the basement of one of the houses and had diarrhea as we were getting ready to attack. I told the platoon sergeant to take the men to the attack position. Then I completely emptied my bowels and hurriedly went to the attack. Prior to the start, a man intercepted me with a letter to his wife. I censored it, signed it, and put it in my left shirt pocket.

"Remembering the Infantry School instruction oft repeated, 'The men will not go if you are not in front to lead them, lieutenant,' I passed through the formation and gave the 'follow me' signal. And so up the hill, my men took up firing on the objective. I turned my back on the enemy position to signal them to increase the volume of fire. I turned back, took a few steps, and was hit in the chest and abdomen and went down on one knee. I jumped to get out of the line of fire and called to the platoon aid man that I was hit. I looked over on my right and saw the man who had given me the letter go down.

"I told the medic to treat him first. He replied, 'I'm sorry, sir. He's dead.' My men were going to take the door off a house to evacuate me, but the aid man had sent someone for a litter, which was produced in a short time.

"We took the hill and the evacuation process began. The aid man had given me a shot of morphine, and soon I was in the battalion aid station. Because of profuse bleeding, they stripped me. The aid station sergeant removed everything from my pockets, including the letter now soaked with my blood, which was placed with all my worldly goods. At the regimental aid station, they gave me another shot of morphine, one of the chaplains anointed me and gave me a blessing, and I was on my way to the division clearing station, this time on the hood of a jeep."

Medics administered more shots of morphine as Randall traveled on a litter atop a half-track until a Mobile Army Surgical Team (MAST; later, in Korea, MASH) operated on him. As the Germans continued to advance in the first days of the Battle of the Bulge, the Stolberg hospital, with Randall and other severely wounded patients, lay in the path of the enemy. The First Army surgeon ordered everyone except volunteers to leave, because, with capture imminent, he wanted American medical personnel to tend to the wounded who would die if moved. "Everyone, doctors, nurses, technicians, ward attendants, all volunteered, so the hospital CO said, 'We all stay.' Fortunately, Stolberg was not captured, and thanks to the courage of our medical personnel, we had treatment as usual."

On a hot summer's day, five months earlier, D Company from the 5th Armored's 81st Tank Battalion, equipped with light tanks, had clattered ashore at Utah Beach. As a unit in CCB, the tankers followed the stampede through the Saint-Lô gap in the German lines, and in the dash through the French countryside on a single day rolled thirty-seven combat miles. Voo Doo Dog (the radio code name for the company), having paraded through Paris, engaged the enemy during September along the Siegfried Line. They spent most of October and November as reserves bivouacked in Luxembourg and Belgium.

On 10 December, along with the rest of CCB, D Company circled its vehicles in the vicinity of Kleinhau. Antiaircraft and American fighters drove off occasional marauding visitors from the Luftwaffe. The tactical experts, recognizing the limitations of light tanks against German armor and the enemy antitank weapons, mainly employed them against selective targets, like roadblocks, snipers, and nonbunkered machine gun nests, and for supply and evacuation of wounded.

Bob Miller, a gunner with the outfit, recalled moving out at dawn on 12 December to carry food, ammunition, and water to the forward troops. When the 2d Platoon tanks neared their destination, they were forced to detour off to the side to get around a disabled Sherman. A mine exploded under the third tank in line, and while a crew worked to extricate an unconscious GI, Pvt. Dominick Colangelo, the other two tanks slowly continued ahead. After depositing their cargo, the pair returned. Miller recalled, "They decided to pass the two knocked-out vehicles on the other side in hopes of avoiding the numerous mines. As Lt. Henry Potts [who had dismounted] guided his tank around, it too struck a mine, killing him and seriously wounded the driver, T/4 Peter Thauwald." Shrapnel struck four of the tankers still laboring to free Colangelo. Among those who picked up a Purple Heart here was Gunner Miller. Another tank was abandoned, because it was too dangerous to attempt to cross what was obviously a heavily seeded minefield.

For nine days, Voo Doo Dog brought supplies forward and on the return trip evacuated the wounded. Infiltrating Germans continued to plant deadly mines. Lieutenant Henry V. Plass solved the problem for one run by shoving a broken-down engineer's truck ahead of him as a makeshift minesweeper. The company's 1st Platoon moved to Strass, where it could directly support the 330th Infantry while the two other platoons continued to perform supply and liaison missions. When CCB lost communications to the 330th Regiment, a tank commanded by Lt. Carlo Lombardi and driven by T/4 Roy Rusteberg scooted over a stretch of mine-infested ground and evaded a gauntlet of antitank weapons to bring its radio to the isolated GIs of the 330th.

The occupation of Gurzenich, opposite the city of Düren on the eastern side of the Roer, and Birgel by the 329th bagged more than 1,000 prisoners. The drive by elements of the 5th Armored and its partners in the 83d Division secured positions along the northern rim of their sector. To the south lay the other objectives—Bergheim, Winden, and other towns astride the Roer.

In the pathway was the well-defended village of Kufferath. A task force of tanks and armored infantry CCA passed through Gey, then fought its way into the settlement of Horm under heavy artillery fire and beset by mines. Fusillades of shells from the 34th Tank Battalion blasted the Horm defenders, smashing self-propelled 75mm and 150mm cannons along with antitank pieces.

A shell pierced the side of a tank commanded by Sgt. Wilmer Doty. The explosion blew Doty out of the vehicle. He climbed back into the burning tank to rescue his gunner, Cpl. Charles Fuller. Having dragged Fuller to safety, Doty again braved the flames to retrieve his driver. Two more rounds crashed into the crippled tank, killing the driver and seriously injuring Doty.

The onslaught by the Americans overwhelmed the resident German soldiers, who began to surrender. Infantrymen from the 83d took over handling the prisoners. The task force rumbled toward Kufferath, only to encounter another savage reception from antitank guns and artillery. B Company of the 34th lost five tanks in the duels but doggedly persisted with only three Shermans and a tank dozer toward Kufferath.

From the skies, a squadron of P-47 fighters hurled their thunderbolts at the Kufferath garrison, the troops in Bergheim, and enemy positions in the woods. The GIs from the 5th Armored besieged Kufferath from three sides. However, the resolute defenders kept up their fire, demolishing a number of the American tanks. Casualties accumulated, but the fighting intensified, making it difficult to spare men for carrying parties.

In the final assault on Kufferath, SSgt. Andrew Hovdestadt from the 46th Armored Infantry volunteered to lead combat patrols to kill or roust the defenders from houses in the town. During one excursion, an artillery shell burst near him. Although mortally wounded, he dragged himself to a protected position from which he urged his companions on, while attempting to succor other injured men before he succumbed.

The Americans swarmed into Kufferath, bagged ninety-eight prisoners, and counted 175 Germans dead or wounded and eleven antitank weapons destroyed. For five days they held on, until fresh forces from CCA reinforced or replaced them. From here the drive resumed toward Bergheim and one of its nearby enclaves, Schneidhausen.

The 5th Armored Division's 71st Armored Field Artillery, as part of CCB, had spent the latter part of November and the first week of December in the vicinity of Aachen, laying down interdiction fire on the foe's pillboxes. Forward observers for the 71st employed both L-4 single-engine airplanes and the M4 tank. Ralph Hendrickson, a cannoneer for an M7, the self-propelled tracked gun, had been drafted into the horse-drawn artillery before the attack on Pearl Harbor. As an original member of the 71st AFA, he had already witnessed combat during the second week of December, when he reached the Huertgen Forest near Grosshau. "Immediately after arriving in our gun position and our guns were laid to fire, I began to make a personal reconnaissance of the battery position. I took extreme care to look the place over good after I saw those bullet-riddled trees and dead bodies. I wasn't about to step on a mine. While checking the area around the dead bodies, I noticed this dead GI sitting on a log with his right arm raised up over his head. His left arm was half raised, and his box of stationery was scattered on the ground. I felt sorry for him and his family, but the only thing I could do was pick up his stationery and secure it for Graves Registration. I did this and protected it with his poncho. All the many other bodies were in a flat position.

"About the third day there, Graves Registration began to pick up bodies. They were not very careful with the bodies. They handled them like dead meat. They actually threw them in the back of a cargo truck and piled them like cordwood. They did all this while we watched. The sitting GI whom I had seen couldn't be laid flat, so they sat him on top of the other bodies behind the driver. When the Graves Registration truck drove by my gun position, the bumps [in the roadway] made my dead friend's upraised right arm wave to me. His right arm continued to wave as far as I could see when the truck was driving away. [The sight] has haunted me all of these years."

German aircraft put in a rare appearance over the encampment of the 71st, bombing and strafing with minor damage, although nearby units of CCB counted eighteen casualties from the raid. Life for the artillerymen was more comfortable than what the infantry endured, and particularly the previous tenants of the turf. When they completed a firing mission, the crews retired to what official communications described as "log huts dug into the ground." The battalion report described them as "fairly comfortable, warm, and splinterproof." With the immediate field of battle advanced some miles, the artillerymen lived more comfortably than the previous residents. James Burrell, a T/5 in A Battery, noted that while some foxholes and dugouts had heavy log and dirt roofs, "not one hole was long or deep enough for us, so off came the tops, and we put in our own addition—namely, stoves made from five-gallon oilcans complete with Boche stovepipe and illumination in the form of flashlights or half-track trouble lights rigged up with lengths of wire. We fired on targets of opportunity and laid down heavy barrages in preparation for the attacks. For the boys that were off duty during the day, there was the usual army time-passers, poker and blackjack games, just laying around and chewing the fat or snatching a little of those forty winks missed the night before while on that firing problem."

Hendrickson remarked that because some congressmen had received mail from mothers about the lack of correspondence from their sons in combat, "a direct order came down that we had to write home regardless of whether it killed us or not. The ink in our pens was frozen."

The 71st AFA had supported the attack by units of CCB coordinated with the 83d Division, aimed at eliminating the Germans from a sector extending from Kleinhau to Winden on the Roer River. While CCB bogged down, the tactical air force dispatched P-47s and P-38s to blast a quarry, a German strong point already a focus of attention from a TOT. The objective finally yielded, after a mad dash across open ground by tanks carrying GIs surprised the Germans in the quarry. The wall of resistance to CCB cracked, and troops from CCB on 16 December occupied the high ground overlooking the Roer River towns of Winden, Untermaubach, and Undingen.

For the task of capturing the major dams, the Schwammenauel and Urft, the First Army chose the latest arrivals to its V Corps, the 78th Infantry Division, which came to the forest with no previous combat experience. Major General Edwin P. Parker, Jr., CO of the "Lightning" Division, expressed some concern about the responsibilities entrusted to his combat novices, but Courtney Hodges dismissed his anxieties, asserting it had been "proven time and time again that our training methods in the United States were not only correct but completely adequate to defeat the Boche." Like a number of other outfits, the division, activated in August 1942, had shipped most of its original complement to France as replacements for the first combat units in Europe. When it came to the Huertgen, many of its members were relatively new to the infantry. A large number were drawn from the now-folded Army Specialized Training Program, which sent men in uniform to college to study languages and engineering. Others carried M1s after duty in the Air Corps, which reduced its flight cadet program.

On 13 December, as a slushy snow covered the ground amid frigid temperatures, the GIs of the 78th's 310th Infantry climbed out of their foxholes and headed for the first objective, Rollesbroich. Fog concealed the Americans until someone tripped a mine and then faint rays of sun pierced the mist, silhouetting GIs for the benefit of German gunners.

According to Adrian E. Sumerlin, of Headquarters Company in the 3d Battalion, "Some of the men froze when they came under fire and couldn't get up and move forward. Lieutenant Colonel [Harry] Lutz, a Michigan State graduate and the 310th's 3d Battalion CO, all six feet six inches of him walked by one man and said, 'What's the matter, son? You pinned down?' The man looked up at him and jumped up and charged forward.

"As the battalion entered the edge of the village, a sniper firing from a large house wounded some of our men. The colonel grabbed a rifle from a nearby soldier, charged the house, kicked the door open, and killed the sniper. Then he continued through the village, clearing out snipers until the village was secure." Although the initiation to battle included a fierce house-to-house firefight, the inexperienced foot soldiers of the 310th captured Rollesbroich with limited losses. On their right flank, the 309th Infantry took Simmerath. However, the 78th now faced its most formidable challenge. The village of Kesternich, perched atop a high ridge overlooking the Roer, controlled a southern approach to the bloody prize of Schmidt. A postmortem analysis reported, "Visual reconnaissance over the battle area was limited due to a dense fog. Observation of Kesternich, the battalion objective, was mostly confined to a map study." Circumstances were propitious for fulfilling General Parker's worst fears.

The battle for Kesternich began with the 2d Battalion of the 309th approaching the town from the northwest. F Company had hardly jumped off before the GIs encountered a thick girdle of wood-encased mines, whose explosions alerted German gunners. Mortars crashed down on the infantrymen trapped in the field, killing and maiming many not already hurt from the mines.

Sergeant William Ryan, a squad leader, recalled, "It was supposed to be a secret and surprise attack on German troops. I was in the file on the left side of the road. There was no order to 'lock and load' so our rifles were empty." This was a precaution taken to avoid alerting the enemy through accidental discharge of a weapon. "The order came to 'fix bayonets,' and we started moving forward. I never did hear a command to load the rifles. Shortly after, ahead and to the left front, the sky began to be lit by German flares.

"Somewhere in a field to the left, I could hear cries for help. I remember thinking to myself that the flares indicated the 'surprise' was gone, and I thought 'into that hell walked the 200' [Company F], and I asked God to protect me.

"First there was the darkness and then a flare and a short period of dark followed by the light of the next flare. As we approached a stone bridge, I could see ahead, perhaps fifty yards, a large dark building, and just beyond it the road began a gentle curve to the left. I remember thinking that this spot has got to be zeroed in. It looked mighty dangerous, so I called back to the men behind me, 'Spread out. I think we're going to be hit.'" Ryan, at this moment on his own, put a clip of ammunition in his rifle.

"Shortly thereafter, as I continued on the road, something caused me to look back. I do not remember hearing any noise or explosions, but in the dark between flares I could see what looked like a series of balls of fire, which seemed to walk down the road between the two files of men. This was when the Germans opened up with mortar fire, and it took out a lot of Company F men as killed and wounded.

"I moved to my left off the road, around the back of the building. I do not know how many were with me, but to the rear of the building, there seemed to be a high mound. We moved forward across the top and entered into a field. I was advancing in a minefield. The ground was frozen and iced up and partially swept clean of snow. I saw a three-prong fuse sticking out of the ground. I was about to avoid it, when off to my right, perhaps thirty yards, I saw a flash of fire about knee high, to the immediate front of three GIs from my company. They had bunched up, probably accidentally, and the flash may have been an 88 that caught them.

"I was distracted as a large 'T' whipped toward me like a boomerang. It was the whole arm with the rifle held at the balance by one of the three men. In that fraction of a second, my right foot caught the fuse, and the explosion messed up my right foot and leg. My left leg was also damaged with puncture wounds.

"Both my legs were [now] bare, the long underwear and pant legs were gone up to my crotch. I could readily see the condition of my legs. I did not need to give myself any first aid, as the right leg did not bleed at all, and the blood from the puncture wounds on my left leg seemed to coagulate or freeze. I felt no sense of panic nor did I have any pain.

"I know the three men on my right were alive for quite some time, as I talked to them about medics coming to help us. I do not think they really knew how bad they were hit, and they did not seem to be in any pain. After an hour or so, I did not receive any more responses."

Ryan lay there for hours, while other soldiers, including his assistant, who spoke with him briefly, passed him by. Almost at dusk, having been on the field for many hours, the sergeant convinced a Company F soldier to summon help for the wounded. Whether or not he delivered the message, Ryan spent the night lying in the minefield.

"The next day I saw men a short distance to my front, and I called to them for some assistance. At first, they seemed to be hesitant, and I suspect they were 'stragglers.' Finally, one man left to get help. It finally arrived in the form of a large bulldozer that came into the minefield from the rear. There was a driver and a man who followed in the path of the dozer track and others who remained outside the minefield. The dozer, as it came toward me, caused many explosions under the tracks as it ran over antipersonnel mines. When it drew near me, the operator called to me to turn away and put my helmet on the back of my head. He then proceeded along the left side of my body about a foot away. When he had cleared me, he stopped.

"The second soldier had climbed up, stood on the track, reached down, and assisted me up. Using my rifle as a crutch, I was able to help him lift. He placed me on the hood facing forward. The operator was then going to take me out, but I convinced him to go over and pick up [another] of the wounded. I remember looking down and seeing one half of one of the eighteen- or twenty-four-inch-wide links in the track missing and hoping it would just hold together.

"The dozer moved with the soldier walking the track and me on board, all the while exploding mines. We reached [the other GI] safely. He was lifted up and placed on the hood, and then the dozer backed out of the minefield. I could see his left foot was missing and his right eye out. There were a series of indents running down his forehead across the eye socket, where the belt of ammo must have been thrown up from the explosion, slapped into his face, and gouged his eye out."

Shock and his injuries clouded Ryan's memory of what occurred subsequently. He dimly recalled futile efforts to find a vein for a needle and a visit from a chaplain who indicated he was dying. However, he survived, only to discover that when he reached a hospital in England, he was believed to be one of some German soldiers who infiltrated the American lines wearing GI uniforms. Ryan, who lost part of his right leg, was rescued from the ignominy of prisoner-of-war status by the accidental appearance of a wounded friend from Company F. The fellow sergeant confirmed Ryan's American identity.

Ryan's rescuers came from the division's 303d Engineer Battalion. According to that organization's history, "A large, well-camouflaged *schu* minefield had protected the approaches to a machine gun nest and had claimed three infantry casualties. Two medics, attempting to aid the men, had also struck *schu* mines and volunteers were called for from the Engineers to get the men out. Captain Woodrow Dennison of the 1st Platoon, A Company, set out and soon probed into a *schu* mine, which exploded in his face. T/5 Raymond Sporenkel then offered to try driving his 'cat' across the field to the wounded, and Pfc. Arthur Reynolds, 3d Platoon medic, climbed on to care for the men as soon as they were reached." The two men were awarded Bronze Stars for their actions.

Troops from Company E headed into the battle aboard Shermans from the 709th Tank Battalion, which slowed and stalled in deep drifts of snow while antitank guns pelted them. Some of the foot soldiers, jumping off the armor, fought their way through mortars, machine guns, mines, and small arms to buildings on the outskirts of town. With the tanks they had left behind still bogged down, the small band of Americans had no radios to communicate with the battalion CP.

Lieutenant Colonel Wilson L. Burley, Jr., the 2d Battalion commander who began the attack riding on a tank but left the vehicle for a shell crater along the main road into town, had little information on the whereabouts of his own troops and knew nothing about the enemy defenders. When he finally contacted the leaders of the two forward companies, he directed them to withdraw to more secure positions. The battalion commander decided to personally investigate the situation in Kesternich, a fatal move; his body was found some time later. With the executive officer missing in action, command of the battalion devolved upon the Company H honcho, Capt. Douglas P. Frazier.

The 3d Battalion of the 309th also participated in the attack on Kesternich. Ray T. Fortunato, who had been a student at Penn State, where his one semester of advanced ROTC qualified him for OCS, led a platoon in Company I. "On 13 December, we attacked across an open field filled with haystacks. The haystacks turned out to be German pillboxes, and as soon as we were out in the open, they started firing. We returned enough fire that white flags appeared from the pillboxes. However, as some of the Germans came out to surrender, some of our soldiers, angered because some of their buddies had been killed or wounded, started firing on the surrendering soldiers. Needless to say, the white flags came down and the battle was on.

"I was hit in the groin by a machine gunner. There were a total of four bullet holes in my trousers. Only one of the bullets did any real damage. It ripped open the inside of my leg. I lay on the battlefield until a medic came up and dressed my wound.

"He suggested that I make my way back to the aid station. I did so on my hands and knees. First, I was put in the basement of a house with some other wounded from my company. We were shelled constantly while there. The next day, I was moved to a battalion aid station, then a regimental aid station, and then to a general hospital in Liège, Belgium." He returned to Company I in the final days of the war.

Unhappy with the results at Kesternich, Hodges groused about the confusion and poor intelligence. He scolded Gerow with a reminder of the debacle involving the 28th Division. The perilous circumstances of the 2d Battalion of the 309th forced Parker to order the 310th's 2d Battalion, under Lt. Col. Byron W. Ladd, to move on Kesternich from the east. Unfortunately, Ladd's troops never acquired intelligence on the defenses, and one machine gun in a concealed bunker wreaked havoc on the unsuspecting GIs. The Americans endured a fearful pounding from automatic weapons and then artillery after they scattered into ground saturated with antipersonnel mines. Ladd's forces absorbed an estimated 25 percent in casualties. Nor had the attack improved the conditions for the men from the 309th. Company E's number of effectives fell to about forty, and the tanks remained out of action, allegedly because of a dispute over whether they should get out in front of a bulldozer assigned to clear the road or follow the earthmover.

Corporal Clete Henriksen, second in command of an 81mm mortar squad with H Company of the 310th, beginning on 13 December, recounted the moments as the outfit moved up and then plunged into the maelstrom. "The weather was cool and the sky was overcast. It was apparently a typical December day. There was snow on the ground. Even though the day was rather cold, it was a perfect day for a long march, as one's body warms while walking, especially if one is carrying extra weight, as we were. We marched in orderly fashion and with very little talk or fanfare. We were told to allow several yards distance between ourselves, so it was difficult to converse with the marcher in front or in back. It was easier to talk with the soldier across the road.

"I began to get the feeling we were approaching the front when I could see some smoke in the distance near the horizon. Also, I could hear muffled sounds that must have been the artillery or gunfire. It was just barely audible at first and only sporadic. The march took us over somewhat winding and hilly roads through countryside that undoubtedly was naturally beautiful, but we were not in the proper mood for enjoying the scenery."

The ominous signs of war, split or broken trees, chunks of metal and wood, and then pieces of discarded or destroyed equipment—a nearly capsized jeep or an American steel helmet sitting atop a ditch bank—obliterated interest in bucolic splendor. The pungent odor of a dead horse and the sound of a human in obvious pain crying out from an adjacent field intensified the anxiety.

The column reached a barricade of dragon's teeth and then entered the village of Simmerath, where the troops experienced their first taste of incoming. "My platoon was directed to a certain location near what appeared to be the center of town. As I came around the corner of a house, oh my God, there lay the bodies of two dead German soldiers not over a yard apart.

"Dawn broke on December 14, and we expected to be called upon to fire our mortars. However, we were restrained and learned later that it was due to the inability of forward observers to pinpoint the exact positions of substantial numbers of the enemy, together with fear of firing on our own forces, some of which were still unaccounted for from the previous day's fighting. We were told that our rifle companies were moving to the attack of a heavily fortified community called Kesternich. Enemy 88 shells were hitting our town again, and there were rumors of individual German snipers still in Simmerath, although the town was essentially in American hands."

Restless members of the mortar section wandered about Simmerath, frequently firing their rifles into the upstairs wreckage of houses as a prophylaxis against snipers. The troops nibbled on K rations and obeyed orders to fortify their mortar positions in the event of a counterattack. "In the late afternoon, we were shocked to learn that SSgt. Raymond Kaster, our able squad leader, had been shot and killed by an enemy soldier. Evidently, Sergeant Kaster had been a bit too trusting in expecting a German soldier to surrender. Instead, the Kraut mortally wounded our brave colleague." As a direct consequence, Henriksen was given command of the squad.

In the dawning hours of 15 December, a coordinated tank, artillery, and infantry attack, with combined forces from the 2d battalions of both regiments, struck at Kesternich. Hard fighting brought some armor and foot soldiers into the town to engage in bitter, bloody, house-to-house struggles. Unfortunately, command and control collapsed. Some soldiers, needed in the event of a counterattack, escorted prisoners to the rear. Others sought protection within the rubble of buildings. Squad and platoon leaders lost contact with their men.

"We were given permission," said Henriksen, "to begin firing our mortars according to prearranged conditions and in support of our troops. In the confusion of battle, we did not get reports of progress or lack of same, but we were given orders to fire and do other things without knowing what the situation really was. If, however, we were ordered to lay a barrage of fire at 700 yards and later were told to fire again at 600 yards, we could be reasonably sure that the enemy was making progress in our direction and this could be very unsettling.

"Not long after we began firing our mortars, the enemy sensed this activity was coming out of Simmerath, and we started receiving incoming artillery fire much closer to our positions. It was during that day that a German 88 shell landed either directly in or at the very edge of one of our mortar emplacements, killing Private Dorn and seriously wounding a fellow squad member. Many other incoming missiles struck in the vicinity of our dug-in positions, and one extremely close hit tore part of the makeshift half-roof off our position. The word we received from the front was that heavy fighting was in progress, and it was reported that the two machine gun heavy weapons platoons of our H Company had also received some casualties. This was distressing news."

The two battalion commanders, Lutz and Ladd, conferred and made plans for the defense of their positions. The men in Kesternich were told to hold the town "at all costs." In the afternoon, the enemy began to bombard the Americans with deepening intensity. The explosions destroyed the telephone lines, and darkness denied any opportunity to reinforce with tanks.

From a heavily wooded area about 300 yards from town, a large number of soldiers from the 272d Volksgrenadier Division advanced under the protective cover of self-propelled guns. Darkness enveloped the counterattackers, rendering the American forward observers unable to spot targets for 78th Division artillery. No one thought to arrange for registration on critical areas, permitting the big guns to fire blind. A message from the 310th's Company E commander reported "an endless line" of Germans accompanied by either a tank or an assault gun.

Rifleman Sol Lederman in F Company of the 310th was among those who left the hedgerows and moved through an open field toward Kesternich. "No sooner had we advanced approximately 100 yards, we were pinned down by enemy fire. A man about fifteen feet to my right was suddenly hit. I asked where he was struck—he said in the belly. I told him to crawl back to the road and wait for the medics.

"I noticed there was enemy fire coming from the haystacks in the field, which were about 1,500 to 2,000 feet to my right. I fired a couple of rounds into the haystack and the shooting ceased. After what seemed an eternity, we were told to advance ahead toward our objective. When we arrived at the top of the open area, we were in Kesternich and the enemy was gone. We received orders to dig foxholes and secure the ridge overlooking a wooded area. My squad leader, Sergeant Suskind, and I dug our foxhole. Then I realized I had to urinate, which I did, but my fingers were somewhat frostbitten. I couldn't close my fly. Did it really matter?

"After a short time, the enemy began to shell our position with 88mm fire. A shell burst about six feet from our foxhole, and it felt like my helmet was pushed over my shoulders. Suddenly, my leg, my shoulder, and my face felt wet and warm. I then realized that I was hit by shrapnel. I had no trouble maneuvering. It was getting toward dusk when our squad was told to find a basement in one of the houses, secure the house, and get some rest. Meantime, another squad had secured our positions overlooking the forest area below.

"We were cleaning out the basement and had men at the doorway to check for enemy soldiers. Suddenly, the man at the door said there were German soldiers coming toward the house that we were in. I asked him if he was sure and he said 'yes' and that they were all wearing overcoats. We were told to shed our overcoats and that anyone we saw with an overcoat we should kill immediately.

"The Germans surrounded the house and started to throw grenades into the basement. Luckily, we had all jumped into the stairs leading down the basement and no one was injured. By that time, it had gotten dark outside, and they could not discern what or how many of us were in the house. We quickly stationed another man on the other side of the door, so that we had one man on either side. I stationed myself about ten feet inside the door, facing out.

"The Germans started to yell '*Kammen ze rause*' [come out]. One man, Beldegay, started being hysterical and said, 'Let's give up and surrender. Think of my wife and two kids.' We had a much greater problem, that our BAR man, Hirshmann, had come to the United States in 1939 from Germany and he was Jewish. We were very concerned about his life. In the meantime, two German soldiers entered the kitchen. As soon as they stepped over the threshold, I and another man by the door opened fire and killed the two Germans, who now lay dead. Another German was running in from the side of the house. I saw his silhouette running toward me, so I fired and must have hit him, because he went down and never moved.

"The Germans kept hollering for us to surrender. We could have killed many more of them because we had grenades, but Hirshmann suggested that we surrender and take our chances. The problem then arose, who would be the first to go out of the kitchen door and have to step over the two dead Germans laying there. I asked Beldegay to be the first one, since he was so adamant that we surrender. He refused, but the Germans were hot under the collar and yelling at us to surrender. No one wanted to be the first to step out over the dead Germans.

"I finally decided that I would be the first and it was scary. I prayed that they would not kill me. I put my hands over my head after laying down my M1 in the dark kitchen and stepped over the two dead Germans. The Germans immediately put me against the wall of the house. I thought that this was it, but instead they did the same thing with the rest of the squad. They frisked us. They took my phosphor grenade, and one of them started to play with the mechanism. I had a hard time trying to tell him not to play with it because it would go 'boom.' He finally realized what I was talking about and left it alone.

"Then the German soldiers marched us toward their lines. We stopped at a German aid station, and they asked us if anyone was wounded and needed assistance. I told them I was wounded and they took me into the bunker. There I met one of our colonels and some lieutenants whom I recognized from our regiment. The German medic checked my wounds, and I think he sprinkled some sulfa powder on them. My hands were frostbitten, and he placed them next to the stove. It hurt like hell! He asked me what was inside my shirt and I told him, rolled-up socks. He took the six pair.

They gave me a medic slip that had my wound, the hour 11:30 P.M., and the date 15 December 1944."

As the enemy approached, other outnumbered Americans still in residence crouched in the cellars. They held out during the night, but the relentless assault featuring automatic weapons and heavier caliber guns led to the surrender of fifty-six soldiers, mostly from Company F of the 310th.

In a frantic attempt to reinforce the besieged Americans, the battalion commander committed Company G. John C. Wagner, with a machine gun section in the ill-fated unit, said, "There were about twenty of us, including my battalion CO [Lieutenant Colonel Ladd] and four other officers in a small house waiting to stop a Jerry counterattack. First, the boys across the street [from Company E], after taking a terrific beating, came out to the shouts of 'Come out! Hands up!' by the cocky Krauts. We were next, surrounded on all sides, and it's in sort of disgraceful tone that I saw we surrendered without much resistance. One wonders if he isn't a traitor giving up instead of battling it out, but I was so tired physically and mentally that I remember telling the battalion CO, 'It's better to be a live prisoner than a dead hero.'

"So, some 100 of us were gathered together, searched, and given water inside fifteen minutes of capture. Although I was searched, they took nothing but some rounds of ammo and a K ration. I had thrown my new .45-caliber pistol in a corner of the room that I had just left. I looked around for buddies and asked how badly our machine gun section was wounded—all the time chain-smoking cigarettes because I knew they would be sought by our guards. I downed two D bars rather quickly, too."

The Volksgrenadiers dispatched their captives toward the rear, and Wagner recalled marching four or five hours ever deeper into Germany. "I, along with everyone else, thought of escape, and it was very possible, but how far had the Germans driven? It was extremely cold. I was too tired to spend the night moving and evading the enemy. We stopped occasionally in order the guards might rest and also to duck intermittent artillery fire. All the while, we were passing German armor. I figured the Jerries were making quite a push." The dispirited GIs from the 78th hiked, rode in wood-burning trucks, and traveled by train to a series of stalags.

Captain Frazier led a patrol from his 2d Battalion, 309th Infantry, to the houses at the edge of town. Hopes that some Americans still clung to a foothold ended when the only voices heard were those of the enemy. Another probe sneaked into a house, from which they quickly retreated behind a screen of hand grenades as the German occupants realized the presence of intruders. A third patrol composed of clerks, cooks, and heavy weapons people entered a few buildings on the outskirts and discovered only dead Americans.

With his mortar squad from Company H of the 310th, Clete Henriksen had endured an uncomfortable night. "We continued to exist on our K rations in the absence of something better. We were getting cold, and sometimes wet feet, and there were reports of fellows being evacuated for trench foot. We continued our firing as directed, but reports of activity to the front were not good. There was talk of heavy losses, especially in the rifle companies of our battalion and even word that some of our men were unaccounted for, either killed, wounded, or captured by the enemy. Sometime during the day, I received the additional bad news that my friend James Penick of the 2d machine gun platoon had been killed by a direct hit from an artillery shell. Jim Penick and I had been air cadet trainees together at the University of Tennessee and were both sent to the 78th Division when the cadet program was shut down.

"As late afternoon approached, a revolting development occurred. We were ordered to knock down our standing mortars, put on light packs, grab rifles and ammunition, and prepare to move up to assist the beleaguered men at the front. I was not sure if the intent was to stem a feared German counterattack or to make a concerted effort to wrest control of Kesternich from the Germans. I remember being scared as I, along with other mortar squad members, began moving out of Simmerath in the direction of Kesternich.

"It was getting dark, and we moved slowly and silently in a single file, dispersed so as to minimize the possible effect of enemy artillery fire. We were being led and directed by Section Sergeant Blackford. I can still see his stern countenance as he admonished us to prepare for the worst. As we left the outskirts of Simmerath and headed into the darkness of the night, I saw a headquarters platoon soldier driving his blacked-out jeep into town from the west and thought how lucky he was to be a jeep driver for some officer and not having to go out to meet the enemy with rifle in hand, as we were.

"Some distance out of Simmerath, Sergeant Blackford had us form a skirmish line, and we hunkered down, each of us approximately ten to fifteen yards apart. We each tried to find a shell hole or previously occupied foxhole for protection and still with a line of sight to the front. With the exception of artillery fire seeming to go over our heads into Simmerath and some sporadic rifle or machine gun fire in the distance, we were without close combat activity.

"After shivering in this manner for several hours—it seemed like all night—Sergeant Blackford came along and said we were going back to Simmerath. That seemed like good news, going back to our heavy weapons and the tools that we felt we really knew how to operate. When we got back, I learned that the jeep driver I had seen heading into town as we trudged out had struck a mine and been killed instantly. And I had envied him for being able to stay back in the relative security of Simmerath."

A day later, Henriksen's outfit boarded trucks for a trip to a rest and relaxation bivouac. They were able to bathe, eat hot food, draw new clothing, and be billeted in private homes. "We were not sure if we were in a German household [or a Belgian one]. Even though we were somewhat wary of staying in that house, we fell in the thick, soft feather bed provided for us and had our first good night's rest in days. Needless to say, we locked the bedroom door and kept our rifles handy."

The engineers from the 303d switched from picking up mines to laying them down to protect the embattled GIs, particularly against tanks. Jeeps carried the devices forward, and then soldiers from A Company of the 1st Platoon plus an additional detail from the 3d platoon hand-carried them into the no-man's-land near Kesternich. Staff Sergeant Gus Schmidt and Sgt. Francis Skelly led the men out ahead of the front lines. Those in foxholes were warned to hold their fire at moving targets that night.

"Jerry is sitting over on that hill, looking down your throats, so don't talk, keep as close to the ground as possible, and don't bang those damn mines together," Sergeant Schmidt reminded the GIs as they began to move forward. Occasionally, a German shell fell short of its destination in Simmerath and exploded nearby.

According to the account of the action, Pvt. John Welch then whispered, "What's wrong with those Heinies? Don't they know how to shoot? One notch down on that barrel, and we're all done."

"Don't worry about a thing," replied Cpl. Leo Larrabee. "If they hit this pile of mines, it'll look like the Grand Canyon around here—you'll never remember it." The mission proceeded, even though at one point the Americans ran into an unexpected obstacle, enemy concertina wire with flares and booby traps. They cut a hole to allow passage for those bearing mines, and the work continued. After six hours and as the sun struggled to appear, the job was done, with 1,000 mines rigged to thwart any approach by armor.

The lines between Simmerath and Kesternich temporarily hardened, and only small-scale actions occurred. The 2d Battalion of the 310th figured its losses amounted to six officers and sixty-three enlisted men killed, five officers and nearly 100 enlisted men wounded, and nearly 300 soldiers MIA. Another seventy-five men were disabled by trench foot or nonbattle injuries. The toll on the 309th was just about as severe.

16

The Capture of the Dams

Although the enemy seemed as determined as ever to resist, in the Huertgen area, it was losing the wherewithal and the will to fight at a quickening pace. A major cause of the decline was a few miles south of the forest. On 16 December, German soldiers, under a strategy devised by none other than Adolf Hitler, crashed through the thinly spread lines of the Americans in the Ardennes, turf dominated by steep ridges overlooking deep valleys, fast flowing streams, and wooded areas. To mount this assault led by Panzer forces, the Wehrmacht had siphoned off all available resources in men, ammunition, fuel, and movable guns.

Failures in intelligence, the thinness of the American lines, the assignment of green troops from the 106th Infantry Division to defend a key area, and the terrible beatings absorbed by the outfits engaged in the Huertgen from September until December left the First Army vulnerable to the attack. Notably caught by the unexpected juggernaut was the 28th Division, still trying to regroup and assimilate replacements. Antitank sergeant John Chernitsky and rifleman Ed Uzemack were among the "bloody bucketeers" taken prisoner. The 1st and 9th Divisions struggled on the northern shoulder to contain von Rundstedt's legions. At the same time, portions of the 4th Infantry Division, like the 28th still trying to regain its strength through infusions of recruits fresh off boats, were overrun in Luxembourg. George Mabry, for his heroism during the Battle of the Bulge, almost became the first American to earn a second Medal of Honor, an award apparently denied because of faulty communications.

As successful as the opening onslaught of the Germans was, there could be no reinforcements or adequate supplies for the troops committed in the Huertgen. To add to the difficulties of both sides, the worst European winter in forty years drove temperatures to record lows, while the skies dumped ever-deeper snows.

In mid-December, Michael DiLeo was with Company B of the 5th Armored Division's 46th AIB as it seized the hamlet of Schneidhausen. "We had lost all of our officers with the assaulting platoons. Sergeant Walter Jones, later commissioned a lieutenant, took command. That night we found a safe basement in a large house in Schneidhausen, where we had the wounded brought. First Sergeant Jones radioed the artillery to drop a flare over the bridge to see from the attic if the bridge over the Roer was still up. I went up to the attic with Sergeant Jones. The flare was fine, but we could not tell whether the bridge was still intact. Jones then led a patrol to check the bridge. Two of the men with him were seriously hurt by antipersonnel mines. Jones continued alone. He found the bridge to be in place.

"We had thirty-two wounded in the basement. T/5 Angelo Aquiieri, the medical aid man, even though he was wounded himself, throughout the night worked on the wounded as they were brought in. 'I was tired and hungry, had no food with me. I found some raw potatoes in the cellar, cleaned them with my hands, and ate them. I found a spot in a coal bin, made myself comfortable, and had a good sleep.' DiLeo spent three days in Schneidhausen. "By morning, around 22 December, news came that we had relief. The 8th Infantry Division was coming in. I was in the first group to leave. Some of our wounded were left behind but help was coming for them."

The status of other 5th Armored units was equally dismal. On 19 December, the 15th AIB seized the tiny enclave of Bilstein with support from the 81st Tank Battalion. The infantrymen, riding on the rear decks of the armor, which raced across open ground, encountered surprisingly little resistance. The enemy appeared to have fled in the face of the tanks' cannons and machine guns after being subjected to heavy doses of artillery shells and bombs from P-47s. But the Americans were not granted rest, as orders directed them to roust the defenders who held high ground west of Winden. Technical Sergeant William H. Guinn of C Company, who in the course of a few weeks in the campaign went from squad leader to platoon sergeant to platoon leader and finally to leader of two combined platoons, said, "There were only thirty-two of us left in our company, and we thought this attack would certainly finish off the rest of us."

Despite their shrinking numbers, the GIs succeeded in pushing the defenders out of their hilltop emplacements and into the village of Winden, the main objective. Still in a loose marriage, the 5th Armored and the GIs of the 83d Division bagged Untermaubach and Udingen also on the western banks of the Roer within a few days.

The push through the forest and to the river had been slow yet inexorable. The casualties had been fearsome during December. The 83d Division counted 589 dead, another 1,400 or so wounded, and almost 800 nonbattle losses. The 5th Armored toll was 70 dead, 505 wounded, and 223 injured or disabled and out of combat.

The American campaign through the Huertgen Forest to the Roer paused during the last week of 1944 and well into January of the new year. Although the German thrust in the Ardennes stalled after its first week of gains, it was not until the end of month that the First Army, aided by the timely intercession of the Third Army under Gen. George S. Patton, Jr., felt secure enough to resume its quest to cross the Roer en route to the Rhine.

However, before directing Courtney Hodges to go on the offensive, Eisenhower, as supreme commander, insisted upon seizure of the Roer dams rather than risk inundation of the American forces. The GIs overran the towns of Konzen, Bickerath, Am Gericht, and Imgenbroich, along with nests of bunkers that succumbed to British-manned Crocodile tanks equipped with flamethrowers. Stiffening opposition at Huppenbroich and Eicherscheid eroded the U.S. forces, but the troops achieved their objectives.

Once again, 78th Division soldiers advanced upon Kesternich, which the enemy had held since it killed, captured, or drove out the GIs who occupied the fringes of the town in mid-December. On this occasion, the Lightning Division was an element in the Ninth U.S. Army. The strategists blocked out a script in minute detail, with specific buildings designated for particular rifle squads in the attacking 2d Battalion of the 311th Infantry.

The soldiers jumped off at 5:30 A.M. on 30 January. Almost immediately, the carefully made plans fell apart. Snow obliterated vital landmarks. The Shermans from the 736th Tank Battalion skidded and slipped on the frozen ground. Mines disabled some, while direct fire knocked out a pair. The armor could not keep pace with the foot soldiers, who became wary of their mechanized companions after the exploding mines injured those around the tanks.

Despite the glitches and the intense enemy resistance, by 9 A.M. Americans entered several houses for the torturous ordeal of a house-to-house battle against a well-dug-in foe. The fighting continued into the night, and the battalion commander, Lt. Col. Richard W. Keyes, later commented, "The battle had lost its coordination and the fighting become piecemeal. It was very difficult to pick out specific buildings indicated on the sketch. Most of them had either been demolished completely or had lost their form. Many elements in the companies were scattered and difficult to control. The tank-infantry coordination was not favorable. The tanks seemed to expect the infantry to lead them and the infantry was prone to wait for the tanks."

Colonel Chester M. Willingham, the regimental CO, admonished Keyes to "keep pushing. [The troops are moving] too slow." He told the battalion leader not to hesitate to commit his reserve tank platoon. Problems of poor communication between armor and infantry persisted. The telephone mounted in the rear of a tank to enable a ground pounder to talk with those inside was frequently inoperable or torn away by shell fire. Frustrated infantrymen pounded on the turret or even covered the periscope in order to get the attention of the tankers.

In the Company E spearhead, SSgt. Jonah E. Kelley, a twenty-one-year-old from West Virginia, led a squad. They engaged the Germans hidden in the houses. Wounded by mortar fragments that rendered his left hand virtually useless, Kelley insisted on continuing after the application of a bandage. Because of his injury, he fired his rifle by laying it across one arm instead of from the crook of the shoulder or from the hip.

Held up by fire from one house, Kelley rushed the building and killed the three defenders, enabling his companions to advance. He managed to shoot down a sniper in an upstairs window with a single shot and drop another soldier running from a cellar. The squad took a defensive position for the night, and in the morning, as they continued deeper into Kesternich, they encountered heavy automatic weapons fire. The sergeant artfully maneuvered around the rubble until he saw a machine pistol firing from the concealment of a haystack. Accurate work with his M1 ended the threat.

An American mortar squad attempted to squelch another machine gun nest farther down the street, but the German fire wounded as many as a dozen men. Kelley rushed the position, whose gunner trained the weapon on him from behind a wall. Hit by several bullets, the sergeant, with his final breaths, managed to empty three rounds through a hole in the barricade, snuffing out the enemy soldier. A posthumous Medal of Honor went to Kelley's mother. Kesternich itself fell after the second day of furious fighting, which reduced every single one of its 112 houses to rubble.

Following the bloody successes culminating with the capture of Kesternich, Clarence Huebner, elevated to commander of the V Corps, emphasized the urgent need for the 78th, now returned to the First Army, to capture the major dams. The pressure on Huebner emanated from Eisenhower through Bradley and Hodges. He assigned CCR of the 7th Armored Division and an extra battalion of combat engineers and bolstered the artillery.

Hodges, determined to end the campaign swiftly, brought on additional forces. He inserted the 82d Airborne Division into the Huertgen with the 505th Parachute Infantry Regiment, a regular component of the 82d, and the 517th Parachute Infantry Combat Team, a formerly independent regiment. Both outfits, designated Task Force A, possessed considerable combat experience and had been rushed successfully into the Ardennes to confront the mid-December penetration.

Major General James M. Gavin, the CG of the 82d Airborne, unlike most of the other division commanders, undertook a personal tour of the territory in which he would operate. "I went to the town of Vossenack on reconnaissance. I found no enemy and, having gone through the town by jeep, reached the trail that crossed the Kall River valley. Accompanied by the division G-3, Col. John Norton, and Sergeant [Walker] Wood, I started down the trail. It was really a reconnaissance, since I did not know what the lay of the land would be, and what, if any, enemy might still be there. Our orders for the following day were to attack across the Kall River valley from Vossenack and seize the town of Schmidt. By now, most of the snow had melted; there was only a small patch here and there under the trees.

"I proceeded down the trail on foot. It was obviously impassable for a jeep; it was a shambles of wrecked vehicles and abandoned tanks. The first tanks that attempted to go down the trail [the 707th Tank Battalion with the 28th Division] had evidently slid off and thrown their tracks. In some cases, the tanks had been pushed off the trail and toppled down the gorge among the trees. Between where the trail begins outside of Vossenack and the bottom of the canyon, there were four abandoned tank destroyers and five disabled and abandoned tanks. . . . All along the sides of the trail there were many, many dead bodies, cadavers that had just emerged from the winter snow. Their gangrenous, broken, and torn bodies were rigid and grotesque, some of them with arms skyward, seemingly in supplication. They were wearing the red keystone of the 28th Infantry Division."

As he continued down the pathway, he came upon a demolished stone bridge. "Nearby were dozens of litter cases, the bodies long dead. Apparently, an aid station had been established near the creek, and in the midst of the fighting it had been abandoned, many of the men dying on their stretchers." The scene matches the account of Bill Peña's November experiences with the 109th Infantry.

In pursuit of their assignment, the 505th Parachute Infantry Regiment troopers wended their way over the same trail. They were en route to the objective of Kommerscheidt, site of the slaughter of the 28th Division GIs retreating from Schmidt three months earlier. Sergeant Bill Dunfee echoed Gavin, "The area became known to us as 'Death Valley.' There were trucks, tanks, jeeps, trailers, tank destroyers, bumper to bumper and all shot to hell. I had been exposed to the carnage of war in four airborne operations—Sicily, Italy, Normandy, and Holland—but I never saw anything that could compare. Freshly killed troops in various stages of dismemberment are gruesome enough for the average stomach. But these men had been through a freeze and thaw. They had lain there since November, and their flesh had rotted and was peeling from the skeletons. Some were in litters. I hoped they were killed outright and not abandoned to freeze to death. There was complete silence in our column, each man handling this horror in his own way. For me, it was the most shocking single experience of the war. If anyone needed an incentive to fight, this gave him ample reason."

The other parachute outfit, the 517th, had moved from quarters in Stavelot, Belgium, one of the key towns in the Battle of the Bulge, to Honsfeld for duty under the 82d Airborne. It occupied a blocking position, while the 325th Glider Infantry, fighting on foot, attacked its objectives. On 3 February, the 517th shifted to the control of the 78th Infantry Division, headquartered in Simmerath for assignment in the attack aimed at Schmidt and the Schwammenauel Dam.

Knowing that Schmidt, perched on a ridge that overlooked the Schwammenauel Dam and its reservoir, served as the key to control, and aware of the misfortunes of the 28th Division when it tried to advance through the Kall River gorge, Lightning Division CG Parker aimed his forces to strike from the south. He left the Kall River approach from the northwest for Gavin's 505th. The 517th would attack from Bergstein, northeast in a "diversion" to prevent a concentration of enemy troops around Schmidt.

The opening gambit, on 3 February, called for an attack by GIs of the 78th to sanitize the territory south of the reservoir, which involved crossing a narrowed Roer and seizing Dedenborn, a tiny village atop high ground. Ordinarily, at this time of the year, the frigid waters of the Roer ran slowly but thawed snows created an icy torrent. Two platoons of riflemen from the 1st Battalion of the 311th Infantry struggled through the chest-deep stream, losing more than a dozen men to drowning or gunfire. However, the two officers and thirty-one enlisted men who clambered up the eastern bank, although bereft of many of their weapons, entered Dedenborn, where, fortunately, no one resisted. The 311th's 3d Battalion encountered more numerous enemy troops as it pursued the objective due east of Kesternich, but the opposition yielded readily.

Two days later, the final push began, with the 309th and 310th Regiments advancing through the rain on Schmidt. The first Germans encountered gave up without a struggle; more than 100 surrendered without a shot. At this point, however, the offensive halted while engineers scoured the roads for mines. An impatient Huebner, hectored by Hodges, widened the front with orders for the 9th Division to ford the Roer near the Urft Dam. The move would forestall any reinforcement from the east to the defenders. The GIs of Gen. Louis Craig streamed across the river and quickly established a block against the Germans.

At the same time, Huebner ordered Parker not to delay further and instructed him to cross the Roer at Roerberg, seize a lesser dam, the Paulushof, and the forested high ground in the vicinity. Parker designated the 311th Regiment for the assignment. Once again, haste wasted lives without reward. Enemy mortars, registered on Roerberg, fell with deadly accuracy. The first half dozen shells hit someone, killing at least seven men, including a pair of war correspondents, and wounding the battalion commander and other key officers. Enemy observers overlooked the site chosen for fording the river and reconnaissance determined the waters ran far too swiftly for the GIs to wade across or bridge them. Huebner cancelled the ill-timed operation.

Parker and Huebner renewed the push toward Schmidt, with the 310th passing through the two other 78th Division regiments. A welter of instructions confused the officers and men at the front with no clear direction to any specific unit. The darkness of the 5 February night forced a halt. In another poorly thought out plan, the 1st and 2d Battalions of the 310th passed through the ranks of the 309th on their way to assault a fortified barracks in Schmidt. The infantrymen moved out at 3 A.M. on 6 February in total darkness with predictable consequences. The soldiers, unable to distinguish their locations, blundered about, falling into abandoned foxholes and shell holes. Seven hours after they started out, they had advanced less than 500 yards and narrowly escaped destruction as they repulsed a strong enemy counterattack. Greatly displeased, Huebner visited Parker to vent his displeasure.

William Sylvan at First Army headquarters reported on 6 February, "Gen. [Hodges] was not too well satisfied with the progress made during the day toward Schmidt. The area was heavily mined and pillboxes strongly defended. Gen. nevertheless felt with all the strength we had in that area, greater gains should have been made. Tonight forward troops advanced in the vertical grid 3,000 yards toward the town. The 517th Parachute Infantry, which attacked south in the vicinity of Bergstein, ran into heavy minefields and small-arms fire; at the end of day made only 800 yards not yet up to the Kall River."

The 8th Division occupied the village of Bergstein after the 2d Ranger Battalion drove the enemy from Hill 400. In the strategy devised by the V Corps with the 78th Division's Parker, the 517th PRCT relieved the foot soldiers in Bergstein for the final assault on Schmidt. Dick Robb, sergeant major of the 517th's 3d Battalion, described the 13th Infantry Regiment that the troopers replaced as "in the worst condition of morale one could imagine. The Germans had them completely cowed. At dusk, Jerry moved up close to the town into trenches and sniped at even the slightest movement. At dawn, they moved back to a wooded area and covered the GIs with rifle and mortar fire.

"Several of us entered a house overlooking the enemy positions. Outside lay a body, a GI. I asked how long he had been there. An officer told us, 'several days.' We learned there were a number of dead that couldn't be recovered because of the situation. We were told the troops were fed only twice a day, after dark in the evening and before dawn of the next day."

The 517th's march toward the Roer dams began badly when regimental CO, Col. Rupert Graves, arrived at Bergstein and immediately sought to reconnoiter the area. Observing the activity, German gunners began dropping shells into Bergstein, which led to protests from the 8th Division GIs. Their commander started to scold Graves, who tartly responded that he could hardly be expected to launch an attack without adequate reconnaissance. The 8th's CG accepted the explanation but insisted Graves should consider himself severely reprimanded.

The 2d and 3d Battalions were to head out at night, cross the steep ravine down to the twenty-foot-wide Kall, wade through the frigid water, and seize control of the high ground overlooking the road to Schmidt. Aside from the firepower, including artillery and mortars, that could be brought down on them, the troopers knew they would contend with a huge minefield.

According to Tom R. Cross, son of the commander of the 121st Infantry and a captain in the 517th, who subsequently investigated the sequence of events, the strategists in charge were well aware that a frontal assault toward Schmidt invited disaster. In fact, the plan envisioned that while the 517th would preoccupy the major German forces, other U.S. units would swing around the defenders and envelop Schmidt. Unfortunately, instead of instructing the troopers to feint and thus distract the foe, they were told to confront and engage the enemy.

At the headquarters of the 82d Airborne, Rupert Graves was informed by the top intelligence and operations officers of the futility of the role assigned to the 517th. Said the 517th's Tom Cross, "Mel Zais [3d Battalion CO] went to the 121st Infantry Regiment of the 8th Division, which was commanded by my father, Col. Thomas J. Cross. My father, who lost a lot of men trying to dislodge the Germans from Bergstein, gave Mel all the details based on his experience in the area. He told Mel that the 517th was facing an impossible task and urged him to relay that to the headquarters committing the 517th to the task. Mel said it was too late. The timetable for the operation would not permit a change."

Lieutenant Colonel Dick Seitz, the 2d Battalion leader, criticized the operation as a classic series of errors. "High echelon strategists can work from a map and aerial photos, but it is an axiom of military operations that battalions or companies should never advance without first-hand knowledge of the terrain. We never had an opportunity to make a foot recon. The plan called for a night attack, which makes the need for good recon, enabling one to recognize terrain features, even more imperative. The plan said we were to advance with the two battalions abreast. We were unable to properly rehearse the operation. The book calls for adequate planning, rehearsals, and to proceed on a narrow front. We violated all of these and jumped off right on schedule.

"I did take out my battalion in a column of companies, which is a narrow front. I thought things were going well, when I learned the

3d Battalion was held up by heavy machine gun fire. They were now holding their position, waiting for artillery fire. We had started without initial arty [artillery] prep to gain the element of surprise.

"My battalion, with [Capt.] George Giuchici of F Company in the lead, continued forward. Suddenly, from the direction of the 3d Battalion, the enemy counterattacked in force. At the same time, the Germans lit up the night with flares; it was like daylight. The enemy cut across between my command group and the 2d Platoon of F Company. I was behind them with the 3d Platoon. Good old George, bless his heart, a great soldier, kept going. I realized that the 3d Battalion was not on line with me, leaving my flank exposed. I ordered a halt and to repel the counterattack."

Private First Class Myrle Traver, toting a BAR, was part of F Company. "In the early afternoon, someone brought word they had found an abandoned cabin. At last, a warm place where we could cook and eat. Joe Martin, Wayne (Willie) Gibbon, Elio Masianti, and I sat and talked after our meal. Word came we were to go at 10 P.M. Boy! We hated to leave that warm place and go out into the snow.

"I remember putting the little white strips of plastic on the backs of our helmets. The strips were fluorescent and would shine at night so we could see the man in front. We moved out and started crawling, keeping in line by following the tape strung out by engineers. Machine guns and flares kept me scared to death. Just keep crawling on the belly, flares and guns flashing, but just keep going. We finally got through the minefield and were moving up and down mountain trails. Sometimes we would fall behind, then play catch up, so as not to lose sight of the white spot on the helmet ahead.

"After some time, I looked back. No one was following. We just kept moving. I ended up in a foxhole with Lieutenant [Warren] Caufield. He told me to keep down. About then, two German officers walked up. Caufield raised up his folding carbine and shot both Germans from about a three-foot range.

"Daylight was breaking and we began to move out again. A few hundred yards further, shells from our own artillery landed right among us. Captain Guichici told Caufield to stay with the wounded and for George Flynn and me to follow him. We ran and ran; if you knew Guichici, you knew he could run. He had his drum-type submachine gun in one hand like a pistol and I dragged the BAR. Flynn carried an .03 Springfield sniper rifle. We stumbled onto a young German soldier. He looked to be about thirteen years old. He begged us not to kill him, and Guichici said to bring him along.

"We reached the area where we were supposed to meet E Company, but there was no one there. We hid in a large shell hole and waited, hoping the infantry would attack on schedule and pick us up. There was no attack during the day. We didn't know it had been called off. We talked about trying to get back through to our lines that night, but what would our chances be, trying to pass through the minefield. We decided to wait, hoping for the attack the next morning. Again no attack. We heard troops fighting, the sounds getting closer, even heard American troopers cussing and yelling but they fell back. That night two German officers stood talking and smoking right above us. Captain Guichici reached up and touched one of the German's boots, just to see if he could do it.

"Later that night, while Guichici was guarding the German kid—we took turns with guard duty at night—Guichici woke me and said the kid was gone. We thought maybe he had crawled out to relieve himself, as we all had done. But he never came back."

Clifford Land, also from F Company, recalled, "As soon as the flares died out, many GIs jumped up and ran. The enemy was aware this would occur, so they sprayed the field the second the flares went out. Many were killed or wounded as a result.

"Concussion from a mortar shell knocked me into a shell hole. I was lying there when I heard my squad leader say, 'All right, men. Let's withdraw.' I rose from that hole and walked off in the direction I faced. It happened I was going the wrong way, into the enemy lines.

"Because of the concussion, I did not know I was alone and headed in the wrong direction. Nor was I aware I was in a minefield and surrounded by the enemy. I stopped once to rest. After hearing a noise behind me, I looked and saw the unmistakable silhouette of an enemy helmet. I began to run down the hill, came to a river, and took a left turn, which was again the wrong direction. I wandered for three days and nights behind the German lines, laying low during the day, traveling at night, digging frozen turnips from the ground with my bayonet for food."

The troopers with Dick Robb had become infuriated by the stiletto-like thrusts of the foe from its well-protected hideouts. "One of their snipers hit one of our guys carrying a plastic water bottle," recalled Robb. "That did it, those bastards were in no way going to move us. On even a suspicion of movement in their area, every rifle of ours fired into their positions. That night, we tried to attack across the open area toward them. Even with the 596th Engineers, we could not get through their mines. We lost men to mines, even those who went out to get them."

Well back in the battalion column marched engineers from the 596th Engineer Company, a component of the 517th, carrying heavy timbers and planks to construct a crude bridge across the Kall. Sergeant Allan Goodman saw the flares illuminate the sky and the incoming fire crash down on anything that moved. Even before dawn, the engineers realized that there was not going to be a river crossing. They discarded their timbers and planks.

"At midmorning," said Goodman, "we were asked to clear a path through the minefield. From the town plateau, the ravine, with sides at a forty-five degree or even steeper pitch, sloped down toward the river. The path was to run halfway up on the pitched sides and mines were plentiful, Bouncing Betty and *schu* mines. They were both trip wire and contact type that lay buried.

"We were under constant mortar fire, but the steep slopes protected us to a degree. We laid a white tape and cleared a foot-and-a-half path on each side as we went. The distance was several hundred yards or more. To do this, we worked all day and night, about thirty-six hours straight, and I got far enough forward to receive direct fire from a machine gun emplacement. I could see German ambulances evacuating their wounded.

"On about the third day, one of the 517th men was brought back up the path after he had slipped off and lost a foot. He actually seemed happy, and we actually envied his leaving, foot or no. That evening I was called to battalion headquarters to be briefed for a night attack. A lieutenant asked if the engineers would lead the way on the path. I interrupted to say we weren't going to be sheep. We had laid the path line and would be close, but we were not point men and we needed both hands to clear mines when needed. The lieutenant didn't like it, but the senior officer backed me up.

"That night my squad was split and my corporal, Dave Pierce, took four men and I took four to each side of the ravine. The night was chaos and the infantry never did reach the objective."

In the three days that the 517th vainly struggled to pass through the minefields toward Schmidt, the regiment lost more than 200 troopers, about a quarter of its already depleted riflemen complement. Said medic John Chism, "When I finally stood in front of the side selected for our aid station and looked at the endless vista both north and south, I felt like I was looking on Dante's inferno. I did not see how anyone could survive this punishment. At night, Bergstein-Schmidt had a yellowish cast caused by the continuous use of various types of flares. Big ones from artillery discouraged troop movement. Little flares conveyed messages about attaining an objective or to fire or lift artillery. The terrain constantly absorbed projectiles of every description. It was laced with beautiful but deadly tracer ammunition from small arms. The combination of all this arcing fire provided depth to the hell washing over the pockmarked mud. The ground was chopped and chewed by round after round into a mass of growing craters. The shell holes served as temporary cover when troops were caught in the open. It was temporary because one had to go forward or backward to survive. To stay meant certain injury.

"From Bergstein down to the river in the approach to Schmidt, there were just so many paths. It was not enough to take a road with shoulders full of mines from friend and foe removed by our engineers. Security had to be provided, because the Germans were adept at letting attackers pass and then sliding their own mines over a previously cleared road.

"Outside the hovel that served as the CP and aid station was a large bomb crater, which had to be negotiated on entering or leaving the building. The mortar platoon had placed one of its section behind the building and the natural berm of the crater. One of the mortar men, seeing a buddy, climbed up on the berm to talk to his friend. A sniper fired one round, hitting him in the head, tearing a huge gash and exposing the brain.

"Captain [Daniel] Dickinson [battalion surgeon] and I happened to be at the aid station, a dozen yards away. We had to treat the man where he lay, which meant we were partially exposed. I assisted Dickinson but felt the need to take cover in case the sniper had any more ideas. Dickinson's attention was undivided. He carried on the examination with the same coolness and devotion to detail as if he were in a stateside hospital. When he finally pronounced the trooper dead, he instructed me how he would like to have him evacuated. He then secured an M1 rifle and went after the sniper. [Dickinson had previously served as an infantryman.] To his dying day he believed he got that sniper. Dickinson never said anything, but I believe he wanted to show any spectators that the care given the dying soldier was available to everyone." And Dickinson was laboring under added stress, because his normal associate, Doc Plassman (another battalion surgeon), at the insistence of Chism, had been evacuated with a case of lobar pneumonia.

Clifford Land, after wandering through no-man's-land, sifted back to the 2d Battalion. "Daylight caught us as we were coming into a clearing at the base of a mountain. A German machine gun opened up and sprayed the entire area. Men ran in every direction, and I made a dive for a foxhole and landed squarely on top of the battalion commander, Lieutenant Colonel Seitz. There were maybe three other men in that hole. I will never forget how mad the lieutenant colonel was, not from me falling on him but because of the situation we were in. He arose from the foxhole and started giving orders. Standing upright, he shouted for every man to gather up all the equipment he could carry and start a withdrawal up the hillside toward our lines. And he walked as straight as any man could up that hill with a string of men following, while bullets flew and mortars fell all around."

Russel Brami, with E Company of the 2d Battalion, had been directed to trail the unit's advance. "Major Dave Armstrong came to me and said, 'Brami, we're going back. You lead us.' There were thirty to fifty guys now behind me. We were all scared shitless. All I could do was walk over the thin path marked by engineer's tape. It was the scariest moment of the war for me."

The trio of Capt. George Guichici, George Flynn, and Myrle Traver of Company F, lost and out of contact with their fellows, their prisoner having vanished, spent the night hoping the attacking troopers would reach them by morning. "About an hour after first light," said Traver, "we saw troops coming our way and the helmets looked like ours. We didn't realize that these were German paratrooper helmets, which did not have the drop side like the regular German ones. The brush was so thick in that direction it was hard to be sure, but we thought they were ours. Six heads and guns came over the rim of the crater and then we knew.

"I asked Guichici, 'What now?' He said, 'To hell with it.' They wanted to shoot Guichici because they were afraid of his size. But the kid we had taken prisoner was with them and I told him we hadn't killed him. He was able to talk the others out of killing Guichici."

Traver spent sixty-four days as a prisoner of war and his two companions a similar amount of time. Traver and Flynn, separated from the captain, tried to escape with a group of other captives but were caught. Guichici slipped away twice only to be recaptured on both occasions.

The 1st Battalion initially had been designated as reserve for the assault on Schmidt. After the first day of the abortive attack, the troopers under Major McMahon started out from Hill 400 toward Zerkall on the left flank of the line. For medic Charlie Keen, the days and nights after the sojourn at Stavelot had been devastating. "We would fight all day and just before total dark, the Krauts, with clockwork precision, would counterattack, employing five tanks and a battalion of infantry. You knew exactly what they were going to do without fail. Someone heard our officers talking about General Gavin speaking on the phone to higher headquarters. He was asked about conditions, and he responded he had all five regiments committed [the 505th and 508th PR were part of the operation] and both flanks exposed for several miles, but not to worry since he still had a company of military police in reserve.

"Around dark one evening, with the snow about a foot deep and still falling lightly, we were subjected to intense, heavy artillery fire, especially to our front. Slim Ford, an old Toccoa [Georgia base] boy, came running back yelling for me to hurry as Doyle Gray had just been hit. I took off full speed as shells were still coming spasmodically, and in the thick woods, a tree burst would get you whether you were in a foxhole or not. The smell of cordite, or whatever the hell they put in besides powder, hung over the place and the air itself was crystallite.

"No one was in sight since Slim and Gray was on outpost. There were no GIs and, thank God, no Krauts. In what you might call my free flight, I saw all the shattered trees and over to one side a paratrooper in a jumpsuit with his head stuck in the snow. It was Gray. I heard some more shells coming in, and, spotting a small hole near him, I grabbed for his webbing to drag him into the hole with me in one leap. Just as my hand touched his webbing, I spotted an ear on a snow-covered bush and knew instantly that the body I held did not have its head in the snow. There wasn't any head. Apparently, a large piece of shell had cut or blown it off.

"The scene will go to my grave with me, but I've often thought at least it was quick. An only child, Gray was always looking for some kind of spot in this life where he could find his place. He did and it was the role of a loner, utterly without fear, who had rather kill the Germans than do anything else. The success he achieved was not the vocation you could take home to civilian life and to a worshipping mother. She wrote the captain and any name she could recognize as having been with Doyle. I should have been the one to answer but I didn't."

On the night of 6 February, H and I Companies were caught in the enemy guns amid the minefield. Platoon leader Ludlow Gibbons from I Company, with a mere fifteen troops left from his normal complement of forty, advanced until they reached a clearing. Gibbons remembered, "We [a scout and the lieutenant] walked twenty or thirty yards into the open field in bright moonlight. The scout and I were facing each other, squatting on our haunches, discussing whether to go right or left to skirt the clearing. I glanced up and directly behind the scout a man's figure appeared. He let out a yell while hitting the scout, who went down. The German ran off to the right as I fired several rounds. I moved back to the head of the column. Moments later the scout showed up."

But with their location disclosed, the men from I Company began taking heavy fire. When dawn broke, the enemy opened up with machine guns from two separate emplacements. The CO, Capt. James Birder, sized up the situation as untenable. He directed a retreat, to be aided by troopers from H Company. As Birder and his people gingerly made their way back, a GI stepped off the tape and onto a mine. Birder carefully followed the wounded man's footsteps and tried to lift him from under his arms. Birder slipped in the snow and sat down on another mine, triggering a second explosion. Both of the badly injured men were carried some two miles to the nearest aid station, where they died.

John Saxion served as a platoon leader for H Company. "All morning I had sat with artillery Capt. Robert Woodhull and two of his observers. We watched the Germans through binoculars as they set up mortars in the valley below us. The captain's 75s could not get enough angle to fire on them.

"About noon, H Company moved around the hill to get a Jerry machine gun. We eliminated the gun and were digging in, eating our rations. The point BAR man brought me two Germans, one of average size was leading a huge soldier whose head was bandaged along with his chest and hands. When we interrogated the smaller prisoner, he told us that after our third attack had been repulsed, the Germans started to celebrate. The big guy, who was arrogant and very much a Nazi, pulled the pin of a potato masher and held it near his head. It had gone off for a self-inflicted wound.

"I turned the big one over to Sergeant Robb to take to the rear. On the way back, Robb ordered him to help carry a stretcher. He refused, citing the Geneva rules. Robb threatened him with a .45, telling him to walk off the tape. The prisoner then helped carry the litter up the hill. Later, I asked what became of him and was told he died."

Robb saw first-hand the somewhat bizarre antics of the enemy. "A group of us topped a rise at the edge of some woods looking across a clearing to another patch of trees. A number of Germans ran out of those woods toward us, shouting and screaming. A turkey shoot; they had to be crazy. These were targets less than fifty yards away. We captured one who walked right into us and surrendered. He told us something about his comrades using drugs. That fit their behavior.

"Our lieutenant requested we be allowed to withdraw unless we could have reinforcements. We were only ten or twelve and way out front with mostly wounded behind us. Permission was granted, and we started back with our prisoner. I was jabbing him in the back with my left fist to move faster, my .45 pistol in my right hand, safety off, my finger very tight on the trigger. We were going by several of my friends lying off the trail. He and I were alone, no one else about. Seeing feet blown off by *schu* mines and now the dead by the trail, I thought perhaps I would kill the prisoner. Why not? No one would know, just a bullet in the back. There would be no retribution for me, even if someone found out.

"I had not completely justified the act in my mind. He was a paratrooper, not an SS man. Suddenly I came on Sgt. Fred Harmon and a lieutenant. They had a stretcher and on it was one of ours, his right leg blown off at the hip, an awful sight. For an instant, I cursed myself for not killing the German while I had the chance. Then I pointed to the lieutenant's end of the litter and shoved him at it. I am sure the German was pleased to take the stretcher because there lay safety for him."

Saxion watched what he described as an endless stream of men carried back on litters. "When mortars started to pound us, our position became exposed, so we withdrew to our starting point. On the way back we passed the bodies of Captain Woodhull and his observers, killed by the mortars that we observed being set up that morning."

One of the wounded from I Company was Lt. Charles Casey, who had been a friend of Saxion through Saxion's difficult days in Italy, then the invasion of southern France, the Bulge, and now the bloody encounter between Bergstein and Schmidt. "Casey came up from the Kall ravine," said Saxion, "blood pouring from an ear, and he had another wound in his hip. He asked me for a cigarette but did not even recognize me." Nothing demonstrated more clearly to John Chism the need to swiftly remove the wounded and begin sophisticated treatment unavailable in an aid station than his three days on the Bergstein-Schmidt front. "Walter Frieble, who came to us fresh out of high school, and Captain Birder both should have survived, although seriously wounded. But the weather and the extra hour required to get them to the hospital was the difference that cost their lives. On the other hand, Hank Wanggrzynowicz was the most seriously wounded person I handled. He was hit by a large caliber bullet or fragment, which all but decapitated him. The missile passed completely through his chin, knocking out teeth and inflicting extreme damage. The little we could do for him was limited to removing loose debris and inserting a tube in order to prevent him from choking on blood. He could not be transported by litter and insisted on sitting up. Roy Dunne, the pint-size ambulance driver, propped him up with an extra blanket and broke all records getting him to Stavelot. Dunne surprised us when he passed the word that he had deposited a living Hank."

Even as they departed the battlefield, having been relieved by other units, the 517th suffered final losses. Charlie Keen was on his way back up the slope to safety. "We all watched as a small ball of fire came across the Roer, traveling slowly about 100 feet in the air and crashed right next to the only house still standing. There was a loud explosion and the concussion from the rocket caused the entire house to collapse. We didn't know it at the time, but a group from B Company's 2nd Platoon was in the building. Many were injured, but the one man killed was big Frank Hayes, the former heavyweight champion of the 17th AB Division. Frank had joined the outfit at Toccoa from Painted Post, New York, and was the last man from the outfit to die in battle."

Clark Archer, 2d Platoon sergeant in B Company, recalled that during daylight hours the men remained under cover in Bergstein. "We had no officers remaining. I placed our first squad in the basement of a two-story building. Evidently, an advance party from the 508 PIR [another 82d Airborne unit] entered Bergstein by jeep and immediately drew a barrage of screaming meemies. The building housing our 1st Squad suffered a direct hit, killing all four of the men in the basement. Four men in the immediate vicinity, including me, were also wounded. I was told in Liège General Hospital that the 'Buffalo,' [a] jeep rigged to carry four stretchers, had detonated a land mine between Bergstein and Brandenberg, killing the driver. I was on the right side and became a patient of the traction ward for three weeks."

The 517th pulled out of the area in a welter of grief, bitterness, and anger. While the firepower delivered by the 517th wiped out most of the German paratroop regiment opposing it and persuaded the enemy to depart without further resistance, the troopers believed that they had been needlessly thrust into battle and had more than 200 men sacrificed. None too robust following weeks of battling to stop the enemy in the Ardennes, the line companies of the 517th, after their tour in the Huertgen, averaged only 39 percent of their normal complement. On the other hand, the fight prevented any reinforcement of the Schmidt garrison.

In the assault on that town, impelled by the unhappiness of the corps commander and First Army, Parker chose to abandon the orthodox policy of retaining a reserve and pitched all three of his regiments into the attack. In a pincers formed with the 82d Airborne's 505th, the 309th moved on Kommerscheidt, northwest of Schmidt and a death trap for the 28th Division in November. Elements of the 310th approached Schmidt from the southeast, while the 311th attacked the town itself.

Godfrey Stallings, a radio operator with K Company, recalled that in the direct assault, his unit would work with armor. "We were to rendezvous with the tanks at the edge of the woods. Some of our men were to ride on top of the tanks across the open space, while the rest of us followed on foot. There was some mix-up in getting the tanks and infantry together.

"Tanks make a lot of noise when they move with their motors roaring, treads clanking and squeaking. When the tanks came roaring up, they were heard and spotted by the enemy. We were coming to the rendezvous through the forest, as this would keep us hidden from enemy observation until the last minute. The enemy spotted the tanks and figured an attack was building up. They were getting their artillery zeroed in on the tanks.

"In the mix-up and confusion of getting the infantry and tanks coordinated, the enemy found out we were in the woods behind the tanks. They changed the artillery range and began a heavy barrage of shells into the woods where we were waiting. They decided to go after the infantry instead of the tanks.

"Our captain, realizing we would be cut to pieces if we stayed there, jumped up and started ordering the men to move forward, out of the woods. He got the men assigned to ride the tanks up on the tanks, and the tanks to move out into the attack. The rest of us followed and started the attack across the open area on foot. It seemed that everything broke loose about that time. Everybody seemed to be firing everything they had, and I do mean everybody was shooting.

"Those of us on foot did not have much protection in the open area. Just blades of grass, weeds, and depressions in the ground left by tank tracks. Our best bet was to keep moving forward. One group would shoot while another moved up. It was sort of a leapfrog action. When you ran forward, it was in a zigzag pattern, and when you hit the ground, you rolled to spoil the aim of any enemy shooting in your direction." He was describing the fire-and-movement tactic.

"When the leading tank got almost to the edge of the village, it was hit by antitank shells and set on fire. The other tanks, seeing that the leading tank had been destroyed, wheeled around and started back toward the woods. The GIs on the ground saw the tanks turn around and thought a retreat had been ordered, so they started back toward the woods, too.

"Captain Feery, my company commander, seeing the attack was faltering, started moving around, getting our men off the tanks and ordered everybody to start toward the village again. He kept the attacking going. There was so much noise it was hard to hear anything. It seemed that Captain Feery was everywhere, urging the men forward. I did the best I could to keep up with him, as I had a walkie-talkie on my back and had to keep in touch with him as much as possible to relay any messages received."

According to combat interviews conducted shortly afterward, the Company A, 774th Tank Battalion, commander refused to order his vehicles forward. He remained adamant despite the demands of the 3d Battalion CO, Lt. Col. Andy A. Lipscomb, seconded by Lt. Col. Harry Lutz, the CO of the 310th's 3d Battalion, which occupied an adjacent area. The tankers balked even when a pair of infantry lieutenants offered to leave their foxholes and personally escort the armor forward.

Companies I and K struggled forward to the outskirts of Schmidt, where they began the systematic but bloody task of routing the enemy from each building. As the night approached, Stallings said his outfit gained a crossroads in the middle of the village. Feery received a DSC for his work.

Believing Schmidt was securely in the hands of his forces, Parker directed the 310th to march through Schmidt on its way to the Schwammenauel Dam. But before they advanced all the way through the village, nasty firefights blazed up, and the drive to control the vast reservoir stalled. From First Army headquarters, Hodges communicated his discontent to corps. Apparently, the 9th Division CO, General Craig, happened to be at Huebner's command post shortly after the call from Hodges. Huebner snatched the opportunity to enlist Craig in the effort and scheduled two regiments of the 78th to serve under Craig for a final assault on the Schwammenauel.

A genuine sense of urgency gripped American field commanders, as intelligence reports on 9 February spoke of an ominous rise in the river level, predicting two feet above flood stage within four days. Troops from the 9th Division achieved their objective, the village of Hasenfeld, which would provide an assembly area for the spearhead (the 1st Battalion of the 309th) against the dam defenders. The infantrymen would be accompanied by a detachment from the 303d Engineers, who would be responsible for dismantling any explosives and inspecting the dam for damage.

Because of the imminent flood threat, the attack, originally scheduled for daylight on 10 February, began during the preceding night. The steep, debris-covered terrain severely hampered the movement of the soldiers, but the darkness and the constant artillery cloaked their approach from the enemy. Only after a commotion created when a GI fell into a foxhole occupied by Germans did the foe come alert. Flares lit up the sky, revealing that the GIs had already entered into the German lines. Furious exchanges of small arms, grenades, and close combat ensued.

Explosions in the dam's valve house building alarmed the Americans, who rushed forward to capture the gatehouse and some other structures. Because of the destruction of the control valves, water gushed through openings in the Schwammenauel. Around 11 P.M., five men from the 303d Engineers first approached the dam itself. As the Americans attempted to cross the top, German gunners tried to blow them away. Lieutenant James Phelan, leader of the group, said, "It was like a ten-minute artillery barrage—repeated every ten minutes; between shell explosions the burp gunners could be heard."

Driven off by the intense fire, the patrol returned around midnight. They planned to sprint across the dam to the spillway and climb down from there to a tunnel in the dam, the most likely place for demolition charges. They covered the 1,000 feet atop the structure, unharmed by sniper bullets and shells of varying calibers. But the spillway had been blown up, leaving a chasm fifty feet wide, forty feet deep, and with vertical concrete walls. The only means to approach was a daring slide down a 200-foot face to the tunnel entrance, which the engineers successfully navigated. They surprised and captured a handful of Germans, machine gunners and snipers, but could not find any explosives. In fact, as GIs swarmed over the Schwammenauel, they discovered no sign of any demolition materials. The only water escaping came from the destruction of the valves and that was controllable.

The Americans were now out of the woods; the five-month battle for the Huertgen Forest was finally over.

17

POSTMORTEMS

The "victory" achieved by the First Army in the Huertgen cost 24,000 dead, wounded, captured, or missing GIs with an additional 9,000 disabled by frozen or wet feet, respiratory ailments, and other nonbattle injuries. For one of the few campaigns of the war, German losses actually were fewer, although the Third Reich was far less able to replace men and equipment than the Allies. The ability of the Nazi government to continue resistance was eroded, but that was not the purpose of the offensive in the Huertgen.

To gain the real estate, the strategists had committed the 1st, 4th, 8th, 9th, 28th, 78th, and 83d Infantry Divisions, the 505th and 517th Parachute Regiments, the 2d Ranger Battalion, the 5th Armored Division, and some attached special tank, engineer, and artillery units. The damage to the American forces seriously weakened the First Army, diluting its extended front line into a thin crust that enabled the Germans to crash through in the initial phases of the Battle of the Bulge. The struggle in the Huertgen left the 1st and 9th Divisions, which had been fighting since the 1942 North African campaign, almost entirely populated by replacements. The 4th and 8th Divisions, veterans from D Day and the Normandy campaign, respectively, likewise suffered huge turnovers. The 28th Division was still trying to replace, regroup, and reequip when von Rundstedt's legions struck on 16 December. Both the 2d Ranger Battalion and the 517th Parachute Regiment came out of the forest as skeletal outfits.

According to the 82d Airborne CO, James Gavin, the German Maj. Gen. Rudolph Gersdorff, chief of staff for his country's Seventh Army, said, "The German command could not understand the reason for the strong American attacks in the Huertgen Forest. . . . The fighting in the wooded area denied the American troops the advantages offered them by their air and armored forces, the superiority of which had been decisive in all the battles waged before."

William Burke, who served with the 803d Tank Destroyer Battalion, remarked, "Some of us with combat experience from the beaches to Huertgen were hard-pressed to understand the tactical wisdom of slogging it out in such an unforgiving environment instead of bypassing it."

Frank Gunn, the commander of the 2d Battalion of the 39th Regiment that captured Merode, said, "In retrospect, it seemed to me that the Huertgen Forest could have been contained rather than assaulted and a large flanking or encircling movement performed by corps. This would have reduced the casualties and still have accomplished the mission of capturing the dams on the Roer River.

Although the reservoirs controlled by the dam system posed a potential for flooding the countryside, they were certainly not the original objectives of the offensive into the Huertgen, and the documents from army sources during the initial phases of the campaign do not even mention them. Had the area been bypassed, the consequences of opening the floodgates is problematical, and it could be argued that the most vulnerable segment of the American forces to inundation were the very GIs dispatched into the forest.

J. Lawton Collins, the U.S. VII Corps commander, argued for the correctness of the plunge into the "green hell." He insisted, "If we would have turned loose of the Huertgen and let the Germans roam there, they could have hit my flank." In theory, the drive through the Stolberg corridor toward the Roer would have been menaced by an attack from the Huertgen on the right flank of Collins's troops. However, Collins based his opinion on the potential of the enemy to strike at him from the forest. The evidence indicates otherwise.

The Westwall was built strictly for defense. It did not provide a launching platform for an attack. The extensive minefields and dragon's teeth were intended to stop invaders. The huge bunkers housed fixed, rather than mobile, guns. This was particularly true in the forest, except for lanes for machine guns that exploited the firebreaks in the cultivated woods. There were few roads built to accommodate the German tanks, which were much heavier than the Americans ones that bogged down in the muddy trails. Any attempt to move in a substantial column would have brought down the wrath of the Allied Air Forces, which ruled the sky. A strong Panzer spearhead, such as that which led the breakthrough in the Ardennes, was out of the question.

Nothing better proved the effectiveness of the forest as a natural defensive redoubt than the experience of the 3d Battalion of the 9th Division's 47th Infantry. As Chester Jordan, the platoon leader, testified, the outfit took over Schevenhutte, well inside the forest and held off strong German counterattacks from mid-September until two months later, when the 47th resumed its advance. No one in First Army, VII Corps, or V Corps appears to have noticed why the battalion was able to maintain its position. Like the German defenders, it capitalized on the forest terrain to defend itself against repeated attempts by the enemy to oust it.

In an oral history, Collins, when asked about training, said, "I think if it is emphasized to the student the importance of terrain, it would be a good idea, because certainly there is no question in the world that you can't always tell what the enemy is going to [do], but the terrain is there, and if you study it, you can make use of it and make the enemy conform to what you want to do." Collins, his superiors—Hodges, Bradley, and even Eisenhower—the upper echelon strategists, and even the division commanders apparently relied on maps to define the battlefield. Theirs was a two-dimensional understanding of the terrain and the defenses. Aerial recon could not detect the true nature of the enemy emplacements. Dick Seitz, who commanded the 2d Battalion of the 517th, pointed out, "High echelon strategists can work from a map and aerial photos, but it is an axiom of military operations that battalions or companies should never advance without first-hand knowledge of the terrain." And, like so many other units, he never was given the opportunity for such a reconnaissance because of the importunate demands of those in charge.

Totally ignorant of the thickness of the forest and the absence of genuine roads through it, the top command sent men into battle.

Perhaps because of the almost impenetrable vegetation, they knew nothing of widespread minefields, the artful tangles of booby-trapped barbed wire, and the plethora of massive pillboxes, impregnable to artillery and to attack from the air.

As far as one can determine, the generals never inspected the area into which they dispatched troops. Not a single source whom this author interviewed recalls ever seeing any of them come forward to observe the killing grounds. Ed Uzemack mentioned getting a hand from the 28th Division CG, Norman Cota, when he left the assembly area, but that hardly put Cota in a position to appreciate what his troops faced. John Chernitsky, the antitank squad leader, complained that he never saw any of the brass near the front. The 28th's assistant division commander, General Davis, was credited at First Army headquarters with having led men to safety but that occurred only after a disastrous attack and was not a substitute for careful inspection of the disputed turf. The same applies to the other divisional leaders. They compounded the problem with schedules that did not permit those expected to carry out the strategy to respond adequately.

Too often, individuals well removed from the combat zone ignored the axiom cited by Seitz. In addition, they frequently dictated tactics. In an article in the July-August 1993 issue of *Armor,* Harry J. Schute, Jr., noted that when the 28th Division jumped off at the start of November, "There were no orders given for preoperation patrolling by any commander, at any echelon, to attempt to find enemy positions or strength or to ascertain the viability of the Kall trail as a division MSR [main supply route]. The absence of patrolling and intelligence gathering gave the enemy an unnecessary advantage by keeping their locations and strength unknown until the attack began."

In fact, the 28th commander, General Cota, had little or no input into the selection of objectives made by the V Corps leader, Gen. Leonard Gerow, and his staff. Cota was expected to contribute at most fine-tuning and to see to the execution of the plan. General officers, of course, cannot be expected to expose themselves to combat alongside their troops. Those in command must stay out of harm's way in order to remain able to plot strategy, direct maneuvers, and maintain overall control of their forces. But that does not mean they should be so removed as to be unknowing of the conditions for which they devise the strategy. In fact, the German generals habitually came forward for a personal inspection before they committed their troops.

In the battle for the Huertgen, American field grade officers, on the other hand, often came under fire while directing their troops, and the casualty rate for colonels, lieutenant colonels, and majors was significant. All three of the battalion commanders of the 22d Infantry who led their soldiers into the Huertgen were either killed or wounded. The 309th Infantry lost two battalion COs at Kesternich. The 109th Infantry's Howard Topping, whom platoon leader Peña had regarded as an overzealous martinet, won the admiration if not the affection of his subordinates. "We had to admit that this truculent man was a damn good front line officer."

Among the company grade officers and noncoms, the numbers of killed, wounded, missing, or captured were so high that command and control became extremely difficult to maintain, one reason for some panicky retreats. The people at First Army and corps headquarters never seemed to grasp how much this affected performance. When Courtney Hodges griped that better progress could be made if the troops went about their tasks appropriately "buttoned up," nothing better demonstrated his unawareness of the battlefield. The solution for the problem of slow progress or failures was to berate both lesser commanders and the troops for a lack of soldierly qualities, rather than accept the responsibility for poor strategy and tactics that sapped morale and the will to fight.

Certainly, those on the firing line can be expected to show some reluctance for advancing toward their potential doom, and it is necessary in war for commanders to push them. George Wilson, as a company commander, at one point wanted to retreat but his superior insisted he hang on. Wilson subsequently agreed the battalion commander had been correct. But in this instance, the order emanated from someone close enough to events for a realistic, if tough-minded, appraisal.

The distance of command from battle sites contributed to other errors. Charles Haley, the executive officer for George Mabry, leading the 2d Battalion of the 8th Infantry Regiment, 4th Division, offered a criticism of the planning and intelligence of the Huertgen operation. "To attack a position a second time from the same direction with the same scheme of maneuver after the first attack has failed, unless unavoidable, is unsound." He noted that the upper echelons ignored the need for rest and rehabilitation of hard-hit soldiers and the lack of training for replacements. He insisted, "Higher commanders must recognize when a unit has reached the point when it is no longer capable of making a successful attack." He concluded that, while the enemy paid dearly for his defense, "the Battle of the Huertgen Forest, as bloody and bitter a fight as any of the war, brought no glorious victory. No major breakthrough was made nor large area overrun by our troops."

Henry Phillips, who fought with the 9th Division during the latter part of November, pointed out that what appeared effective on paper either did not follow the script or the situation was misjudged. "The concept of the First Army offensive was a good one. Execution of the preparatory air strike was faulty due to extreme caution about friendly casualties à la Cobra [the massive air attack near Saint-Lô, where friendly bombs killed several hundred Americans]. The bombs fell too far behind the German lines to be effective. The 1st [Division] attacked on too broad a front. They should have concentrated their punch on the left, where we were ultimately employed, instead of trying to cover their entire sector with advancing infantry. This produced gaps through which we advanced quite easily at first but also salients of German resistance, which were able to pound our right flank. Such errors of commission or strategy originated with First Army or corps." In Phillips's experience, the field grade officers all performed very well.

One particular problem noted by many analysts was the obvious lack of instruction in how to fight in a heavily wooded area. Training courses in the States taught GIs about beachhead landings, combat in the desert, and house-to-house fighting. But the kind of environment presented by the Huertgen was never part of the curriculum. The usual foxhole offered insufficient protection against tree bursts. Visibility fell to within a few feet in the dense vegetation, a condition exacerbated by fog, rain, and snow. Enemy positions enjoyed great concealment, surprising foot soldiers and denying observers sight lines to guide mortars and artillery. The trees thwarted radio signals. The GIs had to learn on the job, at an exorbitant cost. A more general deficiency that manifested itself in other campaigns was ignorance of the best means to deploy armor and a lack of teamwork between tanks and infantry. Henry J. Schute, Jr., commented that the 28th struck with "insufficient armor to hold its position." The analyst remarked on the absence of information on how poorly the Kall trail would serve armor or supply vehicles. Preston Jackson, the 112th Regiment's liaison officer, remarked on that problem. The Keystone Division apparently did not expect to encounter enemy tanks, which played a large role in routing the Americans at Schmidt and Kommerscheidt.

Foot soldiers regarded tanks as magnets for enemy fire and preferred to stay away from them. For their part, the tankers desperately wanted infantrymen close by to ward off the *panzerfausts,* to detect mines, and locate targets. Neither tankers nor infantrymen, except in the armored divisions, were adequately schooled in how to work as a team. The contretemps between the commander of a company from the 774th Tank Battalion and the commander of the 3d Battalion of the 311th Infantry in front of Schmidt exemplified the problem.

The communications gap between the types of soldiers was exemplified by several incidents in the forest. George Wilson of the 22d Infantry denounced a source in an armored unit for insisting that friendly forces held a hill from which his men absorbed deadly fire. On the other hand, the 46th Armored Infantry was falsely assured by 4th Division headquarters about the occupants of a hill, which led to unpleasant encounters with German machine guns.

The fiasco of the Huertgen campaign passed unnoticed, giving way to the drama of the Battle of the Bulge and then the crossing of the Rhine. In war, unlike the mythology attached to sports, the only question is whether you win or lose. That seems particularly true for the most senior commanders. Judging by what happened in the woods, the top ranks were never called to account for the horrific losses in what can only be described as a huge strategic mistake compounded by tactical errors. There was no one to charge those directly responsible with misfeasance. Above Hodges and his corps and division commanders, there were only Bradley and Eisenhower. Bradley undoubtedly approved the proposals of his First Army chief. Although Eisenhower was more removed from the operations than the others, it would seem that he shares some culpability for not calling for a reassessment of the offensive after the first two months of appalling losses without requisite gains. Several field-grade people and some of the company commanders were relieved for allegedly failing in their assignments, but the generals involved never had to explain their decisions that led to such excessive loss of life.

The difficulty is in the nature of a military organization. Prosecution of a war requires executive decisions free of the lengthy discussions of a democratic endeavor. An army cannot be run as a democracy but must be authoritarian, with someone issuing the orders and others carrying them out. Within that framework lies the corpse of accountability. There is no means to question the decision-maker. The crush of war and the filter of information through channels easily defeats effective and intelligent civilian oversight. A congressional committee can look into charges of waste, corruption, or stupidity in the training and equipment of the armed forces during peace. There is neither the time nor the requisite intelligence available in a war for such control. The lower echelons of the military, if aware of the sins of their superiors are stifled by the requirements invested in the chain of command. Woe betide any officer who complains of the mistakes of those higher up.

During World War II, the major case in which someone of the most senior rank was publicly held responsible for failure was that of the two commanders at Hawaii on 7 December 1941. There was no effort to inquire how Douglas MacArthur and his Air Force commander, Gen. Lewis Brereton, were caught with their planes down, some twenty-four hours after the attack on Pearl Harbor, when the Japanese raid on the Philippines destroyed 50 percent of the resident American Air Force.

Dwight D. Eisenhower, as supreme commander of the Allied Forces, fired Maj. Gen. Lloyd Fredendall, the II Corps commander in North Africa, because he set up his headquarters sixty miles behind the front while the Germans then rampaged through American positions at Kasserine Pass. The supreme commander also subsequently banished Fredendall's successor, Maj. Gen. George S. Patton, Jr., for abuse of a pair of soldiers afflicted with combat fatigue. He took no action against Maj. Gen. Mark Clark for the slaughter of 36th Division GIs in an ill-conceived Rapido River crossing. Patton's successor at II Corps, Maj. Gen. John Lucas, lost his post because of a stalemate at the Anzio beachhead. Others, guilty of inadequately thinking out the Anzio venture, escaped discipline. On the other hand, several divisional commanders were dismissed because of alleged failings during the Ardennes campaign, although once again those at the top, Bradley and Hodges, remained untouched.

The sins of strategy and tactics committed by the top brass also resulted from the nature of the chain of command. Officers were aware that their posts and their careers depended upon satisfying the wants of superiors. In the Huertgen, many lesser rank individuals were relieved because of the conviction of their betters that they were underachievers. Because they foresaw the consequences of failure and to meet expectations, some lower echelon individuals supplied false, overly optimistic reports. These in turn fed the wrongheaded approach.

As much as the story of the Huertgen campaign is a tale of bungled management, it is also a testament to the resolve of the men in uniform on both sides, who risked and gave their lives on behalf of their countries. One cannot hear the accounts of the ordeals, the bloody awfulness experienced by those who participated, without wondering why soldiers continue to fight. It is easier to understand the German behavior after years of propaganda in a dictatorship—the desire to defend the homeland and the readiness of their superiors to shoot anyone whose will appeared to flag. American veterans, if asked why they stayed the course, almost invariably list as the first reason their bonds with their fellow soldiers. Men who live, eat, sleep, train, and face death together develop a strong enough tie so that if one moves forward, the other joins him. The writer Paul Fussell uses the word "inertia" to define this kind of momentum fueled by shared experiences and common backgrounds. Under that rubric should be included at least a modicum of commitment to the United States. Although patriotism is often dismissed as a motivation, since no one talks about country while trying to survive an artillery barrage or is engaged in an attack, according to the people this author interviewed, the impetus to volunteer in many instances was a recognition of a threat to the United States. Those who put on uniforms because of the draft seemed equally desirous of preserving the institutions of the country. The American soldiers in the Huertgen for the most part stolidly accepted their responsibilities and performed well despite their lack of proper instruction and the hash of strategy and tactics foisted upon them.

No less an authority than Gen. Matthew Ridgway, who commanded airborne troops, remarked that there comes a time when every soldier reaches a breaking point. That some fled the enemy in the Huertgen cannot be denied. There were moments in the Huertgen when an officer or noncom found it necessary to threaten a GI to prevent abandonment of a position but that was not unique to this campaign. According to David Eisenhower, in his biography of his grandfather, *Eisenhower at War, 1943–1945*, by late December 1944, 40,000 GIs had been accused of desertion since 6 June. Of these, 2,800 faced a general court-martial. The only American to be executed for desertion during World War II was Pvt. Eddie Slovik, a member of the unfortunate 28th Division. But Slovik's crime occurred well before the Bloody Bucket entered the woods. However, it may well be that Slovik, who faced a firing squad on 31 January 1945, was the final casualty of the Huertgen campaign. He probably lost any hope of clemency because of perceptions about discipline drawn from the panicky retreat in the Huertgen and, subsequently, during the Battle of the Bulge.

During war, commanders must have the courage to order the rank and file to engage in actions that may maim or kill them. That is part of the job. But it would be more seemly if those who sent men (and in the future, perhaps women) toward death on a battlefield had some sense of their responsibility beyond just winning. If held accountable not only for what they achieved but what it cost, perhaps the strategists might look harder for a way to gain the objectives. Should that be the lesson of the Huertgen campaign, it would still be too high a price to pay.

Roll Call

Alexis, Jerry. The B Company replacement with the 110th Regiment of the 28th Division survived a prisoner of war camp. "I've often called my combat and POW experiences the defining point of my life. I'm proud of my military record and have no regrets regarding that part of my life." He became a minister and lives in Pittsburgh, Pennsylvania.

Alyea, John. The tank driver for the 707th Tank Battalion lives in Munster, Indiana.

Archer, Clark. The paratrooper with the 517th PRCT has been the historian for the 517th's alumni organization and makes his home in Daytona Beach, Florida.

Beach, John. The West Point graduate and platoon leader of the 1st Division was treated for his wounds by German doctors before he was liberated from a POW camp. Some years after V-E Day, Beach became convinced that the Medal of Honor awarded to Sgt. Jake Lindsey rightfully belonged to Jim Wood, the lieutenant who assumed command of the handful of men left from his and Wood's platoon. Beach tracked down several men, who supplied affidavits attesting to Lindsey's actions. One recanted completely, while another admitted he never saw Lindsey at the time of the action. Nevertheless, the Department of Defense refused to overturn the citation to Lindsey or issue one for Wood. Beach retired as a lieutenant colonel and is deceased.

Boesch, Paul. The one-time wrestler who led an 8th Division platoon wrote a book on his experiences, *Road to the Huertgen: Forest in Hell,* which was privately printed. In 1987 he met Hubert Gees, the German soldier who was among the defensive forces in the Huertgen. According to Gees, they "shook hands in reconciliation across the graves" at a military cemetery. Boesch is deceased.

Boice, Dr. Bill. The chaplain assigned to the 22d U.S. Infantry authored a history of his regiment during World War II. He lives in Phoenix, Arizona.

Burghardt, Al. The mortar squad sergeant with the 110th Infantry recovered from trench foot after prolonged stays in hospitals. "In regard to knowing if the orders were realistic in terms of resources, terrain, and opposition, we were not privy to this information. We just did what we were told. We had little idea of where we were going. Pride kept me going. When the struggle for the Huertgen Forest ended, the original soldiers that I started with were gone. I was the only one left in the mortar section who had been in constant combat since the 28th Division went into combat." After separation from the service, he went into sales and now lives in Tonawanda, New York.

Burke, William. Originally the holder of an ROTC commission from Oklahoma Military Academy, he served with the 803d TD Battalion from February 1942 until the war's end. He remained in the service and led combat units in Korea and Vietnam before retiring as a major general. He lives in Apopka, Florida.

Camm, Frank A. A 1943 graduate of West Point and a lieutenant in the 303d Engineers of the 78th Infantry Division, Camm's father commanded the division artillery in the Huertgen. "We bivouacked behind the front line divisions for a couple of weeks before entering the Huertgen. During this period, selected officers and noncoms visited our counterparts among 1st Division troops engaged north of us on the Aachen front. They acquainted us generally with the combat environment and fearsome ability of German Tiger tanks to run roughshod over American antitank mines. However, we did not hear that three U.S. divisions in succession had failed to take our division objectives in the Huertgen." Camm retired as a lieutenant general and makes his home in Arlington, Virginia.

Carlson, Ernest G. A radio operator in Company D of the 28th Regiment, 8th Division, he said, "We, the lonely infantry man, didn't know what the objective was. Mainly, it was the next hill or valley. I've returned twice to the Huertgen Forest. Visiting the area makes you wonder how it was taken. The Germans had all the high ground and advantage to see all approaches." As a civilian, he worked himself up to supervisor and manager in a manufacturing company. He lives in Erie, Pennsylvania.

Carnivale, Jim. The machine gunner with the 46th Armored Infantry Battalion of the 5th Armored Division lives in Massachusetts.

Chernitsky, John. The antitank crewman with the 110th Regiment of the 28th Division helped his wife, Dorothy, compile the book *Voices from the Foxholes,* which contains oral histories from many 28th Division veterans. He lives in Uniontown, Pennsylvania.

Cohen, Mike. After being wounded by an exploding mine, the lieutenant with the 12th Engineer Combat Battalion went through fourteen months of recovery and married a nurse he met at Rhodes General Hospital in Utica, New York. "There was a lot of pious talk during the war about 'There are no atheists in foxholes.' That's a nice Sunday morning aphorism, but it's not true. A lot of prayers were said, of course, but there isn't much else you can do when those shells are bursting all around you, but nobody believed the prayers were going to help. Foxholes don't convert atheists; they breed them." Cohen retired from a textile manufacturing company as a division vice president.

Coleman, Harper. The 4th Division heavy weapons soldier had two brothers who fought in World War II in the Pacific Theater. He lives in Tucson, Arizona.

Collins, J. Lawton. The VII Corps commander rose to chief of staff for the army and died in 1987.

Crawford, Jack. The recipient of a battlefield commission with the 4th Division reconnaissance unit who met Ernest Hemingway, he endured a year of hospitalization after a mine exploded. An importer, he lives in Wilmington, Massachusetts.

Cross, Tom. The commander of the 121st Infantry in the Huertgen was the commander of the 8th Division during the Korean War. After retirement, he served as a deputy administrator for the Veterans Administration, then headed by Omar Bradley. According to his son Tom, Cross made up a listing of those officers and men who had been killed under his command in the Huertgen Forest. He then embarked on a "full court press to personally visit as many of their relatives as he could locate. It was a noble thought and deed, but after a considerable number of these personal visits, he had to stop them, because of the emotional drain that ensued and which left him somewhat disillusioned and sad. He told me that some of the parents and wives of the deceased appreciated the gesture, while others were only interested in the insurance benefits or were so bitter as to make his visit a dreadful memory. He told me that it was a mistake to undertake such a mission, even if well intended." He died in 1963.

DiLeo, Michael. The rifleman in Company B of the 46th Armored Infantry, 5th Armored Division, recalled, "I saw Lieutenant Smith [who walked off the battlefield] once after the Huertgen Forest while we were camped in Eupen, Belgium. I happened to be on the street when he walked by. He looked like he was in a different world. I saluted him, but no return. He has never been to any of our reunions. We have had fifty-three. Perhaps he would feel embarrassed. Seeing all those dead and wounded soldiers on the battlefield was too much for him. From Normandy to the Elbe River, we had six company commanders." DiLeo lives in Glen Cove, New York.

Dillard, Marcus. The mortar squad member from the 12th Infantry of the 4th Division lives in Largo, Florida.

Eames, Warren. Wounded first on 21 November and again the following day, the rifleman from Company G, 18th Infantry, 1st Division, underwent surgery without anesthesia for ear and scalp repair at a field hospital. He recalled that while at an evacuation hospital with "thousands of patients," disillusion set in. "I had learned all about battle. My idealism was gone. It seemed to me that absolutely *nothing* was worth going through all that hell—not even to win a war." Returned to duty in January while the division maintained a defense of the northern shoulder of the Battle of the Bulge, Eames found no familiar faces in his squad. All had either been killed, wounded, or taken prisoner. He was soon relieved from combat duty because of continuing problems from his head wounds. He lives in East Temple, Massachusetts.

Edlin, Bob. The 2d Ranger Battalion lieutenant returned home to Indiana, where he joined the local police force, rising to command the unit before moving to Corpus Christi, Texas, where he has an auction business.

Faulkner, Don. The replacement officer assigned to the 22d Infantry lives in Winter Park, Florida.

Fleig, Raymond. The 707th Tank Battalion platoon leader who wrote a history of the unit lives in Springfield, Ohio.

Goldman, Jack. Loader and radio operator for the command tank and then supply sergeant in Company B of the 707th Tank Battalion, he became supply sergeant for the unit. "We had an assortment of men from all over the country, all kinds, hillbillies, farmers, New York City college men. I played guitar and joined in with Texans and southerners. At first, like kinds formed separate clans, but this slowly changed and a mutual respect took over and was replaced by the crew clan. Of the original 125 men in the company, only twenty-six survived from the Battle of the Bulge." A retired accountant, he lives in Elkins Park, Pennsylvania.

Gunn, Frank. With a degree in plant pathology and a commission as a second lieutenant through the University of Georgia ROTC, he began as a platoon leader with the 9th Infantry Division and remained with the organization through its combat tour beginning in 1942 in North Africa. During the Huertgen campaign, he served as commander of the 39th Infantry's 2d Battalion. "As a battalion commander through five campaigns, I found my regimental commanders and my division commanders outstanding. I enjoyed having really first class company commanders, although we experienced a large casualty rate in them and platoon leaders. In retrospect, it seems to me that the Huertgen Forest could have been contained rather than assaulted and a large flanking or encircling movement performed by corps and First Army. This would have reduced the casualties and still have accomplished the mission of capturing the dams on the Roer." However, this observation is definitely Monday morning quarterbacking. He retired as a brigadier general and lives in Hampton, Virginia.

Hendrickson, Ralph. The 71st Armored Field Artillery GI who began his military career while horses pulled the guns, briefly left the service to work as an auto mechanic before his National Guard unit was recalled in 1947. He then remained on active duty until he retired as a sergeant major. He lives in Ninevah, New York.

Jackson, Preston. The 112th Infantry platoon leader and OCS friend of Bob Edlin continued his military service until he retired as a major general. He lives in Mississippi.

Jordan, Chester. The platoon leader with the 47th Infantry in the 9th Division recounted his experiences in an unpublished manuscript, *Bull Shots.* He lives in Baton Rouge, Louisiana.

Karre, Albert. The S-3 for the 2d Battalion, 39th Infantry, in the Huertgen, he is deceased.

Kemp, Harry. The Pennsylvania native went on active duty with the 109th Infantry of the National Guard's 28th Division. He remained in the service, commanded a battalion in Korea, and held several staff positions before retirement as a colonel. He wrote a book about the 109th, *The Regiment: Let the Citizens Bear Arms,* and resides in San Antonio, Texas.

Knollenberg, George. The 60th Infantry, 9th Division, rifleman replacement lives on Hilton Head Island, South Carolina.

Kull, William. The rifleman replacement with the 12th Regiment of the 4th Infantry lives in Colorado.

Lamb, Cliff. A member of Company B, 46th Armored Infantry Battalion, 5th Armored division, he is deceased.

Lavender, Don. The replacement rifleman assigned to the 29th Regiment Combat Team, 9th Infantry Division, wrote *Nudge Blue: A Rifleman's Chronicle of World War II.* He lives in Des Moines, Iowa.

Lomell, Len. Commissioned a lieutenant shortly before the 2d Ranger Battalion joined the fighting in the Huertgen, he recovered from wounds received on Hill 400 and became a lawyer. His home is in Toms River, New Jersey.

Mabry, George. The 2d Battalion commander in the 8th Regiment, 4th Division, remained on active duty, rising to the rank of lieutenant general. "He could 'spin a yarn' better than most," said his former comrade John Swearingen. "He used this gift of gab many times for the soldiers as well as for the officers. George was a natural born leader who kept his cool in the best or in the worst of times." He is deceased.

Marshall, John. A CO, 707th Tank Battalion, gunner, and assistant driver, he was appalled by a proposal by a citizen of Holland who sought to erect a memorial in Schmidt to honor both the men of the 707th and German soldiers from the Wehrmacht's 89th Division. In a letter to an official of Schmidt, he wrote, "From 1933 to 1945, Germans really did support Adolf Hitler and really did allow their evil government to perform 'ethnic cleansing' amongst those decreed by Hitler and his henchmen to be *untermenchen* [subhuman]. Of course, there were many proud Germans who did not agree with him but went to war for their country. They had no alternative. I met many of these people, proud and loyal Germans, ashamed of what was allowed to happen. These people felt pain, bled, died, and prayed, just as we American soldiers did. I have corresponded and exchanged Christmas greetings with some of these families for [many years]. . . . I do not hate the Germans.

"The U.S. and German governments came together in friendship decades ago, as did peoples of the two nations. That does not mean, however, that we should begin erecting encomiums to those who fought on behalf of a criminal government, 1939–1945."

Although aware that others in his outfit, notably Ray Fleig and former GIs from the 78th Division, have had friendly reunions with their former opponents, Marshall pointed out that no one has proposed that joint memorials be created in the Pacific to honor both Japanese and Americans, and concluded, "I assert to you and van Rijt [the Dutch proponent] that had it not been for the U.S. war effort by men like us, then the descendants of those soldiers of the 89th whom he would honor would in 1999 have him goose-stepping down the streets of his home town." Marshall lives with his wife, Daisy, in Lincoln Park, New Jersey.

Maxwell, Norris. The captain with A Company of the 121st Regiment, 8th Infantry Division, was convicted in a court-martial of "disobedience," but was restored to duty and in time retired with roughly the same rank and decorations as his peers. He lives in San Angelo, Texas.

Miller, Bob. Headquarters squad GI for Company D, 81st Tank Battalion, 5th Armored Division. He lives in Gilbert, Arizona.

Myers, Tom. As a replacement, he served with I Company, 110th Regiment, 28th Division, until captured after the Huertgen campaign in the Ardennes. He resides in LaPine, Oregon.

Peña, William. As a replacement officer, he came to I Company of the 109th Infantry, 28th Division, as it first reached the Siegfried

Line. Having survived the Huertgen Forest and the Battle of the Bulge, he was still with the regiment in March as it approached the town of Schleiden on the Olef River. When a mine blew up, he was badly wounded, losing his left foot. He later learned he was the last casualty suffered by I Company, as the unit did occupation duty for the remainder of the war. He has corresponded extensively with Hubert Gees, the former German soldier who fought in the same area as Peña and wrote a memoir about his experiences, *As Far as Schleiden.* He lives in Houston, Texas.

Phillips, Henry. The acting M Company commander of the 47th Infantry, 9th Division, wrote several books about specific battles in North Africa and Germany involving the division. He lives in California.

Ragusa, Joe. The member of A Battery, 7th Field Artillery Battalion participated in the 1st Division landings in North Africa, Sicily, and Normandy. He lives in Armonk, New York.

Ramirez, Oswaldo. The regimental liaison officer for the 16th Infantry of the 1st Division who temporarily joined a line company near Hamich lives in Austin, Texas.

Randall, Frank. The replacement lieutenant who joined Company B, 39th Infantry, 9th Division, in the Huertgen, where he was badly wounded, went before a medical board in April 1945, which offered him medical retirement. "I told them to shove it. I had been working out every day in the hospital gym under a doctor's supervision. I went on to serve another twenty years before retirement as a colonel. I then volunteered for Vietnam, but I was advised to 'enjoy my retirement.'" He lives in Jefferson City, Missouri.

Reed, James. The I Company, 109th Regiment, 28th Division, replacement officer, he is deceased.

Salomon, Sid. The C Company, 2d Ranger Battalion, platoon leader at Omaha Beach and later B Company commander lives in Doylestown, Pennsylvania.

South, Frank. The 2d Ranger Battalion medic lives in Delaware.

Swearingen, John C. The S-3 for the 2d Battalion, 8th Regiment, 4th Division, was nominated for the Medal of Honor for his heroism by his superior, Lt. Col. George Mabry, in leading a crossing of the Sauer River late in January. "From September 1944 to February

1945, eight U.S. infantry and two armored divisions were committed in the Huertgen 'Hellfire' Forest. Thirty thousand American doughboys were killed or wounded. During this period, Eisenhower and Bradley lived the good life in Paris with full knowledge that committing U.S. troops in the Huertgen was not necessary. They did not have the guts to admit their decision was a terrible mistake and withdraw all troops." He lives in Columbus, Georgia.

Thomsen, Howard. The maintenance noncom for the 707th Tank Battalion lives in Bennington, Nebraska.

Treatman, Paul. The medic with the 26th Infantry of the 1st Division became a school administrator and lives in Cranbury, New Jersey.

Tschida, Nick. The sergeant with the 2d Platoon, Company B, 46th Armored Infantry Battalion, suffered post-traumatic stress syndrome. "While hospitalized, I made myself a promise that I would forget as much of the war as possible. It took a year and one half until the nightmares and dreams stopped on a steady program." He lives in Saint Paul, Minnesota.

Uzemack, Ed. The rifleman replacement with the 28th Division survived five months in a POW camp after the Battle of the Bulge. He lives in Chicago, Illinois.

Vannatta, Glen. Company commander of B Company, 110th Infantry, 28th Division, during the Huertgen campaign, he became a math teacher, taught in Pakistan, and then served as supervisor of mathematics in Indianapolis public schools until his retirement. He lives in Boca Raton, Florida.

Wagenseil, Arthur. The radio operator with a forward crew for the 56th Field Artillery Battalion of the 8th Division worked for the United Nations for more than thirty years. He lives in Paramus, New Jersey.

Wallace, George. The overage replacement platoon leader with A Company, 16th Infantry, 1st Division, came out of the Huertgen with trench foot and loss of hearing in one ear. He worked in sales promotion for broadcasting and the magazine industry. He lives in Mamaroneck, New York.

Wilson, George. The platoon leader and then company commander with the 22d Infantry of the 4th Division wrote a well-received book about his war experiences, *If You Survive.* He lives in Grand Lodge, Michigan.

Wofford, Stephen "Roddy." The platoon leader with A Company of the 121st Infantry, 8th Division, needed nine months to recover from his wounds. "I think my narrow escape in the Huertgen gave me a sense that each day is a gift from the Lord. Even now I usually get up at the crack of dawn and watch the sun rise and give thanks to Him who saved me from a wretched death." As a civilian, he and his wife bought a moving and storage business where he lives in Beeville, Texas.

Wolf, Karl. The West Point graduate and replacement officer with the 16th Infantry, 1st Division, retired as a lieutenant colonel after earning a law degree. He lives in California.

Wood, James. The platoon leader of the 16th Infantry, 1st Division, was liberated at the end of April 1945 from a POW camp. He is deceased.

Bibliography

Archer, Clark, ed. *Paratroopers' Odyssey*. Hudson, Florida: 517th Parachute Regimental Combat Team Association, 1985.

Baumgartner, John W., et al. *The 16th Infantry, 1861–1946.* Du Quoin, Illinois: Cricket Press, 1999.

Black, Robert W. *Rangers in World War II.* New York: Ivy Books, 1992.

Boesch, Paul. *Road to the Huertgen: Forest in Hell.* Houston, Texas: Gulf Publishing, 1962.

Boice, William. *History of the 22d U.S. Infantry in World War II.* Washington, D.C.: Infantry Press, 1959.

Bradley, Omar. *A Soldier's Story.* New York: Henry Holt and Company, 1951.

Burghardt, Alfred. Privately Printed Manuscript. Tonawanda, New York.

Chernitsky, Dorothy. *Voices from the Foxholes.* Uniontown, Pennsylvania: Privately Published, 1991.

Currey, Cecil B. *Follow Me and Die: The Destruction of an American Division in World War II.* New York: Stein and Day, 1984.

Eames, Warren. *Recollections of War.* East Templeton, Massachusetts: Privately Printed Manuscript.

Eisenhower, David. *Eisenhower at War, 1943–1945.* New York: Random House, 1986.

Eisenhower, Dwight D. *Crusade in Europe.* Garden City, New York: Doubleday, 1948.

Fifth Armored Division. *Paths of Armor.* Atlanta, Georgia: A. Love Enterprises, 1953.

Gavin, James M. *On to Berlin: Battles of an Airborne Commander.* New York: Viking Press, 1978.

Griesbach, Marc F. *Combat History of the Eighth Infantry Division in World War II.* Nashville, Tennessee: Battery Press, 1988.

Jordan, Chester. *Bull Shots.* Baton Rouge, Louisiana: Privately Published, 1991.

Kemp, Harry. *The Regiment: Let the Citizens Bear Arms.* Austin, Texas: Nortex Press, 1990.

Lavender, Donald. *Nudge Blue: A Rifleman's Chronicle of World War II Experience.* Privately Published, 1968.

MacDonald, Charles B. *The Siegfried Line Campaign.* Washington, D.C.: Office of Military History, 1963.

———. *The Mighty Endeavor.* New York: Oxford University Press, 1969.

———. *The Battle of the Huertgen Forest.* New York: Jove, 1983.

MacDonald, Charles B., and Sidney T. Mathews. *Three Battles: Arnaville, Altuzzo, and Schmidt.* Washington, D.C.: Office of Military History, 1952.

Marshall, John. *A Fighter Tanker's Story.* Lincoln Park, New Jersey: Privately Printed Manuscript.

Miller, Edward G. *A Dark and Bloody Ground: The Hürtgen Forest and the Roer River Dams.* College Station, Texas: Texas A&M Press, 1995.

Miller, Robert M. *Voo Doo Dog.* Bleicherode, Germany: Privately Printed Manuscript, 1945.

Mittelman, Joseph B. *Eight Stars to Victory: A History of the Veteran Ninth U.S. Infantry Division.* Washington, D.C.: F. H. Heer Printing and 9th Infantry Division Association, 1948.

Myers, Tom, and Marcel Scheidweiler. *G.I. Tom Myers' War Memoirs:* Luxembourg: Sankt-Paulus-Druckerei, 1991.

121st Infantry Regiment. *Combat History.* Baton Rouge, Louisiana: Army & Navy Publishing Company, 1946.

Salomon, Sidney A. *2d U.S. Ranger Infantry Battalion: 14 November–10 December 1944.* Doylestown, Pennsylvania: Privately Published, 1991.

Sylvan, William. *Diary.* Carlisle, Pennsylvania: U.S. Army Center for Military History.

Thirteenth Infantry Regiment. *Combat History.* Baton Rouge, Louisiana: Army & Navy Publishing Company, 1946.

Tobey, Nelson. *History of the 7th Field Artillery Battalion, World War II.* Las Cruces, New Mexico: Privately Compiled Manuscript.

Twenty-eighth Infantry Regiment. *Combat History*. Baton Rouge, Louisiana: Army & Navy Publishing Company, 1946.

Weigley, Russell F. *Eisenhower's Lieutenants: The Campaign of France and Germany, 1944–1945*. Bloomington: University of Indiana Press, 1981.

Weingartner, Steven, ed. *Blue Spaders: The 26th Infantry Regiment, 1917–1967*. Cantigny, Illinois: 1st Infantry Division Association, 1996.

Whiting, Charles. *The Battle of the Huertgen Forest: The Untold Story of a Disastrous Campaign*. New York: St. Martin's Press, 1989.

Wilson, George. *If You Survive*. New York: Ballantine Books, 1987.

Wolf, Karl. *World War II Combat Experiences*. Corona del Mar, California: Privately Printed Manuscript.

Index

Aachen, 1, 6–7, 12, 16–20, 23, 26–27, 37, 49, 59, 67, 84–86, 181
Adams, Francis, 55–57
A Dark and Bloody Ground, 251
Alexis, Jerry, 95, 113, 122–23, 127, 167–71, 367
Alyea, John, 100–101, 129–32, 161, 367
Alzen, 44
Am Gericht, 334
Anderson, Glen H., 256
Andrus, Clift, 230
Antwerp, 36, 85
Aquitieri, Angelo, 333
Archer, Clark, 351
Ardennes, 8, 12, 65–66, 352
Argonne Forest, 37, 252
Arman, Robert, 244–45
Armor, 359
Army Specialized Training Program (ASTP), 317

Barrileaux, Melvin, 128
Barton, Ralph, 153, 180–81, 191, 251, 308
Bastogne, 33
Battle of the Bulge, 44, 338, 356, 362
Bea Wain, 124, 129, 132–33, 141, 161
Beach, John, 18–20, 25, 62, 185–88, 254, 283, 367
Beldegray, Pvt., 326–27
Berber, Raymond, 112
Bergheim, 314
Bergman, Ed, 34–35
Bergstein, 107, 234, 256, 301, 304, 309, 338, 340, 345, 350–51
Berlin Sally, 180
Berndt, Albert, 151
Bertier, Ralph B., 74
Bickerath, 332
Bilstein, 332–33
Birder, James, 348–49
Birgel, 308, 314
Blackford, Sgt., 329–30
Bland, Tyler, 291, 297
Blazzard, Howard, 219
Block, Walter, 200–201, 244, 247, 304
Boesch, Paul, 237–38, 251, 278, 280–81, 367
Boice, Bill, 203, 206–209, 368
Bond, Van H., 311
Booth, Everett, 195–196
Boudinot, Truman E., 20, 57,
Bovenberg Farm, 224, 227, 273
Bovenberger, 222
Bovenbergerwald, 222
Boyer, Howard, 277

Bradley, Omar, 4, 8, 10, 13–14, 50, 65, 68, 84–86, 94, 146, 184, 189–90, 237, 336, 358, 363, 369
Brami, Russ, 346
Brandenberg, 107, 234, 300, 351
Brereton, Lewis, 363
Briggs, Victor H., 18–20, 255
Brown, Audney, 106
Bulau, Alvin, 285–87
Burrell, James, 316
Burgess, Gil, 100
Burghardt, Al, 89–91, 123, 136–37, 164–67, 368
Burke, Bill, 218–19, 357, 368
Burley, Wilson, 321
Burton, William H., 290, 297–98

Caldwell, Lt., 220, 222, 249, 262–66
Camm, Frank A., 68
Camp Elsenborn, 44, 63
Canham, Charles, 239, 278
Carlson, Ernest, 250–51, 282, 368
Carnivale, Jim, 294–95, 298, 369
Carter, Andrew, 143
Casey, Charles, 350
Castle Hill (Hill 400), 301–305
Casualties, German, 79–80, 84, 160, 193–94, 351, 355
Casualties, U.S., 56, 62, 73, 75, 84, 117, 121–22, 130, 147, 156, 160, 167, 177, 195, 200, 206–209, 227, 281, 299, 304, 308, 331, 334, 352, 355
Caufield, Warren, 342
Caumont, 18–19
Chatfield, Lee W., 74,
Chernitsky, John, 93–94, 167, 332, 359, 369
Chism, John, 345–46, 350–51
Clark, Bill, 243
Clark, Joseph, 111
Clark, Mark, 364
Clayman, Donald C., 222–26
Cliett, John, 278
Cobra, 40
Cohen, Izzy, 232
Cohen, Mike, 3, 268–72, 369
Colangelo, Dominick, 313
Coleman, Harper, 209–11, 369
Colliers, 252
Collins, Joseph Lawton, 8, 12–16, 18, 23–24, 27, 37, 59, 63–64, 67–68, 72, 146–48, 180, 191, 196, 198, 201, 240, 251, 256, 308, 311, 357, 369
Cologne, 65, 68
CCA 3d Armored Division [U.S.], 21, 26–27, 49
CCB 3d Armored Division [U.S.], 20, 49
CCR 3d Armored Division [U.S.], 55–56
CCB 5th Armored Division [U.S.], 6,
CCR 5th Armored Division [U.S.], 256–57, 277, 290, 300, 309
CCR 7th Armored Division [U.S.], 336
Combat Fatigue, 208–209, 249
Corbin, Duane, 229
Cota, Norman, 32, 105–106, 108, 113–14, 123, 127–28, 136, 143, 146, 359
Courtney, Bill, 245–46
Craig, Louis A., 24, 37, 44, 67, 70, 310–11, 339, 354

Crawford, Jack, 153–54, 252–53, 368
Cross, Dick, 256, 300
Cross, Thomas J., 234–35, 239–40, 256, 278–81, 288, 300–301, 341, 369–70
Cross, Thomas R., 300, 341
Crucifix Hill, 26, 181
Currey, Cecil B., 177

Danna, A.V., 45
Davis, George, 105, 108, 123, 136, 146–47, 156–57, 183, 359
Decker, Lawrence L., 73
Dedenborn, 338
DeLille, Lionel, 5–6
DeMarco, Michael, 117
Dennison, Woodrow, 321
DePinto, Count and Countess, 84
Dickinson, Daniel, 346
Diepenlinchen, 55–56
D'Horn, 310–311
DiLeo, Michael, 296–99, 333, 370
Dillard, Marcus, 154–55, 370
Dixon, Benjamin, 49
Doan, Leander, 22
Dorn, Pvt., 325
Doty, Wilmer, 314
Dragon's Teeth, 7, 99–100
Drake, Hubert, 206
Dreher, Bill, 245–46
Dulac, Wilfred, 108, 110–11
Dunfee, Bill, 337–38
Dunne, Roy, 351
Duren, 6, 8, 24, 37–38, 43–44, 68, 184, 314
Dyer, Sgt., 186–87
Eames, Warren, 181–82, 198–200, 227–33, 370
Edlin, Bob, 174–76, 243–48, 370
Eicherscheid, 334
Eight Stars to Victory, 38
VIII Corps [U.S.], 65
Eighth Air Force, 148, 184
8th Infantry Division [U.S.], 63, 202, 234, 256, 267, 280, 282, 288, 299–301, 340–41, 356
8th Infantry Regiment [4th Division, U.S.], 172, 209, 218–19, 278, 280
18th Infantry Regiment [1st Division, U.S.], 84, 181–82, 196, 198–200, 202
81st Tank Battalion [5th Armored Division, U.S.], 307, 333
82d Airborne Division [U.S.], 336, 352, 356
83d Infantry Division [U.S.], 289, 299, 305–306, 314, 317, 334, 356
85th Recon Squad [U.S.], 5
803d Tank Destroyer Battalion [U.S.], 203, 218
893d Tank Destroyer Battalion [U.S.], 117, 128
899 Tank Destroyer Battalion [U.S.], 73
Eisenhower, Dwight D., 2, 4, 8, 13, 65, 68–69, 84–86, 146, 306, 334, 336, 358, 363–65
Elsenborn Ridge, 180
Elwood, Dallas, 110–111, 120
Eschweiler, 6, 23, 26, 234
Eupen, 14
Faulkner, Donald L., 258–62, 266–67, 289–90, 371

Fehrenbach, David, 19–20
Feery, Capt., 353
Ferry, Allan B., 55–57
Fields, Gerald, 155
V Corps, 8, 13–14. 17, 24, 32, 49, 61, 65, 67, 87–88, 101, 105–106, 148, 240, 277, 305, 336
5th Armored Division [U.S.], 5–6, 13–14, 24, 235, 263, 277, 300–301, 305, 307, 309, 314–15, 332, 334, 356
15th Armored Infantry Battalion [5th Armored Division, U.S.], 307–308, 333
56th Field Artillery Battalion [U.S.], 281
First Army [U.S.], 1, 5, 10, 12, 15–16, 35, 49, 65, 67, 69, 84, 86, 101, 108, 135, 148–49, 178, 180, 234, 267, 306, 332, 336, 352, 356
First Army [Canadian], 85
1st Infantry Division [U.S.], 13, 15–16, 18, 23, 25–26, 49, 55, 62–63, 85, 88, 172, 181–83, 185, 190–95, 201–202, 226–27, 234, 283–84, 287, 356
Fitzsimmons, Bob, 246
505th Parachute Infantry Regiment [82d Airborne, U.S.], 336–38, 352
517th Parachute Infantry Combat Team [U.S.], 336, 338, 340–52, 356
Flanigan, Capt. , 205,
Fleig, Raymond, 101, 106–107, 113, 115, 118, 128, 138–39, 365, 371
Flint Harry ("Paddy), 81
Flood, Albert, 117, 143
Flynn, George, 342, 346–47
Follow Me and Die, 177
Ford, James, C. 112
Ford, Slim, 347–48
46th Armored Infantry [5th Armored Division, U.S.], 289–99, 332, 362
47th Armored Infantry Battalion [5th Armored Division], 309
47th Infantry Regiment [9th Division, U.S.], 38–40, 49–50, 55, 59, 71, 144, 171, 184–85, 190, 202, 211, 222–27, 273, 277, 288, 358
4th Cavalry Group [U.S.], 71
4th Combat Engineer Battalion, 253
4th Infantry Division [U.S.], 13–14, 28, 49, 61–62, 88, 144, 152, 155–56, 190–91, 202–204, 209, 211–12, 218, 305, 332, 356, 362
Fortunato, Ray T., 322
Foster, James, 291
Franklin, Pfc., 110
Frazier, Douglas, 322, 329
Frazier, Gael, 226
Fredendall, Lloyd, 363–64
French, Robert, 253–54
Frenzerburg Castle, 273–77
Frieble, Walter, 350
Friendly Fire, 41, 43, 57–58, 141
Fringhaus, 46
Fronczek, Louis, 244
Fry, Edmond, 270
Fuller, Charles, 314
Fussell, Paul, 364

Gallagher, William, 309
Gavin, James, 336–38, 347, 355
Gees, Hubert, 78–80, 103,

158–60, 178, 282–83, 288, 367
Germany (Third Reich), 1, 4–6, 8–10, 63, 86, 355
Germeter, 59, 72, 74–76, 88, 102, 106–108, 120, 150, 161, 203, 243, 248, 252, 267, 269–70, 277
Gerow, Leonard, 8, 13–14, 32, 67, 87, 105, 108, 124, 146–48, 178–79, 251, 280, 287, 301, 305, 322, 359
Gersdorf, Rudolph, 356–57
Gey, 305–306, 314
Gibb, Frederick W., 195
Gibbons, Ludlow, 348
Gibney, J. L., 144
Ginder, P.D., 280–81
Goldman, Jack, 97, 100, 132, 134–35, 161–62, 371
Goodman, Allan, 455–45
Granger, George, 134, 141, 161–63
Grant, Bill, 292
Graves, Rupert, 340
Gray, Doyle, 347–48
Greenlee, Lt., 267
Gressenich, 43, 53, 184–85, 193, 222
Grosshau, 203, 219, 234, 248, 257–58, 260, 262, 265, 288–90, 309
Grosskampfenberg, 34
Guichici, George, 342–43, 346–47
Guinn, William H. 333–34
Gunn, Frank L., 310–11, 357, 371
Gurzenich, 308–309, 311
Gut Schwarzenbroich, 211, 218
Hackard, Clifford, 139
Haley, Charles, 211–216, 360–61
Hamberg, William, 288
Hamich, 24, 182, 184–85, 189, 192–93, 195, 203, 222, 228, 254
Harmon, Fred, 350
Hasenfeld, 354
Hassel River, 39
Hatzfield, Theodore, 128
Hazlett, Robert, 118
Hayes, Frank, 351
Heinsberg, 184,
Heistern, 223, 227, 234, 284
Hemingway, Ernest, 9, 252–53
Hendrickson, Ralph, 315–16, 371
Henrikson, Clete, 323–25, 329
Herman, Bob, 309–10
Hill 400—*see* Castle Hill
Hill 401, 290–97
Hirshmann, Pvt., 327
History of the 22d Regiment in World War II, 203
Hitler, Adolf, 7, 17, 27, 332
Hodges, Courtney, 1, 3–5 , 8, 10, 12–16, 27, 37, 49–50, 59, 72, 84, 86, 105, 114, 123–24, 127, 135, 143, 146–48, 152, 179–80, 183–84, 189–91, 198, 201, 234, 239, 251, 256, 287–88, 306, 317, 322, 334, 339–40, 354, 358, 360, 363–64
Hoefen, 44
Hogan, William, 55–58
Holzinger, Warner W., 5–6, 15
Hopkins, T/5., 307–308
Horn, 314
Hostrup, Bruce, 114
Houston, Jack, 67, 69–70,
Hovdestadt, Andrew, 315
Hucheln, 223, 273
Huebner, Clarence, 23, 183,

196, 198, 201, 284, 336, 339, 354
Huertgen, 24, 61, 75, 87–88, 103, 107, 120, 124, 179, 235, 239, 250, 256, 260, 267, 269, 277–83, 288
Huertgen Forest, 9, 16, 23–24, 37, 41, 43–44, 59–61, 67, 69, 76, 81–83, 86, 89–90, 127, 148, 181–82, 189–91, 253, 267, 269, 292, 302, 334
Huppenbroich, 334

Inde River, 273
Isley, Carl J., 141

Jabos (see P-47s)
Jackson, Langdon, A. Jr., 211, 213–16
Jackson, Preston, 108, 126, 243, 362, 371–72
Jaegerhaus, 75
Jamison, Pvt., 109
Jeter, John R., 235, 256
Johnson, Ralph, 33–34
Johnstone, "Pop", 110–11
Jones, Robert, 240
Jones, Walter, 333
Jordan, Chester H., 40–44, 53–55, 171–72, 224–25, 273–76, 358, 372
Julich, 68, 184
Jungersdorf, 284

Kall River, 37, 113–15, 127, 143, 165, 167, 340
Kall Valley, 126, 136, 140, 144–45, 165–67, 336–38
Karnak, Charles A., 39
Karre, Albert, 76–78, 372
Kater, Raymond, 324
Keen, Charlie, 347–48
Kelley, Jonah, E., 335–36
Kemp, Harry, 9, 89, 93, 105, 112, 372
Kenan, Thomas A., 219–22, 257, 260–61, 263, 266
Kesternich, 24, 318–31, 334, 336, 339
Keyes, Richard, W., 335
King, Raymond, W., 224–25
King, Roswell H., 21, 25
Klaus, Bill, 244
Kleinau, 43, 87, 235, 256, 260, 288, 292–96, 301, 307, 309, 313, 317
Knollenberg, W. George, 87–88, 372
Koblenz, 16
Kommerscheidt, 113–16, 123, 126, 128, 136, 139, 143, 146–47, 150, 156, 165, 337, 352
Konzen, 334
Korb, Charley, 201
Kozlowski, Mike, 124–25, 129–30, 160
Kudiak, Tony, 119
Kufferath, 314–315
Kuhn, Pvt., 186
Kull, Bill, 172–74, 255, 372
Kunzig, Henry B., 278–80

La Barr, James, 39
Lacy, Lt., 123
Ladd, Byron W., 322–23, 325, 328
La Fauci, Rocco, 172–73
Lamb, Clifford, 292–96, 372
Lammersdorf, 46, 48–49, 59–60

Land, Clifford, 343–44, 346
Landesschutzen, 50
Langerwehe, 194, 200, 228
Lanham, Charles, 28–31, 62, 206, 252–54
Larrabee, Leo, 331
Lavender, Don, 81–83, 87, 372
Lazo, Lt., 195
Lederman, Sol, 325–28
Leming, James, 107
Lengfeld, Friedrich, 79, 159–60
Leonard, Turney, 138
Levasseur, Armand, 15–16, 35, 58
Lindsey, Jake, 20, 189, 367
Linguiti, Paschal, A., 117, 125
Lipscomb, Andy, 353
Livingston, Louis, 160
Lloyd, Lt., 260–62
Lombardi, Carlo, 314
Lomell, Len, 301–302, 304, 372
Lovelady, William, 20, 25, 49
Lucas, John, 364
Luckett, James, 155, 181
Lutz, Harry, 318, 325, 353
Luxembourg, 3, 5, 12, 33, 289

Mabry, Benjamin, 216–17
Mabry, George L. Jr., 211, 215–18, 332, 360, 372
MacArthur, Douglas, 1, 363
MacDonald, Charles, 70, 287
Macon, Robert C., 305, 309
Madden, Alan P., 157–58
Maginot Line, 7
Main River, 65
Mallard, Merle, 271
Manning, Clise, 303
Manuel, Ralph, 225–26
Masney, Otto, 303
Market Garden, 36, 50, 65
Marshall, George C., 10, 12, 86
Marshall, John, 97–101, 124–25, 129–33, 141–42, 160–61, 372–73
Mason, Harry, 142
Maxwell, Norris, 237, 238, 240–41, 373
McAulay, Sgt., 233
McBride, Mort, 304
McBride, Patrick, 229
McColligan, William, 6
McCoy, Tim, 84
McGraw, Francis, 196–97
McKee, Richard, 213–16
McKnight, Leonard, 125, 129–32
McNair, Leslie, 41
McWatters, William L., 277
Merberich, 43
Merode, 196, 284–87, 310–11, 357
Mettendorf, 24
Meuse River, 8, 37, 67, 71
Miller, Bob, 313–14, 373
Miller, Edward, 181, 206, 251
Mills, Herbert, 25
Mines, 267–72, 319–21, 344–45
Mobile Army Surgical Team (MAST), 312
Monschau, 8, 16, 24, 37–38, 44, 49, 67, 71, 305
Monschau Forest, 9
Montgomery, Bernard, 4, 36, 50, 65
Montgomery, Champ, 292
Mossback, 58
Muglia, Alfred J., 117, 126
Munsterbusch, 26, 69
Myers, Clarence, 42–43, 275–76

Myers, Tom, 149–50, 163–64, 373

Napolitano, Lou, 294
Nelson, Gustin, 140, 143
Neppell, Ralph G., 309
Newcomb, Arthur, 31–32
Newman, Floyd, 19
Newman, Wayne, 150, 163–64
Nimitz, Chester, 1
Ninth Air Force [U.S.], 13–14, 148, 184
Ninth Army [U.S.], 65, 190, 305, 334
9th Infantry Division [U.S.], 13, 24, 37, 39, 44, 49, 55, 58–59, 63, 67, 69, 78, 83–84, 86, 89–91, 144, 171, 182, 273, 310, 332, 354, 356
9th Panzer Division [German], 17
90th Infantry Division [U.S.], 172
99th Infantry Division [U.S.], 305
IX Tactical Air Force [U.S.], 13, 71
XIX Corps [U.S.], 12, 68,
Norton, John, 336–37
Nothberg, 222
Nuetheim, 22

Oliver, Lunsford E., 308
104th Infantry Division [U.S.], 88, 172, 190–91, 201, 273
105th Panzer Brigade [German], 17
106th Infantry Division [U.S.], 332
109th Infantry Regiment [28th Division, U.S.], 62–63, 88–93, 103, 108, 119, 121–22, 124, 143–44, 147, 153, 179, 202, 237, 240, 302, 337
110th Infantry Regiment [28th Division, U.S.], 33–34, 88, 95, 103, 108, 121–23, 136–37, 143, 147, 164
112th Infantry Regiment [28th Division, U.S.], 14, 49, 88, 106–108, 108, 113–14, 119,
121st Infantry Regiment [8th Division, U.S.], 234–42, 248, 256, 277–81
124, 128, 133, 135–37, 139–40, 143–44, 150–51, 156–57, 179, 200, 243, 288
146th Engineer Combat Battalion, 141, 144
116th Panzer Division [German], 27, 160
Operation Queen, 179–80, 184
Orlando, Guido, 142
Ostrowski, John, 139
Our River, 4–6, 62

Paris, 33, 94
Parker, Edwin, 317–18, 322, 338–39, 352, 354
Paths of Armor, 24
Patton, George S., 3–4, 10, 12–14, 16, 334, 364
Paul, Bruce, 120, 146, 157
Paulushof Dams, 306
Payne, Richard, 139
P–47s, 50, 71, 87, 102, 117, 119, 141–42, 184
P–51s, 141
Pena, Bill, 62–63, 91–93, 102–103, 108–12, 120, 153, 156–58, 337, 373–74
Penick, Jim, 329

Persinger, Stu, 291
Petersen, Carl, 123, 137, 139–40, 143
Petty, William L., 303
Phelan, James, 355
Phillips, Henry, 183–84, 226–27, 361, 374
Pierce, Dave, 345
Pillbox Assault Tactics, 30, 35, 50–52
Porter, Charles, 119
Potter, Pvt., 272
Potts, Henry, 313
Pritts, Marshall, 137
Proximity Fuze, 60–61
Pyle, Ernie, 253

Quarrie, William D., 106

Raffelsbrand, 123
Ragusa, Joe, 374
Ramirez, Oswaldo, 195–96, 374
Randall, Frank, 80–81, 311–13
Ray, Bernard, 215
Reed, James, 144–46, 152–53, 374
Reger, Pvt., 109
Replacements, 34, 64, 80–81, 94–95, 103, 121–22, 149, 195, 249, 267
Reynolds, Arthur, 321
Rhine River, 4, 6, 8, 33, 50, 65, 70, 86, 334
Richelskaul, 74–75, 123
Ridgway, Matthew, 365
Ripperdam, Frank, 116
Ripple, Richard, W., 96, 136–37, 139–40
Robb, Dick, 340, 344, 349–50
Robinson, Sgt., 298
Roddwell, Col., 183
Roer River, 8, 16, 23–24, 37–38, 44, 49–50, 59, 67–69, 273, 305–306, 314, 318, 334, 338–39, 357
Roetgen, 20, 38–39, 45, 277
Roetgen Forest, 9, 38–39
Rollesbroich, 317–18
Roosevelt, Theodore, Jr., 209
Rose, Maurice, 23
Rott, 21, 114, 127
Royal Air Force [RAF, British], 14, 148, 184, 190, 306
Roush, Luther, 40
Rudder, James, 243–44, 248, 302
Ruggles, John, 260
Ruhr Valley, 65
Rundstedt, Karl Rudolph Gerd von, 28, 68, 332
Rusteberg, Roy, 311
Ryan, William, 318–21

St. Lo, 4, 29
Salomon, Sid, 244, 246, 302–303, 374
Saltonstall, 103
Sauer River, 4
Saxion, John, 349–50
Schack, Friedrich August, 17, 27
Scharnhorst Line [Westwall],6, 20, 22–23, 25, 45–46, 48, 59,
Schelde Estuary, 36, 85
Schevenhutte, 38, 43–44, 50, 53–54, 59 , 71, 171–72 , 182–84, 196, 211, 218–19, 273, 358
Schill Line [Westwall], 7, 23–25, 27, 38, 55, 58–59, 69
Schmidt, 6, 24, 69, 71, 74, 85, 102, 105, 113–18, 123–24, 126, 128, 135–36, 139, 144,

147, 150, 161, 178, 183, 301, 318, 337–41, 345, 352–54
Schmidt, Gus, 330
Schmidthof, 21, 25
Schnee Eifel, 62
Schneidhausen, 333–34
Schu Mines, 213
Schute, Harry, J. Jr., 359, 362
Schwammenanuel Dam, 8, 67–69, 306, 354–55
Schwerin, Graf von, 17–18, 27–28
2d Infantry Division [U.S.], 280–81, 305
2d Ranger Battalion [U.S.], 174–76, 200, 202, 242–48, 267, 301–305
Searles, James, 274–75
Seiler, Gus, 140
Seitz, Dick, 341–42, 346, 358
Seitz, John, 196, 284
Sellerich, 30–31, 61
Sevenig, 62
70th Tank Battalion [U.S.], 203
71st Armored Field Artillery [5th Armored Division, U.S.], 315–17
707th Tank Battalion [U.S.], 88, 95–101, 106–108, 113–15, 118, 128–35, 150, 160–61, 337
709th Tank Battalion [U.S.], 321
736th Tank Battalion [U.S.], 335
745th Tank Battalion [U.S.], 284–87
774th Tank Battalion [U.S.], 309, 353, 362
Seventh Army [German], 16, 28
VII Corps [U.S.], 12, 14, 16–17, 28, 55, 59, 65, 68, 86, 88–89, 106, 180, 196, 240, 305, 311, 357–58
71st Armored Field Artillery [5th Armored Division, U.S.], 5, 307
78th Infantry Division [U.S.], 250, 305–306, 317–18. 325, 334, 338–40, 356
Sheldon, Tom, 40, 42, 276
Sheridan, Carl, 275
Shultz, Robert H. 33–34
Sibert, Franklin, 156
Siegfried Line [See also Westwall], 2, 4, 6–8, 14, 23–24, 26, 35–36, 62, 70, 99, 172, 174
Simmerath, 323–24, 329–31, 338
Simonskall, 167
Simpson, William, 65
16th Infantry Regiment [1st Division U.S.], 14, 15, 18, 23, 25–26, 33, 49, 69, 84, 185, 189, 191–96, 202, 223, 254–55, 267, 283–84
60th Infantry Regiment [9th Division U.S.], 37–38, 44, 59–61, 71, 73–74, 87–88, 310
628th Tank Destroyer Battalion [U.S.], 309–10
Skelly, Francis, 330
Slovik, Eddie, 365
Smythe, George, 39
South, Frank, 175–176, 200–201, 242–43, 267, 304–305, 374
Spaatz, Carl, 86
Spencer, Jim, 130, 132
Spooner, Anthony, 115, 139
Sporenkel, Raymond, 321
Squires, Lt., 40–41
Stallings, Godfrey, 352–53

Stalcup, Joe, 241
Stephenson, Lt., 229–30
Stewart, Archie, 271
Stolberg, 6, 20, 22–24, 26, 37, 55, 58–59, 67, 185, 189, 201, 234, 273, 313, 357
Strass, 305–307
Strickland, Sgt., 186–87
Stroh, Donald A., 234–35, 239, 251, 278, 288, 301
Stroud, Pfc., 110
Stumpf, R. H., 45–46, 76
Sullivan, William B., 71–73
Supplies, Shortages, 31, 38, 56, 63,
Supreme Headquarters, Allied Expeditionary Force (SHAEF), 68
Suskind, SSgt., 326
Sussman, Lawrence, 260, 262
Swearingen, John, 212, 214, 372, 374
Sylvan, William, 3, 4–5, 8, 14–15, 35, 49–50, 59, 83–84, 105, 108, 114, 123–24, 127, 135, 143–44, 146–48, 179–80, 189–91, 201–202, 239–40, 251–52, 306, 339–40

Tait, William, 137
Tanks [American], 57, 96–99, 101, 118–19, 134, 138, 283–87
Tanks [German], 96, 116–17, 118–19, 138, 192–93, 301
Tank Destroyers, [U.S.], 218, 301, 309–10
Tanner, William, L., 226
Task Force Boyer, 277–78
Task Force Davis, 144, 161
Task Force Doan, 22
Task Force Lovelady, 20–22, 24, 38, 49, 190
Task Force Mills, 25, 190
Task Force Ripple, 136–38
Teague, Arthur L., 206
10th Tank Battalion [5th Armored Division, U.S.], 277, 288, 309
Terry, John R., 271–72
Thauwald, Peter, 313
Thibodeaux, Clifton, 197–98
Third Army [U.S.], 4, 8, 10, 13, 16, 49, 334
3d Armored Division [U.S.], 13–14, 16, 20–23, 28, 38, 49, 55, 185, 190
33d Armored Infantry [3d Armored Division, U.S.], 20, 190
13th Infantry Regiment [8th Division, U.S.], 63, 248, 279–81, 340
30th Division [U.S.], 85
34th Tank Battalion, 314
39th Infantry Regiment [9th Division, U.S.], 38, 45–48, 59, 71, 74–78, 80–81, 310–12
Thomsen, Howard, 96, 98, 133, 151, 161, 375
Thompson, Evan B., 276
Thompson, Oscar, 74
303d Engineer Battalion [U.S.], 321, 330, 354–55
309th Infantry Regiment [78th Division, U.S.], 322–23, 339, 352
310th Infantry Regiment [78th Division, U.S.], 317–18, 322–28, 331, 339, 352–54
311th Infantry Regiment [78th

Division, U.S.], 334–36, 338–39, 352, 362
325th Glider Infantry [82d Airborne Division, U.S.], 338
329th Infantry Regiment [83d Division, U.S.], 308–309
330th Infantry Regiment [83d Division, U.S.], 306–307,
331st Infantry Regiment [83d Division, U.S.], 306,
Topping Howard, 89, 92, 111, 120–21, 145, 156, 360
Traska, Henry, 102
Traver, Myrle, 342–43, 346–47
Treatman, Paul, 197–98, 375
Tree Bursts, 60–61, 103
Trench Foot, 122, 183, 185
Tucharelli, Carmen, 193
Tschida, Nick, 290–92, 375
12th Army Group [U.S.], 4, 63, 65, 69, 94, 105, 183
12th Infantry Division [German], 28, 58
12th Infantry Regiment [4th Division, U.S.], 144, 152, 160, 172, 179–180, 203, 235, 237, 252, 282
12th Engineer Combat Battalion [U.S.], 3, 267–72
20th Engineer Combat Battalion [U.S.], 115, 117
22d Infantry Regiment [4th Division, U.S.], 28–32, 49, 61–62, 172, 203, 210, 219, 235, 240, 252, 254, 256–57, 290, 299
26th Infantry Regiment [1st Division, U.S.],15, 20, 22, 196–97, 202, 234, 284, 287
28th Infantry Division [U.S.], 13–14, 32–33, 49, 84, 88–90, 105–106, 108–14, 127, 139, 143–44, 146, 152, 171–72, 177–79, 180, 183, 202, 235, 243, 250, 282, 302, 359
28th Infantry Regiment [8th Division, U.S.], 234, 239, 248, 250, 300
272d Volksgrenadier Division [German], 325
275th Infantry Division [German], 78, 282

Undingen, 317, 334
Untermaubach, 317, 334
Urban, Hubert, 222–23, 274, 276
Urft Dam, 8, 68, 306, 339
Uzemack, Ed, 95, 113, 121–22, 332, 359, 375

Vannata, Glen, 34, 142–43, 375
Vechte, 38–40
Vechte River, 24–25, 39
Vipond, Loren L., 6
Voo Doo Dog (D Company, 81st Tank Battalion), 313–14
Vossenack, 24, 74, 76, 106–108, 113–14, 128–29, 133, 136, 141–43, 150, 200, 250, 252

Wagenseil, Arthur, 230, 238, 281–82, 375
Wagner, John C., 328
Wallace, George, 191–92, 375
Wanggrzynowicz, Hank, 350–51
Warner, Don, 206
Weaver, Walter, 288, 301
Weeces, Clyde, 197–98
Weissenburg, 56–57

Weisser Wehe, 74, 79, 155
Welch, John, 331
Wenau, 202
Wenau Forest, 9, 38,
West, George, 106, 134–35, 160
Westwall [see also Siegfried Line], 4, 6–7, 14, 16, 23, 25, 32, 35–36, 39, 44, 48, 50, 62, 64, 70, 357
Widdon, William, 33
Wilde Sau, 153, 159–60, 178, 282
Wilhelmshohe, 273
Wilson, George, 28–32, 50, 61–62, 180, 204–206, 219–22, 248–50, 257–58, 262–66, 289–90, 360, 362, 375–76
Winden, 314, 317, 333–34
Wofford, Stephen, 235–37, 240–42, 376
Wolf, Karl, 25–26, 69–70, 184, 192–94, 376
Wolfson, Mike, 311
Wolters, Wheeler, 151
Wood, James H., 19, 185–86, 188–89, 254–55, 267, 283–84, 367, 376
Wood, Walker, 337
Woodhull, Robert, 349–50
Wounded, Treatment of, 117, 156–58, 201, 206–209, 232–33, 319–21

Yeager, Harold R. 34
Yergau, Paul, 241–42
Youngman, Pfc., 188

Zais, Mel, 341
Zeppenfeld, 1st Sgt., 79
Zweifall, 38–40, 59